TRYING CASES
TO WIN

Anatomy of a Trial

HERBERT J. STERN
STEPHEN A. SALTZBURG

TRYING CASES TO WIN

Anatomy of a Trial

HERBERT J. STERN
STEPHEN A. SALTZBURG

THE LAWBOOK EXCHANGE, LTD.
Clark, New Jersey

Copyright © 1999 by Herbert J. Stern

ISBN 978-1-61619-349-2 (Vol. V Anatomy of a Trial)
ISBN 978-1-61619-344-7 (set)

THE LAWBOOK EXCHANGE, LTD.
33 Terminal Avenue
Clark, New Jersey 07066-1321

*Please see our website for a selection of our other publications and
fine facsimile reprints of classic works of legal history:*
www.lawbookexchange.com

Library of Congress Cataloging-in-Publication Data

Stern, Herbert Jay, 1936-
  Trying cases to win / by Herbert J. Stern. -- Lawbook exchange edition.
    volumes cm
  Includes bibliographical references and index.
  ISBN 978-1-61619-344-7 (set : hardcover : alk. paper) -- ISBN 1-61619-
344-1 (set : hardcover : alk. paper) -- ISBN 978-1-61619-345-4 (v. 1 : hardcover :
alk. paper) -- ISBN 1-61619-345-X (v. 1 : hardcover : alk. paper) -- ISBN
978-1-61619-346-1 (v. 2 : hardcover : alk. paper) -- ISBN 1-61619-346-8 (v. 2
:hardcover : alk. paper) -- ISBN 978-1-61619-347-8 (v. 3 : hardcover : alk.
paper) -- ISBN 1-61619-347-6 (v. 3 : hardcover : alk. paper) -- ISBN
978-1-61619-348-5 (v. 4 : hardcover : alk. paper) -- ISBN 1-61619-348-4 (v. 4
: hardcover : alk. paper) -- ISBN 978-1-61619-349-2 (v. 5 : hardcover : alk.
paper) -- ISBN 1-61619-349-2 (v. 5 : hardcover : alk. paper)
  1. Trial practice--United States. I. Saltzburg, Stephen A. II. Title.
  KF8915.S736 2013
  347.73'75--dc23

2013003867

Printed in the United States of America on acid-free paper

Author

Herbert J. Stern is nationally known as a skilled trial lawyer and recognized as one of the nation's finest teachers of trial lawyer techniques and strategies. A partner in the Florham Park, New Jersey, law firm of Stern & Kilcullen, Mr. Stern is a former Federal Judge, having served as United States district judge for the District of New Jersey from 1974 to 1987.

After graduating from the University of Chicago Law School, Mr. Stern began his career as an assistant district attorney for New York County in the Homicide Bureau under the legendary District Attorney Frank S. Hogan. During that time he conducted the grand jury investigation into the death of Malcolm X and ordered the arrests of the men convicted of the assassination.

Mr. Stern established his reputation as an advocate while serving as a trial attorney with the Organized Crime and Racketeering Section of the United States Department of Justice after trying significant cases against such notable adversaries as Edward Bennett Williams, Simon H. Rifkind, and Frederick B. Lacey. Later, while serving as United States Attorney for the District of New Jersey from 1970 to 1974, Mr. Stern won a national reputation for unprecedented convictions of public officials, including the mayors of Jersey City, Newark, and Atlantic City.

Mr. Stern hold five honorary degrees and has taught at the University of Chicago, Harvard, Yale, and Columbia law schools and lectured nationwide for state bar and CLE programs. He has served as co-director of the University of Virginia Law School Trial Advocacy Institute since 1980.

In addition to the *Trying Cases to Win* volumes, Mr. Stern has authored *Judgment in Berlin*, an account of his experience as a United States judge for Berlin presiding over the trial of two fugitives from East Berlin who were accused of hijacking a Polish plane to West Berlin. Mr. Stern is also the author of *Diary of a D.A.*, published by Skyhorse Publishing, 2012.

Stephen A. Saltzburg has been the Howrey Professor of Trial Advocacy, Litigation and Professional Responsibility at the George Washington University Law School since 1990. Before that, he taught at the University of Virginia School of Law from 1972 to 1990, and was named the first Chairholder of the Class of 1962 Endowed Chair. Professor Saltzburg served as Reporter for and then as a member of the Advisory Committee on the Federal Rules of Criminal Procedure and as a member of the Advisory Committee on the Federal Rules of Evidence. Professor Saltzburg was the Reporter for the Civil Justice Reform Act Committee for the District of Columbia District Court and then became chair of that Committee. Professor Saltzburg has served as a Special Master in two class action cases in the District of Columbia District Court, and continues to serve as a mediator for the United States Court of Appeals for the District of Columbia. He also has mediated a wide variety of disputes involving public agencies as well as private litigants and has served as an international arbitrator.

From 1987 to 1988, Professor Saltzburg served as Associate Independent Counsel in the Iran-Contra investigation. In 1988 and 1989, Professor Saltzburg served as Deputy Assistant Attorney General in the Criminal Division of the Department of Justice, and in 1989 and 1990 was the Attorney General's ex officio representative on the United States Sentencing Commission. In June 1994, the Secretary of the Treasury appointed Professor Saltzburg as the Director of the Tax Refund Fraud Task Force, a position he held until January 1995. Professor Saltzburg is the author of numerous books and articles on evidence, procedure, and litigation.

Table of Contents

Acknowledgments

As with the preceding volumes, this volume of the work is the product of the efforts and contributions of many people. First, I must acknowledge Marc P. Gallant and Aspen Law & Business, who provided the initial impetus and encouragement for the work. I must, of course, acknowledge Professor Stephen A. Saltzburg, who located the transcript that we have used and provided many suggestions and very helpful contributions to the work. David Johnson, who edited the first four volumes, was good enough to reenlist and with his enormous understanding of the work provided all of the cross-references to the entire work as a whole. Finally, I would like to thank and acknowledge Madelene Magazino for her patience and enormously helpful typing and retyping.

Herbert J. Stern

Introduction

It has been more than a dozen years since I began to write the first volume in this series. I never thought it would take ten years to produce the four volumes in print; and I believed that with the publication of Volume IV, *Summation,* I would be finished—or if not finished, at least done.

Yet, as the years have clicked by, it has occurred to me that what we do and what we teach about what we do in the courtroom is not susceptible to one exposition, one demonstration, one practice session. Although each new lesson and practice session may not actually impart dramatically new matters, the person practicing will hear and see new material because of a heightened sensitivity and awareness. One makes muscles by repeating exercise.

Thus it also occurred to me that for those who have been exposed to the contents of *Trying Cases to Win,* in its four volumes or in any one of them, there would be a need for fresh opportunities to work through the principles and techniques in these volumes with new cases and materials. And that, of course, brought forth the concept of this supplement, first suggested to me by Marc Gallant of Aspen Law and Business. The notion was, initially, to produce an opportunity to experience the trial work of others and to perfect one's own, designed for those who have some background in the approach to the trial of cases laid out in the underlying work. However, this begat a dilemma.

How can one be sure that the readers have all the previous material in mind as they go through the trial and its critique? More than just cryptic references to the series had to be made. As these references gave birth to longer exposition, it became clear to the authors that this work had the ability to stand alone from the others, although its readers would be better informed with reference to the underlying work.

A word now about the use of the word "he" and also to the fact that there are now "authors," whereas before there was but one. When I first entered law school, more than 40 years ago, less than 5 percent of our class were women. Now, as often as not, in any given class women may constitute the majority. The use of the word "he" in this work, and in the prior ones, is meant to be gender neutral, the equivalent of "humankind," and should not be taken in any other way or for anything more than the avoidance of a continual and often clumsy "he or she."

As for why there are now two authors, well, the addition of Professor Saltzburg adds a depth that only another insight can afford. Steve Saltzburg and I have been teaching together for nearly two decades. Together, we founded the Advocacy Institute at the University of Virginia Law School, and, as co-directors, have just graduated our 18th yearly crop of practicing lawyers and law students. It is my hope and expectation that together we will be enabled to provide additional training and teaching materials to the trial bar.

One final word. It would not be inappropriate for one to ask of me, "What have you learned in these past few years? What would you have written differently, taken away, or added if you were to write the entire four-volume work over again?"

The entirely truthful answer is that I do not regret and would not withdraw a word, for all that I have seen, done, and taught has confirmed the *maxims* and *lessons* that dot the work. There is one subject, however, that I would greatly expand on and make an even higher imperative in the art of advocacy: the overwhelming importance of emotion in the decisional process of anyone and everyone—and therefore the overwhelming importance of having the trier commit emotionally at the outset of hearing the controversy.

The events of the last few years have convinced me that people—*all* people—decide as they *want* to, and then use intellect to justify that decision, not the other way around. Moreover, because the stated intellectual "reasons" rarely actually drive the decision, the reasons that are given are usually makeshift and often inappropriate as a matter of plain logic, reason, and even common sense. And that is why questioning jurors after verdict is so darn frustrating. Their reasons rarely make sense. The basic explanation for this phenomenon is that they simply did what they *wanted* to, and then found a reason —any reason—to explain the result. The late Robert F. Hanley said it very well in a passage quoted in Volume I:

> In life, people make decisions first and then find the arguments to rationalize them, though rarely is this sequence consciously appreciated. Few people argue matters out, either in their heads or with their friends, and make their decisions based on the results of the debate. Human beings may be a rational species, but, more often than not, the reason proceeds from the emotion, not vice versa. These basic thoughts come booming forth from Aristotle's text.

If you doubt that, just regard the judgment of judges—the equivalent of verdicts by jurors. The difference is that judges usually give fairly detailed reasons for their decisions, whereas jurors use general verdicts and sometimes answer special interrogatories. The fact of the matter is that very often—all too often—the reasons given by judges in opinions are as wide off the mark, or nearly so, as the reasons the jurors give you when you ask them after their verdict. Why? For the same cause: the decision is an emotional one, and the reasons are the intellectual footnotes sought out and then offered to justify a decision that often was previously made on a different level or basis. Reflect on your nonjury cases. Will it matter which judge hears it? If so, why? Because of the different emotional baggage the one or the other will bring to the case, correct?

The same is true when people—all people, judges and jurors—debate behind closed doors in an effort to arrive at a collegial decision. During the course of mock trials, we have (with permission, of course) listened in and even sat in as mock jurors made arguments to each other—arguments that made no sense, but that advanced a position obviously held for quite other reasons which are not articulated.

Look at the Supreme Court of the United States, for example, the highest court of all. The record comes to it frozen.

There are no facts to be found. The law applicable to the case resides in books. And yet we *know* that in a host of cases, a court comprised of Warren, Brennan, Marshall, and Douglas, on the one hand, and Burger, Rehnquist, Frankfurter, Scalia, and Thomas, on the other, will more often than not see the record and the precedents differently. Why? Because they *want* to, that's why—and for reasons that will not appear in their decisions. Indeed, the truth is that all too often judges, on all sides of issues, will actually malform the record and even the precedents in order to come out where they want to.

Let us go back to our trial setting. How could one jury, an all-white jury, acquit police officers of assaulting Rodney King in the face of the actual video of the beating of the man as he lay helpless on the ground? They said they had a reasonable doubt, because they wanted to. Why is it that more Democrats than Republicans believe that President Clinton did not lie before the grand jury, and why is it that more Republicans than Democrats believe that such perjury, if committed even in a private lawsuit, is an impeachable offense? The answer is obvious. We all answer factual *and* legal issues the way we want to, and then muster support in the evidence, or the lack of it, or in constitutional imperatives put forth to buttress our position.

Well, what has all that to do with you and with me, in the more routine cases that we handle in our courtrooms, where jurors do not automatically line up emotionally before the case is heard, because no great social issue or cause immediately strikes them? The answer, for me, is of the utmost importance. It is this: once we appreciate that our jurors will try to vindicate their own positions, as advocates we must invest them on our side at the earliest possible moment, so that all that emotional stuff will work for us. And that, of course, brings us to the overwhelming importance of the opening as a tool of advocacy. Neither jurors nor anyone else will keep an open mind for as long as they can avoid it. Even as you read these words, you say "yes" or "no" to yourself. It is difficult to wait even for the end of the paragraph, much less the end of the book or even the introduction. The point is simply this: if your opening can persuade a juror that he is on your side, then that will be his side, and he will hear the trial with the same bias that he would bring to one of the great out-of-court issues that he has taken an out-of-court position on. Volume I describes, in greater length than is available here, the reasons for this, and how to implement the tools of advocacy to achieve this in opening.

But now, as our trial is about to begin, as you, the reader, observe as it progresses, I suggest you do so at various levels. Put yourself in the position of counsel, to be sure. But also watch the trial unfold through the eyes of the jurors. Listen to the judge and see if you can follow his instructions. Listen to counsel as they open. Are they clear? See if you are asking yourself immediately, "Who is right here?" And most importantly, "Who am I for?" And then, as the trial proceeds, listen to the examinations. Test them, to be sure, against the principles of the underlying work, but also watch yourself. See if you are unconsciously rooting for the side you have already espoused. See if you use rationalization and denial to deal with what you do not want to hear (Volume I). See if opening is an argument (Volume I), and if both direct and cross-examinations are arguments, too (Volumes II and III). And, finally, when you get to summation, see how much the arguments mattered to the jury, or, for that matter, to you (Volume IV).

There is, of course, yet another level upon which you should function to get the maximum benefit from the exercise; after all, that is also what this is, an exercise performed by *you*, as you add muscle and tone to your own advocacy. Even as you listen to the transcript the way a juror would, with another part of your mind listen to the arguments and the examinations the way a trial lawyer does. Focus on the way each question is crafted, and consider what might be done to improve it. I am often asked how I came to certain insights about trial advocacy, and, of course, there is no one simple answer. Doing and the study of doing, reading books about doing, and watching others do are all ingredients in the mix. But one of the most beneficial tools for me has been the study of the transcript of other trial lawyers, past and present. It began when I was a youngster, reading trial records that I discovered in my father's closet. If you were a surgeon taking training, you would watch other surgeons and study their techniques. If you were a musician, you would take training with a teacher or coach who would critique you as you did your exercises. Athletes undergo the same training, practicing under the eye of a coach and studying films of themselves and others as they perfect their own technique. Unfortunately, our own profession does little or nothing similar to train its members. For us, the reading and analysis of transcripts can and should be a coaching experience for trial lawyers. But that reading must be done in a disciplined and uncompromising way—unsatisfied with any effort that falls even one hair short of the best that can be *imagined,* even if only rarely attained.

And here, I fear, we may in this work be doing some injustice to the fine attorneys who appear in the record we are about to present. For this disciplined, uncompromising training requires them to be held against a standard that no lawyer can possibly attain all of the time, and that includes the authors. But no one—not them, or us, or you—can continue to advance if we do not, as the poet noted, reach beyond our grasp. The attorneys who appear herein have our unqualified admiration and our gratitude. And, with that, let us commence our work.

Come, the judge is entering the courtroom. The trial is about to begin.

May 1999   *Herbert J. Stern*

Chapter One

Opening Instructions

THE COURT'S INSTRUCTIONS

THE COURT. Let's swear in the jury.

[Comment] Sit in the box with the lay jurors—see if you can follow this. You are the jurors. You have never been to law school, perhaps not even college. Now listen.

(Jury panel sworn)

THE COURT: You've now been sworn as the jury to try this civil case in which the Plaintiff is suing the defendants, seeking money damages that he claims resulted from the defendants' conduct.

In this case there are several different parties representing separate and distinct claims. The law permits joining of these claims for trial because they arise out of the same subject matter.

Although these different claims will be tried together, each is separate from the other and each party is entitled to have you consider each claim separately as it affects that party.

Therefore, you should consider the evidence as it relates to each party or claim separately as you would if each claim had been tried before you separately.

Your oath as a juror has committed each of you to be an active participant in the administration of justice. The trial will develop questions of fact upon which the parties do not agree. It is your duty as jurors and yours alone to determine the facts from the evidence presented during the trial.

Questions of procedure and of the law to be applied to the facts will also occur during the course of the trial. It is my duty as the trial judge to make certain that the trial is conducted properly and according to the rules of law, and I will instruct you after all of the evidence has been submitted as to the law which you will apply to this case.

Now, I will tell you some general things about the procedure we will follow and how you are to perform your duties. First, the Plaintiff's attorney may make an opening statement outlining his case.

Immediately thereafter, the Defendant's attorney may also make an opening statement outlining his defense or he may do so later in the case.

The Plaintiff presents his evidence first, and when he is finished, the Defendant may present his evidence. Evidence in rebuttal may also be presented. The direct examination of all witnesses is conducted by the attorney calling the witness and all witnesses may be cross-examined by opposing counsel.

I may ask questions of a witness in order to obtain information to bring out some facts that are not fully developed by the testimony. Please do not consider my questions any more or less important than those of the attorneys.

At the end of all of the evidence, the attorneys may make their closing arguments; in these arguments, the attorneys will give you their views of what the evidence proves on the questions you have to decide, and these arguments should be given due consideration, but they are not evidence.

[Comment] What are the chances that the jurors follow all of this, or any of it? And here come a whole lot more instructions.

Only the evidence which has been admitted during the trial can be considered by you in determining the facts.

The admission of evidence in court is governed by rules of law. During the trial the attorneys may deem it necessary to make objections, and it then becomes my duty to rule on those objections, and to decide whether certain evidence can be admitted for your consideration.

You must not concern yourselves with the objections or my reasons for my rulings. You must not consider testimony or exhibits to which I have sustained an objection or which I have ordered stricken from the record. None of my rulings should be regarded as an indication of my opinion as to what your findings should be.

You should not take any questions that I may ask witnesses as any indication of my opinion as to how you should determine the issues of fact.

Any opinion which you think I have, as to the facts, would not be at all important. For you and you alone are the sole finders of the facts.

You must consider and weigh the testimony of each witness, and give it as much weight as in your judgment it is fairly entitled to receive.

The matter of credibility of a witness, that is, whether his testimony is believable in whole or in part, is solely for your determination.

[Comment] Too much, too soon. If we really want jurors to be able to apply this stuff, why not give them a written handout that they can keep with them? But here comes another deluge.

I will mention some of the factors which might bear on such determination:

Whether the witness has any interest in the outcome of the case or has friendship or animosity toward other persons concerned in the case. The behavior of the witness on the witness stand, and their demeanor. Their manner of testifying, and whether they show any bias or prejudice which might color their testimony. The accuracy of their memory and recollection. Their ability and opportunity to acquire knowledge of or to observe the matters concerning which they testified. The consistency or inconsistency of their testimony, as well as its reasonableness or unreasonableness in light of all of the other evidence in the case.

Both parties may call—are there any expert witnesses in this case?

MR. LONGER: No, Your Honor.

MR. SONNENFELD: No, Your Honor.

[Comment] The next instruction is both clear and memorable.

THE COURT. Okay. Do not discuss this case or anything connected with it amongst yourselves or with anyone else until all of the evidence is in and you have received final instructions from me and have retired to the jury room for deliberations to reach your verdict.

Do not permit others to discuss the case with you or in your presence. If such a thing should occur, you should advise me promptly. In addition, do not talk to counsel or the parties or the witnesses on any subject.

If you were to do so, even though innocently, it could be misinterpreted and could create serious problems.

Counsel and I are required by law to take up certain matters out of your hearing; we may do this at the bench or in the chambers, or I could ask you to leave so we can do this in the open courtroom. You should not concern yourself with any such proceeding.

[Comment] Now comes the burden of proof, on top of all this other stuff.

In civil cases, the Plaintiff has the burden of proving those contentions which entitle them to relief. Defendants are not required to offer evidence on their own behalf.

When parties have the burden of proof, their contention must be established by a fair preponderance of the evidence. A fair preponderance of the evidence means you are persuaded that a contention is more probably accurate and true than not.

To put it another way, think, if you will, of an ordinary balance scale with a pan on each side. Onto one side place all of the evidence favorable to the Plaintiff. Onto the other side, place all of the evidence favorable to the Defendants. If after considering the comparable weight of the evidence you feel that the scales tip ever so slightly or to the slightest degree in favor of the Plaintiffs, your verdict must be for the plaintiffs. If the scales tip ever so slightly or to the slightest degree in favor of the Defendants or they are equally balanced, your verdict must be for the Defendants.

While you must follow my legal instructions, you are the sole fact finders.

Your recollection, not mine, nor counsels' controls. You must decide all questions of credibility, weight and fact, including the inferences to be drawn from the facts.

The trial should take probably two or three days, probably three days. We'll be in court from roughly 9:30 to 4:30, with periodic recesses. And what I do is I break about every hour and then we'll break for lunch for about an hour and a half. If you need additional recesses, please raise your hand and I'll accommodate you right away.

[Comment] By this time, the last instruction will be closely followed. The good news is that the trial will be short.

My last direction is you are not to take any notes during the trial. These preliminary instructions have been presented prior to opening statements and testimony so that you may better understand the issues involved, evidentiary rules and courtroom procedures.

I'll give you other instructions in addition to these and my final charge. You should consider all instructions a connected series. Taken together they constitute the law. Thank you.

[Comment] The rest is bad news. Heads must be swimming in the jury box by now. And the dual news that they cannot take notes and that there are even more instructions to come can hardly be welcome news to the prisoners of the jury box.

Counsel, you may address the jury.

ANALYSIS OF THE PRELIMINARY INSTRUCTIONS

The trial judge has defined the burden of proof and demonstrated how slight it is in a civil case. The judge also has described the procedures that will unfold, so that the jury is prepared for the order of proceedings. As a result, counsel should feel no need for a "warmup" when they open to the jury.

The judge has precluded the jury from taking notes. No explanation is offered to the jury. But counsel are now aware that the jury is not going to be able to jot down names of witnesses or to write down reminders about evidence.

These instructions are almost entirely procedural. The judge, who probably knows little about the facts of the case, describes it in a bare sentence. He does tell the jury that there are two defendants and that the case against each should be analyzed separately, but in giving this instruction he cannot know for sure how the parties will deal with any differences that exist between the defendants.

[Comment] Of what value were these instructions? How much of them could these jurors possibly understand, particularly since they were lumped together in what is obviously a pro forma speech?

Chapter Two

The Opening Arguments

THE PLAINTIFF'S OPENING

The Opening Argument

[Comment] We call an opening an argument, for that is what it is—or should be. To vault over objections, particularly "argumentative," it must be disguised as an offer of proof. See Vol. I, pp. 142–147. The fact that there is nothing in most codes or rules of evidence forbidding "argument" in opening, and the further fact that no satisfactory definition of the prohibition exists, matter not. The objection lingers on, more from tradition than anything else; so, to be able to speak the advocate must disguise his argument as an offer of proof. But it is an "argument" that must be crafted and delivered. Vol. I, pp. 128–132. Before one can open, or do anything else in the courtroom for that matter, one has to decide the purpose of the task. That is, what is the object, the goal to be attained? For us that is clear: It is to argue your case and prejudice the tribunal so that they agree with you and take your side, as it were, so that your side becomes their side. If you achieve this, they will try to hear testimony and exhibits thereafter your way—because, you see, it will be their way. Some of this is in Stern's introduction, but the truly organized presentation of the power and purpose of opening arguments is one of the main themes of Volume I.

THE COURT: Counsel, you may address the jury.

MR. LONGER: Thank you, Your Honor. Good morning, ladies and gentleman.

THE JURY: Good morning.

MR. LONGER: My name is Fred Longer, and I appreciate your time, and I appreciate your attention today. My client is here because <u>he feels cheated</u>. <u>He feels like</u> he's

lost an opportunity that was his. <u>He feels like</u> he did work
that he should be paid for, but he's not getting paid for.

*[Comment] No personal advocacy. The attorney puts the client
in front of him and even at that the client only "feels" cheated.
This is not a persuasive way to argue. See Vol. I, pp. 22–24. It
should be: "We will prove to you that he performed a service for
this large insurance company, which then cheated plaintiff out
of his commission." It is the lawyer who must advocate the justice of the cause, not the client.*

Mr. Sussman is the President of Tower Financial
Planning Associates Incorporated. Mr. Sussman brought
together Blue Cross and Blue Shield with the Ironworker
District Council 17 Health and Welfare Fund here in
Philadelphia, brought them together, and allowed them
and enabled them and <u>influenced</u> them to agree to a contract. Because Mr. Sussman had familiarity with a co-
chairman of the Board of Trustees of the Ironworkers
Welfare Fund.

*[Comment] Not a felicitous presentation. Sussman is hardly
presented in his best light. It would be easy to point to his prior
relationship in selling insurance to the Union, and therefore the
"access"—the word of art of the day—which he enjoyed.*

It's because of Mr. Sussman's <u>connections</u>, his hard
work and because of his idea, that Blue Cross/Blue Shield
was able to get together with the Ironworkers, and enter
into a multi-million-dollar contract. It's because of his
efforts, his ideas, that Blue Cross/Blue Shield now has a
contract with approximately 2000 new clients,
Ironworkers, for his efforts, for his ideas, for his influence. Blue Cross/Blue Shield has given Mr. Sussman
nothing. Nothing.

*[Comment] Much better. The word "connections," however, on
top of the earlier "influenced," does not advance the cause.*

Now, as you heard Judge Kaffrisen mention, you folks
will decide the facts in this case, and you, it's your burden

to decide whether or not I've satisfied my burden. I have to prove to you by a preponderance of the evidence that Mr. Sussman was wrong[ed] and he should be right.

Mr. Sussman gave Blue Cross/Blue Shield a multi-million-dollar contract, gave them thousands of new clients, but he did it based on his influence, his ideas and his hard work. And the evidence will show to you that the balance on the scales of justice weigh[s] in my client's favor.

[Comment] The message is a good one. The words might be better chosen. And the constant reference to "client" is a violation of Rule I. See Vol. I, p. 36. Juries want to know whether lawyers — whom the jurors believe know the truth — themselves believe in what they say, or are merely taking a "client's" position.

Now, this is my opening statement. I get to preview for you the evidence that you'll hear, and what we'll see in the next day or two or three. And what I intend to do is have Mr. Sussman get on the stand, Mr. Sussman will testify, along with other witnesses, and Ms. Hardy, seated over here to the right of Ms. Bennett. Mr. Craggs will come and testify, he's the Plan Administrator. You'll also hear other witnesses, that Mr. Roberts, who is an associate in Blue Cross/Blue Shield, these people will all testify. Mr. Sussman will tell you that he's an insurance agent. He grew up in South Philly. He lived in So. Philadelphia. He started working at Sears after high school, went on into the insurance business about 30 years ago. Started selling life insurance, all sorts of insurance, casualty insurance as well, but then he focused on life insurance, which is health insurance and life insurance.

[Comment] It would be better for counsel to say "I will prove" than to use Sussman's proclamation as the vehicle of speech. See Vol. I, pp. 22–24. Now comes, in our view, one of the best portions of the opening.

He started with other agencies and in time he started to work on his own, because he liked meeting the people that would come in and helping them out and he also liked the challenge that selling insurance offered to him.

Mr. Sussman, about 25 years ago, started Tower Financial Planning Associates. It's an insurance broker-age agency. It sells insurance. Mr. Sussman is the agent that brokers the business through Tower Financial. Over the years he's met many people, sold many people insur-ance, and over the years, the way he's made his money, by selling insurance, is by receiving commissions when he makes a sale of insurance.

The insurance companies pay him that commission. The clients, the insureds, do not pay him the commission. It's the insurance company that does.

[Comment] Although the jury and you, the reader, are not presently in a position to know it, the most important words counsel has uttered are the last: "clients, the insureds, do not pay him the commission. It's the insurance company that does."

Mr. Sussman has been doing this, as I said, for over 30 years, he's made a lot of connections selling insurance. People tell him about—refer friends to him. Other clients come to him and that's how he gets his business. Other people come to him.

One of the people that he's met over the years is a gen-tleman by the name of Robert Sweeney. Mr. Sweeney is a friend of Mr. Sussman's, or was a friend until recently. He, as I said before, is an Ironworker, but he's more than an Ironworker. He's the President of the Local 399 in New Jersey. And he's more than just that.

As the President and Business Agent of Local 399, he's a member of the Board of Trustees for the Welfare Fund. He's more than just a member of the Board of Trustees for the Welfare Fund. He's the Co-chairman of the Welfare Fund. The Welfare Fund has a Board of Trustees, there's 22 of them. There are 11 Locals that comprise the Welfare Fund. Each Local presents a Trustee.

[Comment] So far, he is excellent. His introduction of the plaintiff, what he does, how he earns his livelihood and the transition to the introduction of the union and Sweeney are very good indeed. As you will see, something more must be done, either here or later, to anticipate whether Sweeney will be adverse to Sussman. Indeed, we will later see him testify that Sussman is entitled to nothing.

On the other side of the Union side of the Welfare Fund is the Management side. They [re]present a Local. There are 11 Management Trustees and 11 Union Trustees. There are only two chairmen. They are Co-chairmen, Mr. Sweeney is a co-chairman on the Union side of the Board of Trustees. He's an influential person on the Board of Trustees. Mr. Sussman had a very good relationship with a very influential man on the Board of Trustees, the Ironworkers Welfare Fund.

Mr. Sussman, because of his <u>relationship</u> with Mr. Sweeney, was able to sell to him and the Ironworkers, in 1994, a contract with a Preferred Provider Organization, a PPO.

[Comment] Notice: "influence" and "connections" have wisely been elevated to "relationship." And now we are introduced to an important point of the case.

Preferred Provider Organization has networks of doctors who offer discounts on their prices by joining that network and people can save money on their insurance costs, their health benefits by going to PPOs. Mr. Sussman suggested to Mr. Sweeney in 1994, that they go to the PPO, by the name of Preferred Care.

Mr. Sussman has a contract—I'm sorry, the Ironworkers now have a contract with Preferred Care. Mr Sussman receives commissions on that contract with Preferred Care. But, when the contract was being started, Mr. Sweeney had some concerns about the reach of the networks, what doctors were in the networks, some of the other locals were concerned that the networks didn't reach far enough.

So Mr. Sussman, because it was his client, because it was his friend, because it was his job, thought that he should look for other providers on behalf of the Ironworkers.

[Comment] This is a critical point, as we shall see. Just who is the plaintiff representing in seeking to find better insurance for the Union? Is it the Union or the new insurance company? And notice, Sussman has a commission in place with the company he is working to replace.

Mr. Sussman, in 1994, called Ms. Hardy. He told her the situation going on with the Ironworkers. Ms. Hardy had been trying to get the contract with the Ironworkers for years. It's a big account. There are thousands of members, Ironworkers to insure.

[Comment] Very good. It might have been wise, however, to introduce just who Hardy was to the jury and to us.

And Blue Cross/Blue Shield didn't have their account. They had it a long time ago, but they lost it, and they couldn't get it back.

[Comment] It would be better for plaintiff to start with Blue Cross/Blue Shield seeking the union than the plaintiff seeking a new insurance company for the union. And now he makes that point. And very well, too.

The Ironworkers had no interest in Blue Cross/Blue Shield. In 1992, Ms. Hardy wrote a memorandum that said that there was a total lack of interest by the Ironworkers [in] Blue Cross/Blue Shield, and she concedes that that total lack of interest sustained itself in 1993, and in 1994, until Mr. Sussman. After Mr. Sussman got Ms. Hardy involved with him and Sweeney, she noticed an interest in the Ironworkers.

[Comment] We still do not know much about Ms. Hardy, or what she has at stake in this prospective contract.

The Ironworkers were now interested in Blue Cross/Blue Shield. They, however, were going forward with the Preferred Care contract that Mr. Sussman had arranged with them.

Mr. Sweeney wanted more time to see how things worked for Preferred Care, to get some experience under his belt. After several months passed by, we go into the new year of 1995. Mr. Sussman wants to talk to Mr. Sweeney again, because of some problems that they were still experiencing with the Preferred Care organization.

He calls Ms. Hardy, they have at least two more tense meetings in 1995, Mr. Sussman and Ms. Hardy and Mr. Sweeney, each one gets better than the next. At the end of March, Mr. Sweeney is talking about Blue Cross/Blue Shield. He's interested in moving to a new provider.

[Comment] Notice that counsel has swung from the past tense into present-tense storytelling. Not so good. Better to stick with arguing — using "I will prove," or its equivalent. See Vol. I, pp. 202–203. Unfortunately, counsel does not use the tools of argument in opening — "I will prove," "The evidence will conclusively show," etc.

The two of them, Mr. Sussman and Ms. Hardy, had been providing him information that allowed him to do that. They got him doctors' listings, they took ZIP Code listings of where the Union members were so that they could understand and inform you of where the networks were based on ZIP codes, they figured that out.

At the end of March of 1995, Mr. Sussman and Ms. Hardy had met with Mr. Sweeney, Mr. Sussman understood that they were going to go forward with Blue Cross/Blue Shield. They are seriously thinking of going for and contracting with Blue Cross/Blue Shield.

[Comment] This is a little confusing. There is a mere chronological listing of events. The argument ought to be that the

plaintiff introduced Blue Cross/Blue Shield to the union and obtained for Blue Cross/Blue Shield an insurance contract long sought by the company, but which it simply could not get, and this argument should be developed in more detail. And why was Sussman doing all this? Here it comes.

At that time, Ms. Hardy told Mr. Sussman for the first time, you won't get a commission, Mr. Sussman, unless you have a broker of record letter. What's a broker of record letter? It's Blue Cross/Blue Shield's policy to have the client in a letter saying I recognize you, agent, in this case Mr. Sussman, to be the broker on this contract.

Mr. Sussman spoke to Mr. Sweeney and told him, I need my broker of record letter. Mr. Sweeney told Mr. Sussman, I won't give it to you because you should have gotten your protection and your commission from the insurance carrier.

For 30 years Mr. Sussman has always gotten his commissions from the insurance companies, not from the client. Ms. Hardy is telling Mr. Sussman that the broker of record letter makes the client pay the commission.

[Comment] Good, but will the jury understand? Do you? And did you know that there were conversations between plaintiff and Hardy about a 1–3% commission for Sussman prior to the meeting with Sweeney? No? Well, neither do the jurors.

Mr. Sussman didn't know what to do at first. He spoke to people that he knew to find out where to go. People that he knew in the insurance business told Mr. Sussman, don't deal with Helen Hardy, she's bad news. You should go to speak to the Broker Department at Blue Cross/Blue Shield and deal with a fellow, a gentleman by the name of Eric—Brian Sullivan.

[Comment] How do these nameless informant whispers about Ms. Hardy's unreliability get into evidence? And if they don't, how can this be argued in opening?

Mr. Sullivan and Mr. Sussman met in early April with Mr. Sweeney and proposed alternatives to what Ms. Hardy had been talking about with Mr. Sweeney. Those alternatives also sounded interesting to Mr. Sweeney.

Mr. Sussman provided doctors' listings and other information to Mr. Sweeney about what Mr. Sullivan could offer. This was in April of 1994. In between April of 1995 and the end of July of 1995, it was the Fund that had decided to go forward with Blue Cross/Blue Shield.

They got involved, their consultant, an actuarial consultant in New York City, a man by the name of Charles Maresca, he has a company called the Segal Company, to speak to Ms. Hardy.

[Comment] All these dates and all these names are flooding the jurors with information which they have to process and discern the significance of, instead of it being marshaled into an argument to prove a point. Not so good. See Vol. I, pp. 203–205.

Mr. Maresca and Ms. Hardy spoke. <u>You're going to find that Mr. Maresca told Ms. Hardy</u>, we're not going to pay commissions.

<u>We're</u> not going to increase our risk in this. Mr. Sussman is not in this contract. He's out.

Ms. Hardy knew that by not putting the commission in she could go forward with this contract now <u>at a reduced price</u>. The price was Mr. Sussman's commission.

[Comment] Will this be understandable to the jurors? Is it to you? He is saying that the union saved money on the premiums by not giving Sussman the broker letter. Well, if so, and if it was the union's decision, as counsel says, the union's instruction to Ms. Hardy not to pay a commission, why is Blue Cross being sued for interference with Sussman and the union?

In August of 1995, Mr. Sussman tried again to bring Mr. Sullivan back to Mr. Sweeney, and they met again, but Mr. Sweeney had already decided, <u>because of what he was hearing from his consultant</u>, that they were going

to go with Blue Cross/Blue Shield through Ms.
Sullivan—I'm sorry, Ms. Hardy, and Mr. Sussman was
out.

*[Comment] See—it was a pure union decision—counsel
argues.*

Now, Mr. Sussman makes a living through commissions. This was a big account.

His commissions would have been very big because of
the size of this account. He had estimated at one point in
time, based on a conversation with Ms. Hardy, that his
commission would be around $150,000 for selling this
contract. And it's not just a one-year deal. Every year that
the contract is renewed into the future, he would get a
commission. It adds up after time.

*[Comment] What is he asking for? How much? No one can
know. It will be a recurring problem for him.*

But, Blue Cross/Blue Shield wouldn't recognize him,
and today, still doesn't recognize him to be the broker.
They don't even recognize him to be involved in the sale,
but words speak louder—what's written there speaks
louder than what you're going to hear today.

I'd like to show you something. This is a memorandum that Mr. Sullivan wrote in October of 1995. He was
looking to get compensated himself for the contract that
Mr. Sussman was able to broker on behalf of the
Ironworkers.

And in this paragraph here, he says: "I must say, that
my broker, Mr. Sussman, did start the group up again in
looking at Blue Cross." Mr. Sussman started this group
up. The Ironworkers to looking at Blue Cross, not Ms.
Hardy, not Mr. Sullivan, it was his hard work and it was
his efforts and it was his connections that got the
Ironworkers to contract with Blue Cross/Blue Shield.

And the evidence will show that Mr. Sussman
deserves a commission because of his efforts and his hard

work and the compensation that he's seeking is <u>not something excessive</u>.

[Comment] Well . . . what is it that he is seeking that is so modest compared to what he is entitled to? And what is it that he is entitled to?

It was understood to be this way, by the normal course of business in this line of business.

And Mr. Sussman is not looking for anything unjust or unreasonable, he's looking for just and fair compensation. And at the end of this trial, we'll be asking you to render a verdict in my client's favor. I thank you for your time right now. Thank you for your attention.

[Comment] The trouble with not indicating what the plaintiff is entitled to is that it sounds as though there was no agreement *and that he therefore is not* entitled *to anything.*

Analysis of Plaintiff's Opening Statement

There would be no better way to analyze the success of an opening argument than to ask the jurors who heard it what they understood the plaintiff's argument to be. We cannot ask the jurors, but each of us who reads the transcript can decide what we think plaintiff's counsel was arguing. Before reading further, stop and ask yourself what the theme of the plaintiff's case is. The ease or difficulty you have is some indication of the effectiveness of the argument.

We think that the strength of this opening argument is that it has a central theme, and for us it comes through clearly: namely, Mr. Sussman had arranged for health insurance for a union welfare fund with a preferred provider network. The fund had some concerns with the network and had some interest in considering an expanded network. Mr. Sussman's once good friend, Mr. Sweeney, was president of a local ironworker's union and co-chair of the board of trustees of the welfare fund. Mr. Sweeney was a powerful union figure. Mr. Sussman contacted Blue Cross/Blue Shield to see what sort of package it might provide. Up until then, the insurer had had no success

in interesting the welfare fund in obtaining insurance with it.
But it is obvious that the fund represents thousands of workers, and a contract would be of great interest to the insurer.
Mr. Sussman's contact with an official at the insurer, Ms.
Hardy, ultimately led to the insurer's providing a health plan
for the welfare fund. At some point during the negotiations,
Ms. Hardy informed Mr. Sussman that he would not receive
any commission because he did not have a "broker of record"
letter. Sussman regarded such a letter as being outside the
usual insurance practice, and tried to go around Ms. Hardy to
another person at the insurer, Mr. Sullivan. But we do not
understand what the broker letter means in terms of who pays
the commission—that is, not who writes the check but whose
money it is, the union's or the insurance company's.

Bottom line: Blue Cross/Blue Shield gets a major new
client; Mr. Sweeney's welfare fund gets a good deal; and Blue
Cross is able to make a greater profit and offer a favorable contract by not paying Sussman a commission.

Plaintiff's counsel wisely lumps the two defendants
together in the opening. The suit is against Blue Cross/Blue
Shield, and the fact that there might be two named defendants
is not important in this opening argument. Notice that there is
no "windup." Plaintiff's counsel has left for the trial judge the
entire task of explaining the procedures to the jury. There is no
effort to avoid the burden of proof, weak as it is in a civil case.
Plaintiff's lawyer wisely assumes the burden without trying to
minimize it. (See Vol. I, pp. 146–151.)

Plaintiff's counsel is at his best when he lays out Mr.
Sussman's background. Is it relevant that Sussman grew up in
Philadelphia, lived in South Philadelphia, worked at Sears,
and started his own business? In a strictly legal sense, maybe
not. But nothing could be more important to a jury. Is it relevant that Mr. Sussman started his business 30 years earlier
and has been selling all kinds of insurance? Again, it may have
small probative value in a strictly legal sense, but the jury
surely understood that Mr. Sussman worked his way from
Sears to his own business and that his business is providing

insurance for people about whom he cares. All of this is calculated to endear the plaintiff to the jury and to move them to
want to find for him. And if they want to find for him, they
will. If not, not.

Plaintiff's counsel is not as strong when he describes how
Mr. Sweeney and Ms. Hardy attempted to exclude Mr.
Sussman from the final dealings. It is virtually impossible, for
example, for anyone to understand exactly what the Segal
Company in New York and Mr. Maresca have to do with the
case.

It is also unclear from the opening argument exactly what
roles Mr. Sullivan and Ms. Hardy each played at Blue
Cross/Blue Shield. It seems as though Ms. Hardy must have
personally received some type of bonus or reward for landing
the welfare fund account, and Mr. Sullivan wanted to capture
for himself whatever Ms. Hardy got. If this is so, imagine how
much more powerful the opening statement would have been
had counsel said:

> I am going to prove to you that Blue Cross/Blue
> Shield deliberately set up a system that encouraged
> their employees to cheat innocent outsiders like Mr.
> Sussman for their personal profit, and that the sys-
> tem promoted so much greed that even inside the
> company its agents attempted to cheat each other. I
> will prove to you that Ms. Hardy, an agent who had
> no ability to interest Mr. Sweeney and his welfare
> fund in her company, signed up the fund as a major
> client solely because of Mr. Sussman and then
> turned on Mr. Sussman to deny him the commission
> that he had earned. And I will also prove that inside
> the company Mr. Sullivan memorialized for Blue
> Cross/Blue Shield the truth, which was that Mr.
> Sussman was solely responsible for the insurer
> being able to obtain the welfare fund as a client. Mr.
> Sullivan didn't care, however, about Mr. Sussman.
> He didn't care that Ms. Hardy had cheated him out
> of a commission. Mr. Sullivan wanted the reward

and the credit that Ms. Hardy got for landing the welfare fund and for cheating Mr. Sussman.

Plaintiff's counsel emphasizes that Mr. Sussman will testify and promises what Mr. Sussman will deliver. Counsel misses opportunities for personal advocacy, to promise what *he will prove* and use his personal credibility to bolster the forthcoming testimony of Mr. Sussman. More personal advocacy and avoidance of the term "my client" would likely improve plaintiff's counsel's standing with the jury.

Plaintiff's counsel obviously understands that, just as it is important for the jury to think that Mr. Sussman is the kind of person who should win, the jury will not be happy with Sussman if they think that Sussman is seeking a windfall from the defendants. That is why counsel tells the jury that Sussman is seeking a standard commission, which is substantial in this case. There is some defensiveness in the exclusive focus on what Sussman is seeking. Consider how much easier the point goes down if made this way:

> I shall prove to you that Mr. Sussman created a wonderful opportunity for the welfare fund and its thousands and thousands of union members. He created for them the opportunity for excellent medical care at a reasonable cost with a broad and talented pool of doctors. Mr. Sussman created for Blue Cross/Blue Shield an opportunity for profit that the company longed for but had been unable to get a foot in the door for years. He will have made millions of dollars in revenues for Blue Cross/Blue Shield over many years. That is just what he was asked to do, get the best possible coverage for the workers at the best possible price from a company that would make a fair profit. Mr. Sussman seeks the usual commission an agent typically receives for putting together this kind of package. We will prove to you that an insurance company like Blue Cross/Blue Shield that signs on thousands and thousands of new clients typically pays a commission to

the insurance agent who makes it possible for the company to receive millions and millions of new dollars in revenue, but in this case Blue Cross/Blue Shield departed from the standard practice late in the negotiations between it and the welfare fund because it sensed that it could cheat Mr. Sussman out of the fee he had earned.

It is clear from the plaintiff's opening that the villain from the plaintiff's perspective is Blue Cross/Blue Shield, not the welfare fund. However, the opening does not clearly indicate the plaintiff's view as to the conduct of Mr. Sweeney, other than to refer to him as someone who once was a friend of the plaintiff. The plaintiff might have benefited from explaining how the insurer's actions attempted to pit Mr. Sweeney against Mr. Sussman, and the conflict that the insurer created for Mr. Sweeney.

Consider the following argument, for instance:

Blue Cross/Blue Shield said it would not pay any commission to Mr. Sussman because he had no broker of record letter. Now, this was the same Blue Cross/Blue Shield that had been dealing with Mr. Sussman over months of negotiations without a mention of such a letter. When Blue Cross/Blue Shield said to Mr. Sussman that he needed the letter, the company was really saying that the welfare fund should pay any commission. I'll prove to you that this not only was inconsistent with the industry practice, but, more than that, Blue Cross/Blue Shield understood that Mr. Sussman came to it so that the union could see about getting a better deal for its members, not so that it could pay a commission that it never before paid. We will prove that if Blue Cross/Blue Shield had even hinted that it would want to have the welfare fund pay the broker's commission when Mr. Sussman first approached the company, there would have been no contract because Mr. Sussman would not have participated on that basis. It was after Mr. Sussman had made contact with the welfare fund and assured that there eventually would be a contract, one that Blue Cross had been salivating about, that Blue Cross/Blue Shield said to Mr. Sussman that he needed to get his commission solely from the fund. Now Mr. Sussman knew that Blue Cross could pay him a commission. He knew they could do this if they wanted, but he had no choice but to report to Mr. Sweeney what the company had said. This put Mr. Sweeney between a rock and a hard place. Mr. Sweeney knew his unions did not pay the broker's commission. He also knew that, as a result of Mr. Sussman's efforts, his welfare fund was about to enter into a good contract with Blue Cross/Blue Shield. His duty was to obtain the health insurance for the men and women he represented as trustee and co-chair of the welfare fund. So, Mr. Sweeney did what he had to do, which was to get the insurance coverage for the workers. We will prove to you that Mr. Sussman understood the position that Mr. Sweeney was in, that Mr. Sussman never wanted the welfare fund to pay his commission, and that Blue Cross/Blue Shield purposefully acted to drive a wedge between Mr. Sussman and Mr. Sweeney.

It is important to note that plaintiff's counsel does not get into the law upon which he relies or the precise legal theory that justifies relief. The jury understands that the plaintiff feels that Blue Cross/Blue Shield cheated him. Plaintiff's counsel made a strategic judgment that it was not important early in the case to get into elements of a cause of action. The jury understands an allegation of cheating.

In sum, plaintiff's counsel chose a strong central theme and understood the importance of emphasizing Mr. Sussman's background, which would appeal to the jury and make them want to find for him, while attempting to anticipate an argument that Mr. Sussman was greedy. We have made some suggestions as to how the execution of the theme might have been improved.

One last caveat before we move on. There is a point during the opening argument when plaintiff's counsel states that Mr. Sussman made inquiries about Ms. Hardy and was told not to deal with her because she is "bad news," and that he should deal with "a fellow" or "gentleman" named Sullivan. The juxtaposition of the criticism of Ms. Hardy with the references to Mr. Sullivan could be heard as gender bias. It seems clear to us that this was not intended, but it is a reminder of the care that must be taken when making references to anyone's gender or in making any comparison between individuals that might imply bias.

THE DEFENDANTS' OPENING

Defendants' Opening

MR. SONNENFELD: May I proceed, Your Honor?

THE COURT: Please.

MR. SONNENFELD: Good morning, again. This is our second day together. I want to begin again by thanking you for coming here to serve as jurors.

You serve a very important part in our judicial system and Mr. Longer and I are both very appreciative of you coming in and spending your time with us today and for the next two days. We will try to minimize our imposition on your time by moving this forward.

The jury system really is a wonderful system. Here we have eight people from every part of Philadelphia, from the Northeast, Mount Airy, Germantown, South Philadelphia, West Philadelphia, and you're going to gather together and bring together your collective judgment in deciding this case.

[Comment] Do you think that the jury is impressed with this flattery from a suitor who they know wants only their votes and has no intention of ever seeing any of them again?

Now, as I told you yesterday, in this case, I represent Independence Blue Cross and Pennsylvania Blue Shield. They are two companies that are both nonprofit companies, they have no shareholder. They are owned by their members, the people who get their health insurance through Blue Cross and Blue Shield, and they have been sued for money by Mr. Sussman, actually his company, Tower Financial Planning Associates.

[Comment] This is excellent. It is Rule III stuff (see Vol. I, pp. 88–93), calculated to make jurors want *to find for the defendant.*

One thing I want to ask you, in this case, is to remember the old story, how there are two sides to every story. You have now heard Mr. Sussman's side, and you'll hear his evidence first, as the case goes forward. I want to ask you to not make any judgments or conclusions about the case until you've heard both sides, until you've heard the evidence from Independence Blue Cross and Pennsylvania Blue Shield, as well, and then once you have heard all of the evidence, then you can form your judgments about what this case is about.

[Comment] This is an argument that should not *be made. First, on the upside, no one will or can obey the request. So there is no upside. On the downside, the request implies that unless it is obeyed the jury could find for the plaintiff on the basis of his case alone. In other words, there is an implication that there are two cases heard right after each other, first the plaintiff's and then the defendant's. Not so. The defendant will be making its case during its cross, while the plaintiff is presenting his. The jury should not be asked* by counsel *to keep an open mind until the very end of both direct cases, because it is an argument made from what may be perceived to be weakness. In any event, the jurors won't do it because they simply cannot do it. Only lawyers see two cases. The jurors see only one. For a full discussion of the principles underlying this point, see Vol. I, pp. 209–211.*

Now, Mr. Longer began his opening to you by saying that his client is cheated or <u>feels</u> cheated and, therefore, is seeking compensation or money from my clients, Blue Cross and Blue Shield, to compensate him for work he had done.

[Comment] Nice play on "feels," a gift which plaintiff's counsel gave him.

To the contrary, I think <u>the evidence will show</u> you that, if anything, Mr. Sussman is <u>seeking something for nothing</u>. He is, in essence, trying to take advantage of a friendship he once had with Mr. Sweeney, of the Ironworkers over in New Jersey, and trying from that to get something that he didn't work for, a commission on a contract that did take place between Blue Cross and Blue Shield and the Ironworkers Health and Welfare Fund, but one that Mr. Sussman <u>had nothing to do with</u>.

[Comment] It would be stronger to assume the burden of proof, even as the defendant, with a "we will prove." It is our view that all litigants, regardless of whether they are prosecuting or defending any case, should assume the burden of proof in opening. See Vol. I, pp. 148–156. That said, counsel has been very clear and firm in his assertion that Sussman did nothing. The jury will likely hold him to that assertion. And if the promise of proof comes true, then the defendant will very likely prevail. But if it is not true that the plaintiff had "nothing" to do with this deal, what then? Having made such a strong claim, if it turns out to be incorrect, is the defendant likely to be able to prevail on any alternate theory it may have? See Vol. I, pp. 82–84.

Now, at the end of the case, Judge Kafrissen will instruct you on the law to apply to your deliberations, and he'll instruct you at the end of the case, that in this case, what the Plaintiff is claiming, what Mr. Sussman and Tower is claiming, is that Blue Cross and Blue Shield intentionally or negligently interfered with Mr. Sussman's prospective, that means future, relationship with the Ironworkers District Council.

I'll repeat that, because I know that is complicated. What Mr. Sussman's claim is, is that somehow Blue Cross and Blue Shield intentionally interfered with his relationship, his future relationship, with the Ironworkers. And in order to prevail, Mr. Sussman and his company Tower, as Judge Kafrissen will instruct you at the end of the case, will have to show in his evidence, four things. He'll have to show that he had a prospective future relationship with the Ironworkers. He'll have to show secondly that Blue Cross and Blue Shield somehow interfered with the relationship between Mr. Sussman and the Ironworkers.

[Comment] This is, in fact, the defendant's stronger argument. The plaintiff has not sued Blue Cross in contract for money owed him by Blue Cross for past service. He is suing in tort for disturbing an ongoing or prospective relationship between himself and the union. Although counsel has not made that as clear as he might have, he has gone a long way. But now he returns to the definitions, only to make them cloudy.

He'll have to show that this interference was <u>without a privilege or justification</u>, meaning that Blue Cross and Blue Shield had no <u>right to this alleged interference</u>. And fourth and finally, he'll have to show that he was in some way damaged as a result.

[Comment] That may well be an element, but it may sound to the jurors as though there was a disturbance here caused by Blue Cross—although with the right to do so.

I submit to you that the <u>evidence that you will hear</u> in the next three days will establish none of those four elements of the claim of intentional or negligent interference with a prospective contractual relationship between the Ironworkers and Mr. Sussman.

[Comment] I will prove.

And the reason that it won't is because the Ironworkers didn't want to have anything to do with Mr. Sussman. And Mr. Sweeney, who is the co-chair of the Ironworkers District Council, will make that clear in his testimony.

[Comment] The last two paragraphs strike hard, shrewd blows. But they should be expanded upon. Rather than going through a chronological telling of events, as he is about to do, he should promise to produce Sweeney — and other representatives of the union — who will swear to the jury that they did not want Sussman to get a fee, that he had no relationship with the union which Blue Cross interfered with, and that they believe he is entitled to nothing. *In other words, it is essential that counsel immediately vindicate the claim he has made by footnoting its bona fides with the witnesses and what they will say. Vol. I, pp. 199–200. Remember, the organization of what you say is as persuasive as what you have to say. Vol. I, pp. 203, 205. Instead of an argument, we are about to get a witness-by-witness account.*

Let me instead review for you the time line of what happened here and what you will hear in the evidence to be presented in the next several days.

As you're going to hear from Ms. Hardy, from Independence Blue Cross, Ms. Hardy is in charge of the department at Independence Blue Cross that deals with unions and union health and welfare funds. She is in charge of that department. She is the manager of that department. And <u>you will hear</u> that virtually every union in the Philadelphia area provides health coverage for its members through Independence Blue Cross and Pennsylvania Blue Shield.

[Comment] Well, at least now we know who Ms. Hardy is. But notice "You will hear" instead of "we will prove." The witness has become the facilitator of the speech in order to avoid the objection, "argumentative." Better to use counsel's "I will prove" or "establish" and so forth. See Vol. I, pp. 142–144.

And <u>Ms. Hardy will explain to you</u> that it is virtually unheard of for a union to use a broker. There is no need for a broker. For the most part, a broker doesn't confer any value or benefit. Most unions use a consultant, who consults with them and advises them on their compensation, and the consultant is paid not by a commission, but by an annual fee that is negotiated and set in advance. And indeed, here the Ironworkers had had a relationship for some 40 years going back to the 1950s with a consulting company used by many unions and health and welfare funds in New York, known as the Segal Company.

[Comment] This is really very good. The jurors understand that the consultant charges the union a fee and that the insurance company pays people like Ms. Hardy. But, again, it is Hardy — the witness — who is the projector of truth, not the advocate.

Now, <u>as Ms. Hardy will explain to you</u>, it is true that although the Ironworkers District Council at one time had Blue Cross and Blue Shield health insurance, at some time they dropped that and became self-insured. And Ms. Hardy had called upon, as was her job, the Ironworkers from time to time, to try to reinterest them in going with Blue Cross and Blue Shield.

[Comment] Ditto.

And some time in 1994, in the spring of 1994, Ms. Hardy herself called upon Mr. Sweeney. You're going to hear a lot about Mr. Sweeney. Ms. Hardy called upon him, introduced herself and made a presentation to him on behalf of Blue Cross.

Now, it's important to understand exactly who Mr. Sweeney was. Mr. Sweeney is the President and Business Manager of one local of the Ironworkers Union. There are 11 locals in the Tri-State Area, South Jersey, Pennsylvania, Eastern Pennsylvania and Delaware, that comprise the Ironworkers District Council Philadelphia and Vicinity Health and Welfare Fund. He is the head of the one of the 11 locals that comprise that fund. The Fund itself is governed by the Board of Trustees. The Board of Trustees has 22 members, 11 management and 11 union. One from each of the 11 unions. Mr. Sweeney is one of the 11 union members on the Fund. He is the Co-chair of the Fund, along with Mr. Reith, who is the management co-chair. The Fund meets quarterly. The Trustees of the Fund meet quarterly. There are minutes of the meetings and the Fund can only act by an action approved by the Board at a quarterly meeting and reelected in the minutes.

   <u>Neither of Mr. Sweeney or any of the other 21 other Trustees on their own can bind the Fund to anything</u>.

[Comment] Well, we certainly have a good picture of who Sweeney is, and his importance. But who is more helped by this point, the plaintiff or the defendant? And in light of that, what is the point of the last sentence (even if technically true), that Sweeney cannot himself contract? By the end of this case, one thing will surely be clear: What Sweeney wants, Sweeney gets.

   In any event Ms. Hardy, in the spring of 1994, called upon Mr. Sweeney. That was a meeting set up by another union leader. And at various times Ms. Hardy called upon other Trustees of the Ironworkers District Council trying to interest them in Blue Cross and Blue Shield. Roughly a month later, at the end of May, beginning of June 1994, in that time frame, Mr. Sussman called Ms. Hardy up on the phone, introduced himself and suggested that he would like to bring her to meet with Mr. Sweeney. So, Ms. Hardy went with Mr. Sussman to meet with Mr. Sweeney and had a second meeting. She already had one meeting.

[Comment] The chronology continues. But you will learn, much has been skipped over that took place between Sussman and Sweeney and between Sussman and Hardy before the meeting. Now, as you read the next portion, remember that defendant's counsel claims that Sussman did nothing and is entitled to nothing.

They had a second meeting, <u>nothing came of it</u>. It was a meeting that lasted about a half hour and <u>nothing came of that meeting</u>. They met, and that was it. One important thing happened on the way to that meeting. Mr. Sussman suggested that Ms. Hardy meet him at the Woodcrest Shopping Center in New Jersey and that they drive to Mr. Sweeney's office together in Mr. Sussman's car. That is the first time that Ms. Hardy and Mr. Sussman ever met face-to-face, and in the car, Ms. Hardy explained to Mr. Sussman that if he expected to earn a commission here, he would have to have a broker of record letter from the Ironworkers, naming him, appointing him and authorizing him as their broker. And that letter had to come not from Mr. Sweeney, as an individual, but it had to come from the Board or authorized by the Board of the Ironworkers District Council Philadelphia and Vicinity Health and Welfare Fund. And there is a reason for this broker of record letter.

[Comment] Ah so, before the meeting there was talk of a commission, and even Blue Cross says Sussman was told how to get one.

One may wonder if the jurors understand how the defendant can claim that Sussman is taking advantage and being greedy in asking for anything at all from the jury while having been advised by Hardy as to how to get a commission. Counsel knows—but neither you nor the jury does yet—that Hardy wrote a memo referring to the potential for a 1–3 percent commission she discussed with Sussman. It seems to us that the examiner must bring it out himself, having been given the opportunity by the plaintiff's failure to mention it first, and make clear that it was the parameters of a fee to be paid by the union, through its premiums, which its broker of record letter will authorize Sussman to collect from Blue Cross from the union's premiums, not to be paid by the company from its profits.

But we left off the argument with counsel about to make an excellent point, "And there is a reason for this broker of record letter."

It is not mere paperwork that serves no purpose. There is a reason for it and the reason is, the broker's fee is built into the premium or the administrative fee charged by Blue Cross and Blue Shield, for administering the program. It's built into that. So ultimately, any commission that would be paid, that is built into the fee, winds up being paid by the Health and Welfare Fund, winds up being paid by the members of the unions who are part of the Health and Welfare Fund. So, to make sure that that commission is authorized and authorized to be built into the premium, Independence Blue Cross and Pennsylvania Blue Shield require that the broker first obtain a broker of record letter. And Ms. Hardy told Mr. Sussman about that on the way to the very first meeting with Mr. Sweeney, so that was clear. In any event nothing came off of that meeting. That was a meeting in May or June of 1994. Nothing came of that meeting. In the meantime, Mr. Sussman went on to other things.

[Comment] Now this is excellent. *For the first time the jury can understand what this broker of record letter means — and who pays the fee if Sussman gets the letter from the union. Unfortunately, instead of concluding with the point that Sussman's beef is with the* union, *because the* union *did not give the letter because the* union *did not want to pay the fee, counsel closes the main point of his case by returning to the less likely theme that Sussman did nothing and is therefore entitled to* nothing from Blue Cross.

Among other things he went on to was his friend Mr. Sweeney introduced him to the Ironworkers up in North Jersey, as well, and the evidence will show that he was told the same thing, he needed a broker of record letter. This happens later in 1994.

We then get to 1995, and some time around March of 1995, Mr. Sussman again calls Ms. Hardy. This is nine months later. Again, he calls Ms. Hardy and tentatively sets up a meeting with Mr. Sweeney. Again, Mr. Sussman never confirmed the meeting and the meeting didn't take place.

That would have been the end of March of 1995, some nine months later. Again, no activity. Then, in April of 1995, Mr. Sussman called up another person at Independence Blue Cross, Brian Sullivan, and sets up a meeting for Mr. Sullivan, so he and Mr. Sullivan went down to meet with Mr. Sweeney. This is some nine months after the first meeting and that meeting, again, didn't go anywhere.

There was some discussion, Mr. Sullivan asked for some information, Mr. Sussman had provided the information and it didn't go anywhere.

[Comment] Not only is this chronology unclear, but the point of inserting it into the argument is also unclear, until counsel gives us this explanation:

Basically, what Mr. Sussman is asking you in this case, is to award him hundreds of thousands of dollars for having set up these two meetings, one with Ms. Hardy back in May or June of 1994 and the one with Brian Sullivan in 1995, and for that he is asking you to award several hundreds of thousands of dollars for doing basically nothing.

[Comment] Then the chronology begins again.

Now, what did happen, was Ms. Hardy continued to meet with other members of the Board of Trustees of the Ironworkers District Council Health and Welfare, and doing that in the spring of 1995, and at the June 1995 quarterly meeting of the Ironworkers Trustees, the Trustees directed their Investments Committee, which is the committee that deals with insurance, to look into an alternative to their then existing health coverage, and the Trustees at the Investment Committee to work with their consultant. The consultant is the Segal Company up in New York and Mr. Maresca, whose testimony you'll hear in this court, directed him to look into alternatives.

Mr. Maresca then set up a meeting with Ms. Hardy, of Independence Blue Cross. That meeting took place in July, 1995. Now, more than a year after this meeting that Mr. Sussman had set up with Ms. Hardy, July of 1995, Mr. Maresca came down from New York from the Segal Company, went with Mr. Sweeney and some others, met with Ms. Hardy and some others at the offices of Independence Blue Cross over at Market Street. You can see it if you look out this window you can see it seven blocks over. It has a Blue Cross on the top of the building and they met there on July 5th of 1995. They met at some length.

Later in July, July 31st, Mr. Maresca from the Segal Company sent to Blue Cross a letter on behalf of the Ironworkers Health and Welfare Fund, requesting that they make a formal proposal.

In August of 1995, Independence Blue Cross sent to Mr. Maresca at Segal Company a proposal on behalf of the Ironworkers District Council, a proposal for health insurance for the Ironworkers District Council, and the proposal was the size of probably these two books here put together.

It was a thick proposal that went to Mr. Maresca. Mr. Maresca and the Segal Company studied that proposal. When at the end of August, 1995, the Segal Company, Mr. Maresca made a recommendation to the Ironworkers District Council that they go with Blue Cross and Blue Shield along the lines of this proposal that was submitted a few weeks earlier.

That recommendation was then considered and approved by the Investment Committee at a meeting in September of 1995 and then by the whole Board of the Ironworkers District Council later in September of 1995.

In all of this, Mr. Sussman and Tower had nothing to do with this. He simply was not involved. Mr. Sussman never presented a bid on behalf of Blue Cross or Pennsylvania Blue Shield to the Ironworkers. Never sub-

mitted an insurance contract on behalf of Blue Cross or
Blue Shield or the Ironworkers District Council.

*[Comment] This last is the real point. Plaintiff did not repre-
sent Blue Cross; if he represented anyone, it was the union,
which would neither pay him nor authorize Blue Cross to pay
him by issuing the appropriate letter. Where does this point
belong? It belongs at the very outset of the argument, and then
again throughout the argument. We suggest it belongs, for
example, when we first learned of the union's decision, upon the
advice of its professional consultant, Maresca, not to issue the
broker letter—and then argue the chronology to show no
Sussman involvement after the introductory period, after which
the* union *wanted him out of the picture.*

*Now, counsel wisely deals with the technical claim made in
the complaint.*

> And most importantly, Mr. Sussman will acknowledge
> that he was never told by anyone either at the
> Ironworkers or in Blue Cross that anybody at Blue Cross
> had directed the Ironworkers not to deal with him. That
> was simply a decision that the Ironworkers, as Mr.
> Sussman must acknowledge and as Mr. Sweeney will tes-
> tify, and his co-chair, Mr. Reith, will testify, and Mr.
> Craggs, who was their administrator, will testify and Mr.
> Maresca will testify, it was simply a decision that the
> Ironworkers made on their own and on the recommenda-
> tion of their consultant of 40 years, Mr. Maresca, of the
> Segal Company.

*[Comment] This is an excellent exposition of the insurance
company's best position.*

> So, what then happened is this lawsuit has now
> ensued and Mr. Sussman has also sued Blue Cross over
> in New Jersey and sued the Ironworkers in New Jersey
> as well.

> MR. LONGER: Your Honor, I have an objection here.

> THE COURT: Sustained.

MR. SONNENFELD: And he is seeking damages here. The damages that he is seeking are ridiculous as the evidence will show. This is a cost-plus contract between the Ironworkers and the Independence Blue Cross Pennsylvania Blue Shield. Blue Cross and Blue Shield, because of their size and negotiating position, negotiated discounts with hospitals and providers of medical service. Those discounts are then passed on to that subscriber. What Blue Cross and Blue Shield do in this contract or under this contract with the Ironworkers, is bill the Ironworkers what they pay out to the hospitals and apply to that an administrative fee.

[Comment] Good, but make even clearer. The letter that the union would not give would have increased premiums to the working men and women who are its members.

Somehow here Mr. Sussman is trying to claim credit for something that <u>he had nothing to do with</u>, trying to claim a commission which he may describe is based on savings which he had <u>nothing to do with</u>, those are the Blue Cross discounts or based on work he claims that he did, which he didn't do. So, to summarize, in contrast to what you heard from Mr. Longer, I would, again, submit to you that this is a case of somebody trying to get something that they're not entitled to, <u>something that ultimately will be passed on either to the union members making up the Ironworkers Health and Welfare Fund or to the subscribers of Independence Blue Cross</u>. It is simply something that is not warranted by the evidence that you will hear, from the witnesses who will testify over the course of the next three days.

[Comment] We again hear the "did nothing" claim, which we suggest is an unnecessary reach. As for the rest, it is strong, emotional stuff. It is powerful and aimed at making the jurors want to find for Blue Cross. But we are not too sure that all of it — especially the reference to the subscribers of Blue Cross — would usually be allowed, particularly as several of the jurors are such subscribers (as you will learn).

Again, I want to thank you for your time and patience
and we appreciate your service.

Analysis of Defendants' Opening

Here defendants' counsel begins with a "windup." The jury
awaits his response to the claim that plaintiff's counsel made,
that the plaintiff was cheated. Defense counsel does not step
up to the plate and say right off the bat that there was no
cheating, there was no unfairness, and there was no injustice.
Instead, he runs through the geography from which the jury
comes. Like plaintiff's counsel, he refers to the defendants as
his clients. The jury understands that he is a paid advocate
and is not really interested in the fact that the jurors reside all
over the city. They want to know whether what plaintiff's
counsel said is true.

Once the windup is complete, defense counsel does a good
job of trying to personalize the companies. They are nonprofits.
They are owned by the people who buy insurance. Why, it
seems that they are owned by the union members whom they
serve. This is good stuff. Counsel says it at the beginning of the
opening and repeats it at the end. It is a strong performance.

The opening statement is more of a chronology than the
plaintiff's, but the chronology is used here to make the argument. The argument is that Mr. Sussman arranged a couple of
meetings over several months, and that these meetings were
unsuccessful. Thereafter, the unions received help and guid-
ance from the Segal Company (that company mentioned but
unexplained by plaintiff's counsel) and Mr. Maresca (also mentioned without any identification by plaintiff's counsel).

As with the plaintiff's opening, it is useful here to ask what
was the central theme of the defense. It seems to be: If
Sussman was anyone's agent, he was acting for the union, not
the company. That is why he was told about the need for a broker of record letter if he wished to be paid.

Bottom line: Sussman unilaterally sought to become a
negotiator for the unions, who did not want his help. The *final*
deal had nothing to do with him, and any fee would increase

health care costs for union members. Sussman did nothing to justify a fee.

The last point is less important—for Sussman really did do something or there would be no rational basis for any discussion with Hardy about a fee to be paid by anyone. But the real issue for the defendant seems not whether Sussman is entitled to anything—both sides seemed happy enough to use his services at some point—but rather whether he had a deal that his fee would be in addition to the base premium (in which case the union would pay it) or would come from the profits of Blue Cross on the deal, in which case the insurance company would pay it . . . or, as may most likely be the case, he did not take the trouble to pin down the deal clearly enough to protect himself and provide for an entitlement from either.

Defense counsel knows that it cannot be good for his clients if the jury thinks that the companies, nonprofit or not, are making a killing on the deal. Thus, the argument is that Blue Cross/Blue Shield get nothing but an administrative fee (the amount of which is not mentioned) and the unions pay a lower than market rate to doctors and are well served by the arrangement the insurer made for them.

It is apparent that defense counsel understands as well as plaintiff's counsel that, if the jury thinks that Mr. Sussman is a small businessman who was cheated by the insurers, he will win the case. Defense counsel reaches for the fact that Sussman has sued not only the Pennsylvania insurers but also a New Jersey insurer and, more importantly, a New Jersey union. The judge sustained an objection to the argument. Plaintiff's lawyer sought no limiting instruction, and probably was correct in concluding that the less said about the other suit the better. Defense counsel hoped that the additional litigation would suggest that Sussman was greedy and was not content with complaining about insurers; he also sued a union.

The final suggestion that any award that the defendants would pay would be passed on either to union members or to subscribers seems, at least to us, to be impermissible.

KEEPING SCORE

We believe that people begin to make up their minds as soon as possible. The opening argument is a powerful tool in any trial because it has the potential to affect how the jury perceives all of the evidence that follows the openings. Therefore, we suggest that each reader ask himself at this point whose opening was more powerful, which was more effective, and which made it easier for the jury to follow the evidence.

As you look back on these openings, recall that plaintiff's counsel had the opportunity to address every piece of evidence and each potential witness first. He could have dealt with the Segal Company and Mr. Maresca and put them in some perspective. He did not do so. He did reach for an internal memorandum made by Mr. Sullivan, an agent of a defendant. If this was his "smoking gun," it might have been used in a more dramatic way and might have received more emphasis. Moreover, you will learn of a memo written by Ms. Hardy in which she refers to a 1 to 3 percent commission for Mr. Sussman. This is never mentioned by the plaintiff, when it should have been a centerpiece of the opening argument. Why? Because it is an amazing admission that directly refutes one chamber of the heart of the defendant's argument, that Sussman is entitled to no commission; and damages the other, that commissions are the responsibility of the union, not of the company.

The defendants did not go near the Sullivan or Hardy memoranda. Indeed, while plaintiff's counsel painted a picture of a competition between Sullivan and Hardy, defense counsel's picture was of two company employees approached by a hapless Sussman who was unable to accomplish anything.

Look back on defense counsel's argument. Is it consistent, or does defense counsel argue against himself? If the Ironworkers and Sweeney wanted nothing to do with Sussman, why does it matter that Sweeney had no authority to act on his own?

Opening argument is the most influential weapon of the advocate, because it comes at the beginning of the case, and is the most difficult to employ—for precisely the same reason. It is not so much that it is difficult to speak without running afoul of prohibitions against being "argumentative," which most of us learn how to overcome, sooner or later. The truly great difficulty lies in the predictive nature of openings—the promises of proof in a world of many unpredictabilities, such as judicial rulings and witness recollections and even the performance of adversaries. And yet, it must be done: to the extent that the advocate is more and more timorous in his predictions, he is less and less effective in shaping the judgments of the jurors which are being made as he speaks. Nevertheless, a weapon aimed at an adversary will backfire if strong promises are unfulfilled, particularly if they are believed when made. Therein lies the rub. The jury believes or not, as you argue. If they believe, they will subliminally hear and see and emotionally work at keeping to those beliefs.

But what if later they are forced to admit that they are mistaken, forced to change because an advocate misled them? The pendulum then can swing very far back indeed. And that is why, before opening, counsel must play the trial out in his mind, the direct and cross of all witnesses, searching for what he can relatively safely promise and, for those weak aspects, which he must have, where a promise will more likely make the jurors find that the fact has been proven. For a full exposition of these critical considerations, see Vol. I, pp. 79–82. Once you have finished reading this trial record (that is, the remainder of this book), you may wish to return to these openings. You will then be in a position to evaluate how counsel could have opened, and what could *reasonably* have been expected of each of them, given what they knew about the case before they opened it.

Chapter Three
The First Witness

One of the most, if not *the* most, difficult decision for trial counsel is choosing the order of his witnesses. It is the decision that trial lawyers make last, and the one that requires the most knowledge about the case. See the full discussion in Vol. II, pp. 215–220. Here, the plaintiff has no choice to make. He himself is really all he has.

DIRECT EXAMINATION OF THE PLAINTIFF'S FIRST WITNESS

Text of the Direct Examination of the Plaintiff

THE COURT: Call your first witness.

MR. LONGER: I call Mr. Sussman to the witness stand.

THE CRIER: State your name, spell your last.

THE WITNESS: Leonard Sussman, S-U-S-S-M-A-N.

LEONARD SUSSMAN, WITNESS, having been duly sworn, was examined and testified as follows:

BY MR. LONGER:

Q: Good morning, Mr. Sussman. Are you the President of Tower Financial Planning Associates?

A: Yes.

[Comment] The next question is not so good.

Q: Why are you suing Independence Blue Cross and Pennsylvania Blue Shield?

A: Because I believe I'm owed a commission that I was never paid.

[Comment] Poor. Puts the burden on the witness. He thus has to become his own advocate — and will not be a good one. No

one can advocate his own case from the witness stand. For example, he does not even say he is owed a commission, only that he believes so. As we noted in reference to opening, one cannot hope to do any task in the courtroom — not opening, not direct, not cross, and not summation — unless one understands the purpose of each of them. And the purpose of direct, for you the advocate — is to argue your case through the witness to the jury. To do that you must use your questions, lots of questions, to make the argument. Questions on direct are the tools of the argument. Counsel are to argue with questions. Witnesses are not to make arguments through long narrative answers. We must learn how to "lead without leading," Vol. II, pp. 19–21; loop each answer by the next question, Vol. II, pp. 17–18; how to get testimony repeated as many times as you wish, Vol. II, pp. 22–31; and why not to use long narrative answers. In the final analysis, the purpose of a direct is to do your opening right through the witness, limited only by the witness's window of knowledge about the case and the rules of evidence, which can limit what people can say from the stand.

Q: <u>Now, before we go into that,</u> I would like you to tell the jurors some background first and why don't we begin by telling them where you were born?

[Comment] Good, a nice transition. And now the examiner wisely takes charge of the examination.

A: Born in Philadelphia.

Q: Where did you go to school?

A: South Philadelphia High School.

Q: Maybe you could bring the microphone closer to your mouth. What's your birthday?

A: June 1st, 1939.

Q: That makes you 58?

A: 58, correct.

Q: And after high school, what did you do?

A: I went to Penn State Ogontz Center for one year and then I went to Temple Night School also for two years and that was the end of my education.

Q: Did you go to night school because you were working during the day?

A: I started work in 1957 at Sears.

[Comment] Look how nicely he loops each question into the last answer. Small chunks and pieces, easily understood. See Vol. II, pp. 17–18. So much better than merely saying: "Give us your background and education," calling for a long, Vesuvius-like response.

Q: And how long were you at Sears?

A: Five years.

Q: What did you do vocationally after Sears?

A: Went in business with my father for four and a half years, and then after that, I went into the insurance business.

Q: Why did you go into the insurance business?

A: It was something that I always wanted to do. The building business with my dad didn't work out very successfully, and back when I was in high school, I had put in my yearbook that I thought I would like to be an insurance salesman, so I thought that was my next vocation, I was going to give that a try.

Q: What is it about insurance that was so interesting to you?

A: Well, I found it very challenging and something I could excel at, and I liked to be in that environment. It was something that worked for me.

Q: Did you like meeting with the clients that you dealt with?

A: Yes.

[Comment] Splendid. Breaks it up—the examination becomes a conversation and can achieve the Wimbledon effect of getting jurors' heads swinging back and forth. Watch how short questions are met by short answers in a volleying back and forth. And look how Sussman is made into an appealing and sympathetic figure by his lawyer, someone the jurors will want *to find for. It is the advocate who is achieving this with his questions and organization, not the witness.*

Q: How did you begin in the insurance industry?

A: I started out my training with Equitable Life Insurance Company. And I was with them for about six months. Then I went to Pacific Mutual, and I was with them for about six months. Then I went to work for an agency in Northeast Philadelphia called Lyons & Cohen.

Q: What sort of business is Lyons & Cohen?

A: They're in the casualty business and I was the life insurance agent that handled the life insurance for that agency.

Q: So you began dealing with life insurance about a year after getting into the insurance business?

A: Well, actually, I started with Equitable.

Q: <u>And</u> this is what year?

A: Towards the end of 1966.

Q: That's when you started with Equitable?

A: Yes.

Q: So you started with Lyons in about 1967; is that about right?

A: Yeah, around the early part of 1967.

Q: And for how long were you with that entity?

A: I would say about two years.

Q: <u>And</u> then what did you do.

A: I opened my own agency.

Q: And what was the name of that agency?

[Comment] Very lovely up to this point. But here he could have done some looping—which he now does; watch.

A: It was called the Leonard Sussman Insurance Agency.

Q: And what was the business of Leonard Sussman Insurance Agency?

[Comment] See?

A: I took a general agency with a company called Pilot Life, and I was to go out and recruit agents to work through my agency.

Q: What did you do?

A: I was their recruiter and I sold insurance.

Q: And how long were you operating the Leonard Sussman Insurance Agency?

A: I'd say about two years.

Q: And what happened?

A: I was bought by a company called Bala Cynwood Associates up on City Line Avenue. They had bought my agency and I went to work for them as their life insurance salesperson.

Q: And how long were you with the Bala Group?

A: About a year.

[Comment] Counsel is becoming addicted to beginning each question with "and," as so many do. It is a way of catching a breath before the next question must be asked. Unfortunately, this unconscious mannerism is distracting. Fortunately, he stops.

Q: What did you do after that?

A: Then I formed Tower Financial Planning and it's been that since.

Q: What year approximately was Tower formed?

A: Tower is about—I've been in business about 31 years, and Tower is about 25 years old, so it would be about 1972.

Q: 1972?

A: '72.

Q: And where was Tower located?

A: Tower originally was located in Philadelphia in the Lewis Tower Building at 15th and Locust Streets.

Q: Is it there now?

A: No.

Q: Where is it now?

A: On Route 73 in Marlton, New Jersey, and we've been there for about 20 years.

Q: Is it a New Jersey corporation?

A: Yes.

[Comment] Excellent—counsel has shown the witness as an insurance man for his whole life. Now we also see that others work for and are dependent upon him for their livelihood. Does this bear directly on the facts? No. Will it have an impact on the outcome of the case? Very likely. Why? Because it will likely draw the jurors emotionally to his side of the case.

Q: Do you have other employees besides yourself at Tower?

A: Yes.

Q: How many?

A: Currently, we have five additional employees.

[Comment] Even more might have been attempted: Who are they? What are their names? And so forth. Of course, sooner or later there will be an objection. So what? The examiner will not be hurt. At some point the objection will be sustained, but the adverse counsel would suffer a deep wound if the direct continues in this way.

Q: What does Tower do?

A: Tower is a life insurance brokerage agency.

Q: Can you explain to the ladies and gentleman of the jury what that is?

A: A brokerage agency is where we represent multiple companies and we're the agent for those companies and other life insurance agents will come to us for a particular product if they need a competitive term or a hard to please case, Tower solicits their brokerage business.

Q: You solicit their business and broker it to the insurance companies; is that correct?

[Comment] The answer was not clear, and so counsel clarifies it. Excellent.

A: Yes. I'm like the wholesaler in the life insurance business.

Q: You act as the middle man between the agents and the insurance companies?

A: That's correct.

[Comment] The examiner is in there pitching, making the testimony clear with his follow-up questions. A really fine piece of work.

Q: <u>And</u> what do you do as the president of Tower?

A: Obviously, I run the company and look to promote the brokerage business, and I also sell personal business myself, where I have my own clientele, that I write their business for.

Q: Has Tower ever received any awards or honors?

A: Many, many awards.

Q: <u>And</u> what are <u>they</u> in the nature of?

[Comment] Excellent as this is, he should take the opportunity to loop and groove, i.e., "Tell us the kinds of awards that . . ."

A: Well, they are always for production. Companies reward you for the amount of business that you do, and I have won awards personally for a leading producer for many companies, and the agency has won awards for being in the leading production agencies for those companies.

Q: When you say, "production," do you mean sales?

A: Sales, yes.

Q: <u>And</u> sales are the life blood of the company?

A: That's what we do. We're a sales organization.

[Comment] Again, excellent. Counsel has made the testimony clearer with his follow-up questions.

Q: How does—how do your sales generate income to you?

A: The companies pay me a commission.

Q: And the companies being the insurance companies, correct?

A: Correct.

[Comment] Well done. Commissions are to Tower what sales of goods are to retailers. This is the heart of the case. The issue here really is who is responsible for paying Sussman. So the next question is key.

Q: In your 30 years of experience, have the insurance companies always paid you a commission?

A: Yes.

[Comment] Very good. But now is the time to hammer the point. Counsel must do more. "Would you represent a company for nothing?" "Why not?" And so forth. Unfortunately, he moves on.

Q: What sort of insurance products do you sell now?

A: Well, we sell all forms of life insurance. All forms of health insurance, disability insurance, and annuities.

Q: <u>And</u> you've been doing that with Tower for the past 20, 25 years?

A: Since I've been in the business.

Q: Now, what sort of clientele do you have?

*   *   *

[Comment] There was a recess before the answer was given. Counsel skillfully picks up the examination after the break.

Q: I believe before the break, I'd just begun asking you to tell us about your clientele and would you please tell us.

A: The clients that I have personally range from individuals to corporations, they just kind of go the gamut. I've been in the business for so many years that we just meet a lot of different people and do a lot of different business.

Q: Do you have any Union clients?

A: The only Union clients that I would consider myself having is the Ironworkers of Philadelphia Council.

Q: <u>And</u> how did you achieve that client?

[Comment] That is a little lazy for a good transition. We suggest, instead, to repeat, loop, and groove. "I would like to ask you some questions about the Ironworkers. First, how did you obtain this Union as a client?"

A: I had been friendly with a fellow by the name of Bob Sweeney. He's the business agent for the Local. I've been friendly with him for about 15 years, maybe a little bit more.

Q: <u>Would</u> you <u>describe</u> your friendship with Mr. Sweeney?

[Comment] "Would you" and "could you" are not good ways to begin questions, for the answer to both is "yes." And asking for a "description" of a relationship is to call for a speech from the witness. Counsel was probably concerned about leading. But, by use of alternatives (Vol. II, p. 20), this can be surmounted. "Were you close friends, or casual acquaintances?" for example, and so forth.

A: <u>I thought we were very good friends</u>. We've known each other for all these years. We've been very good friends.

[Comment] Now, that is a much more important answer than the jury or, for that matter, you the reader, are likely to appreciate. Sweeney, as we shall see, is entirely on the side of the defendant and will testify on its behalf that Sussman is entitled to nothing—no commission. Counsel, therefore, has two jobs. One, which he does well, is to demonstrate that Sussman and Sweeney were close, which is why Blue Cross used Sussman—and owes him a commission. The other job is to prepare the tribunal for the fact that the Sussman-Sweeney relationship has changed.

Q: Have you sold Mr. Sweeney any insurance?

[Comment] He means personal, but does not say.

A: Yes.

Q: Have you sold any of Mr. Sweeney's friends or associates insurance?

A: Yes.

Q: Has Mr. Sweeney referred to you any business?

A: Yes.

[Comment] All this needs to be developed more. It is the heart of the plaintiff's case and Sussman's relationship with Sweeney is really all he had to offer Blue Cross. Moreover, as we shall see, Sweeney is not going to be helpful.

Q: Have you ever—you mentioned that he was with the local, what was his position, there?

A: Business agent.

[Comment] Do we all know what that is? That a business agent is the de facto boss of the union?

Q: Did you understand that he was also associated with the Welfare Fund?

A: Yes.

Q: Did you understand what his position was with the Welfare Fund?

A: Yes.

Q: What is that?

A: He was co-chairman.

[Comment] As a suggestion, this might be a good spot to argue Sweeney's importance in the union's decision as to which insurance to take.

Q: Have you ever spoken to Mr. Sweeney about the Ironworkers' Employee Health Benefits?

A: Yes.

Q: Tell us <u>about</u> conversations that you've had with Mr. Sweeney about the Ironworkers' Welfare Benefits.

[Comment] Not a proper question. "Tell us about . . ." calls for a selective summarization. "What did he say to you about . . ." or vice versa is the way. See Vol. II, pp. 21–22. Otherwise, the attorney abandons the examination and turns his role over to the witness.

A: We <u>would</u> talk about the Welfare Benefits numerous times in reference to their claims experience, how the Fund was doing with their financing. He had told me that they were experiencing—

MR. SONNENFELD: Objection, Your Honor, to what Mr. Sweeney told him.

THE COURT: Sustained.

[Comment] Not clear if judge's ruling is right, but the question "Tell us about the conversation" is at the root of the problem. Should have been specific. If Sweeney had merely said that he was dissatisfied with the prior insurance, it would not be hearsay because it was not offered for truth. Fortunately for the examiner, we believe, he is forced to take control again.

BY MR. LONGER:

Q: When did you have these discussions with Mr. Sweeney about the Welfare Benefits?

A: It was over a period of our friendship.

Q: Did the conversations that you've ever had result in you taking any action as an insurance agent on behalf of the Welfare Fund?

A: I made recommendations to him that they implement some cost saving measures. Some of them, obviously, he listened to; some, you know, he took—he used, and some he didn't.

Q: What were <u>the ones</u> that he took?

[Comment] Excellent. Examiner is in control and exercising good management. As a suggestion, he might have looped by asking, "Which of your money-saving suggestions were implemented by the union?" Better looping that way.

A: I recommended that they go to a Preferred Provider Organization. The Union at the time was paying all their own medical bills and I thought they could save a substantial amount of money if they brought in a Preferred Provider Organization that would give them discounts if the members used the group of physicians that were in that organization.

Q: Okay, that's a lot to digest. When did you have this conversation with Mr. Sweeney?

[Comment] Right on; counsel knows that he must break it up.

A: Some years ago. I mean, we talked about it many times.

Q: And when did you suggest to him to use the Preferred Provider Organization?

A: I'm sure sometime back in '94, in the early part of '94, maybe late '93.

Q: And you have used the term Preferred Provider Organization. Tell us what a PPO is.

[Comment] Good loop and groove, from question to answer to question.

A: PPO is a—companies put together PPOs which stand for Preferred Provider Organizations, where they go to various doctors and they get discounts from them, and then whoever joins in that PPO gets the discount from that organization.

Q: And you mentioned this to Mr. Sweeney because you thought that it could save the Ironworkers money by going with a PPO?

A: That's correct.

[Comment] This is excellent advocacy right through the witness.

Q: And you had also mentioned that the Ironworkers were paying their own bills, is that also called self-insured?

A: Right. The Ironworkers are self-insured.

Q: Now, in using a Preferred Provider Organization, does that status change?

A: No. They still stay self-insured, it's just that the bills that they'll be paying for the medical services to their members, would just be at a discount.

Q: Did the Ironworkers contract with the Preferred Provider Organization that you are talking to Mr. Sweeney about?

A: Yes.

Q: What—that is Preferred Care?

A: Preferred Care, correct.

[Comment] This is an excellent pace for a direct. A juror is quite likely able to follow, understand, and remember it. The next question, however, falls out of this pattern and turns the examination over to the witness, who goes on and on.

Q: <u>Would</u> you tell us how it came about that you contracted with the Ironworkers for Preferred Care?

A: I had spoken with Mr. Sweeney numerous times, as I had said, told him about how I thought they could save some money. Had a few meetings with him with someone that was very familiar in selling these Preferred Provider Organization.

We had some meetings. We got them involved with the Union, and eventually, a contract got signed between Preferred Care and the District Council of Philadelphia.

[Comment] Counsel takes control again.

Q: And the person that was involved in your meetings with Mr. Sweeney, was who?

A: A fellow by the name of Roger Halverson.

Q: And together, did the two of you broker a contract with the Ironworkers?

A: Yes.

Q: And do you receive a commission from Preferred Care based on the contract?

A: Yes. I get a commission from Preferred Care.

[Comment] Excellent—now he authenticates the point. Notice the careful organization of the direct. Much better than the organization of the opening. He is doing well in his arguing here. And he sure is establishing that Preferred Care, an insurance company, paid Sussman a commission after Sussman introduced the contract. All of this prepares the way, of course, for Blue Cross, which did not pay.

Q: I'd like to ask you to turn to Exhibit Number-1, which is in the notebook right beside you.

A: I don't know what you're—

Q: Why don't you turn to—there are several fax cover sheets in the beginning, but why don't you turn to the page that says: "Marketing Service Agreement."

A: I have that.

Q: Do you recognize this document, Mr. Sussman?

A: Yes.

Q: What is this?

A: This is the Agreement that I entered into with Preferred Care as to our commission.

Q: And where in the document, does it refer to your commission?

MR. SONNENFELD: Your Honor, while Mr. Sussman is looking, I'd like to object. I don't think the commission, if any, he receives from Preferred Care is relevant to this case.

THE COURT: Overruled.

MR. LONGER: Thank you, Your Honor.

[Comment] The objection is late. It should have been made earlier to have any hope of surviving the ruling. The point is

one that the defendant should try very hard to keep out, for the reason in the last comment. By the same token, it is a vital point for the plaintiff.

BY MR. LONGER:

Q: If I could help you, I believe it's on Page 4.

A: Okay, thank you. It's on the bottom of the page.

Q: And what is the commission agreement that you have with Preferred Care?

A: The commission that I have is that Preferred Care pays a 20 percent commission for the amount of money that they make off the Union, and that Roger and myself split it, so that we get 10 percent each.

[Comment] That is a substantial percentage. Now counsel nails it down, preparing the way, of course, for what will come later.

Q: <u>And</u> this document indicates that the network agrees to pay Tower Financial Planning 10 percent commission of the fees?

A: Correct.

Q: <u>And</u> is this a document which you've signed in June of 1994?

A: Yes.

Q: <u>And</u> this document was amended, was it not, by exhibit, if you would turn to Page 2, to reflect that the contract was specific to the Ironworkers; is that right?

A: Yes.

Q: Did you sign Exhibit Number-2?

A: Yes.

MR. LONGER: Your Honor, just as a procedural matter, should I wait to introduce exhibits or is your practice that we do it as we go along?

THE COURT: Well, why don't we label the exhibits and introduce them as we go and then at the end you sort of wrap it up after the evidence is all over.

MR. LONGER: We'll wrap it up after the evidence is over.

THE COURT: In other words, if you just mention for the record the exhibit number you're utilizing and keep a record of what you've used as opposed to what you've got until your case is over and then we can admit it or have any arguments or any agreements.

MR. LONGER: Thank you, Your Honor.

THE COURT: By the way, just so that you'll understand one quick thing, exhibits are all prenumbered to get it ready for trial, those numbers don't mean anything. All they mean is that these documents were all given numbers. They may be number one and then number 16 and then number four, don't attach any importance to the numbers, and left out numbers simply means that something somebody thought might come up wasn't important and didn't come up, also has no importance.

So, the numbers are really just so that if we have to go back and look at it later we can and know what paper we're talking about, because as you can see, from the number of papers that have been numbered, it would be difficult without some system. Okay.

MR. LONGER: Thank you, Your Honor.

BY MR. LONGER:

[Comment] The above exchanges are almost unintelligible. The judge and the parties have agreed to allow premarked exhibits to be read from without the formality of introduction of exhibits. This follows the suggestion of Vol. II, pp. 176–180. Do not introduce items that you do not need during direct; wait until the end of direct to avoid a potential voir dire, which, at a minimum, is directus examinationus interruptus, so to speak, and, at a maximum, is who knows what.

Q: Now, you entered into a separate agreement with Preferred Care. Did Preferred Care enter into an agreement with the Ironworkers?

A: Yes.

Q: I'd ask you to turn to Exhibit Number-4, do you recognize that exhibit?

A: Yes.

Q: What is that?

A: That's the Agreement that Preferred Care entered into with the Council Ironworkers of Philadelphia Council.

[Comment] Good use of physical exhibits to footnote the credibility of testimony on direct. Vol. II, p. 155.

Q: Now, if you look at the back, it's not signed, is that the Agreement that they actually entered into?

A: This is a copy that I had in my file that Roger had sent to me, so I would be aware of what was going on and what was about to be signed.

Q: So this was a draft, is that your understanding? This was a proposed Agreement that hadn't been signed yet? <u>And</u> you're aware that the Ironworkers did enter into an Agreement with Preferred Care, correct?

A: Yes.

Q: <u>And</u> is the Agreement they actually entered into, Exhibit Number-5, to your knowledge?

A: Yes.

Q: <u>And</u> that is dated what?

A: August the 1st, 1994.

[Comment] The document corroborates the testimony, or, better put, the document authenticates the testimony, rather than the other way around. Look how nicely he argues as he goes from here on. Unfortunately, he is back to his "ands."

Q: Now, you received commissions from Preferred Care; is that right?

A: Yes.

Q: <u>And</u> have you received them since August 1, 1994?

A: Yes.

Q: <u>And</u> since August 1, 1994, approximately what are the commissions that you've received from Preferred Care based on the contract that they had with the Ironworkers?

A: Approximately $20,000.

Q: <u>And</u> is that your 10 percent commission?

A: That's my 10 percent and then Roger—whatever I have gotten, he has gotten identical dollars.

Q: So 20 percent commission all told that you split with Mr. Halverson has been about $40,000?

A: Yes sir.

[Comment] This is an important point, for it is what he is giving up. Why would he look to replace a company that was paying him with one that would not? That's the point of all this. Unfortunately, this was not mentioned in opening. Therefore, what chance is there for the jury to understand this point, if these few questions are all that are asked without opening argument? Some additional questions along this line must be asked. If not now, then surely later.

Q: Are you familiar with the document called a broker of record letter?

A: It's something that Blue Cross and Blue Shield has. I'm familiar with it now.

Q: <u>And</u> you mean Independence Blue Cross and Pennsylvania Blue Shield?

A: Yes.

Q: And what is a broker of record letter?

A: It's a letter that the employer is supposed to give you appointing you as the broker to represent them to Blue Cross and Blue Shield.

Q: Did you need a broker of record letter to receive your commission from Preferred Care?

A: No.

[Comment] He is striking hard blows.

Q: Did anyone at the Ironworkers tell you that you needed a broker of letter to get—a commission from Preferred Care?

A: No.

Q: Do you consider yourself to be the broker on that Preferred Care contract with the Ironworkers?

A: Yes.

[Comment] Good—the implication is that the broker letter was an extra, unusual requirement imposed by the defendant.

Q: Now, as I understand it, you were talking to Mr. Sweeney at some point with respect to Blue Cross and Blue Shield, when did those discussions begin?

A: Prior to them signing the contracts with Preferred Care.

Q: And how did the topic come up?

A: Mr. Sweeney had expressed—

MR. SONNENFELD: Your Honor, I object to what Mr. Sweeney expressed.

THE COURT: Sustained.

MR. SONNENFELD: Thank you, Your Honor.

[Comment] Probably wrong ruling. The testimony is not offered for the truth of its content. It is merely an expression of

Sweeney's displeasure with the current insurance. But plaintiff's counsel does not fight. He simply goes after the same conversation from another direction.

BY MR. LONGER:

Q: Did you have discussions with Mr. Sweeney about the effectiveness of the networks with Preferred Care?

A: Yes.

Q: Did you speak to him about the need for perhaps to use a different entity rather than Preferred Care?

A: Yes.

Q: Was that because of his interest in using or not using Preferred Care?

A: Yes.

[Comment] Used alternative to avoid an objection for leading. See Vol. II, p. 20. He is skillfully avoiding the prior ruling. Excellent—he got the point in without objection. Now watch him use his next question to loop into the subject of the last answer.

Q: What did you do as a result of the discussions with Mr. Sweeney about his concerns with the network with Preferred Care?

A: I recommended to him that Blue Cross and Blue Shield of Pennsylvania would be a really good alternative because of the extensive networks that they had, and would probably cover the areas in which his concerns were about.

Q: What did you do after you expressed that to Mr. Sweeney?

[Comment] The use of "that" passed up an opportunity to loop. Moreover, counsel still has not argued that the plaintiff was shifting out of a company that was paying a 20 percent commission. And now we meet the defendant Blue Cross and the principal person on the other side, Ms. Hardy.

A: I called Helen Hardy and set up a meeting so she and I go can out there and visit with him.

Q: And approximately when did you call Helen Hardy to visit with Mr. Sweeney?

A: Before they signed that contract with Preferred Care.

Q: And did you talk to Ms. Hardy?

A: Yes.

Q: What was your <u>discussion</u> with Ms. Hardy <u>about</u>?

[Comment] Not the proper way. Turns examination over to the witness. See Vol. II, pp. 21–22. He asks for a summarization, which is not only objectionable but also not as effective as, for example, the way he handled the Sussman-Sweeney conversation, piece by piece.

A: I had told her that it would be a good idea to get a meeting together with the three of us, that the Ironworkers were going to go with Preferred Care. Bob wasn't all that excited about the network and that we'd have a really good opportunity and get a good audience at this point, because they're thinking in terms now of going outside of their—of what they were currently doing.

Q: And did you discuss with her getting together with Mr. Sweeney?

A: Yes, I set up a meeting.

[Comment] "Why did you set up the meeting?" And so forth. This is the heart of the plaintiff's case. Indeed, as we shall see, the majority of what he conferred on both the union and the company was in the introduction of the parties.

Q: And if you would, just for the benefit of getting a time reference, turn to page—I'm sorry, Exhibit Number-S, can you identify this document?

A: Yes. That's a letter that Helen Hardy had written to me on June the 3rd, 1994.

Q: And was it about June of 1994, or maybe just days before that you had this conversation with her about setting up a meeting with Mr. Sweeney?

A: Yeah, obviously, we had met, and she was writing a letter to basically thank me for the meeting, to discuss what she was, you know, the issues that we had discussed.

Q: So, approximately how many days in advance of your meeting with Ms. Hardy and Mr. Sweeney did you have this initial phone call with her?

A: I don't remember exactly. I'd say within a few weeks.

Q: So either May or early June of 1994?

A: Correct.

[Comment] Unfortunately, we may get confused, because counsel is taking us back and forth in time, before and after two separate meetings: one with Sussman and Hardy alone, and one with them and Sweeney. And it is the meeting between Sussman and Hardy that is the more important one.

Q: You met with Ms. Hardy and Mr. Sweeney; is that right?

A: Yes.

Q: How did you go about setting up that meeting with Ms. Hardy?

A: I had called her on the phone and told her that, you know, it would be a good opportunity to meet with Mr. Sweeney. Called Bob Sweeney, got a date, we set up, you know, we set up the time, we met, and we drove to the Union Hall together.

[Comment] Counsel knows this narrative answer is not clear. So he uses questions to break it up, get repetition, and dwell on this activity of Sussman's.

Q: You met Ms. Hardy?

A: Yes.

Q: And drove to the Union Hall together?

A: Yes.

Q: And did you talk to Ms. Hardy in the car about what you were hoping to do with Mr. Sweeney and the Ironworkers?

A: Yes.

Q: What was the substance of your discussion?

A: The substance of the conversation was that I felt that they were not totally happy in the direction that they were going and that it would be a good opportunity again for the Blues to come in there, and we would have a favorable meeting. I think that this is a situation that we would be able to get the Blues to come into—that it would be better for the Union and be an opportunity for the Blues.

Q: When you say it was a "favorable meeting," do you say that because of your relationship with Mr. Sweeney?

A: Yes.

[Comment] He led because he had to. Indeed, he should go even further. This is really Sussman's biggest contribution to Blue Cross. And so the examiner begins to use questions to make the point.

Q: What did Ms. Hardy say to you when you told her that?

A: She had told me that she had some conversations and had met with some of the people from the Local prior to this and she has not been very successful in these meetings, and where did I think it was going to go, and I said let's go together and I think you're going to be very surprised to see where it's going to go.

[Comment] The "that" passed up the opportunity to loop. For example, "when you told her that you could change the climate to a more favorable one."

Q: You say that she had other conversations with other people in the Local, what do you mean by that?

A: She had told me she had spoken with Nick Craggs. She had told me that she had spoken with some of the other labor people that are involved in the Council, and she had said that she had spoken with Bob Sweeney at one time.

[Comment] Excellent. We get the picture of a frustrated saleswoman for a frustrated company.

Q: Now, who is Mr. Craggs?

A: Mr. Craggs is the person that administrates the Pension and Health and Welfare Fund for the Iron-workers.

Q: And she indicated to you, Ms. Hardy indicated to you, that she had spoken to Mr. Craggs?

A: Numerous times.

Q: And what did she tell you about her conversations with Mr. Craggs?

A: She wasn't able to get to first base with him. Meaning, that she was not able to—

MR. SONNENFELD: Your Honor, I object. This is leading, and I think the witness can—

THE COURT: Sustained.

[Comment] Counsel for Blue Cross objects. Not because the question is leading—indeed, the ruling is wrong. Look at the question. Counsel objects because he is getting hurt, although the use of the word "meaning" by Sussman could be objected to as Sussman's interpretation of what is in Hardy's mind. But, the wrong objection having been made, the examiner seized on the word "meaning" and does it again.

BY MR. LONGER:

Q: What did you understand her to <u>mean by</u> that?

A: I'm sorry, could you repeat the question?

Q: What did you understand by Ms. Hardy's comment to you that she couldn't get to first base with Mr. Craggs?

[Comment] Good for him. He not only led, but looped the last answer with his next question. Because of the objection counsel got to do it again.

A: She had told me that she had numerous meetings or conversations with Mr. Craggs, the [Blues] would love to have this account, they weren't able to get it. They had it some years ago and they lost it and she was just unable to break the door, break into this Union. She had told me that the Blue Cross and Blue Shield insured most of the contractor—or construction unions in the Philadelphia area, and they were doing extremely well with them and she had gotten a lot of referrals from those particular labor people, and she still couldn't get near to get a proposal into the Ironworkers.

Q: And you told her that you think that you could get a favorable—

A: I told her if she comes with me, I'm sure that we will get a favorable meeting and most likely this will go somewhere.

[Comment] He might have asked "Were you in court when counsel told the jury that you had done nothing *for Blue Cross and were entitled to nothing . . . ?" That is not to say he did not do well, for he did.*

We are still in the pre-Sweeney meeting, the meeting in which Sussman was alone with Hardy. Now counsel, having demonstrated a reasonable basis for compensation, approaches the payment to the plaintiff, but he tries to deal with the broker of record letter first. Do you agree? Or should it be the promise, first, before any mention of the need for a letter done after Sussman had performed the introduction?

Q: And did she mention to you, in this car drive, that you would need a broker of record letter in order for you to get a commission?

A: No.

Q: Did you talk about a broker of record letter being necessary to get a commission in your conversation with her setting up the meeting with Mr. Sweeney?

A: No.

Q: Did you talk about commissions though?

A: Yes.

[Comment] See why we suggested to go here first? Now counsel goes for the money. He might use the Hardy silence on the letter after he brings out her holding out the prospect of a commission.

Q: <u>And</u> what did you talk about with respect to the commissions with Ms. Hardy?

A: I told her that I would hope to get the same commission that I was currently getting with Preferred Care.

Q: <u>And</u> that is—

A: Based upon—that that commission is based upon the savings that the Union has in their billing where the company that is billing them get[s] a fee, I would get a percentage of that fee.

[Comment] Three "ands" in a row force us to break our no comment vow. Now, the answer.

Q: <u>And</u> what was the percentages that you were telling her that you expected to get?

A: We were getting 20 percent of the savings—of the—excuse me, we were getting 20 percent of what the Union was paying to Preferred Care.

[Comment] Unfortunately, that is a bit confused. Is he saying he wants 20 percent of the entire premium, or 20 percent of the

difference between what the union saves over the Preferred Care deal, or the same commission as before? Unfortunately, counsel does not clarify this portion of the key conversation in the case.

Q: And what did Ms. Hardy say to you in response to you discussing with her your commissions with Preferred Care?

A: Well, in that particular meeting, or in the car, she said she wasn't sure that that was doable, that the Blues had a totally different type of commission structure and we would discuss it.

[Comment] He should have first pointed out the agreement in principle to pay a commission, then pointed to the failure to mention in that conversation the need for any letter from the union—and all this before Sussman changed the climate for Blue Cross in the first meeting with Sweeney.

Q: Now, you're driving to the Union Hall, you got there, what did you two do when you met with Mr. Sweeney?

A: Well, obviously, I introduced Ms. Hardy to Bob Sweeney, they had met, they knew each other. I told them, you know, I said to Bob, "I think you got to sit down and listen to her now for, sure, this is something you should be doing." I gave my best sales pitch that I could to get him interested, and he said that at this point they weren't going to do anything. He really—he understands how good the Blues are, but they've already made a commitment to Preferred Care. He's not going to go back to the Committee and tell them that he recommended something that wasn't good, let's give it a try and let's see how it goes, and if it's really all that bad, we'll talk about it next year, and so we thanked each other and we walked out and got back in my car and I drove her back to her car, and I told her in the car that I will continue to, you know, have conversations with him and see if I can't move it off of dead center.

And she thanked me, and obviously, she sent me this letter.

[Comment] Wow! That sure is a lot of stuff in one narrative burst, and before we have it all down we are on to a letter sent by her to him after a meeting we have not fully grasped. We suggest that counsel should go back over portions of the last answer before leaving the conversation and entering the letter.

Q: Right, that's where I was coming back. That letter indicates that she was confirming 85 percent of the doctors located in Pennsylvania are contracting with Pennsylvania Blue Shield under the UCR Program, correct?

A: Right, I had asked her to send me, just so I could put it in front of him, to send me a provider list, so that I could let him see how broader the provider was with the Blue Cross; and Blue Shield was over the Preferred Provider list.

Q: If you would, let me point you to Exhibit Number-19, which was a letter dated June 6th, 1994—

A: I see that.

Q: Do you have that in front of you?

A: Yes.

Q: Is that a letter that you received?

A: Yes.

[Comment] Good. We now know *that such a letter was indeed sent; again, we know the exhibit authenticates the testimony.*

Q: Did Ms. Hardy on June 6th, or thereabouts provide you with the listing of doctors?

A: Yes.

[Comment] Here is another opportunity to emphasize that plaintiff was working himself out of one established commission, with the promise by Hardy of a commission on the new deal. But we still have not gotten the full story of why Hardy sent Sussman the letter. Perhaps we can glean the reason from the next series of questions.

Q: What did you do with that list?

A: I took that list to Bob Sweeney and again went through it with him and told him to pick out some doctors that he and his family uses, the kids use, see if these doctors are in there, could it be a list that he'd be happy with and to pass it around to the other Locals and see if they'd be happy with it.

Q: Did you attain any information from him?

A: At that meeting, no.

Q: I see. Let me go back to the Exhibit Number-8.

[Comment] Good, but could be better. The "I see" is a subliminal admission of failure.

The last paragraph of that letter: "It was a pleasure meeting with you and Bob Sweeney. I look forward to continuing our dialogue so that we can hopefully meet objectives which are beneficial to all of us."
What did you understand the mutual benefit to be?

MR. SONNENFELD: Objection, Your Honor.

THE COURT: Overruled.

THE WITNESS: It was my interpretation of this letter that we were going to work this account jointly and I would be receiving a commission.

[Comment] In our view, counsel got a gift on that ruling — allowing the witness to "interpret" himself a commission.

BY MR. LONGER:

Q: And is that based upon the conversation that you had with her prior to your meeting with Mr. Sweeney?

A: Yes.

[Comment] Excellent looping back into earlier testimony. Another opportunity to say "Would you have done all this and lose existing . . . for a total of nothing?"

Unfortunately, counsel has interrupted the point he was making earlier: why Hardy sent Sussman a list of doctors. Unhappily, this happened because he used the wrong exhibit, #8 instead of #10. He will do that now, but each of these points should be entered separately and closed separately before a new one is begun.

Q: I'd like you to look at Exhibit Number-10. Can you identify what Exhibit Number-10 is?

A: Yes.

Q: What is it?

A: It's a bill that Bob Sweeney's, one of his grand-children received from the hospital.

Q: And what is it <u>representing</u>?

A: It represents a copy of a bill that the insured received or the employee received just showing what the costs of that hospital stay was.

[Comment] The lawyer passes the baton. What he wants to do is show that Sweeney was unhappy, personally, with the other insurance company and that this dissatisfaction paved the way for Sussman to bring in Blue Cross. Unfortunately, counsel does not see how to make this clear. As with all of us, if we do not see the way to do it with questions, we are sometimes forced to seek help from the witness, and so he asks the witness to explain the document's "significance."

Q: Well, what is <u>significant</u> about this document?

A: Well, I had asked Bob to get together a group of these for me so that we can get Blue Cross and Blue Shield to reprice these up, using this same type of proce-dure, what would be the savings to the Union.

[Comment] Putting aside the fact that the question was objec-tionable, as much as witnesses are allowed to "interpret" the materiality of documents to cases, is the answer what counsel

wanted? We think not. A review of the last two questions may be helpful.

Q: And what did you do with that document?

A: I gave these to Helen Hardy.

Q: So that she could do this, repricing that you're—

A: Right. So that we could come back and say, this is what Blue Cross would pay the provider and what the savings would be.

[Comment] How might the goal have been achieved? "Was Sweeney happy with the way his grandchildren's bills were handled?" "What was your purpose in using his own family's bills?" Many questions might be asked now. "Did you do this to help Sweeney or the Blues—why? Was it gratis?"

Q: Would you turn to Exhibit Number-11—I'm sorry, yes, Exhibit Number-11. And what is that document?

A: That's a computer run that I got from the Union showing the distribution of the Union employees, where they are by ZIP Code, so that they would get a feel to see where all the—where their members are, to see if they have good coverage by their network.

Q: You used the word, they'll be able to see that.

A: They'll being Blue Cross and Blue Shield.

Q: Did you give that ZIP Code listing to people at Blue Cross and Blue Shield?

A: Yes.

Q: Who did you give that to at Blue Cross/Blue Shield?

A: Helen Hardy.

Q: And when did you give Ms. Hardy Exhibit Number-11 and Exhibit Number-10, if you can recall?

A: I don't recall the exact date.

Q: Was it in proximity to the June meeting in 1994?

A: It would have to have been, because I started to call Nick Craggs and tell him the information that I needed so that we can start looking at the Plan.

[Comment] And this is the man whom the defendant, in its opening, claims did nothing! *Again, we suggest that the jury should be reminded of that in the here-and-now with a question, rather than wait for summation. For example: "Were you in court when counsel for Blue Cross told this jury that you had done nothing, made no contribution . . . ," etc.*

Q: Mr. Sussman, I would like to direct your attention to Exhibit Number P-7, and ask you to tell us what that document is?

A: It's a copy of a notebook that I would keep on my desk to remind me to make phone calls.

Q: If you would turn to the page which has the numbering at the lower right-hand corner, TF, Tower Financial 7—I'm sorry, I take that back, the next page, Page 8. There's an entry there on Wednesday, the 1st, of—is this the 1995 calendar?

A: I'm looking at it, but I don't see it.

Q: Do you understand this to be your 1995 calendar?

A: Yes.

Q: There's an entry on Wednesday the 1st, is there not?

A: Yes.

Q: And, what does it say there?

A: It says that I have an 8:30 appointment with Blue Cross and Blue Shield meeting.

Q: And who did you understand that you were meeting with on Wednesday the 1st of March, at 8:30, 1995?

A: With Bob Sweeney and the gal from Blue Cross and Blue Shield, Helen Hardy.

Q: And why did you have a meeting in March of 1995 with Ms. Hardy and Mr. Sweeney?

A: Because I had had numerous conversations with Bob during the year since Preferred Care was in and they were not happy with the networking that was going on, and I thought it would be time to kind of get started early to get Blue Cross back in there, start getting all the information, get everything cooking, so maybe by September when the policy came up for renewal, because they don't move all that fast, we would be in a position to put Blue Cross/Blue Shield in there.

[Comment] Excellent. Notice the use of the document to authenticate the testimony. And then we see short questions and answers leading to the final point. The jurors' heads were likely swaying back and forth between the examiner and the witness. The next few questions are not so good. Counsel begins to lean on the witness to carry the ball when he asks the witness to tell "about" the meeting, and the answers become fuzzy.

Q: And tell us about what happened at that meeting?

A: Went back with Helen, obviously, and Bob, and we discussed what was going on with Preferred Care and Helen had assured him that they have a much better way of doing the job, and we agreed that we'll start taking a look at it, and he said it's probably something we should be doing.

Q: And what did you do after that meeting? Let me ask you this: It sounds like there was more interest than before, would you agree with that?

A: Well, there was a lot more interest. The interest was that they weren't—I was getting calls from Bob that the network wasn't—working all that well.

MR. SONNENFELD: Objection, Your Honor.

THE COURT: Sustained.

[Comment] The ruling is wrong. Apparently, the judge thinks this is hearsay, which mere complaints about prior insurance are not. But the ruling helps counsel get back in the saddle.

BY MR. LONGER:

Q: Because of this new interest that you had—that you were receiving, what did you do?

A: I told Helen that we have an opportunity now to really get onto this thing and whatever she has to do to get a hold of Nick, and you know, whatever information she needs, we should get working on it and start putting together a proposal.

Q: And what work did you do to start working on a proposal?

A: I think that's—at that meeting we just left it at that way. I don't think we did very much, other than I had Bob call Nick to tell Nick to receive Helen and whatever information she's going to need, to make sure that she gets it.

Q: And did you have another meeting with Mr. Sweeney and Ms. Hardy after that?

A: Yes.

Q: When did you have another meeting with Mr. Sweeney and Ms. Hardy?

A: I'm not sure of the date but it's probably a month or two after this.

[Comment] How many meetings are we up to? How many meetings were there? Shouldn't counsel remember for us by numbering them? Counsel needs to show how much more Sussman was doing and for whom. We might also be reminded that the man was in business and expected to be compensated. "Did you think you were doing all of this for nothing?"

Q: Well, let me direct your attention to Page Number 9, Exhibit Number-7, and there's an entry dated March 27.

A: There was a meeting that I had set up with Helen to meet with her and there, was miscommunications. I was there, she wasn't, and we never made that meeting. And then I reset it for another time.

Q: And if you turn to the page, you have an entry on your diary for Friday, March 31, Bob Sweeney, Helen Hardy?

A: We went back on that Friday.

Q: And what happened at that meeting?

[Comment] Again, an open-ended question. The witness is on his own.

A: He just reinforced that we should get involved with Blue Cross and that Helen should get involved on a more serious basis, and that he felt that this is an avenue that they should be going to.

[Comment] This answer is not so good. Who is "he"? Whoever he is, the focus has shifted from Sussman to him.

Q: Did you have the <u>sense</u> that the Ironworkers were going to go with Blue Cross at that time?

A: Yes.

[Comment] The word "sense" could have been objected to but, given the next Q&A, counsel was probably wise not to.

Q: And was that a sense that was conveyed to Ms. Hardy at the same time?

A: I don't think it was totally conveyed by Bob Sweeney at the time, but I think I conveyed it to her.

Q: What did Ms. Hardy say to you after you told her that you understood that the Ironworkers were interested now in going with Blue Cross/Blue Shield?

A: She was really excited, because <u>it was something that she could never have done</u>.

[Comment] The last answer, if conclusory, would be objected to. Counsel, we think, sensed it, and asked the correct question.

Q: What did she tell you?

A: She just told me how thankful she was and how excited she was and how excited she was to work on the case, and hopefully they were going to get it.

[Comment] Notice, the answer is more limited now that the actual conversation has been requested. This sets the stage for the money.

Q: Did she mention—did you talk about your commissions at this conversation?

A: <u>Probably</u>—yes, I'm sure I did mention some <u>sort of</u> commission.

[Comment] Not good. Weak answer and sounds speculative.

Q: Did you have a discussion about a broker of record letter at this conversation?

A: No.

Q: When did Ms. Hardy first tell you that you needed a broker of record letter?

A: <u>Probably</u> after <u>maybe</u> a month or two after this.

[Comment] The thought is good, but counsel might have argued through his question that this first mention of that letter came long after Sussman had performed for Blue Cross. Now counsel abandons all control and turns the accelerator over to the witness to go as far as he wishes, as the witness selects events covering the next two-month period.

Q: And what transpired between March and a month or two after?

A: Well, she was gathering information, to the best of my knowledge, because I had set up for her to go down and visit with Nick Craggs and get all that information, whatever it was that she was needing.

Bob had told me she was down there having meetings with him. Really nothing other than my knowing that she was getting together enough information to go out and get a quote.

Q: Did it concern you at all that Ms. Hardy was talking to Mr. Craggs—

A: No.

Q: —so frequently?

A: Not at all.

[Comment] Now counsel again takes command—and when he does, things go crisply.

Q: Did you take any other action on behalf of the Ironworkers? Let me ask you a different question.

Let me ask you to turn to Page 11 of Exhibit Number-7.

A: Yes.

Q: There's a entry there dated Friday, April 7th, which is just about a week and a half since that last meeting on March 31, correct?

A: Right.

[Comment] We are now to be introduced to Brian Sullivan. But who is he?

Q: You had a meeting—you have an entry there that indicates Brian Sullivan, with a telephone number.

Did you meet with Mr. Sullivan just a week and a half after your meeting with Mr. Sweeney and Ms. Hardy?

A: I think that was just a phone call. I don't remember meeting with him that quick. I don't remember if I met with him or if it was just a phone call.

Q: You did have a meeting with Mr. Sullivan and Mr. Sweeney?

A: I had two meetings with Mr. Sullivan and Mr. Sweeney.

[Comment] We still do not know who Sullivan is, unless we remember the opening. It would be wise to reintroduce us to him as he enters this stage of the account.

Q: And this entry of yours, is that reflecting a meeting or a phone call?

A: I would have to say that that was a meeting, because I usually met with Sweeney on Friday mornings.

Q: Now, what happened between March 31 and April 7th, that caused you to speak to Mr. Sullivan?

[Comment] Same observation.

A: Helen Hardy had given me a buzz and told me that unless I got a broker of record letter, that I was not going to be able to collect any type of commission from Blue Cross and Blue Shield.

Q: So she did talk to you about a broker of record letter after the March 31 letter?

A: That's right. That's what precipitated from me calling Brian Sullivan.

[Comment] Unfortunately, we have not been prepared for any of this, unless we remember who Sullivan is. Do you? Do you think that the jury does?

Q: What precipitated—how did you know to contact Mr. Sullivan?

A: I have a—some friends of ours that are, you know, in the group business and they do a lot of business with Blue Cross and Blue Shield and I had a meeting with them, and I told them what was happening and my conversation with Helen Hardy. They told me—

MR. SONNENFELD: Objection to what they told Mr. Sussman.

THE COURT: Sustained.

MR. SONNENFELD: Thank you, Your Honor.

[Comment] Counsel does not accept defeat. So he tries the back door.

BY MR. LONGER:

Q: What was your understanding after this meeting with these people that you just—actually, what are their names, the people that you met?

A: Dick Sidenberg and Eric Raymond.

Q: After you have this conversation with Mr. Sidenberg and Mr. Raymond, what was your understanding about what you should be doing?

A: They said—

MR. SONNENFELD: Objection, Your Honor.

BY MR. LONGER:

[Comment] He does not wait for the ruling, and wisely so, for the objection is correct in that the question calls for conclusions. The examiner really wants to hear what they said about her. So he tries another back door. This, too, could have been objected to, but wasn't.

Q: Without disclosing what they said, what was your <u>understanding</u> about what you ought to do?

[Comment] "Understanding," from whom? Same problem. Should have been the same objection. But there is none so the testimony rolls in.

A: I need to get onto Brian Sullivan because he's someone that would—he handled the brokerage side of it, and whatever would go down, and if we can get him involved in it, <u>then for sure that I'll get a commission.</u>

[Comment] Well, one might think that this is what counsel wants to hear, but it isn't. Remember his opening, when he spoke about Hardy's bad reputation? That is what he wants to hear. Watch.

Q: Did you have any understanding about Ms. Hardy after that conversation?

A: I don't understand the question.

[Comment] Uh, oh. Counsel was caught between his fear of leading and his fear of hearsay. So he threw the ball to the witness. The witness had a chance to bang Hardy, because of the failure to object, but did not take it, so counsel has to do it again. Guess what happens.

Q: Did you get information about Ms. Hardy during that conversation?

A: They—

MR. SONNENFELD: Objection, Your Honor.

THE COURT: Sustained. Well, he can answer yes or no, but he can't give—

MR. LONGER: Thank you, Your Honor.

BY MR. LONGER:

[Comment] He has failed again. But the judge's splitting of the baby has given him another opportunity. So now he tries to say it himself by offering an alternative to avoid the objection "leading." His adversary wisely stops him.

Q: And was it favorable information or unfavorable information?

MR. SONNENFELD: Objection, Your Honor.

THE COURT: Sustained.

[Comment] The hearsay nature is just too much. Counsel has failed, so he must move on.

BY MR. LONGER:

Q: You then called Mr. Sullivan; is that correct?

A: Yes.

Q: Because you understood that working through him, you would be able to get a commission?

MR. SONNENFELD: Your Honor, objection. It's leading, hearsay.

MR. LONGER: I'm just repeating his testimony, but if you'd like, I'll—

THE COURT: You can ask the question. Go ahead.

[Comment] The examiner has won. Unfortunately, he seems to forget that he has. So, instead of repeating the same question and harvesting the answer, he goes on to another question. He has persisted because he needs to explain why Sussman turned from Hardy to Sullivan. We guess that, in the end, he did. After all, the jurors did hear his attempts to question, if not all of the answers.

BY MR. LONGER:

Q: You had this conversation with Mr. Sidenberg, right?

A: Right.

Q: And they told you what?

MR. SONNENFELD: Objection, Your Honor.

THE COURT: Sustained.

[Comment] The defendant's attorney stepped in and stopped him.

BY MR. LONGER:

Q: You took action after this meeting based upon something that you heard, and what did you do?

A: I called Brian Sullivan.

Q: Thank you. And you called Mr. Sullivan because you had an understanding about your commissions; is that correct?

A: That's correct.

Q: And what was your <u>understanding</u> about commissions with Mr. Sullivan that was different than with Ms. Hardy?

A: I was assured that if we can move—

MR. SONNENFELD: Your Honor, I object. This is getting in what Mr. Sidenberg told him.

[Comment] The word "understanding" has not helped. It sounds speculative and interpretive rather than an account of a conversation. In any case, Sullivan is a Blue Cross/Blue Shield man. His statements to Sussman are admissible but the questioning is unclear at this point. Even the defense is confused about which conversation is being elicited. What then is going on with the jurors?

THE WITNESS: This is not—

MR. LONGER: It's not getting into that, it's what he understood.

MR. SONNENFELD: His understanding of what Mr. Sidenberg told him is the backdoor to getting in what Mr. Sidenberg—

THE WITNESS: No, it's Brian Sullivan.

MR. LONGER: It has to do with his understanding of the relationship between Mr. Sullivan and a commission and Ms. Hardy and a commission.

THE COURT: I'll let him answer. Go ahead.

THE WITNESS: My <u>understanding</u> was that if Brian and I can get this together and, you know, with the Blues, working through him, that I would be <u>assured of receiving a commission</u>.

[Comment] It finally came out, as it was bound to. Statements of Sullivan, as a representative of Blue Cross, are not hearsay. And sooner or later the jurors were bound to hear of his

promises to Sussman. And yet, we suggest that the last answer is not as definitive as to Sullivan promising a commission as could be elicited by a specific question; for example, if he had been asked: "In substance, Mr. Sussman, what did Sullivan say to you about a commission?" Vol. II, pp. 210–214.

BY MR. LONGER:

Q: And would you need a broker of record letter working with him?

A: No.

Q: That was your <u>understanding</u>?

A: That's correct.

[Comment] What is the "understanding" based on?

Q: And so on April 7th, you met with Mr. Sullivan and Mr. Sweeney; is that right?

A: Correct.

Q: And what did you do at this meeting?

A: I brought Brian in, introduced him and told him that he was also from Blue Cross and Blue Shield. That he had a different way of doing with the group, different than what Helen Hardy was proposing, that would probably be the same cost to them, but just at a little different twist, and that it would move it off dead center, because <u>if you're not giving me a broker of record letter</u>, I have no way of getting paid, so if Brian and I can work this out, everybody gets satisfied. It will be good for you and good for me. He said, "I really don't have any objection to doing that, but"—

[Comment] This is now a hodgepodge, with all the "he's" and "him's." Actually, it contains much that is helpful to the defendant, such as the fact that it was the union that was preventing Sussman from getting paid. Defense counsel steps in to clarify, but, we suggest, not the most important point.

MR. SONNENFELD: Could I just ask who the he is, Your Honor?

THE WITNESS: Yes, Bob Sweeney said, "I really don't have any objection doing that, but we're really pretty far ahead, and I don't know what the—what's going to be the doctors and, you know, where are you coming from?" So Brian said "I will get to you a list of all the providers in the State of Pennsylvania and New Jersey that we have under contract," and he did. I mean, we left it that Bob will take a look at it.

BY MR. LONGER:

Q: All right. And this list of providers, did Mr. Sullivan give it to you or did he give it to Mr. Sweeney?

A: Well, he dropped it off at my office. He had a courier drop it off at my office. It was a box about that big [indicating], and then I made arrangements to get it over to Bob Sweeney's office and drop it off to him.

Q: And that was part of the service that you provided in trying to broker this contract?

A: Yes.

[Comment] Again, we see the man who was described as having done nothing, doing yet something else to achieve the contract between the union and Blue Cross.

Q: And what did Mr. Sweeney do with that listing?

A: Not very much.

Q: Did you have discussions with him about it?

A: Yes.

[Comment] Not so good. It were better not asked. Counsel wisely moves away and asks a nicely formed question.

Q: What was the next thing that <u>you did to try to sell Blue Cross/Blue Shield to the Ironworkers</u>?

A: I had set up another meeting with Brian. And we went back to see Bob Sweeney and we discussed why he didn't think it was a good idea for us to get involved at this time, and he told us and he said if you really are persistent and what we did is we turned it over to Charlie Maresca, write a letter to Charlie Maresca, and if he wants to listen to your proposal or this second proposal, what-have-you from Blues, then let him deal with it, but I'm out of it at this point.

[Comment] The answer is obscure. Too much, too soon. And now we have ushered in another person, a Mr. Maresca, who needs to be reintroduced to us. Unfortunately, we get no help from the next question.

Q: That second meeting with Mr. Sullivan, is that indicated—was that—when did that take place; is that later in the year?

A: It was not all that much further than the—you know, after we had our first meeting. It was only a few weeks after.

Q: Well, let me draw your attention to Exhibit Number-13. That's a letter dated July 31, 1995, to Ms. Hardy from Charles Maresca, and it refers to a meeting that those two had on July 26th, correct?

A: Yes, that's correct.

Q: Have you ever seen this document before?

A: Yes.

Q: When did you have the occasion to see this July 31st, 1995 letter?

A: I don't remember the date that I got it, but Bob Sweeney gave it to me.

Q: And he showed it to you, and <u>what did you understand</u> when he showed it to you?

A: I <u>understood</u> that they've, from what he told me, and giving me the letter, that they <u>made up their mind</u> to go with Blue Cross and Blue Shield.

[Comment] The reader should recognize that, whether or not one decides to object, the question in that form is objectionable, and that the answer is as well.

Q: And is it that you understood that they were now going to go with Blue Cross/Blue Shield, that you wanted Mr. Sullivan to meet with Mr. Sweeney again?

A: Yes.

Q: And that's the second meeting that you were referring to?

A: Right.

Q: And that took place after July 31, 1995?

A: I would think so.

Q: So sometime in August, you had your meeting, or August or thereafter, you had that meeting?

A: The second meeting with Brian.

[Comment] This is better, because counsel is now moving crisply.

Q: Did you have concerns about you getting your commission based on the work that you did, the meetings that you set up with Ms. Hardy, and Mr. Sweeney, and that's why you brought in Mr. Sullivan?

A: Yes.

Q: Why did you have those concerns?

A: Well, because I just said earlier, I knew that I wasn't going—they were not going to give me a broker of record letter. They told me—

MR. SONNENFELD: Could I ask who they is?

[Comment] This turns out to be a great objection. Watch the witness demonstrate that it was the union, not the insurance company, that was stopping the paying of a commission to him.

THE WITNESS: Bob Sweeney had said to me, was questioning me, "Where is your commissions going to come from?" And I said, "They're going to come from Blue Cross and Blue Shield." He says, "<u>I don't think so</u>." And I said, "Bob, I've always dealt with insurance companies, I get paid from the insurance companies. You're currently with Preferred Care, they pay me. I would expect Blue Cross to pay me." And he said "<u>That's not the case, and I cannot in good conscience go back and give you a broker of record letter knowing that it's going to cost the Union any money.</u>"

[Comment] The point the plaintiff should be making is that his deal with Blue Cross was that his commission would come from Blue Cross's end; that the premium would be the same, Sussman or no Sussman. But, of course, that is not the theory of the complaint, which sounds in tort rather than contract.

BY MR. LONGER:

Q: Did you have discussions with Ms. Hardy about where your commission would come from?

A: No.

Q: Did you have discussions with Mr. Sullivan about where your commission would come from?

A: Yes.

Q: Did you <u>understand</u> that the commission would come from—where did you <u>understand</u> the commission would come from?

[Comment] When counsel wants to avoid the underlying conversations, he goes to the witness's understandings and conclusions. This is improper. Now, having thrown a general ball to the witness, the witness hits it foul. Watch.

A: With Ms. Hardy I had <u>hoped</u> that we would strike the same similar kind of contract that I had with Preferred Care. With Brian it was a different situation. He said there would be so much per head per month, and that's where the commission would come from. It would be built into the administrative fees.

[Comment] The "hope" is not a good word. We thought that the suit was premised on a Hardy promise, not one from Sullivan. Counsel wisely shifts hope into "understanding." He now has testimony that Sullivan, not Hardy, promised that the commission would come from Blue Cross, but Sullivan did not get the deal, Hardy did. Can the jurors, or even the judge, follow this?

Q: And was it your <u>understanding</u> that you would share the administrative fees with Blue Cross/Blue Shield?

A: It was my <u>understanding</u> that I would share a <u>portion of</u> that, yes.

[Comment] "Understanding" from whom? A "portion"? How much? Just what is the claim here? But there is no objection.

Q: And what became after that meeting with Mr. Sullivan and Mr. Sweeney in August?

A: Nothing. They just went full steam ahead and wound up going with the Blues.

Q: Did Mr.—you had mentioned that Mr. Sweeney told you to speak to their consultants, didn't you?

A: Mr. Sweeney asked us to write to Maresca and outline what we thought would be our proposal to him, and Maresca never answered our letter.

Q: And at that point, did you understand the deal to be over?

A: At that point, when he didn't answer our letter, both Mr. Sullivan and myself decided there's no sense going any further with it. There's no place for us to go.

[Comment] Counsel is ready for his finale.

Q: And what happened after that, did the Ironworkers contract with Blue Shield/Blue Cross?

A: To the best of my knowledge, yes.

Q: That was after you got Ms. Hardy in to meet with them, right?

A: That's right.

Q: That was after you had tried to get all of this listings of doctors and information back to Blue Cross and over to the Ironworkers; isn't that right?

A: Yes.

[Comment] Good—but now he puts the onus on his client with the words "you," and "feel" and "like."

Q: And do <u>you feel like</u> you were cheated?

[Comment] Is "feel" a good word?

A: Yes.

Q: Do you <u>feel</u> like you were treated unfairly?

[Comment] Again.

A: Totally.

[Comment] Counsel for the defendant should be objecting to these conclusory allegories and accusations from the plaintiff. But, since there is no objection, the testimony of the mental workings of the plaintiff rolls on, and on.

Q: Why?

A: Well, as a salesperson and working on commission, I don't know what was in it for me to bring in another carrier <u>when I was already getting a commission</u> from the current place. I just cut my throat. I just gave up my salary.

[Comment] Finally we hear that he replaced the paying Preferred with the nonpaying Blues.

Q: Does that make sense?

A: Well, I would hope at my age I knew better.

Q: You wouldn't have brought her in if you knew that you were going to be shut out after having brought her in, would you?

A: Not in a heartbeat. Why would I do that?

[Comment] This is excellent. Now counsel is using his questions to argue his case—and very well, too.

Q: And you didn't talk about a broker of record letter with her until after you had assurances with Mr. Sweeney that this contract was going forward; isn't that—

A: Yes.

MR. SONNENFELD: Objection, Your Honor. Leading. Asked and answered.

THE COURT: Sustained.

MR. SONNENFELD: Move to strike the answer that was given.

THE COURT: Stricken.

BY MR. LONGER:

[Comment] The examiner has done well. The striking means nothing and the objection has given him another shot. It is now he—not his client, but he, the advocate for Sussman, not Sussman himself—who smites the defendants.

Q: In your entire career, in the insurance business, the 30 years that you've been in this insurance business, have you ever been treated like that?

[Comment] We suggest that this is objectionable.

A: No.

Q: Have you ever lost a commission after you've gone through all of this work and seen the clients contract?

A: No, never.

[Comment] We suggest that this is objectionable, too.

Q: Do you think Blue Cross/Blue Shield did this to you intentionally?

MR. SONNENFELD: Objection, Your Honor.

THE COURT: Sustained.

BY MR. LONGER:

Q: Do you think Ms. Hardy knew what she was doing when she shut you out?

MR. SONNENFELD: Objection, Your Honor. Argumentative.

THE COURT: Sustained.

[Comment] Not only argumentative, but requires Sussman to be a mind reader.

BY MR. LONGER:

Q: Did Ms. Hardy ever say anything to you that made <u>you think</u> she was trying to negotiate with the Union, the Welfare Fund, based on your commission?

MR. SONNENFELD: Objection, Your Honor. Leading.

[Comment] The objection should have been speculative.

THE COURT: Overruled.

THE WITNESS: No.

[Comment] A good question and answer, if he was suing Blue Cross for a broken promise, rather than a tort. But the answer implies that she did not discuss Sussman's commission. If so, where is the interference?

BY MR. LONGER:

Q: Do <u>you think</u> that you provided a service to Blue Cross/Blue Shield?

A: Yes.

Q: Do <u>you think</u> you should be compensated for that service?

A: Yes.

Q: Tell everyone why?

A: I only work on a commission. I don't get anything else.

[Comment] This, except for both "you thinks," which could have been excised, and was objectionable, was all superb. It sounds like the client is doing it, but it was the lawyer. Now he begins to approach damages.

Q: Explain how you calculate your commission.

A: I <u>would hope</u> that I would get a percentage of the savings that the Union is getting as part of my commission. Ms. Hardy had talked to me and said that there was <u>anywheres</u> from a one to three percent commission, <u>but I'm not sure what</u>—if that was on billing or how that was going to you know, what the prime was at, <u>I think it was too early in the game to understand where that was coming from.</u>

[Comment] This answer does not help. It is conflicting as to who pays, on what basis, and on how much. His use of "hope" could set him up for a directed verdict. Counsel would have done better to use questions, as he has up until just now.

Q: Well, do you know what the—let me show you, direct your attention to Exhibit Number-15. Have you ever seen a document like this before?

A: Yes.

Q: What is it?

A: It's called a 5500 and employers need to file this with the federal government any time they're providing employee benefits.

Q: This is a Form 5500 for the Ironworkers District Council Philadelphia Vicinity Welfare Plan, is it not?

A: Yes.

Q: Does this document indicate the benefit payments of the Welfare Plan made from October 1, '94 to September 30, 1995?

A: It should, yes.

Q: I draw your attention to Page 6, Item 8.

A: I see that. It says: "benefit payments and things provide benefits direct to participants or beneficiaries, 13 million—"

MR. SONNENFELD: Objection, Your Honor, and move to strike. This is benefits that were paid during the year that ended three months before the contract of Blue Cross went into effect. This has nothing to do with benefits that were paid under Blue Cross. It has nothing to do with Blue Cross.

THE COURT: Sustained.

MR. SONNENFELD: Thank you.

BY MR. LONGER:

Q: Mr. Sussman, how big did you understand the account to be with Ironworkers?

A: Bob had told me that at one year it was 17 million dollars.

MR. SONNENFELD: Objection, Your Honor. Objection.

THE COURT: Sustained.

MR. SONNENFELD: Thank you, Your Honor.

BY MR. LONGER:

[Comment] Plaintiff's counsel does not blink. He goes at it again and, this time, firmly in control and squarely in the sad-

dle. The words of the union man might well be hearsay, but not if the words come from Ms. Hardy, the Blue Cross representative.

Q: Did you discuss with Ms. Hardy the size of this Welfare Fund?

A: Yes.

Q: Did you discuss with Ms. Hardy how much money was at stake here?

A: Yes.

Q: How big is the Welfare Fund, when you talked to Ms. Hardy?

A: I had told her that I was told that it was about 17 million dollars.

Q: And did she agree with you?

A: I don't think she could—there was nothing to agree or disagree, I was giving her the number.

Q: Now, you talked to Ms. Hardy and she told you that you said that you could expect between one to three percent of a commission; is that right?

A: Yes.

[Comment] Counsel led, and he really had to.

Q: If you would, turn to Exhibit Number-17, Page IVC-470.

A: I remember that.

Q: This is a document that Ms. Hardy produced to us, it's dated September 22nd, 1994; do you see that?

A: Yes.

Q: And it says; "Call Len Sussman, Re: Compensation"; do you see that?

A: Yes.

Q: There it says: "One to three percent"; do you recall that?

A: Yes.

[Comment] *Great document. It should have been used in the opening. It should have been used earlier in direct. Indeed, it should have been used repeatedly in both—early and often.*

Q: She told us in her deposition—

MR. SONNENFELD: Objection, Your Honor. This is not proper for Mr. Longer to tell us what Ms. Hardy testified to at her deposition. It's not a proper way to introduce testimony.

THE COURT: Well, let me hear the question.

MR. LONGER: I can do it a different way, Your Honor.

THE COURT: Go ahead.

BY MR. LONGER:

Q: Do you recall what Ms. Hardy was saying when you were talking about one to three percent commission of billing?

A: Well, it was not—yes, it was basically billing. We were originally trying to steer the Union to go with an HMO or point of service kind of a plan, and not to be totally self-insured.

Q: And you understood, you said earlier, the billing was 17 million dollars?

A: That was the impression that I was under.

Q: Now, you went to South Philly High, can you do the mathematics of what one per cent of 17 million dollars would be?

A: One hundred and 70 thousand dollars.

Q: And you went to South Philly High, and you can understand what three percent is, can you?

A: Yes.

Q: What is three percent of 17 million dollars?

A: Three times 170 is $510,000.

Q: You were expecting a big commission after you talked to Ms. Hardy, weren't you?

A: Yes.

MR. SONNENFELD: Objection, Your Honor. Leading.

THE COURT: Overruled.

[Comment] But it is leading. Moreover, Sussman's "expecta-tions" are objectionable. Nevertheless, counsel is slamming home his points with a sledgehammer. And it is effective, pre-cisely because he is doing the advocating through the witness.

BY MR. LONGER:

Q: You thought that this was going to be a big payday, didn't you?

A: Yes.

Q: And this is what Ms. Hardy was telling you, right?

A: Correct.

Q: And these contracts continue year after year, don't they?

A: Yes. I think it's already past its—it's definitely in its second year.

Q: And these things just keep going and going. They have a life of their own, don't they?

A: Yes.

Q: And you would expect to receive $170,000 to $510,000 for every year for a long time based on that con-versation, correct?

A: Hopefully, yes.

[Comment] An excellent ending, with counsel summing up his case with his questions, marred only by the answer evidencing "hope" rather than an agreement.

MR. LONGER: Thank you, Mr. Sussman. I have no further questions.

THE COURT: I think it's probably a good time to break for lunch. We'll do the cross-examination after lunch. It's now 12:00, if you could be back at about 1:45, that would be good, quarter of 2:00. Have a nice lunch, don't discuss the case with each other or anybody else, and we'll see you at quarter of 2:00.

THE CRIER: Everyone remain seated while the Jury leaves the room.

[Comment] We can see now the deficiency in the plaintiff's position caused by the failure to ask for what he wants. He is all over the lot—$170,000 to $510,000 for just one year. And he wants more than one year. Well, what is it that he thinks he is entitled to? And it sure sounds as though we are being forced to guess at his entitlement. This failure to be specific actually undercuts his position on liability. "Hopes" are not contracts, agreements, or even understandings between parties. And yet, counsel has established a solid quantum meruit *claim, which is likely to persuade the jury that Sussman has been cheated out of at least something. Let the lawyers and the judges focus on the niceties of the* law. *These jurors are going to want to do* justice.

- - - -

[Jury exits.]

Analysis of the Direct Examination

The direct examiner begins, as he did in the opening argument, by introducing Mr. Sussman and tracing his career. The examiner shows how Sussman came to have his own business and ties him to Philadelphia and elicits testimony that Sussman's company, Tower, began in Philadelphia but later moved to New Jersey.

The direct examiner asks a series of questions that permit Sussman to explain how his company serves as a wholesaler between insurance companies and agents. The lawyer is arguing his case through the witness to the jury and making the point that agents and companies depend on Sussman to be in the middle. Through effective advocacy, the examiner demonstrates that Sussman has lived on a commission basis for 30 years and that it is a commission business for all sorts of insurance, including health insurance. It is all excellent, and calculated to make us want to find for Sussman.

The examiner moves from the insurance background to Sussman's relationship with Sweeney. They were friends. Sweeney and he did business. Sweeney sent him business. Sussman, it seems, had the confidence of the unions. We also get a hint that they are friends no longer.

The examiner moves to the health insurance problems that the welfare fund was having. There is an objection based on hearsay that the judge sustains, but it does not deter the examiner, because he knows that inevitably Sussman will be permitted to relay the advice he gave to Sweeney and explain the basis for the advice.

The direct examination moves inexorably toward the Blue Cross/Blue Shield deal, first by developing the preferred provider organization that Sussman recommended, how it worked, and how Sussman was paid a commission—by the insurance organization. The examiner shows Sussman a document containing the agreement. In the moment, the examiner corroborates for the jury the truth of what Sussman is saying. The document is dated June 1994.

Note that the trial judge gives some confusing instructions on documents, but his approach is one that affords the maximum tactical judgments for an advocate. The judge appears to say that counsel should mark and identify all exhibits shown to a witness and may use the exhibit, but the exhibit need not be formally offered into evidence until later in the case. This permits counsel to corroborate testimony without being required to publish an exhibit and interrupt the flow of the examination. No voir dire will therefore interrupt the direct.

Counsel uses a second document in conjunction with the first. The first document is Sussman's contract with the provider, and the second is the welfare fund's contract. The two documents indicate that Sussman negotiated for the fund, arranged its contract, and then signed a separate agreement with the provider. It begins to look like the health insurance industry does not operate as uniformly as defense counsel suggested in his opening statement.

The trial judge sustains a second objection to what Sweeney told Sussman. This is probably an incorrect ruling, as the conversation does not appear to be offered for the truth of anything, but to explain why Sussman did what he did. Plaintiff's counsel does not make this argument, however, and probably has decided that the information will work its way to the surface anyway.

The direct examination moves from having Sussman testify about the preferred provider network to his contacts with Ms. Hardy at Blue Cross/Blue Shield. Another document is used. It is Hardy's letter dated June 1994. Again, Sussman's narration of how events unfolded is corroborated with a document. There can be no doubt that Sussman contacted Hardy to discuss the possibility of "the Blues" insuring the unions. The direct examiner scores when Sussman relates how he explained that it could be good for the unions and good for the Blues. This is what a wholesaler is supposed to do, right?

Sussman testifies that he told Hardy in the car on the way to meet Sweeney that he hoped to get the same commission arrangement on any contract that he had with the provider organization and that it was a 20 percent arrangement. Counsel is careful to emphasize that the broker gets 20 percent of the fee that the insurer receives as a result of saving money for union members. The jury, it is hoped, will understand that the union saves on health insurance, the Blues get a fee for arranging the savings, and Sussman wants a percentage of the Blues' fee for putting the deal together. The jury well may understand that Sussman wants no higher a percentage than he is already receiving and which must be known to Sweeney and the welfare fund.

Sussman explains that Sweeney does not want to jump to the Blues because it might make his decision to go with the provider organization look bad. The direct examination continues with Sussman explaining how he left things with Hardy. Hardy provides him with information and writes Sussman a letter, which is exhibit 8, in which she says she hopes they can meet objectives that will be beneficial to all, including Sussman. The examiner asks Sussman what he thought Hardy meant. Now there is an objection. Why? Will the jury not be asking itself the same question? Of course it will! But defense counsel knows that Sussman's answer will emphasize, repeat, and highlight what is key in this case.

The direct examination oddly becomes truncated rather than expansive when the questioning turns to the commission arrangement and why Sussman feels he was cheated. Sussman testifies that the first mention of commissions took place in the car as he and Ms. Hardy were driving to meet Sweeney. Sussman says that he explained his arrangement with the preferred provider organization, and that Hardy's response was that a similar arrangement might not be "doable," because Blue Cross/Blue Shield had its own commission structure. Think back to the defense opening statement. Defense counsel argued that Blue Cross/Blue Shield did not pay commissions, and that fees were paid by unions. This would have been a good point at which to bring forth the exhibit in which the 1 to 3 percent commission was specifically mentioned and to ask Sussman some of the following questions (the answers to which you know):

Q: [After the witness identifies the exhibit] Did you and Ms. Hardy discuss a commission?

Q: Did you talk about a range of 1 to 3 percent?

Q: What did you tell her about your existing commission on the Ironworkers' account?

Q: How long did you and Ms. Hardy talk about the commission?

Q: Would you say that you were clear or unclear about your interest in a commission?

Q: At the time you made clear your interest in a commission, what did Ms. Hardy say about a broker of record letter?

Q: Did Ms. Hardy seem confused at all about your interest in a commission?

After Sussman and Hardy meet with Sweeney, who understandably is not thrilled with going to his board to say that the deal that the Ironworkers just consummated in 1994 with Preferred Care was not the best deal available, Sussman asks Hardy to provide him with information he can transmit to Sweeney. We know she did so, because there is a letter from Sussman to Sweeney, but the letter is not used to make an argument. It would not have been hard to argue through Sussman about the importance of the letter:

Q: Let me take you back to your first telephone discussion with Ms. Hardy. What did she tell you about the history of Blue Cross/Blue Shield with the union?

Q: How excited was she at the prospect of restoring the union as a client?

Q: In that first conversation, what did Ms. Hardy say she thought the likelihood was of being able to restore the union as a Blue Cross/Blue Shield client?

Q: Now, let's go back to the meeting that you and Ms. Hardy had with Mr. Sweeney. How anxious was Mr. Sweeney to renew a relationship for the welfare fund with Blue Cross/Blue Shield?

Q: Based on your long experience with Mr. Sweeney and the Ironworkers, tell us, when you and Ms. Hardy left the meeting, if you had given up on trying to persuade Mr. Sweeney, what chance would Ms. Hardy and Blue Cross/Blue Shield have had to land the fund as a client?

Q: Did you give up after the meeting, or did you continue to work to land the fund for Blue Cross?

Q: Did you speak again with Ms. Hardy about continuing to work on Mr. Sweeney?

Q: Did you ask her for any information?

Q: Did she agree to provide any information?

Q: What information did she provide?

Q: Is this the letter she sent to you?

Q: Why was the letter sent to you rather than to Mr. Sweeney?

Q: At the time Ms. Hardy sent the letter, were you working for Blue Cross/Blue Shield as an employee?

Q: But you were spending time on Blue Cross/Blue Shield's behalf?

Q: Did you understand that you were to get nothing for all these efforts, or that you were to be compensated?

Q: Did you reveal or conceal from Ms. Hardy that you were spending time?

Q: What was your goal in putting Blue Cross/Blue Shield together with the welfare fund?

Q: Was there ever a time that you did not make clear to Ms. Hardy that you expected a commission?

Q: As you continued to work to land the fund for Blue Cross, did Ms. Hardy remain excited or lose interest?

Q: When you and Ms. Hardy spoke, how interested did she seem in your efforts to land the fund?

Q: At the time Ms. Hardy was interested and excited, did she mention a broker of record letter?

Q: At the time she sent you her letter, did she mention a broker of record letter?

Q: Turning your attention to the last paragraph of the letter, where it reads, "It was a pleasure meeting with you and Bob Sweeney. I look forward to continuing our dialogue so that we can hopefully meet objectives which are beneficial to all of us." What did you understand this to mean?

Q: Did you think "all of us" in a letter written to you included you or excluded you?

The use of the information about the hospitalization of one of Sweeney's grandchildren is clever. It shows a personal relationship between Sweeney and Sussman and also reminds the jury that the purpose of the insurance plan was to protect union workers and their families. At the same time, it demonstrates that Sussman is thinking about making the case for Blue Cross/Blue Shield and is actually making it. But, the fact that Sussman turned the letter over to Hardy offered the opportunity to argue the case once more as follows:

Q: Why did you rather than Ms. Hardy seek this information from Mr. Sweeney?

Q: At the time you conveyed the information you obtained from Mr. Sweeney to Ms. Hardy, were you working for Blue Cross/Blue Shield as an employee?

Q: But you were spending time on Blue Cross/Blue Shield's behalf?

Q: Did you conceal from Ms. Hardy that you were spending time gathering this information?

Q: Why did you spend your time and effort in gathering this information from Mr. Sweeney and then sending it to Ms. Hardy?

Q: While you were doing this work, did you do anything to suggest to Ms. Hardy that you no longer expected a commission?

Q: At the time she sent you the letter, did she mention a broker of record letter?

Later in the trial, there will be some question about whether Ms. Hardy actually received the information about Sweeney's grandchild. This might be because Sussman did not identify the information as such. It will be conceded by the defendants that Hardy received some request from Sussman for repricing of certain procedures. If, in fact, Sussman asked for repricing of Sweeney's grandchild's procedures but did not reveal that fact, the point should be made on direct. No one but Sussman can know which procedures he chose to have repriced and why.

The line of questioning set forth here concerning repricing could be repeated with respect to the ZIP Code listings. The power of the documents is that they corroborate Sussman's testimony—but they become more powerful when used as part of an argument made through questions to the witness. The documents also corroborate Sussman's claim that it was his effort and his relationships that enabled Blue Cross to land the Ironworkers account.

The direct examiner moves from 1994 to 1995 without making clear how much time has passed. Sussman testifies that he and Sweeney have spoken during this time, and that Sweeney has expressed concerns about the provider organization. It is important that Sussman has been working the problem for 12 months while Blue Cross/Blue Shield has been on the sidelines, and the point could easily be made with a few questions:

Q: How long was the contract between the welfare fund and the preferred provider organization?

Q: At the end of the first year, what choice did the welfare fund have regarding health insurance?

Q: Did you and Mr. Sweeney speak about the health insurance provided by the preferred provider organization?

Q: How often did you speak with him?

Q: At the time you spoke with him, were you receiving your commission from the preferred provider organization?

Q: Even though that organization was paying you a commission, were you anxious to see the contract renewed if it was not in the best interests of the welfare fund?

Q: As the first year of the preferred provider plan was coming to an end, had you reached any opinion as to how Blue Cross/Blue Shield's plan compared to the preferred provider plan?

Q: Who was it that decided to recommend that Blue Cross/Blue Shield take another shot at insuring the welfare fund?

Q: Had Blue Cross/Blue Shield, to your knowledge, done anything during the year you were speaking with Mr. Sweeney about the problems with the preferred provider plan?

Q: When you decided that Blue Cross/Blue Shield should take another shot, what did you do?

Q: Did you and Ms. Hardy meet again with Mr. Sweeney to talk about Blue Cross/Blue Shield's interest in insuring the welfare fund?

Q: Who arranged the meeting?

Q: At the time you arranged the meeting, were you more or less optimistic than the previous year about Blue Cross/Blue Shield's chances?

Q: Why were you more optimistic?

Q: To the best of your knowledge, did Ms. Hardy or anyone else at Blue Cross/Blue Shield have any information about how the preferred provider plan was working?

Q: Now, when did you and Ms. Hardy meet with Mr. Sweeney?

Q: At the conclusion of the meeting, had Mr. Sweeney made any commitment to Blue Cross/Blue Shield?

Q: At the conclusion of the meeting, had you made any judgment about the likelihood that the Ironworkers would switch to Blue Cross/Blue Shield?

Q: What did you say to Ms. Hardy about your judgment?

Q: What was her reaction?

Q: Did she say anything at that time about the work you had done?

Q: Did you talk again about a commission?

Q: Did Ms. Hardy express any hesitancy in talking about a commission?

Q: What mention did Ms. Hardy make at that time about a broker of record letter?

Notice that Sussman makes a mistake in testifying about when, after he and Hardy met with Sweeney, Hardy first mentioned the broker of record letter. Plaintiff's counsel wisely uses documents to refresh recollection without ever using the words "refresh recollection" and pins the dates down. In doing so, it might have been a good idea for counsel to ask, "So how long after the two of you met with Mr. Sweeney and you told Ms. Hardy that you thought Blue Cross/Blue Shield would get the Ironworkers business was it that Ms. Hardy raised the broker of record letter for the first time?

Plaintiff's counsel promised in his opening statement to prove that Sussman was told not to do business with Hardy, but the judge sustained objections to questions seeking to elicit information about what Sussman was told. Even though the information might not be offered "for its truth," it might well be prejudicial. Plaintiff's counsel could have pursued a non-hearsay argument and opposed the objection, but did not.

Sussman testifies that he telephoned Brian Sullivan who also worked for Blue Cross/Blue Shield, because he believed that if Sullivan rather than Hardy represented Blue Cross/Blue Shield he would be able to receive his commission. The testimony about the Sussman-Sullivan meeting with Sweeney

is disjointed. Apparently, in this discussion, Sussman candidly
tells Sweeney that Blue Cross/Blue Shield will provide essentially the same deal through either Hardy or Sullivan, but that
Sussman only gets his commission through Sullivan. Not surprisingly, Sweeney has no objection to Sussman's commission
being paid by Blue Cross/Blue Shield if the terms of the deal
are the same, but he does not want to go back to square one.
Sussman's testimony that he met again with Sweeney and provided him information that Sullivan had gathered paints the
picture of a man, Sweeney, who does not want to go back to his
board and tell the members that the negotiations they have
been engaged in should start over, especially with the same
Blue Cross/Blue Shield organization to reach the same result.

Sussman testifies that Sweeney told him to contact Charlie
Maresca. It is impossible to believe that any juror could follow
this part of the testimony. Sussman says he wrote to Maresca
but does not identify who Maresca is or why Sweeney would
tell Sussman to contact him. Sussman is asked about a letter
from Maresca to Hardy that apparently confirms that the
union will sign on with Blue Cross/Blue Shield. Sweeney gave
the letter to Sussman, but Sussman is not asked why Sweeney
gave it to him or what Sweeney said in giving it. After seeing
the letter, Sussman and Sullivan meet with Sweeney a second
time.

It is at this point in the direct examination that Sussman is
asked about a critical conversation he had with Sweeney in
which Sweeney said that he would not provide a broker of
record letter to Sussman, because it would cost the union
money. It is unclear when this conversation took place or how
it arose. Did Sussman ask for such a letter? Was Sweeney told
by Hardy that such a letter was needed if Sussman was to get
a commission? This is too important to be left hanging.

Apparently, Sullivan described the Blue Cross/Blue Shield
commission arrangement to Sussman. Sussman candidly
states that in talking with Hardy he had hoped for a percentage arrangement similar to the one he had with the preferred
provider. It was Sullivan who described a different sort of commission arrangement based on a per head basis. Yet, later in

his testimony, Sussman says that Hardy had mentioned a 1 to 3 percent range on commissions. When did this conversation take place? Is this not one of the most critical points in the direct examination? Plaintiff's counsel asks Sussman to do the math based upon a $17 million fee, and in the process counsel reminds the jury where Sussman went to high school. Missing, though, is any detail about when the conversations about the percentages took place, where they took place, and how those conversations fit in with the events as they unfolded. This is especially surprising given that plaintiff has a memorandum written by Hardy that refers to Sussman and "compensation" and contains the 1 to 3 percent figure. With the document to corroborate Sussman, plaintiff's counsel could have dwelled on the conversation surrounding the document without fear of contradiction. Indeed, plaintiff should have been using the document throughout the direct, and even before that, throughout the opening argument.

CROSS-EXAMINATION OF THE PLAINTIFF'S FIRST WITNESS

Text of the Cross-Examination of the Plaintiff

[Jury enters.]

[Back on the record in open court.]

THE COURT: Sir, you're still under oath. Cross-examine.

[Comment] This is one of the most important moments of the trial. In most cases, if the plaintiff leaves the stand believed, he will almost certainly win the case. By the same token, if he is not believed, he will almost certainly lose the case. In most cases, therefore, parties on the stand force credibility contests, because their testimony, if credible, is usually outcome-determinative. See Vol. III, pp. 20–23. But not always. And the purpose of cross-examination of any witness is not necessarily to impeach. The purpose of cross is, of course, the same as direct. It is to argue your case right through the witness to the jury. Now, however, it is easier by far to do that, as you not only may

*but are encouraged to lead. Let us watch the cross-examiner as
he crafts his questions. Let us also see which of the three meth-
ods of cross he employs: impeachment, limiting, or hitchhiking.
See Vol. III, pp. 13–16. This may be one of the very rare
instances in which a party can be crossed by "limiting," for here
the plaintiff has sued Blue Cross for interference by Blue Cross
with the plaintiff's relationship with the union, whereas what
the plaintiff really wants is money from Blue Cross for services
performed for Blue Cross. Thus, it may be possible for the
defendant to take everything the plaintiff has to say at face
value, without any need to force a credibility fight, and still win
by limiting the testimony to the claim. Put another way, aside
from his position that Blue Cross refused to pay him directly,
what evidence does Sussman have that Blue Cross told the
union not to give him a broker of record letter?*

MR. SONNENFELD: May I proceed, Your Honor?

THE COURT: Please.

MR. SONNENFELD: Thank you.

Q: Good afternoon, Mr. Sussman.

A: Hi.

Q: Can you hear me without difficulty?

A: Yes.

Q: I believe you told us, this morning, that you are the
President of Tower Financial Planning Corporation; is
that right?

A: Yes.

Q: And you founded that at some 25 or 26 years ago;
is that correct?

A: Yes.

Q: And I believe that you told us that Tower is located
in Marlton, New Jersey; is that correct?

A: Yes.

Q: And you, yourself, live in Voorhees, New Jersey, do you not?

A: Yes.

Q: And is it correct that your wife is the sole shareholder of Tower?

A: Correct.

Q: And you are a licensed insurance broker, are you not, sir?

A: Yes.

Q: Licensed in the State of New Jersey, and in Pennsylvania?

A: Yes.

Q: And is it correct that you are the only licensed insurance broker employed by Tower?

A: No. There's another fellow, Andy Fisher.

[Comment] Counsel is in control. This is good. But counsel is wrong in his assertions. Not so good for him. So while he is in excellent control of the witness, where is it taking him? What is he trying to tell us through the witness that is of significance to this case?

Q: At the time that you were dealing with the events in question here, in 1994, 1995, were you then the only licensed insurance broker at Tower?

A: No. My partner, Arthur Pearlson.

Q: He's no longer your partner?

A: He died.

[Comment] Again, not good. Moreover, where is he going? We must remember that, unlike a direct, which must present a complete picture (especially from a party), the great strength of a cross-examination lies not only in the ability to use leading questions, but also in the ability to pick the subject matter to which to apply the tools of cross. See Vol. III, pp. 57–62.

Q: Do you recall when that was?

A: Two years ago this Christmas.

[Comment] How is it relevant when the man's partner died?

Q: Now, Tower is involved, I believe, in all lines of the life insurance business; is that correct, sir?

A: Yes.

Q: And your experience has been primarily in life insurance, has it not, sir?

A: Yes.

Q: And is it correct that your experience with health insurance has been a lesser component of your business than life insurance?

A: Not necessarily. It depends on the year.

Q: Would it be correct to say that, in recent years, your health insurance business has been about 25 percent of your business?

A: I don't know the exact number. Health insurance makes up a large percentage of my income.

[Comment] Is this a point worth making? If it is, counsel has not made it. Nor will he, unless he has the ammunition to control the witness. If he doesn't have material to confront Sussman with, the witness can make any answer that he wants to and the examiner can do nothing about it.

Q: But isn't life insurance a majority of your income?

A: Are you talking about Leonard Sussman, the agent, that writes business?

Q: Yes.

A: Or Tower Financial Planning, the agency?

Q: Well, is there a difference?

A: Yes.

Q: Well, let's ask about Tower Financial Planning?

A: I'd say that Tower Financial Planning, the group premium is substantially more than the life premium.

Q: What about Leonard Sussman?

A: The life premium is more than the group premium.

Q: So therefore, the work that you, Leonard Sussman, has done, has been more with respect to life insurance as opposed to health insurance?

A: In proportion to my income, yes.

[Comment] OK, but is this important? He is using the doctrine of limiting, but not to any important purpose. And because Sussman and Tower seem to be indistinguishable, he seems to have taken a long time to make a distinction without a difference. In any event, he now decides to change topics — notice how well he can lead to control the subject matter, but wisely never *tries to compel the witness to answer yes or no. See Vol. III, pp. 24–25.*

Q: Now, is it also correct that before 1994, when you called Ms. Hardy to try to introduce her to the Ironworkers, that you had not previously, you, yourself, had not previously done business with Independent Blue Cross?

A: Correct.

Q: And, in fact, you had never previously even been to the offices of Independent Blue Cross here in Philadelphia; is that correct, sir?

A: Correct.

Q: Now, the Ironworkers has about 2500 employees or members; is that correct?

A: Yes.

Q: The Ironworkers Fund. And some of your work that you do at Tower is with groups, is it not?

A: Yes.

Q: And I believe you have one group that's about 1800; is that correct?

A: Yes.

Q: And one group that's about 1000?

A: Yes.

Q: And the other groups you have are all 100 employees or less; isn't that correct?

A: Correct.

Q: So, therefore, the Ironworkers is the largest group that you had ever dealt with; is that correct?

A: Yes.

[Comment] He certainly has established the point, and used his questions in a most able way to draw the lines of probability (Vol. III, pp. 177–184) to force the witness to give the answers that the examiner wished. But are these points worth making?

Q: The Ironworkers District Council has employees, or I guess members of the various Locals in the Tristate Area, Southeastern Pennsylvania, Southern New Jersey and Delaware; isn't that correct?

A: Yes.

Q: And isn't it correct that you only got one other group that has members or employees in the Tristate Area?

A: Yes.

Q: And is it also correct that the Ironworkers District Council Philadelphia Vicinity, Health and Welfare Fund, is the only Health and Welfare Fund that you had ever represented as a broker?

A: Yes.

Q: And indeed, the contract between the Ironworkers and what you called Preferred Care this morning, that is the only contract you've brokered on behalf of the Ironworkers; is that correct, sir?

A: Yes.

Q: And is it also correct that as of the time of the events in question, 1994, 1995, you were not aware of any other Health and Welfare Fund using a broker for its health insurance; is that correct, sir?

A: I need the question again.

Q: As of the time of the events in question, in this case, 1994, 1995, isn't it correct that you were not aware of any other Health and Welfare Fund that used a broker to place its health insurance?

[Comment] We begin to suspect that at least some of these questions are written down. If so — and we cannot know — it would be an error.

A: I don't know of any other Fund.

Q: And so, therefore, is it correct that you don't know of any other Fund that was using a broker to place its health insurance?

A: That would be correct.

[Comment] Again, counsel is in magnificent control. But is he addressing the issues that will be important to the jurors? Put another way, counsel has conducted a technically proficient examination in the last portion, but has he made any points of value?

Q: Now, you told us that the first meeting that you arranged between Ms. Hardy, seated across the room, and Mr. Sweeney, took place in late May or early June of 1994; is that correct?

A: Yes.

Q: And indeed, you got a letter from Ms. Hardy dated June the 3rd, 1994, thanking you for the meeting; isn't that correct?

A: Yes.

Q: So, therefore, that initial meeting that you set up took place sometime within a few days preceding June 3rd, 1994; is that correct sir?

A: I would think so, yes.

Q: And it's correct, is it not, that that meeting lasted about a half hour?

A: I would say somewheres between half hour and an hour.

Q: Isn't it correct that nothing came of that meeting?

A: Well, no, that's not correct.

[Comment] Counsel ought not to be surprised at this last answer, for, in a sense, the whole deal emanated from this meeting, or at least the plaintiff will so contend. However, counsel is wise indeed to skip over the preliminary meeting between Sweeney and Hardy, and that is the great power of cross—you can do that sort of thing.

Q: That's not correct? Well, you knew at that meeting, did you not, that Ms. Hardy had previously met with Mr. Sweeney?

A: Yes.

Q: You learned that at the meeting?

A: At the meeting, right.

Q: That Ms. Hardy, on her own, without any involvement by you, had previously met with Mr. Sweeney, correct?

A: Yes.

Q: And it's true, also, isn't it, that shortly after the meeting, the Ironworkers District Council chose to enter into a contract not with Blue Cross or Blue Shield but with Preferred Care?

A: Correct.

[Comment] Which meeting? Was it the one that Hardy attended without Sussman, or the later one, with him?

Q: And you informed Ms. Hardy of that sometime in mid-June of 1994, did you not?

A: Yes.

Q: And that contract was effective as of August of 1994, was it not?

A: Correct.

Q: Now, your next involvement in meeting with Ms. Hardy and Mr. Sweeney, was then by your testimony, in March of 1995; is that correct, sir?

A: Yes.

Q: And you told us that you believed you had two meetings, one on March 1st, one on March 31st of 1995; that was your testimony, sir?

A: Yes.

Q: How long were each of those meetings, sir?

A: Maybe half hour to an hour?

Q: And is it your testimony that each of those meetings also took place at the offices of Mr. Sweeney's Local in South Jersey?

A: Correct.

Q: For either of those meetings, did you ever receive a letter back from Ms. Hardy thanking you for those meetings?

A: I don't remember.

Q: And do you have any such letter with you today?

A: I don't have one with me, no.

Q: And did you ever send her any letter concerning either of those two meetings?

A: No.

Q: Now, you next say that you met with Brian Hardy—excuse me, you next met on April the 7th; is that correct?

A: Right. Yes.

Q: And as of April the 7th, when you had your next meeting, you knew then, did you not, that in order for you to receive a commission, you would have to have a broker of record letter?

A: By the time I met Brian, yes, I knew I needed a broker of record letter.

[Comment] Excellent—he has skipped over the stuff he does not want to deal with in the conversations with Hardy and uses the phrase "You would need" and the witness buys it. The cross-examiner then pushes forward.

Q: And you knew that because Ms. Hardy had told you that; is that correct?

A: Yes.

Q: And by going and meeting with Brian on April the 7th, you were trying to circumvent or go around Ms. Hardy?

A: Yes.

[Comment] Excellent. He has made the plaintiff look like he was cheating. The chronology of events is collapsing.

Q: And at the meeting with Brian, on the 7th of April, you were discussing with Mr. Sweeney and Brian, an alternative to Blue Cross coverage known as Blair Mill; is that correct?

A: Correct.

Q: And Blair Mill is a subsidiary of Blue Cross?

A: Yes.

Q: Or an affiliate of Blue Cross. I believe you told us that you were told by Brian Sullivan, that, if you went with Blair Mill, that your commission would then be included in the administrative fee charged by Blair Mill; is that correct?

A: Yes.

Q: Now, Blair Mill is what's called a third party administrator, is it not?

A: Yes.

Q: That is Blair Mill administers claims for groups that are self-insured; is that right?

A: As far as I know, yes.

Q: So it passes onto the group what it pays in paying the claims and then charges to the group on top of that an administrative fee; is that right?

A: Typically, that's what they do.

Q: So, therefore, if your fee, your commission has been included in an administrative fee charged by Blair Mill, and if the Ironworkers had gone with Blair Mill, then the Ironworkers would have winded up paying your commission as part of the administrative fee to Blair Mill?

A: Correct.

Q: And in order to do that, Blair Mill or Blue Cross would have first had to have gotten the permission, someone would have had to disclose this to the Ironworkers, wouldn't they?

A: I would think so.

[Comment] Excellent. This is a fine use of the Rules of Probability to ask questions in series to force a conclusion that the witness would otherwise not want to give (see Vol. III, pp. 177–184); here, that he knew the union would have to pay his commission and that he knew he needed their permission. This is, or should be, the heart of the defense, given the styling of the complaint.

Q: And by the time you had this meeting with Brian Sullivan on April the 7th, you already knew from Mr. Sweeney, did you not, that the Ironworkers would not give you a broker of record letter?

A: Correct.

[Comment] Bang! He got it. Time to close the point (which is that the decision to deny Sussman a commission was made by the union, not by his client, Blue Cross). Instead, counsel moves a little off the subject. In our judgment, this is an error. When you enter a point, close it. (Vol. III, pp. 61–62).

Q: And in any event, it is true, is it not, that the Ironworkers never went with Blair Mill; isn't that true, sir?

A: That's true.

Q: And they never met with the alternative that you had discussed with Brian Sullivan in going with Blair Mill?

A: Correct.

[Comment] Excellent. The impression is given that the Sullivan deal would have been more expensive to the union because of the Sussman commission, and so was rejected—but is it true that the Sullivan deal was more costly than Hardy's? Or is it true that the difference between the two would have affected the amount of profit of Blue Cross?

Q: And is it also correct that between May or June of 1994, when you had that first meeting with Helen Hardy and Mr. Sweeney of the Ironworkers, and March of 1995, you didn't have any other meetings with Mr. Sweeney and anyone from Blue Cross?

A: That's correct.

[Comment] Now, that is an eight-month period. Counsel might have helped with that: "So you agree that during those eight months you did nothing?"

Q: And is it also correct that you, yourself, never attended any meetings between Ms. Hardy and Mr. Craggs; is that correct, sir?

A: That's correct.

Q: And Mr. Craggs is the Administrator employed by the Ironworkers; is that correct, sir?

A: Right.

Q: He's not one of the Trustees?

A: That's correct.

[Comment] Now the cross-examiner enters one of the most important lines of his cross: just who it was that decided that Sussman was not entitled to a commission.

Q: Now, you then said, I believe, that Mr. Sweeney, your friend, showed you a letter that he received from Mr. Maresca, a copy of the letter from Mr. Maresca, dated July 31st, 1995; do you recall that?

A: Yes.

Q: And I believe that letter, and I'll tell you the exhibit number, it's Plaintiff Exhibit-13. Do you have that, sir?

A: Yes.

Q: And Plaintiffs Exhibit-13 is a letter dated July 31st, 1995, from Mr. Maresca to Ms. Hardy; is that correct?

A: Yes.

Q: And it's on the letterhead of the Segal Company in New York, is it not?

A: Yes.

Q: Now, you knew when Mr. Sweeney gave you this letter, that the Ironworkers had used the Segal Company as a consultant for quite some time, did you not?

A: Yes.

Q: You knew they had used them going back 25, 30 or more years, did you not?

A: Yes.

Q: And you knew that the Segal Company was paid not a commission as a percentage of insurance but an annual fee for consulting with the Ironworkers?

A: Yes.

Q: You also knew that the Mr. Maresca had a long standing relationship with the Ironworkers, did you not?

A: Yes.

Q: You knew he was the Official of the Segal Company?

A: I didn't know if he was an official.

[Comment] Counsel is in complete control. He says what he wants to the jury through the witness. It is a fine piece of cross-examination, and the witness's quibble here does not help him, for we now know who Maresca is.

Q: Now, if you'll look at this letter, this is a letter dated July 31st, 1995, from Mr. Maresca to Helen Hardy, Blue Cross, it says: "It was a pleasure meeting with you and your colleagues on July 26"; do you see that first sentence?

A: Yes.

Q: And then in the next sentence it says, "In terms of your providing a proposal for introducing a managed care PPO program on a voluntary basis, effective January 1st, 1996, we enclose the following," meaning Mr. Maresca is sending Ms. Hardy the following. And first he sends a copy of the plan currently in effect. Do you see that?

A: Yes.

Q: You never sent a copy of the plan currently in effect to Ms. Hardy, did you, sir?

A: No.

Q: And next it says: "That we enclose a demographic distribution of the active eligibles," do you see that?

A: Yes.

Q: Do you have an understanding of the meaning of the term "a demographic distribution of the active eligibles"?

A: I think so.

Q: Can you tell us what you understand that term to mean?

A: I think it means where the active eligible members are looking.

Q: And is it correct that you—well, doesn't demographics refer to things like age and gender and so forth?

A: Yes.

Q: And you never sent a demographic distribution of the active eligibles to Ms. Hardy, did you?

A: No, I didn't.

[Comment] All well and good. Counsel is in control, but we wonder if these points—that Sussman did not participate in these matters—are points that are worth making, going as they do to the he "did nothing" defense.

Q: And third, it says that Mr. Maresca sent to Ms. Hardy a copy of the last two years' claims experience by line of coverage, do you see that?

A: Yes.

Q: And it's correct, isn't it, that you never sent to Ms. Hardy, a copy of the last two years' claims experience by line of coverage for the Ironworkers?

A: That's correct.

Q: And see the last paragraph on the first page, Mr. Maresca says to Ms. Hardy: "Your proposal should include a comparison of benefits with those currently in effect for Philadelphia Blue Cross and the other Blue Cross plans that will be involved in terms of covering the Tristate Area"; do you see that?

A: Yes.

[Comment] Again, counsel is masterful in his technique. He is clearly arguing that the plaintiff did little or nothing to put this deal together, and the jury will certainly understand his point. The question is: will they buy the claim that Sussman did nothing? If they don't, will that rejection hurt the other defense, that it was the union that decided not to pay him a commission and not Blue Cross?

Q: You never received a proposal from Blue Cross, did you?

A: No.

Q: And you never sent to the Ironworkers any proposal from Blue Cross, did you, sir?

A: No.

Q: Would you look at the top of the next page, Mr. Maresca says to Ms. Hardy: "You should confirm that you will coordinate all of the necessary informational material for distribution to the participants and be available to address Local membership meetings if asked to do so"; do you see that?

A: Yes.

Q: You never made such a request, did you, sir?

A: No.

Q: And the next paragraph says: "You should indicate the percentage of hospital discounts in each of the areas"; do you see that?

A: Yes.

Q: "Hospital discounts" refer, does it not, to the discounts that Blue Cross negotiates with the hospitals, correct, sir?

A: Yes.

Q: Using its superior bargaining power and purchasing power to get a lower rate, correct, sir?

A: Yes.

Q: You never got that information or hospital discounts from Blue Cross for the Ironworkers, did you, sir?

A: No.

Q: And the letter then goes on to say: "Finally, provide a breakdown of your administrative charges by item, related to your estimate of dollar claims that will be processed through the Blue Cross/Blue Shield office"; do you see that, sir?

A: Yes.

Q: You never obtained and provided to the Ironworkers, did you, a breakdown of the Blue Cross/Blue Shield administrative charges by item related to an estimate of dollar claims?

A: No.

Q: And the letter shows, does it not, a carbon copy to Robert Sweeney and John J. Reith; is that correct, sir?

A: Yes.

[Comment] Again, the same point. And very well made too. But are we to believe that because Sussman did not do everything, he is entitled to nothing? All well and good to point out that the Segal Company took over the negotiations, but the point is that it did so because the union *wanted it to. What of the fact that without Sussman's initiative, none of this would be happening?*

Q: Mr. Sweeney and Mr. Reith are the two co-chairs of the Ironworkers District Council Philadelphia Vicinity Health and Welfare Fund; is that correct?

A: Yes.

Q: As you know, and as the letter states, the Fund consists of 11 Local unions; is that correct?

A: Yes.

Q: And therefore, there are 22 trustees, 11, one from each of the Unions and 11 from Management; is that correct?

A: Yes.

Q: And Mr. Reith is the Management co-chair of the Fund; is that correct?

A: I don't know.

Q: You don't know that?

A: No.

Q: Mr. Sweeney though, you do know, is the Union co-chair of the Fund?

A: Yes.

Q: I take it, you, yourself, have never met with Mr. Reith, have you sir?

A: That's correct.

Q: Nor have you met with anyone else whom you understood to be the Management co-chair of the Fund; is that correct, sir?

A: I don't remember.

Q: Well, do you remember any time ever meeting with any of the other 21 Trustees of the Fund, other than Mr. Sweeney, along with anyone from Independence Blue Cross?

A: With Blue Cross and Blue Shield, no.

Q: And you never met with Mr. Craggs, the Administrator of the Fund, with anybody from Blue Cross and Blue Shield, did you?

A: No.

[Comment] We are now ready to show that the plaintiff, who seeks something large for very little, did an end run around the person who was actually doing the work, that is, Helen Hardy. But, again, why Hardy? If Blue Cross did not counsel against Sussman's commission, why does Blue Cross war about whether he is entitled to one?

Q: Now, after you received from Mr. Sweeney a copy of this July 31st, 1995 letter, which Mr. Maresca had sent to Ms. Hardy, you then called Mr. Brian Sullivan from Blue Cross again, did you not?

A: Yes.

Q: And you did that because you wanted to set up a second meeting between Mr. Sullivan and Mr. Sweeney; is that correct, sir?

A: Yes.

Q: And, in fact, that second meeting took place on August the 21st, of 1995, did it not, sir?

A: I believe so.

Q: And just so you see that I am not asking you to guess at something, would you please look at Exhibit-7,

Plaintiff's Exhibit-7. Do you have plaintiff's Exhibit-7 before you, sir?

A: Yes.

Q: Page TF-15, this is your calendar, your pocket calendar or your calendar?

A: Yes.

Q: If you look there on your calendar, on Monday, August 21st, 8 o'clock, you show Woodcrest Shopping Center, Brian Sullivan?

A: Right.

Q: So that would be the second meeting that you had with Mr. Sullivan and Mr. Sweeney?

A: Yes.

Q: And again, you met with Mr. Sullivan at the shopping center and he went down with you in your car and you went to Mr. Sweeney's office to his Local, the Ironworkers; is that correct, sir?

A: Yes.

[Comment] This last line of questioning is to set up the plaintiff's asking the union for a commission, and it is well done.

Q: Your purpose of that meeting was, again, to try to get a commission; is that correct, sir?

A: Yes.

Q: Is it your testimony that at that meeting that Mr. Sweeney said it was out of his hands, to talk to Mr. Maresca?

A: Correct.

Q: How long did that meeting take place, sir?

A: A while.

Q: Half hour—?

A: Approximately.

[Comment] Instead of focusing on the length of the meeting, it might have been well to point out that Maresca was the paid consultant of the union, not Blue Cross. And that, by his own statements, the plaintiff was seeking a commission from the union, and that the union referred him to the union's paid consultant — Maresca — on this very subject. Defendant's counsel should seek to keep Blue Cross out of this business of the dialogue between plaintiff and union over a commission. Unfortunately, his next questions put his client right into the thick of it.

Q: Now, I believe your testimony was that following this meeting, you sent a letter to Mr. Maresca?

A: No. Mr. Sullivan did.

Q: Oh, Mr. Sullivan sent a letter to Mr. Maresca?

A: Right.

[Comment] When a lawyer repeats an answer on direct, it usually is a good thing. When a lawyer repeats an answer on cross, it is usually a sign of trouble. See Vol. III, pp. 59–60.

Q: Did you ever get a copy of that letter?

A: I don't remember.

Q: You, yourself, never wrote to Mr. Maresca, I take it?

A: No, Mr. Sullivan was writing to him.

[Comment] Unfortunately for counsel, he gets to hear again about his own representative entering the subject of a commission for Sussman.

Q: And you don't have a copy of any such letter?

A: I don't think so.

Q: And in any event, you never had any further contact with Mr. Maresca; is that correct, sir?

A: That's correct.

[Comment] The point is, all in all, that the plaintiff's commission was going to have to be paid by the union under the Sullivan deal, and they did not want to pay it. Unfortunately, in our view, counsel did not close the point.

Q: Now, is it also correct that you have never made any presentation on behalf of Blue Cross or Blue Shield to the Board of Trustees of the Ironworkers?

A: Correct.

Q: And that Board meets quarterly, does it not?

A: I believe so.

Q: And you never submitted to the Ironworkers, any contract or proposed contract between Independence Pennsylvania Blue Cross and Pennsylvania Blue Shield and the Ironworkers; is that correct, sir?

A: Yes.

Q: You never submitted any contract; is that correct?

A: Yes.

Q: Is it correct that you never made any written analysis, never transmitted to the Ironworkers any written analysis of what you claim they would save by going with Blue Cross or Blue Shield; isn't that correct, sir?

A: Yes.

Q: Now, I believe you testified that Ms. Hardy had given you a list of providers at some time?

A: Yes.

Q: And that is of providers of medical services with whom Independence Blue Cross contracts?

A: Correct.

Q: That was a printed document of some thickness?

A: Right.

Q: Isn't that something anybody could get by calling up Blue Cross on the telephone and getting that?

A: I believe so.

Q: Have you ever tried?

A: Yes.

[Comment] Counsel is now in his end game and these last five questions do not belong here, because he has Sussman back doing things with Hardy to get the contract. Counsel now moves to the actual allegation in the complaint, "tortious interference." Unfortunately, he is not clear.

Q: And isn't it also correct that Mr. Sweeney never told you that any representative of Blue Cross or Blue Shield—excuse me, isn't it correct that Mr. Sweeney never told you that any representative of Blue Cross or Blue Shield told any representative of the Ironworkers to avoid doing business with you or Tower?

A: I'm sorry, I need that question again.

Q: All right. Did Mr. Sweeney ever tell you that any representative of Blue Cross or Blue Shield told any representative of the Ironworkers to avoid doing business with you or Tower?

A: I don't really—you have to read it one more time.

[Comment] Interesting answer. Seems like counsel read that question and the question is not clear. Certainly, the witness knows that it is a reading from a script.

Q: Did Mr. Sweeney ever tell you that any representative of Blue Cross or Blue Shield told any representative of the Ironworkers to avoid doing business with you or Tower?

[Comment] It is now clear that the question is written, for the question is word-for-word the same, all three times.

A: What he said to me—

Q: Can you answer yes or no?

A: Mr. Sweeney—

Q: Can you answer with a yes or no?

A: No, I can't answer with a yes or no.

MR. SONNENFELD: Your Honor, may I ask that the witness be directed to answer yes or no.

THE COURT: Repeat the question.

BY MR. SONNENFELD:

Q: Did Mr. Sweeney ever tell you that any representative of Blue Cross or Blue Shield told any representative of the Ironworkers to avoid doing business with you or Tower?

[Comment] This is the fourth time that the question has been read, word for word. We afforded all counsel an opportunity to review and comment on the manuscript prior to publication. Mr. Sonnenfeld advised us that he was indeed reading on this one occasion, but from the witness's deposition testimony, in order to make him conform to that prior testimony, which the witness saw in counsel's hand. This is a fine technique.

THE COURT: You can answer with—you'll have to answer yes or no and then you may explain your answer.

THE WITNESS: No.

MR. SONNENFELD: Thank you, sir.

[Comment] The "thank you" obscures the opportunity to explain. The failure is that of plaintiff's counsel, who might have asked for the explanation, assuming there was one to be had. Defendant's counsel has also passed up the opportunity to confront the witness with the fact that not only is the last answer "no," but also that the witness has no evidence of any kind that Blue Cross told the union not to pay him or in any way interfered with the union paying him, and that his claim

for tortious interference is really nothing but a claim that Blue Cross should pay him a commission.

Now counsel is ready for his finale. He wants to finish strong. He sees it as a gift he has been given during the direct when the plaintiff swore that he had never been cheated before. It was a great piece of testimony, and it provides counsel with a finale. Watch as he asks questions in a series that could not have been written, to argue right through the witness to the jury.

BY MR. SONNENFELD:

Q: Now, I believe you also have contended here that you have been cheated by Blue Cross; is that correct, sir?

A: Yes.

Q: And I think that this morning you were asked by Mr. Longer, whether you had ever before been cheated, I think was the question, in your 20 or 30 years as a broker; is that correct, sir?

A: Yes.

Q: Wasn't your answer no?

A: Yes.

Q: But, in fact, don't you also have a dispute with New Jersey Blue Cross?

A: Yes.

Q: And isn't that dispute also involving a broker of record letter?

A: Yes.

Q: And, in fact, wasn't it back in November of 1994, that you knew that to get a commission from New Jersey Blue Cross, you would need a broker of record letter from the New Jersey Ironworkers?

A: Yes.

Q: And just because we have a few new faces in the courtroom that we haven't introduced, do you see Mr. Sullivan here, do you recognize him?

A: Yes.

Q: He is the gentleman sitting back there?

A: Right.

Q: And Mr. Craggs of the Ironworkers, is the gentleman back here?

A: Right.

[Comment] That was an excellent ending; well delivered and clear.

MR. SONNENFELD: Your Honor, I have nothing further of Mr. Sussman, at this time.

THE COURT: Redirect.

Analysis of the Cross-Examination of the Plaintiff

Defense counsel is prepared and uses leading questions. He has thought out his lines of examination and proceeds to the issues he wants to address. He does not make the mistake of repeating the direct examination. He begins where he wants to, not where the direct either began or ended.

His first point is that Sussman is more involved with life than health insurance, and that this was the first time he had ever dealt with Blue Cross/Blue Shield as a broker. His second point is that Sussman is unaware of any other welfare fund that uses a broker to obtain health insurance. Neither point seems so worthy that the first part of the cross should be dedicated to it.

In asking Sussman about the first meeting he and Ms. Hardy had with Mr. Sweeney, the cross-examiner emphasizes that Ms. Hardy previously had met with Sweeney. Does any of this really help the defense? The first and second points seem inconsequential, and the third establishes that Hardy really wanted the account and had been unable to get it on her own.

The cross-examiner has Sussman admit that he and Ms. Hardy met a total of three times with Sweeney for perhaps an hour and a half. He emphasizes that Sussman got a thank-you letter from Hardy after the 1994 meeting but not after the 1995 meetings, and that Sussman did not write to Hardy. This is a potent, emotional appeal, demonstrating that the plaintiff seeks a great deal for a few minutes of effort. But counsel must resist, as he did not earlier, the suggestion that Sussman did *nothing*. Moreover, later Hardy will deny that some of these meetings took place. If, in fact, the defense is going to contest them, this is the place to start.

The cross-examination establishes that Sussman knew that Mr. Maresca and the Segal Company had represented the Ironworkers for many years. The letter that Maresca sent to Ms. Hardy evidences that Maresca and the Segal Company played an important role in advising the Ironworkers on whether to go with Blue Cross/Blue Shield. By comparing the work that Maresca did with that of Sussman, the examiner is trying—and succeeding—to suggest that Sussman's role was not all that important. The best of the examination was counsel's establishing that Sussman knows that it was the union that refused to pay his commission. Unfortunately, he did not close the point and show that the claim of tortious interference by Blue Cross with Sussman's contract with the union is a sham to sue Blue Cross for the union's refusal.

The cross-examination ends with an attack on Sussman's credibility. On direct examination, Sussman had claimed he had never been cheated before, and he is forced to concede that he is in litigation with another of the Blues over a commission. This is potentially a highly significant moment. If Sussman swore on direct examination that he had never been cheated and had lied, he would be found to have lied to the jury that would decide his case. No jury is likely to tolerate a party's lying to it. Moreover, the credibility of the direct examiner who led Sussman to say he had never before been cheated could be severely damaged. But the point is not made clearly. Is the New Jersey suit one in which Sussman claims to have been cheated? If not, the fact that he has litigation pending is not evidence of a lie. We simply don't know, because the examiner did not pursue the point. If the New Jersey case is different, we might expect on redirect examination to have clarification. Has the defendant taken an unnecessary chance? As we shall see, the answer is no, because redirect did not touch the point.

The questioning about the New Jersey suit strongly suggested that in late 1994 Sussman was aware that New Jersey Blue Cross/Blue Shield required a broker of record letter. It is unclear why this did not lead to a line of questioning like the following:

Q: You knew New Jersey Blue Cross/Blue Shield required a broker of record letter?

Q: You knew that you could not receive a commission from New Jersey Blue Cross/Blue Shield without such a letter?

Q: You had no experience prior to 1994 with any of the Blue Cross/Blue Shield organizations?

Q: This was the first time that you had been asked for a broker of record letter?

Q: You did not know whether the letter was required of all Blue Cross/Blue Shield organizations or only the New Jersey organization?

Q: When you contacted Ms. Hardy in 1995, it was after you knew that a broker of record letter was required in New Jersey?

Q: When you contacted Ms. Hardy in 1995, you deliberately chose not to ask whether such a letter was required?

It is, of course, likely that the plaintiff will make the point that Sussman first contacted Blue Cross/Blue Shield in early to mid-1994, not in late 1994, and that no broker of record letter was discussed at that time. But, if the defense can show that not long thereafter Sussman became aware of the possibility that such a letter might be required and failed to ask about it, the jury might be somewhat less sympathetic to a claim that he feels cheated. Part of the problem is that the plaintiff has not set up his case properly. It is not that he needed or did not need such a letter; it is that Ms. Hardy promised him a commission and then reneged using a "requirement" that the insurance company had the power to waive.

REDIRECT EXAMINATION OF THE PLAINTIFF'S FIRST WITNESS

The question of whether to redirect or not is always a difficult one. It boils down to a weighing of risks, for to do it will open the door to another cross. Have you been hurt enough to take that risk? That is the equation. For a full discussion, see Vol. II, pp. 408–409.

The one advantage that redirects do have is that most judges allow far more leading at this stage than on direct itself.

Text of Redirect Examination of the Plaintiff

BY MR. LONGER:

Q: Mr. Sussman, are you in the habit of writing letters to people after you've had meetings with them?

A: No.

Q: So it's not uncommon that there would be no followup correspondence with your March 1995 meeting with Ms. Hardy; is that fair to say?

A: Yes.

[Comment] See, sounds more like a cross than a direct. And well done at that.

Q: Plaintiff's Exhibit-8 is Ms. Hardy's June 1994 letter to you, June 3, 1994?

A: Yes.

Q: There's nothing in that letter that indicates that you need a broker of record letter back in June of 1994, is there?

A: No.

Q: And as far as you knew, dealing with Independence Blue Cross, as opposed to New Jersey Blue Cross, you didn't need a broker of record letter back in June of 1994; is that right?

[Comment] All of this is highly leading. So counsel objects. But judges do allow much, much greater latitude on redirect. Watch.

MR. SONNENFELD: Objection. Leading.

THE WITNESS: That's correct.

THE COURT: Overruled. But try not to lead the witness.

MR. LONGER: Thank you, Your Honor.

[Comment] See, you can lead, but hold it down to a dull roar. But counsel does not. Indeed, he goes much further.

Q: The first time that Ms. Hardy told you about a broker of record letter was in 1995?

A: Yes.

[Comment] Counsel might have profitably pointed out that this was many months after the 1–3 percent commission conversation that preceded the first Sussman-Hardy-Sweeney meeting.

Q: Now, I'll direct you to plaintiff's Exhibit Number-13, Mr. Sonnenfeld spent some time on that letter with you. That's a copy of the July 31st, 1995 letter from Mr. Maresca to Ms. Hardy, correct?

A: Yes.

Q: Now, at the time that you met with Ms. Hardy, March—the last meeting that you had with Ms. Hardy and Mr. Sweeney, you said it was at the end of March, 1995?

A: Yes.

Q: At that time, you felt—is it accurate that you thought that Mr. Sweeney had told you that there was a very strong interest in Blue Cross?

MR. SONNENFELD: Your Honor, this is leading.

THE COURT: Sustained.

MR. SONNENFELD: Thank you, Your Honor.

[Comment] Neither the objection nor the ruling lasts beyond the next question.

BY MR. LONGER:

Q: At the last meeting in March of 1995, with Ms. Hardy and Mr. Sweeney, what was your understanding of what the Ironworkers were going to do with Blue Cross and Blue Shield?

A: They were going to consider using them. He felt very strong about using Blue Cross and Blue Shield.

Q: It's no surprise to you then, that this letter from the consultant of the firm came out?

A: No, not at all.

Q: And the information that's contained in this letter, is that the ordinary sorts of requests that a consultant would make?

A: Yes.

Q: This is a letter for a request for a proposal; is that right?

A: Yes.

Q: And consultants, when they request proposals, ask for a lot of information, is that right?

A: Yes.

Q: And this is, again, something that you would have expected from a consultant—is that right?

A: Absolutely.

Q: Would you have done this as a broker, necessarily?

A: If I was handling the case direct with another company, I would have asked the same information.

Q: But because you were dealing with Helen Hardy, you didn't feel it was necessary?

MR. SONNENFELD: Objection, Your Honor. It's leading.

THE COURT: Sustained.

MR. SONNENFELD: Thank you, Your Honor.

BY MR. LONGER:

[Comment] Counsel has won. But has he? Watch as the examiner gets to do it again, and then again, and then again and again.

Q: Did you feel it was necessary, having Ms. Hardy by your side?

A: No.

MR. SONNENFELD: Could I—I couldn't hear the question.

BY MR. LONGER:

Q: Did you feel it was necessary having Ms. Hardy at your side?

MR. SONNENFELD: I don't understand the question. It sounds argumentative. I don't know what he means by having Ms. Hardy at his side.

BY MR. LONGER:

Q: Did you feel it was necessary working with Ms. Hardy to make those requests?

A: No.

MR. LONGER: I have no further questions.

THE COURT: Recross.

Analysis of the Redirect Examination of the Plaintiff

On redirect, the examiner reminds us that Sussman was unaware of any broker of record letter requirement when he first contacted Pennsylvania Blue Cross/Blue Shield and began to lay the foundation to have the Ironworkers sign on with that insurer. He also has Sussman say that nothing that Maresca did was surprising and that Maresca basically was performing a role that differed from Sussman's.

Plaintiff's counsel could have anticipated both of these points and brought them out on direct examination, where he could have had Sussman address them without appearing to need an explanation because an accusation had been made. It is doubtful at this point that further examination will change the jury's view of Sussman as a witness and as a plaintiff.

Notice that the redirect examination stayed away from the New Jersey litigation.

On balance, then, the cross scored and kept its point. A word about style: As we can see, a redirect can often be more like a cross, in that the rules of leading are relaxed in practice. This allows counsel to argue through the witness more on redirect than on direct. However, no examination can legally end with a direct. The cross-examiner is always entitled to the last word, and any re- or even re-redirect, can be followed by another cross.

RECROSS-EXAMINATION OF THE PLAINTIFF'S FIRST WITNESS

Text of the Recross-Examination of the Plaintiff

MR. SONNENFELD: Very briefly.

Q: Mr. Sussman, you called Ms. Hardy, she didn't call you; is that correct, sir?

A: That's correct.

Q: And you never had any written agreement with Independence Blue Cross over any commission; is that correct, sir?

A: Correct.

Q: At all times you were acting here on behalf of the Ironworkers, not on behalf of Blue Cross; they were your clients?

[Comment] That is a dangerous question, and one that goes to the very heart of the case — who owes the commission. Counsel is not likely to get a good answer. He doesn't. Although he does ultimately establish that Sussman viewed the union as his "client," Sussman also points out that it is the insurance company that usually pays the commission. Isn't that what all of us experience when we buy insurance?

A: Well, I think that's not the case. I think that typically how I sell insurance is I present the company and I'm the agent. I wasn't representing—was representing the best product for my client.

Q: And your client was the Ironworkers?

A: My client, I believe, was the Ironworkers.

MR. SONNENFELD: Thank you, sir.

THE COURT: Sir.

MR. LONGER: No further questions,

Analysis of the Recross-Examination of the Plaintiff

Does it help the cross-examiner to remind the jury that Mr. Sussman was the moving force in this case and that he contacted Ms. Hardy? She could have told Sussman that Blue Cross does not deal with brokers—but she didn't. The evidence seems to be that she welcomed another approach to a union with which she had had little success.

Will a jury understand why it matters who "the client" is when it has heard evidence and seen a document showing that Ms. Hardy talked to Sussman about paying a commission of from 1 to 3 percent? If Ms. Hardy was not caught up in who the client was, will the jury be? And you, dear reader, who pays the commissions to the agents who sell insurance to you?

All in all, it is our judgment that the direct examiner might well have forgone his redirect, at least as he gave it. Once given, the recross was also without effect, all given the issues that both sides selected to argue through the witness: that is, the plaintiff's argument that he did not know of the requirement of a letter, and the defendant's argument that the plaintiff was never really helping or representing the insurance company.

It remains our view that the plaintiff's best argument was that the insurance company made a promise to the plaintiff, to the effect that if he could persuade the union to switch plans, costing him one commission, Blue Cross would have it replaced by another. The insurance company, he claims, broke its promise by the "requirement" of a broker letter, which the company imposed later, after the promise and his performance, a requirement that the insurance company could have waived. The defendant, in contrast, should argue that the plaintiff's failure to nail down, even at trial, any specific sum owed demonstrates the lack of a firm or mature deal with the insurance company; that, although any commission check would be written by the company, it would be included in the union's rate; that Sussman knew this required union approval; that Sussman knows that the commission was not paid because the *union* refused to pay it and withheld the letter; and that Blue Cross did not persuade the union to refuse the letter or the commission and that even Sussman himself does not claim knowledge that Blue Cross did anything of the sort.

Moreover, the specific charge in the complaint—that the company interfered with a relationship between Sussman and the union—is a sham, a substitute for the actual claim that the company owes a commission. The real claim cannot be made because no deal was agreed to—for any percentage or commission, which is why the plaintiff must speak of "hopes" of an agreement and cannot specify any certain sum as owed.

Chapter Four

The Second Witness: Nick Craggs

TEXT OF THE DIRECT EXAMINATION

MR. LONGER: Plaintiff calls Nick Craggs.

MR. SONNENFELD: Your Honor, with the court's permission, my colleague, Ms. Bennett, will conduct our examination of Mr. Craggs.

THE COURT: Very well.

THE CRIER: State your name and spell your last name.

THE WITNESS: E. W. Nick Craggs, C-R-A-G-G-S.

E.W. NICK CRAGGS, WITNESS, after having been first duly sworn, was examined and testified as follows:

BY MR. LONGER:

Q: Mr. Craggs, you are the plan manager for the Ironworkers Health and Welfare Fund?

A: That's correct.

Q: And you've been the plan manager since 1979; is that correct?

A: That's correct.

Q: Some time in 1993 or 1994, you met with Mr. Sussman in your office with Mr. Halverson; is that correct?

A: That's correct.

[Comment] He is leading, heavily leading. These first questions are probably all right because they merely get things started. But if he keeps it up, and he does, he will be stopped, and he is.

Q: And Mr. Sussman introduced you to Mr. Halverson to bring to you, as being an independent salesman for PPOs; is that correct?

A: That's correct.

Q: And at that time, Multi-Plan was the Fund's PPO for hospitalization; is that right?

A: That's correct.

Q: And you didn't think that a different PPO for doctors would be necessary at that time; is that correct?

A: I think at the time I told them that if we were interested in having a PPO to handle medical coverage, we could very easily go through Multi-Plan that we had on board for hospitals.

Q: You thought you could expand Multi-Plan's services to include—

A: They had already requested that, yes.

Q: But the Fund ultimately entered into a contract with Preferred Care for doctors, didn't it?

A: That's correct. With the understanding that what they couldn't provide, Multi-Plan would provide.

Q: Now, to your right, there's a notebook, and there's Exhibit P-5, which is behind Tab Number 5. Do you have that in front of you, sir?

A: Yes, sir.

Q: And that's the agreement between Preferred Care and the Ironworkers District Council Philadelphia Vicinity Health Benefit Plan; is that correct?

A: That's correct.

Q: And it's dated August 1, 1994?

A: That's correct.

Q: And it bears your signature at the end of the document?

A: Yes, that's correct.

Q: And this is an accurate copy of the document?

A: It appears to be, yes.

Q: This is a document that the Fund keeps or you keep for the Fund in your ordinary course of business; is that correct?

A: That's correct. Yes, sir.

Q: Now, you understood Mr. Sussman to be working together with Mr. Halverson to sell the Fund a contract with Preferred Care; did you not?

A: He introduced Mr. Halverson. I understood Mr. Halverson to be in that businesses. I never knew Mr. Sussman was in that type of business. I figured they had some kind of arrangement, though.

Q: And you understood that they would be compensated together from Preferred Care, did you not?

A: Yes.

[Comment] Excellent. He has made the point that it is the insurance company, not the union fund, that pays the commission. But now he tries it again.

Q: Now, Mr. Halverson was the person you dealt with with respect to the Preferred Care contract?

A: That's correct.

Q: And, he told you, Mr. Halverson told you, that he and Mr. Sussman were going to be compensated together—

MS. BENNETT: Objection, Your Honor. That's hearsay what Mr. Halverson told him.

THE COURT: Sustained.

BY MR. LONGER:

Q: You understood that Mr. Halverson and Mr. Sussman were going to be compensated from Preferred Care, did you not?

MS. BENNETT: Objection. Your Honor, that's a leading question.

[Comment] It is, but the real vice is that it calls for hearsay, although disguised by counsel's device of calling for an "understanding" based on a conversation that has been excluded as hearsay. We have seen him do this with the first witness.

THE COURT: Sustained.

[Comment] A left hook, hearsay. As we have seen, this judge is death on hearsay. Then the right cross, stopping the leading. In fact, she waited too long as to that, for most of the examination has been leading thus far.

BY MR. LONGER:

Q: Do you have an <u>understanding</u>, Mr. Craggs, that Mr. Halverson and Mr. Sussman were going to be compensated by Preferred Care?

[Comment] Now that is the same question. Just take a look back and see. The judge has ruled not only that it calls for hearsay, but also that it is leading—but there are other problems, like conclusory and no foundation. But watch what happens when counsel objects again.

MS. BENNETT: Objection. Your Honor, it's still a very leading question. You've given him a lot of leeway, so far. It's very leading.

THE COURT: Well, I'm going to let him answer.

[Comment] The trouble is that she made the wrong objection. Leading it is, but it is based on the same "hearsay" that the judge prohibited just two questions ago. But who knows if anything could have helped her? Plaintiff's counsel has just lost two in a row, and judges often like to keep things looking even.

No one bats 1000 in a courtroom, or even much more than 500. Why? You know why.

THE WITNESS: The way the arrangement worked is the discounts that we received through Preferred Care, Preferred Care would receive 25 percent of those discounts. Yes, I <u>assumed</u> that Mr. Halverson would be paid out of that 25 percent. It did not add any extra cost to the Fund, to our Fund, the Ironworkers Fund, because we had to pay the 25 percent anyway.

[Comment] The illegality of the answer is betrayed by "I assume." This answer really does not hurt the defendant, nor does it help the plaintiff, because, in the case on trial, if the union had given the broker of record letter it would have cost the union. Of course, the plaintiff wants any commission to come out of the Blue Cross end.

BY MR. LONGER:

Q: Now, you never gave Mr. Halverson a broker of record letter, did you?

A: No. He was not working for us.

[Comment] This is a bad answer for the examiner. So he tries to massage it away.

Q: A broker of record letter was not necessary for the contract between Preferred Care and the Ironworkers in order for Mr. Halverson to receive a commission; is that your understanding?

MS. BENNETT: Objection, Your Honor. Leading and argumentative.

MR. LONGER: I will go with his prior answer.

[Comment] Good for her. The examiner knows he is going to lose, because even if the word "argumentative" does not fit, leading certainly does. In going with the "prior answer," counsel is putting the best face on it that he can.

BY MR. LONGER:

Q: Did you <u>understand</u> that Mr. Halverson was working together with Mr. Sussman?

A: I <u>assumed</u> they were. I was never told that, no.

[Comment] All of this testimony is objectionable for reasons already given. Note the continued, and so far largely successful use of the "understand" device. In any event, so far this is not a great witness for the plaintiff. But then, none of the union people will be. Why, then, was he called, and called so early? The next line of questioning will show us. It will show us the money. And that, we believe, was what the witness was really called to do. If so, the beginning portion of the examination could have been dispensed with.

Q: Now, I would like you to turn, if you will, to Exhibit Number-14, in that notebook. Can you identify that document for me?

A: That's a 5500, which is a document that's required by the federal government for all plans such as ours. it explains to the federal government how much money we take in, in the course of our year, and how much money we pay out.

Q: And is this a document that you keep in the ordinary course of your business?

A: Yes. That's correct.

Q: Are you responsible for preparing this document?

A: No, I'm not.

Q: Does your accountant prepare it and you sign off on it at the end?

A: The way it's prepared is the actuarial firm, Segal Company, requires information from our office, which we furnish them, so that they can prepare the portion that they prepare for this. Our accountant requires information from our office and we furnish that information to the accountant, and then the whole thing is put together by the accountant and submitted by the accountant.

Q: And you're responsible for maintaining those documents in the offices of the Welfare Fund, correct?

A: That's correct.

Q: And is this a true and accurate copy of—

A: Yes. It appears to be, yes.

[Comment] Now, here comes the testimony about large amounts of money, and, of course, the defendant tries to keep it out.

Q: Now, in 1993, is it accurate that the Fund paid health care benefits in the amount of 12 million—

MS. BENNETT: Objection, Your Honor. There's been no foundation for this question, as to its relevance.

THE COURT: Overruled.

THE WITNESS: What was the question?

BY MR. LONGER:

Q: For the period October 1, 1993, through September 30, 1994, is it accurate that on Page 6, Item E, Expenses, benefit payments, payments to provide benefits, the Fund expended $12,889,338?

A: Where do you get that figure?

Q: I'm sorry. On Page 6, right here, that Line E, Expenses.

A: That's correct, $12,889,338.

Q: And I would like to—do you know, in terms of the Philadelphia vicinity, if the Ironworkers Fund is one of the largest funds paying health benefits?

A: No, I wouldn't say we were, no. On a scale of 1 to 10, I would say we're around 4 or something like that.

Q: Now, Exhibit Number-15, would just like to ask you a similar question. That's a Form 5500 for the following year; is that correct?

A: That's correct.

Q: So, that's for the period October 1, 1994 through September 30, 1995; is that correct?

A: Yes, that's correct.

Q: And on Page 6 of that document, is it accurate for that period, the Fund expended $13,301,496?

MS. BENNETT: Your Honor, I would just like to state my objection <u>for the record</u>.

[Comment] Having said that she is speaking only for "the record," the ruling is predictable.

THE COURT: Overruled.

THE WITNESS: That's correct.

BY MR. LONGER:

Q: And is this document a document which you're responsible for keeping at the fund?

A: That's correct.

[Comment] He hasn't touched all the basics of business records, but who's counting? The defendant is wise not to object, because if she does, he will complete the record and, in this case, this judge has signaled that the material is coming in.

Q: And is it a document that you keep in the ordinary course of your business?

A: Yes.

Q: And it was prepared at about the time that's indicated on the document?

A: Yes, that's correct.

Q: Now, Mr. Craggs, you're appearing here pursuant to a subpoena which I had served on you, are you not?

A: Yes, that's correct.

Q: I want to just go back and ask you, if you would, the dates that these documents were prepared, Exhibit Numbers-14 and 15. Exhibit Number-14 was signed by Mr. Reith to Mr. Sweeney on the 23rd of June, 1995; is that correct?

A: Yes, that's correct.

Q: And Exhibit-15, these documents were signed by the same gentleman, June 17th, 1996; is that correct?

A: That's correct.

Q: And, in my subpoena to you, I requested a Form 5500 for the current year, the current year past; is that correct?

A: That's correct.

Q: And did you bring it with you today?

A: No. Because it's not available to me.

Q: Did you have any draft available to you?

A: No.

Q: Do you have the information available in the draft to you?

A: No.

Q: And do you know what the payments are approximately, for health benefits for the year October 1995 to September 30th, 1996?

A: Not off the top of my head, no.

Q: Can you give us a ballpark?

A: I would say it was somewhere near what it was last year, if I would guess.

[Comment] This testimony is aimed at damages, or so we think. But will the jury think so? In any event, "near what it was last year" is not good enough. His next questions ought to have draped $12 million around us again.

Q: And do you know what the retained charges are, that Blue Cross/Blue Shield is charging for?

A: Blue Cross and Blue Shield stated that they would charge us an administrative fee of 10.2 percent over what the actual charges were, actual claims that they paid.

Q: Do you know approximately what the actual claims paid were? You're saying they were the same figure as last year?

A: Somewhere near the same figure, yes.

[Comment] Another missed opportunity.

Q: So, there is a 10.3 percent [*sic*] administrative fee added onto that?

A: Yes. That's correct.

Q: And so we're talking approximately 10 percent of $13,301,496?

A: No, that's not correct.

Q: What is the 10 percent of?

A: The 10 percent—first of all, may I explain that in our office, we handle all types of claims. We handle hospital and medical, we handle drugs, handle dental, handle disability claims, weekly disability claims, that sort of thing, which all comes out of the Health Plan. The Blues only administer for us the hospital and medical. They have nothing whatsoever to do with drugs, optical, what-have-you, that sort of thing.

Q: That figure is the total?

A: Right. That's included in that, yes.

[Comment] All of our figuring is now knocked askew. What is the figure that the plaintiff wants either 1 or 2 or 3 percent of, and for how long a period does he want it?

Q: Do you know approximately how much less of that total figure are the benefits that Blue Cross/Blue Shield was paying or were charging a 10.2 percent administrative charge?

A: I wouldn't know that off the top of my head, no. I would have to have it in front of me.

Q: Is it over 10 million dollars?

A: I doubt it very much.

Q: Six million dollars?

A: Somewhere around there, would <u>guess</u>, 5 to 6 million. It's only a guess.

[Comment] We are now in the area of supposing. An objection might be in order.

Q: So, 10 percent of 6 million, <u>if</u> it were 6 million, is $600,000?

[Comment] Imagine: "If."

A: That's correct.

Q: And that's the profit—

[Comment] Finally, defense counsel steps in.

MS. BENNETT: Objection, Your Honor. He's asking the witness a question—he's only providing a guess as an answer, and now he's asking him to draw a conclusion from his speculation and guess. I mean, I would just like to make it clear that, you know, to <u>make it clear to the Jury</u> and the rest of the court <u>that it's a guess</u>.

[Comment] She has made a good objection, but sought the wrong relief. She really wants the testimony stopped, not admitted as a guess, but the judge comes to the right result.

THE COURT: I don't think that's the purpose of the objection, but I'm not sure that—I'll sustain the objection, however.

[Comment] She should now move to strike his present answer and the preceding guesses, but she does not. At least some of this is now in the record, available for summation and appeal.

BY MR. LONGER:

Q: Do you know how much you are paying Blue Cross and Blue Shield this year?

A: No. I don't think any of their clients know what they're paying them.

Q: You're the plan administrator, and you don't know what you're paying Blue Cross/Blue Shield?

A: That's correct. I can explain, if you'd like.

[Comment] Counsel must have been unenthusiastic about hearing the explanation, because the judge steps in.

THE COURT: You can explain.

THE WITNESS: The reason we don't know is the Blues will not reveal what their discounts are, so that <u>we have no way of knowing</u> what they are actually making. In other words you gave the example of 6 million dollars, 10 percent would be $600,000, and you would jump to the conclusion that that would be their profit. Well, what I'm trying to explain to you is that their profit <u>may</u> very well be much greater than that, because they may get a 50 percent discount and give us a 30 percent discount, and therefore, garner out more profits.

[Comment] Plaintiff's counsel must have loved that answer, although he obviously had not sought it himself. It was all found money for him, and defendant's counsel failed to object to something the witness testified to without the slightest knowledge.

BY MR. LONGER:

Q: But you understand that you're paying approximately 10 percent of the balance of 6 million dollars to Blue Cross/Blue Shield for administrative fees?

A: Yes. We understand that yes.

[Comment] Counsel has put in a $6 million figure from nowhere. Indeed, the earlier $5–6 million questionnaire testi-

mony had been successfully objected to. Unfortunately, instead of objecting, counsel for the defendant sat silent.

Q: How long have you been with the Ironworkers?

A: With the Ironworkers, per se?

Q: You're an ironworker, aren't you?

A: Yes, that's right.

Q: You go back a long time, right?

A: Since 1953.

Q: You used to be a Trustee on the Board of Trustees for the Welfare Fund; is that correct?

A: That's correct.

Q: And, the Ironworkers Fund used to have Blue Cross/Blue Shield as a health care provider, didn't they?

A: That's correct.

Q: What was the reason that the Ironworkers dropped Blue Cross/Blue Shield a long time ago?

[Comment] If you represented the defendant, would you object to that? Who knows what is coming — nothing good for the Blues. And what about materiality? But no objection came.

A: In 1974, when I was a Trustee, we had disgruntled members, and we thought that we could self-administer the plan and handle the claims in-house and save money by doing so, and that's what we chose to do.

Q: And they were disgruntled because they didn't like the services that Blue Cross/Blue Shield was providing; is that correct?

A: We had disgruntled members, but you have them all the time, that's for sure.

[Comment] The lawyer was worse for the defendant than the witness. But again, no objection.

Q: And Blue Cross/Blue Shield—well, were you a disgruntled member?

A: Yes.

Q: You didn't like Blue Cross/Blue Shield?

A: No, that's correct.

Q: And in 1995, you didn't look with great favor on Blue Cross/Blue Shield, did you?

A: That's correct.

Q: And how do you feel today having a year or so of experience with Blue Cross/Blue Shield?

A: They're very nice people but I still don't care for their service.

[Comment] The last questions and answers, in our judgment, go too far. In the absence of objections, counsel, feeling his freedom to do anything he wishes, actually made his witness a biased one against the Blues. Not only that, he has not helped his client—who, after all, was the one who got the union to take the Blues in, or so he proclaims. In any event, the silence of counsel for the Blues is difficult to justify.

Q: The contract that went into effect with Blue Cross/Blue Shield, is that Exhibit Number-25?

A: Yes, that's correct.

Q: That went into effect January 1, 1996?

A: That's correct.

Q: And here we are it's June 17th, 1997, right?

A: That's correct.

Q: So, has that contract been renewed for 1997?

A: It automatically renews.

Q: And, do you expect that it will renew again in 1998?

A: I have no reason to think otherwise.

[Comment] We are now in the area of prophecy. The plaintiff is seeking a percentage into the future, the witness is prognosticizing, and the defendant says nothing.

Q: Do you have <u>any reason to believe</u> it will be canceled in 1999?

A: I <u>have no reason to think</u> that either.

Q: Do you <u>think</u> it will go on for a long period of time?

A: If the Trustees see fit, yes.

[Comment] Really? This bad service is going to be renewed?

Q: The exhibit that I have asked you to look at, Number-29, is this a document which you're responsible for keeping at your offices at the Fund?

A: That's correct.

Q: And, is this a document which [you] maintain in the regular course of business?

A: Yes, that's correct.

Q: And is this an accurate copy of the one that you maintain in your offices?

A: Yes, it appears to be.

MR. LONGER: Thank you, sir. I have no further questions.

THE COURT: We'll take a short recess and then do the cross-examination.

THE CRIER: Everyone remain seated while the Jury leaves the room.

[Jury exits.]

ANALYSIS OF THE DIRECT EXAMINATION

This witness establishes that Sussman never hid from the Ironworkers his interest in a commission and that when Sussman arranged the preferred provider deal everyone thought he would get the commission that he in fact received. Thus, the witness supports the argument that everyone knew that Sussman wanted compensation for his work on health insurance for the Ironworkers.

Although the witness may not actually know what Blue Cross/Blue Shield receives from the welfare fund, or at least the minimum amount that the company receives, plaintiff's counsel manages to convey the message that Blue Cross receives slightly more than 10 percent of all the claims paid. So, if the company pays $6 million in claims, it gets slightly more than $600,000 as an administrative fee. The witness volunteers the most useful point of the examination: that the Blues won't share information about the nature of what they actually pay to doctors and hospitals. The suggestion is that the Blues may do well by pocketing a portion of the discount. If the jury believes that this is possible, it may well believe that Blue Cross easily could have paid Sussman a commission from its profits.

More leading questions are asked here than typically are asked on direct examination. The fact that Craggs has been subpoenaed is some evidence that the Ironworkers are not happy to be involved in the case. They surely are not out to favor Sussman. Moreover, although Craggs does not have much good to say about the Blues, it is not apparent that he thinks much of Sussman. This shouldn't be surprising. Craggs works for the union. He is probably a salaried employee who does not have the opportunity for the kind of percentage deal that Sussman claims he had with Blue Cross. It ought not to be surprising if Craggs resents the claim that Sussman is making.

The examination indicates the danger of pushing a point too far. Each time Craggs indicates that he does not care much for the defendants, the plaintiff damages his own claim to have benefited the Ironworkers by getting them into the deal with Blue Cross. Note, as you read the cross-examination, that the cross-examiner does something similar. She will emphasize that Blue Cross has saved money for the Ironworkers, which is the benefit Sussman claims to have provided to the union.

TEXT OF THE CROSS-EXAMINATION OF THE WITNESS

THE COURT: Cross-examine.

[Comment] This is an interesting opportunity for the defendant. The witness is clearly not partial to the plaintiff. Nevertheless, because the plaintiff has called him, the defendant will be permitted to cross and therefore to lead. There should be a lot of "hitchhiking" here, that is, opportunities to bring out good stuff for the insurance company. See Vol. III, pp. 13–16.

BY MS. BENNETT:

Q: Good afternoon, Mr. Craggs.

A: Hi.

Q: I'm going to direct your attention again to Plaintiff's Exhibit-15—

A: Do you want me to use this book or that book?

Q: The blue book—the black book, those are Plaintiff's. I believe that was the exhibit that Mr. Longer was previously asking you questions about. Turn to Page 6, please, if you will.

A: Yes.

Q: Line E-1, I believe this is where Mr. Longer was asking you to state the number that was listed there. Could you read what Line E-1, the text of that line?

A: "Directly to the participants or beneficiaries."

Q: And the number again?

A: $12,889,338.

Q: I just want to make clear from your earlier testimony, that that number represents payments in addition to payments made to Independence Blue Cross and Pennsylvania Blue Shield for hospitals and doctors' payments; is that correct?

A: No, because this report that I'm looking at is for the time period, if you turn to the front of it, it goes to September 30, 1994, and we didn't use the Blues until '96.

Q: You're right. I'm sorry. I meant payments other than hospitals and doctors?

A: Yes. That's all inclusive. All the payments that were made, yes, ma'am.

[Comment] Unfortunately, she has not begun well. And beginning well really matters. Moreover, repeating these enormous numbers is not good for the defendant.

Q: And am I correct that your contract with Independence Blue Cross and Pennsylvania Blue Shield only pertains to hospital payments and doctors' bills; is that correct?

A: That's correct.

Q: And again, directing your attention to Exhibit-15, which is the 5500 Form, for the following time, following the one we just looked at, correct?

A: Yes, ma'am.

Q: What is the year of this the time period that this covers?

A: This covers October 1, 1994, and ending September 30, 1995.

Q: And again, this covered a time period before you had contracted with Independence Blue Cross and Pennsylvania Blue Shield?

A: That's correct.

Q: And again, directing your attention to Page 6, Line E-1.

A: The number?

Q: Yes. The figure referenced there is approximately 13 million dollars?

A: That's correct.

Q: And again, that includes payments made by the fund for things other than hospital bills and doctors bills?

A: That's correct.

[Comment] The chance that the jury has followed any of this is nil to none. Have you been able to? This much we know: There is a lot of money at stake every year. Now comes an interesting line of questions.

Q: Mr. Craggs, now that the Fund is with Independence Blue Cross and Pennsylvania Blue Shield, have the Fund members saved money?

A: The Fund members, yes, they have.

Q: And that's because there is no deductible?

A: That's correct. Previously, there was a $250.00 per person deductible and a $500.00 deductible per family, and if the member chooses to go and use the Blues as their PPO, there are no deductibles.

[Comment] Counsel is happy. Her next "thank you" shows that she is. But . . . to the extent that the jury finds that Sussman was the cause of this benefit, a benefit both to the union and to the Blues, a benefit that did not benefit him, what then? We guess she was stung by the prior criticism of the Blues by the witness and so embarked on this line of questioning.

Q: Thank you, Mr. Craggs. We're going to be focusing our attention on the blue notebook, so if would like to—

A: Fine.

[Comment] You may see that he is happy to help her, if he can. But has he?

Q: Mr. Craggs, you are the administrator of the Ironworkers District Council Philadelphia Vicinity Health and Welfare Fund, are you not?

A: Not to be picayune, but I'm the plan manager. The Trustees are the administrators.

Q: Okay. Thank you for correcting me. I am just going to refer to that as the Fund from here on in.

A: Sure.

Q: Where is your office located?

A: At 6401 Castor Avenue, Philadelphia, PA.

Q: That's in the Northeast?

A: In the Northeast, yes, ma'am.

Q: <u>Can</u> you tell me what is the Fund? <u>Can</u> you give us a brief description of what the Fund is for the Jury?

A: The Welfare Fund for the Ironworkers, we have affiliated with our office 11 local unions, one in Wilmington, Delaware, three in New Jersey, and the remainder in Pennsylvania. And we take in contributions that are made by the employer paid on an hourly basis, so much per hour or each employee, and we take that money and in turn pay the medical bills, bills, dental, drug, and what-have-you.

[Comment] "Can" is not a good way to ask questions. It usually invites narrative answers.

Q: And who governs the Fund? Who is the decision making body of the Fund?

A: The Board of Trustees, the 22 Trustees.

Q: Okay. And, who are those Trustees? Not by name.

A: Each local union has a Trustee, invariably the Trustee to the Fund is the elected Business Agent for that particular local. And the employer group has an equal number of Trustees that are a counterpart. In other words, an employer from Atlantic City and an employer from Camden, an employer from Scranton, and so on.

Q: Would be—

A: Would counterpart be on Trustees, that's correct, yes.

Q: Are there Chairmen on the Board of Trustees?

A: There are co-chairmen, you, one for the union side and one for the management side.

Q: And who are they by name?

A: On the union side, Mr. Robert Sweeney. On the management side, Mr. John Reith, R-E-I-T-H.

Q: Do either of these men individually, or the two of them acting together even have the power to bind the Fund to anything?

A: No.

[Comment] The purpose of this is to vindicate co-counsel's opening, we suppose; the point that Sweeney alone could do nothing. But is it a point worth making? Will it be believed on this record? For example, if Sweeney was so impotent, why were Hardy and then Sullivan knocking, knocking at his door?

Q: How does the Fund bind itself, for example, a contract?

A: Well, first it has to be approved by the full Board of Trustees. When there are any negotiations to be done, further along the way, the Trustees have formed an Investment Committee. The Investment Committee is comprised of three members from the union side and three members from the management side. And they more or less take care of the everyday workings of what you're trying to do, come back and report to the full Board of Trustees, and then the things are approved.

[Comment] Notice, nearly all the questions have been nonleading, even though she is on cross. And more effective for it too. Effective though she is, she is about to draw an objection. Watch how brilliantly she handles the judge.

Q: And you referenced the Investment Committee. Is one job that the Investment Committee might have, would it be to investigate insurance?

MR. LONGER: Your Honor, I'm going to object. The past two questions and now this question are all well beyond the scope of the direct examination.

THE COURT: Sustained.

MS. BENNETT: Your Honor, while I understand you're sustaining Mr. Longer's objection, the reason I'm doing this now is so that we don't have to call Mr. Craggs back in our case. We would be happy to do so, but I don't think Mr. Craggs would be happy that we do so. Like I said, we would be happy to call him back in our case; it's obviously up to Your Honor.

THE COURT: Go ahead.

[Comment] Bang! She changed the judge's ruling by threatening a longer trial. Good for her! To shorten a trial, a judge will even change his mind. Her adversary knows he has been had.

MR. LONGER: Your Honor, just so that it's clear, I appreciate Your Honor's ruling. I just want it clear for the Jury that this is not part of my case, it's the defendant's case that they are now presenting through the testimony of Mr. Craggs.

THE COURT: Very well.

[Comment] Absolutely brilliant! She moved that judge by threatening a prolongation of the trial. And plaintiff's counsel's attempt to save face was met with the same indifference from the judge as it undoubtedly met from the jury. From this point on, she swings into a direct examination mode, and very well too.

BY MS. BENNETT:

Q: We've already established your position within the Fund. Could you describe for me in general terms your duties and responsibilities?

A: Yes. I oversee the running of the office, the Fund office, and I supervise all the personnel. I am the go-between, between doctors, hospitals, providers of all sorts, insurance companies, lawyers, and what-have-you.

Q: Do you have any decision-making powers on behalf of the Fund, yourself?

A: Any what type of powers?

Q: Decision-making powers?

A: Oh. On a working day basis, yes, but only within the confines of the dictates of the Trustees.

Q: So, does that mean, then that you don't have any powers to bind the Fund to any contractors?

A: That's correct. I do not.

[Comment] OK. But so what? No one says that he did.

Q: I would like to direct your attention to Exhibit-7 in the blue notebook, Defendant's exhibits. Can you identify this document for me?

A: It's a copy of the minutes of the meeting of the Board of Trustees held on June 23, 1995.

Q: And who prepared these minutes?

A: A representative of Segal Company, our actuarial firm.

Q: Are you the custodian of these minutes?

A: Yes, I am.

Q: Were these minutes duly approved by the Trustees at a duly convened meeting of the Board of Trustees of the Fund?

A: Yes.

Q: And are these minutes prepared in the ordinary course of business of the Fund?

A: The minutes are taken at the actual meeting by the representative of Segal Company, yes.

Q: And they then prepare them after the meeting?

A: Yes, at Segal Company.

Q: How often does the Board of Trustees meet?

A: Quarterly.

Q: Did you attend this meeting?

A: Yes.

Q: I'm going to direct your attention to Page 4 of this document. And the first full paragraph there—

A: "A motion was made, seconded and unanimously adopted authorizing the committee to meet with the consultants to review consideration of a PPO (Preferred Provider Organization) program and to report their findings at the September 1995 meeting."

Q: And to whom does that term committee refer to in this paragraph?

A: It refers to the Investment Committee.

Q: Of the Fund?

A: Of the Fund, yes.

Q: And to whom does the term consultant refer?

A: Segal Company.

Q: Who is the Segal Company?

A: The Segal Company is an actuarial firm. Our particular office that we deal with is located in New York, but they have offices throughout the country, they perform actuarial duties. Actuarial duties being they tell you how much money you need to run a program, what benefits you can pay, how long your members are going to live, and that sort of thing.

Q: And who is the Fund's primary contact with the Segal Company?

A: I am.

Q: From the Segal Company, who is the representative?

A: Their representative? Charles Maresca.

Q: How long has the Segal Company been a consultant to the Fund?

A: Since the inception of the plan, that being the one plan in 1952 and the other in 1953. They have been consultants ever since.

Q: So, in essence, about 40 years?

A: Yes, ma'am.

[Comment] She is really very facile. She can do what she wants to do. But what is her point? Do you know? Would the jury?

Q: Back to the paragraph you read in this exhibit, did this resolution made at this June 23rd, 1995 meeting, didn't it initiate the Fund's consideration of entering into a contract with Independence Blue Cross and Pennsylvania Blue Shield?

A: Yes.

Q: And, <u>can</u> you tell me what action was taken as a result of this resolution?

A: Mr. Maresca met with the representatives of the Blues, and laid the ground work and we had several meetings after that, and finally came up with a plan furnished by the Blues that met with the approval of the Trustees, and they decided to go with the Blues.

[Comment] Watch as she turns the examination into a conversation. Very good. But the point of it all remains shrouded.

Q: I'm going to break that down a little bit for you, as well. Do you recall when any of the meetings that were held in response to this resolution—were there any meetings held between Segal Company and Independence Blue Cross?

A: Yes. There was one meeting that I attended in New York with representatives of the Blues, and representatives of Segal Company. And there was another meeting that Mr. Maresca, Mr. Sweeney and myself attended at the office of the Blues.

Q: Do you remember the date or even the month and year in which this occurred?

A: Somewhere in these records it's recorded, but I don't recall, no.

Q: That's fine. I completely understand, it was a very long time ago. I am going to direct your attention to Exhibit-13 in the same blue book.

Q: Can you identify this document, sir?

A: It's the Minutes of an Investment Committee meeting held on September 5th, 1995.

Q: And where was this meeting held?

A: It was held at the offices of the GBCA is the General Building Contractors Association, in Philadelphia.

Q: Is that Mr. Reith's office?

A: That's Mr. Reith's office, yes, ma'am.

Q: Who prepared this document?

A: The representative from Segal Company.

[Comment] Watch as she goes on and on and on in building a foundation for a document that no one intends to object to.

Q: Are you the custodian of this document as well, given that it is Minutes of—

A: Yes, I am.

Q: Were these Minutes approved by the Board?

A: Yes, ma'am.

Q: Are they, again, prepared in the ordinary course of the Fund's business?

A: Yes.

Q: Did you attend this meeting?

A: Yes.

Q: Who else attended this meeting?

A: There was Ms. Hardy, Michael Young of Independence Blues, and Charles Maresca, and John Cassaro, who is Mr. Maresca's assistant—who was Mr. Maresca's assistant at the time and they are both from the Segal Company.

Q: And a Fund representative, as well?

A: Yes, myself. I said I was there, yes, ma'am.

[Comment] As with many lawyers, particularly young ones, the examiner has over-foundated, that is, overprepared for a point that will be suffocated in its introduction.

Q: I'm going to direct your attention to a number of the short paragraphs in this document, and there is one that begins, "The committee noted." [W]ould you read that, please.

A: "The committee noted the Trustee's authorization (at the June 23rd 1995 meeting) to meet with the consultants to review Consideration of a PPO (Preferred Provider Organization.)."

Q: Did that, in fact, happen at this September 15th meeting?

A: Yes.

Q: The next paragraph—and feel free, if you don't want to read, you can paraphrase if that's quicker for you, that line.

A: Consultants reported on matters discussed at the initial meeting with Independence Blues on July 26th, 1995.

Q: Does that refresh your recollection as to when one of the meetings with Independence Blue Cross had occurred, July 26th, 1995?

A: No. I couldn't give you a date. Some time after that, yes.

Q: But that, in fact, happened at this meeting, that the consultants reported of the matters discussed?

A: Yes.

Q: And the next paragraph, and again, you can feel free to paraphrase.

[Comment] She really should have drawn an objection on that invitation.

A: Consultants then reviewed their Memorandum dated August 24, 1995, regarding specific matters discussed at their formal proposal from the Blues.

Q: And did that, in fact, happen at this September 5th meeting, that the consultants reviewed their memorandum analyzing Independence Blues proposal?

A: Yes.

Q: Turning over to the next page, the paragraph that begins, "After lengthy"—

A: "After lengthy discussion and a question and answer period of Blue Cross representatives, the Committee unanimously agreed to approve the concept of a voluntary PPO and hospitalization program through

Independence Blue Cross. The committee unanimously agreed to approve implementation of the program to the Trustees at the meeting scheduled for September 22, 1995."

Q: And again, Mr. Craggs, did this, in fact, happen at this September 5th meeting, this discussion and question and answer session?

A: Yes.

Q: And the committee agreed to recommend the implementation of Blue Cross?

A: Yes, that's correct.

[Comment] All is done well and professionally. But what is she trying to say to us through the witness?

Q: I am going to direct your attention to Exhibit-12. And after you have had a chance to look at this document, can you identify it for me?

A: It's a memorandum from Charles Maresca and it was sent to those members of the Investment Committee.

Q: Were you copied on this documents, sir?

A: Pardon me?

Q: Were you copied on this document? I believe if you turn to the next page.

A: Yes.

Q: Are you the custodian of this document, as well?

A: Yes.

Q: And this was an attachment to the Board of Directors minutes that we just reviewed?

A: The Investment Committee ma'am.

Q: And can you tell me briefly what this memorandum is?

A: I can read it quicker than tell you, I guess. As directed at the last meeting, we contacted Independence Blue Cross to examine the availability of implementing a feasible PPO to offer to the covered membership on a voluntary basis. Blue Cross was selected since they have relationships with other Blue Cross plans enabling coverage for the Tri-State Area covered by the District Council.

[Comment] What is all this about? Is it an effort to suggest that Blue Cross was chosen on merit and that Sussman's "access" was worthless?

Q: Does that refresh your recollection just reading that first paragraph? You, obviously, can read more.

A: Yes.

Q: If you can answer, is this memorandum prepared by the Segal Company reviewing the proposal provided to them by Independence Blue Cross?

A: Yes, it is.

Q: Did the Investment Committee rely on the memorandum prepared by the Segal Company in making their recommendations to the full Board of Trustees?

A: This and all the questions and answers of the Blues' representatives, yes.

Q: Thank you. I'm going to direct your attention to Exhibit-14, and can you identify this document?

A: It's a contract between the Ironworkers District Council of Philadelphia Health and Welfare Fund and Independence Blue Cross and Pennsylvania Blue Shield.

Q: I'm sorry. 14—

A: 15, you said.

Q: I'm sorry, 14.

A: Okay. This is a copy of the minutes of the Board of Trustees held on September 22nd, 1995.

Q: And who prepared this document?

A: The representative of Segal Company.

Q: And you are the custodian of this document?

A: Yes, I am.

Q: Were these minutes approved by the full Board of Trustees?

A: Yes, they were.

Q: And are they prepared in the ordinary course of business?

A: Yes, they are.

Q: Did you attend this meeting?

A: Yes, ma'am.

[Comment] Very well. But to what end? We know the Trustees had to approve the deal. We can expect that they would give reasons. We also understand they are not likely to say that they are doing so because Sussman is a pal of Sweeney's.

Q: I am going to direct your attention to Page 4, large Roman Numeral V. Can you read that, please?

A: "The Trustees reviewed the Minutes of the Investment Committee meeting held on September 5, 1995. A copy of these Minutes is attached to these Minutes, as Exhibit B."

Q: And does that represent the exhibit we were just referring to?

A: Yes.

Q: Could you go on, please?

[Comment] That is a cry by the examiner for help from the witness.

A: Sure. "It was noted that the Committee was authorized to meet to review and consider a Preferred Provider Organization (PPO) for the Health Benefits Fund. A consultant then reviewed in detail a proposal from Independence Blue Cross to provide a Tri-State hospitalization program, Blue Shield, and a Tri-State PPO program. Cost savings both to the Fund and direct to the participants were noted."

Q: Let me interrupt you one second. I just want to go into a little explanation. Consultants, again, is that the Segal Company?

A: That's correct.

Q: And Tri-State PPO program, can you explain to me what that Tri-State is?

A: Sure. Tri-State are the three states of Delaware, New Jersey, and Pennsylvania.

Q: So, the PPO program was to cover all three states.

Q: So, if you can just read the portion where it says a motion was made.

A: "Motion was made, seconded and unanimously adopted to approve and implement the Independence Blue Cross proposal, with an effective target date of January 1, 1996, on a voluntary choice basis for all participants."

Q: And does this accurately reflect what actually occurred at this September 22nd meeting?

A: Yes, it does.

[Comment] One can only imagine the attention awarded by the jury to this recurrent reading of less-than-scintillating prose.

Q: Did the consultant, Segal Company, ever meet with representatives of Independence Blue Cross to finalize the details of this agreement?

A: Yes.

Q: Do you know how many times approximately?

A: Two that I was involved with, and I don't know of any others.

Q: So, you were involved in two of the meetings?

A: Yes, ma'am.

Q: Around what time period did they occur? You can give me in terms of the season of the year or—

A: I would say it occurred quite close to the starting date of the program. So, I would say in November or December of the preceding year.

Q: The start of the program as when?

A: January 1, 1996.

Q: And who was primarily responsible for negotiating with Independence Blue Cross as to rates and things like that?

A: Charles Maresca of the Segal Company.

[Comment] Well, the point—if it is the point—that the union relied on the Segal Company has been made. Now she addresses the precise allegation in the complaint.

Q: To your knowledge, did anyone at Independence Blue Cross or Pennsylvania Blue Shield ever tell you or anyone associated with the Fund to avoid doing business with Mr. Sussman or Tower Financial Planning?

A: Not to my knowledge, no.

[Comment] That is very good indeed; and shouldn't that have been the focus of the examination, rather than one question in the midst of it?

Q: Was Mr. Sussman ever authorized to act on behalf of the Fund as a broker?

A: No, absolutely not.

Q: Was he ever authorized to investigate any savings on behalf of the Fund through Independence Blue Cross or any other?

A: When you threw in "any other," I would have to say yes. Mr. Sussman came in and represented a company called AmeriCare. That's a PPO in South Jersey. He did represent them, and he came with their representatives to make a presentation at the plan office. It never amounted to anything, but yes.

Q: How about if I take back—let me go back to my original question. Was Mr. Sussman ever authorized to investigate any savings that Independence Blue Cross might offer the Fund?

A: Absolutely not, to my knowledge.

[Comment] If you have any doubt whose witness this really is, just re-read the last several questions and answers, as the witness guides the advocate to dock the ship.

Q: Did Mr. Sussman or Tower Financial ever provide the findings for a proposal on behalf of Independence Blue Cross?

A: No.

Q: Did Mr. Sussman or Tower Financial ever make presentations to the Board of Trustees on behalf of Independence Blue Cross?

A: No.

Q: Do you know of any work performed by Mr. Sussman or Tower Financial that helped the Fund enter into a contract with Independence Blue Cross and Pennsylvania Blue Shield?

A: No, I did not.

Q: In your view is Mr. Sussman entitled to a commission as a result of the contract between the Fund and Independence Blue Cross?

[Comment] Plaintiff's counsel knows he must object to that last lethal question, and so he does. But what does the jury think? Suppose counsel, instead of objecting, had demanded to

know if the witness was being asked to opine about a commission from the union, or from the Blues?

MR. LONGER: Objection, Your Honor.

THE COURT: Sustained.

MR. LONGER: Thank you, Your Honor.

BY MS. BENNETT:

Q: Did you ever meet with Helen Hardy of Independence Blue Cross in 1994?

A: No.

Q: Did you ever provide Helen Hardy with any information in 1994, any information such as claims experience?

A: I never provided that to her <u>directly</u>, no.

[Comment] These questions are not so good for her. It puts Hardy on the same non-footing as Sussman. The "directly" was the witness's attempt to help her.

Q: Did you ever meet with Helen Hardy in 1995 other than the meetings that [we] have discussed here, and you have identified one meeting that you attended on September 5th, 1995, where you were present and other Trustees? Other than that, were there any other meetings that you attended?

A: No. I didn't meet with her, but I've been in <u>Helen</u>'s company at various meetings through administrative groups that I belong to, and she attended. So, I've been in her company, but never met for the purpose of carrying on any business, no.

[Comment] The use of Hardy's first name is not so good for Blue Cross.

Q: And did you personally ever provide Helen Hardy with any information about the fund, such as—

A: Not directly, no.

[Comment] Even the witness's efforts to help the examiner are put aside in the last question and answer.

> Q: One more question. In your opinion, or to your knowledge, did Mr. Sussman or Tower Financial <u>have anything at all to do with</u> the Ironworkers' decision to enter into a contract with Independence Blue Cross?

[Comment] Great question . . . if she is sure of the answer. But plaintiff's counsel can't take a chance, so he doesn't. He objects and wins.

> MR. LONGER: Objection. Your Honor. Calls for a conclusion.

> THE COURT: Sustained.

> MS. BENNETT: I have no further questions.

ANALYSIS OF THE CROSS-EXAMINATION

The cross-examination of Craggs bolsters the lines of argument that we saw when Sussman was cross-examined. Craggs makes clear that Sussman was not involved in the actual negotiations with Blue Cross, and that the Segal Company advised the Ironworkers. Craggs also describes how the Board of Trustees gave authority to the Investment Committee, and it could not be clearer that the board made the final decision to go with Blue Cross/Blue Shield. But this is not disputed. Sussman never claimed that the board did not make the final decision. His claim is that he got the ball rolling and that it was his work that resulted in the board's eventual vote.

The cross-examiner also makes a couple of points that were made on Sussman's cross-examination. One is that no single trustee, not even co-chair Sweeney, could authorize a contract with Sussman. We think that the value of this is suspect. Sweeney was not likely just another voter on the board. A second is that Blue Cross never did anything to discourage the Ironworkers from dealing with Sussman or Tower. That is the heart of the case, at least from a technical point of view. Sussman claims tortious interference with a relationship with the Ironworkers, and there is no evidence to suggest that the Ironworkers wanted him to make their deal. Our cross-examiner is concerned, however, that the jury will consider whether Sussman "earned" a commission regardless of the technical legal theory being pursued. That is why she makes the effort to show that Sussman had nothing to do with the Ironworkers' decision to go with Blue Cross.

A major problem for the defense is that none of the points being made are really disputed by the plaintiff. Sussman does not claim that he had a contract with the Ironworkers. His theory is that he never expected to receive anything from the Ironworkers, but expected a commission from the insurer. Sussman's theory is that he opened the door to the deal and that is what a broker does. Craggs's overall testimony during cross about his feelings about the Blues may support Sussman's theory that Sussman's friendship with Sweeney gave the Blues an opportunity they otherwise would not have had. And that is *not* good for the Blues.

Indeed, the cross-examiner makes a mistake in asking Craggs whether Sussman was ever authorized to investigate any savings on behalf of the welfare fund through Blue Cross or anyone else. The answer was "yes" and Craggs explained that Sussman had been authorized to make a presentation on behalf of another company, AmeriCare. The cross-examiner immediately backs away from the question. Quite surprisingly, the plaintiffs never refer to this testimony in the trial. It suggests that Sussman had reason to believe that the Ironworkers respected his thinking about saving them money in insurance programs.

We see here a judge changing his mind about the scope of direct to spare a witness from being called twice. This is a reminder that the direct examiner should never assume that a trial judge will strictly enforce the usual limit on the scope of cross-examination.

TEXT OF THE REDIRECT EXAMINATION

MR. LONGER: I have a few questions, Your Honor. Let's start with the last one first.

*[Comment] Again, the direct examiner must weigh the proba-
bilities and decide whether to examine again, which will open
another opportunity to cross. He has decided to do so. This
decision, as we will see, proves to be a mistake. This witness is
no friend to the plaintiff. He was, obviously, called to put in
some figures to be used for damages. This has been done. To
keep him on the stand is to invite disaster.*

BY MR. LONGER:

Q: You said that you never gave any information
directly to Ms. Hardy, right?

A: That's correct.

Q: You gave it indirectly to Ms. Hardy through Mr.
Sussman, didn't you?

A: No.

Q: No?

A: No.

*[Comment] Again, when a cross-examiner is tagged, or thinks
that he is, he often repeats the last answer in his next question.*

Q: Mr. Sussman never got information from you
about Zip Code listings?

A: Yes, but not for the Blues. It was for the other plan
that I explained to you called the AmeriCare that was in
South Jersey. I did give Mr.—well, the men that he
brought along. I gave them the information, yes.

Q: Was that about the same time as the Blue Cross?

A: No, it was after we had the Blue Cross. That's
when we told them we weren't interested, we already had
the contract with the Blues.

Q: Do you know if he gave that information to Ms.
Hardy?

A: I have no idea what he did with the information. There would be no reason for him to, because we were already signed with the Blues at that time.

[Comment] All in all, counsel at this point is going in reverse.

Q: Ms. Bennett asked you to take a look at Page 4, which says, "After discussion, motion was made, seconded and unanimously adopted authorizing the Committee to meet with the consultant to review consideration of a PPO program and to report their findings to the September '95 meeting." That's what it says, right?

A: Page 4?

Q: Page 4, at the top of the page.

A: Yes.

Q: And the PPO that they were talking about there was Blue Cross/Blue Shield, right?

A: That's correct.

Q: Now, do you know if Mr. Sweeney made that motion, to have them consider Blue Cross/Blue Shield as a PPO?

A: No. I couldn't say who made the motion. It was—as I recall, there were quite a few of the union Trustees that were interested in going with the Blues in order to save the members money.

Q: That's right. The union Trustee members were sponsoring that motion, right?

A: The union Trustees were sponsoring the motion, yes.

Q: The union Trustees wanted Blue Cross/Blue Shield, right?

A: Yes.

Q: And Mr. Sweeney is the co-chairman of the Trustees, right?

A: Yes, but he has—

Q: And Mr. Sweeney—

THE COURT: Wait. Let him finish.

MR. LONGER: I'm sorry.

THE WITNESS: Mr. Sweeney <u>had no influence</u> over the Union Trustees in this matter, <u>in my opinion</u>, because they came to the meeting with that <u>in mind for them-selves</u>. You didn't have to tell them or suggest anything to them.

[Comment] This witness is going to hurt the plaintiff when he can, so the lawyer appeals to the judge. This is a mistake, because the witness's answer, although not what the examiner wants to hear, is not likely to be believed. No answer can hurt you unless it is believed, and one that is discredited by the jury will actually help. Most of the false rules of cross are predicated on the fear of witnesses, which is not necessary if you pick the topic of their testimony on the basis of your ability to punish them with prior statements or evidence, or the rules of probabil-ity, if they make inappropriate answers. See Vol. III, pp. 54–58.

MR. LONGER: Your Honor, I'm going to move to strike—

THE COURT: Stricken.

MR. LONGER: Thank you.

BY MR. LONGER:

Q: Just so it's clear, Mr. Sweeney was the co-chairman on the Union side of the Trustees; correct?

A: That's correct.

Q: It was the Union side of the Trustees that were sponsoring this motion to get Blue Cross/Blue Shield, wasn't it?

A: That's correct. The Union Trustees told Mr. Sweeney that's what they wanted.

[Comment] See. He just proved the unlikeliness of the answer that he moved to strike. Imagine, Sweeney is out there meeting with Sussman and with Hardy but it is not him reporting to the Union trustees. Oh, no—the trustees are telling him. Sure.

Q: Second question, let's take us back to Exhibit Number-12, which was the second copy, I think, Ms. Bennett asked you to take a look at. Do you have that in front of you?

A: Yes, I have it.

Q: Exhibit Number-12 is dated August 24th, 1995, and it's a letter from Charles Maresca to the—

A: Investment Committee, yes.

Q: And in this memorandum, Mr. Maresca has done some analyses, has he not?

A: Yes.

Q: And it's this memorandum which says that [with] respect to surgical medical he expected the fund to have some savings with respect to Blue Cross/Blue Shield's program, correct?

A: Yes.

Q: And you expected them to have some savings of about $200,000; isn't that right?

A: Yes.

Q: Now, he then talks about hospitalization. And let me be clear. Surgical medical is the Blue Shield aspect of this program, right?

A: That's correct.

Q: Blue Shield provides the physicians' services and compensates the physicians for the work that they perform, correct?

[Comment] One begins to wonder if we are in the right case. What has all this to do with the complaint or its defense?

A: That's correct.

Q: Now, Blue Cross is the hospitalization insurance end of this, right?

A: That's correct.

Q: And it's the next paragraph that I would like you to look at on Page 2, that talks about hospitalizations?

A: Yes.

Q: I see that you just turned the page, so now we're on the same page.

A: Yes.

Q: There's a paragraph there in the middle of the page that says Surgical Medical claims paid 12 months ending May 31, 1995, 4.1 million dollars, right?

A: Right.

Q: So, for the calendar year, June 1994 to May 31, 1995, the Fund paid 4.8 million [sic] dollars for surgical medical doctors' payments, correct?

A: That's correct.

Q: Then it goes on to read, "Through network 65 percent, 3.1 million, would add 20 percent co-insurance currently through fund producing a total of 3.9 million dollars in claims paid." Now, that means that if 63 percent of the Ironworkers went through the network that the amounts would be 3.1 million?

A: No. I think what it means is out of the original 4.8 million, if you deducted the co-payments that the members had to pay on their own, you would come up with 3.9 million that the plan itself had to spend.

Q: But let me use his phrase, because it is what I was going to say anyway. "The bottom line for the Fund would be almost cost neutral. We estimate a modest savings of approximately $200,000," right?

A: That's correct.

Q: Now, with respect to hospitalizations, he says he couldn't figure out what the savings would be; is that right?

A: That's correct.

Q: Did he later tell you what the hospitalization savings would be?

A: No. As I testified before, there is no way in God's world that anyone could tell you.

[Comment] Whatever counsel is intending to do is not being done. What can the jury be thinking? He should get this witness off the stand before disaster strikes.

Q: But it's somewhere about $200,000, isn't it? Doesn't generally hospitalization run in excess of the surgeon's fees?

A: Not necessarily, no.

Q: Your experience is that hospitalization costs exceed surgeons' costs?

A: At times, yes.

[Comment] This witness wants to hurt the plaintiff, and is doing so. Counsel had his numbers on direct. He is not advancing beyond that on redirect.

Q: Let me go back to the last question last, and bring it up. I'm going to ask you to look at the black notebook.

A: What number?

Q: Exhibit Number-11.

A: Yes.

Q: Now, just a moment ago, you were talking about Zip Code listings. And you said Mr. Sussman speaking about AmeriCare after Blue Cross/Blue Shield was in place.

A: That's correct.

Q: Now, Blue Cross/Blue Shield came into place on January 1, 1996, correct?

A: That's correct.

Q: This document, this Zip Code listing, has a date, does it not?

A: If it does, I can't see it.

Q: Well, let me read it to you. It says, 4-18-94 on the first page. That's well before Blue Cross/Blue Shield, right?

MS. BENNETT: Your Honor—

THE WITNESS: You have something I don't have.

MS. BENNETT: If he could just point out the date to the witness, I would be grateful.

THE WITNESS: Oh, I see. That's right.

BY MR. LONGER:

Q: The third page of the document, that's dated 4-18-94, isn't it?

A: That's correct.

Q: And that's well before Blue Cross/Blue Shield came into the picture, isn't it?

A: That's correct.

Q: And you gave this to Mr. Sussman?

A: That's correct.

Q: So, earlier you were mistaken, is that correct?

A: No.

[Comment] This fellow is tough. He is not going to give this plaintiff the time of day.

Q: Now, Ms. Bennett asked you, to your knowledge did anyone at Blue Cross tell you to avoid doing business with Mr. Sussman, and you answered no.

A: Correct.

Q: And they didn't have to tell you, did they? You knew that you could avoid the condition—

MS. BENNETT: Objection.

BY MR. LONGER:

[Comment] He abandons the one question, but puts it all in another form, and will be stuck with a predictably hurtful answer, for he has nothing to use to contradict the answers of this witness.

Q: You knew that Blue Cross/Blue Shield was going to tack on a broker commission, right?

A: I hadn't the slightest idea that there was a broker involved, because I never knew Mr. Sussman to do anything whatsoever, so therefore, he would not be entitled to any commission. Commissions never crossed my mind.

[Comment] Bang! Counsel got it right between the eyes. Now he tries to bandage the wound.

MR. LONGER: I'm going to move to strike, Your Honor, as nonresponsive.

THE COURT: Overruled.

[Comment] Bang! Bang! He really got hurt on this. Not only has the witness hurt him, but after appealing to the judge, the judge has agreed with the witness. Vol. III, pp. 49–53.

BY MR. LONGER:

Q: You know Mr. Sweeney?

A: Yes. I would like to think I do, yes.

Q: He was friendly with Mr. Sussman, was he not?

A: Yes.

Q: He's not anymore; is that right?

A: That's right.

Q: And he's not enamored with Mr. Sussman because of this lawsuit; is that correct, sir?

A: No. It has to do with the New Jersey—the North Jersey lawsuit, is why he's not enamored with Mr. Sussman. Because Mr. Sweeney was—

MR. LONGER: Thank you, Mr. Craggs. I have no further questions.

[Comment] Counsel has very wisely retired from the field while he, and his client, yet live—for this witness, figuratively, intends to kill them both.

THE COURT: Recross?

MS. BENNETT: No, Your Honor.

[Comment] A wise decision, indeed.

ANALYSIS OF THE REDIRECT EXAMINATION

The problem the direct examiner is having is that Craggs knows that Sweeney is no longer friendly with Sussman, and Craggs clearly does not want to volunteer anything that will help Sussman. Indeed, Craggs takes every opportunity to hurt the plaintiff. The direct examiner would have been better off to have been leading with questions Craggs could not avoid answering the way the direct examiner wanted.

The examiner should have used Craggs to remind the jury that Hardy thought Sweeney was key. After all, that is why she went to see him, not other trustees, on her own. Sussman thought Sweeney was key, and that is why he brought Hardy with him to see Sweeney. And, lo and behold, somehow Sweeney, having been courted by Sussman, presides over a meeting in which union trustees move the proposal that leads to the Blue Cross contract. You can see the argument that should have been made. It is the examiner's job to make it.

You can see how bogged down the examination got when the examiner attempted to examine on the amount of claims paid. It was complicated, and it is doubtful that any juror would understand what argument was being made.

The examination also demonstrates the price an examiner pays for throwing in a question without adequate preparation. Counsel asks Craggs whether he knew the Blues were going to tack on a broker commission. It should have been obvious that the witness was not going to help Sussman on this point. The question led the witness to volunteer that he did not know Sussman did anything that entitled him to a commission, thus offering an opinion that the judge earlier had not permitted. The examiner moves to strike the answer and loses.

All in all, Craggs is useful to the plaintiff for the money, and only the money. In our opinion, that is all that should have been attempted with him.

Chapter Five

The Sweeney Deposition

TEXT OF THE PLAINTIFF-DESIGNATED TESTIMONY

MR. LONGER: We are going to read the designations from Mr. Sweeney's transcript.

[Comment] When counsel says "designations," he means he will read less than the whole of the deposition. Usually, the party against whom it is read has the right to ask for additional portions, under the Rule of Completeness. See Fed. R. Evid. 106. Because there is no fighting, we take it that counsel agreed to the designated portions that both wanted before they presented the designations to the court.

THE COURT: How long will you be?

MR. LONGER: Fifteen minutes, according to my compadre. We're going to read Mr. Sweeney's testimony into the record as we designated it. Would Your Honor care to explain to the Jury what we're doing, here?

THE COURT: This is the deposition taken of Mr. Sweeney at a prior time. And it's going to be read into the record as testimony. It's just being done this way so that it will make more sense and it will seem more like Mr. Sweeney is talking. This is not Mr. Sweeney, he is just going to read Mr. Sweeney's answers so that we can keep it in a question and answer format. Mr. Sweeney, I assume, is not here for some proper reason?

MR. LONGER: Mr. Sweeney is the Trustee of New Jersey and he is beyond the subpoena power of the Court, Your Honor.

THE COURT: That's why it's being done this way. Okay.

[Comment] Well, that is the legal reason. As we shall see, there is another. Mr. Sweeney is the ex-friend of Sussman. He will actually come to court later on behalf of the Blues.

DONALD HAVILAND, sworn, to read the testimony of Mr. Sweeney truly and accurately.

THE COURT: He is not attesting to the answers themselves. He is swearing that he will read them accurately. The testimony, however, is sworn, is taken under oath, and it's the same as though he were here.

[Comment] This is an excellent way of dealing with the introduction of deposition testimony. Using two people, one to read questions and the other to read the answers, is a refreshing change from just one person reading both.

MR. LONGER: All right to begin, Your Honor?

THE COURT: Yes.

MR. LONGER: Our first designation is from Page 4, Line 12, through Page 7, Line 15.

BY MR. LONGER:

Q: "Good morning. My name is Mark Sonnenfeld. I'm an attorney with the law firm of Morgan, Lewis and Bockius, Philadelphia. I represent Independence Blue Cross and Pennsylvania Blue Shield, in a lawsuit filed by Tower Financial Planning Associates. I have certain questions to ask you that relate to that lawsuit this morning, and as you may know, you are under oath and your testimony can be used in court, in accordance with the applicable rules.

Could you please tell us your full name?"

[Comment] Interesting. The plaintiff chooses to read, as his first portion, the testimony adduced by his adversary. And, wisely, the defendant's counsel makes this clear to the jurors.

MR. SONNENFELD: Just so the Jury is not confused, this was the portion of the deposition that I took, and that Mr. Longer is now reading. We haven't changed names.

[Discussion off the record.]

THE WITNESS: "Robert Carlton Sweeney."

BY MR. LONGER:

Q: Where do you live, sir?

A: 142 Greenvale Road, Cherry Hill, New Jersey.

Q: How old are you, sir?

A: 64.

Q: You're here with your counsel, is that correct, sir?

A: Yes.

Q: Who is that, sir?

A: Michael Fagan.

Q: And he's sitting to your right?

A: Yes.

Q: Did you have a chance to meet with him before the deposition?

A: Yes.

Q: By whom are you employed, sir?

A: Ironworkers Local 399.

Q: What is your position there?

A: I am the President and Business Manager.

Q: Where is your office located?

A: 409 Crown Pointe Road, Westville, New Jersey.

Q: How long have you held that position?

A: I've been the President for 25 years and I've been the Business Manager for 15.

Q: Do you also hold a position with the Ironworkers District Council Philadelphia and Vicinity Health Benefits Fund?

A: Yes, I do.

Q: Is that the correct name of the Fund?

A: Well, I'll call it the Philadelphia District Council Benefit and Pension Plan—Ironworkers Philadelphia District Council Benefit and Pension Plan.

Q: What position do you hold with that plan?

A: I'm a Trustee.

Q: How long have you been a Trustee, sir?

A: In excess of 20 years.

Q: What geographic area does the Fund cover?

A: I guess the Southeastern Pennsylvania, Southern New Jersey and Northern Delaware.

Q: And is the Fund made up of more than one local within the Ironworkers Union?

A: Yes, it is.

Q: How many locals are there?

A: Eleven.

Q: And does each local have a Trustee?

A: Yes.

Q: How many Trustees are there altogether?

A: Twenty-two.

Q: And are some of those labor and some of those management Trustees?

A: Equal numbers.

Q: Eleven of each?

A: Yes.

Q: Where are the offices of the Philadelphia local?

A: 6801 Castor Avenue, Philadelphia, PA.

Q: 6401?

A: 6401. I'm sorry. 6401.

Q: And is there a person who runs that office?

A: Yes.

Q: An office manager?

A: Yes.

Q: Who is that?

A: Nick Elmer Craggs.

[Comment] *Up until now, has any point been made, or is this still pedigree?*

MR. LONGER: We're going to skip now to Page 9, Line 6 through Page 10, Line 9.

BY MR. LONGER:

Q: Are you familiar with a company called Segal, S-E-G-A-L, Company?

A: Yes.

Q: Where is the Segal Company located?

A: On Park Avenue in New York City.

Q: What is their relationship of Segal Company to the Fund?

A: They're consultants to this plan.

Q: And how long have they been the consultants to this plan?

A: In excess of 25 years, that I know of.

Q: How is the Segal Company compensated?

A: Annually.

Q: It's an annual fee?

A: Yes.

Q: Negotiated?

A: Yes. They get a fee, and if they want a raise or something, they have to come before the Board and state why they want the raise and stuff like that. But it's an annual thing.

Q: Does the Segal Company get a commission on insurance that's placed?

A: No.

Q: Is there an individual with the Segal Company who works with the Fund?

A: Yes.

Q: What's that individual's name?

A: Charles Maresca, M-A-R-E-S-C-A.

[Comment] All of this is very clear, but it is not as clear why the plaintiff is offering this. How does it help him? Well, perhaps this was designated by the defendant, for Maresca will help Blue Cross quite a good deal later.

MR. LONGER: We're now going to skip to Page 29, Line 13 through Line 13 [*sic*].

BY MR. LONGER:

Q: Did anyone from Blue Cross or Pennsylvania Blue Shield discuss with you, or to your knowledge, anyone from the Ironworkers, that you should avoid doing business with Tower and Sussman to avoid his commission?

A: <u>No. Our consultant told us that, Maresca</u>.

[Comment] Now, that sure does not help the plaintiff, who is suing Blue Cross for tortious interference. But, perhaps it was a portion demanded to be read by the defendant.

MR. LONGER: We'll skip to Page 35, Line 20 through Page 40, Line 23.

MR. SONNENFELD: So the Jury is not confused, at this point in the questioning it's Mr. Longer at the deposition who was asking the questions.

[Comment] Defense says this, and he is wise to point out that the unhelpful information that the plaintiff's counsel is reading was adduced by the plaintiff himself. It leads us to believe that the earlier portions were adduced by the defendant.

MR. LONGER: Thank you.

[Comment] We don't think he really means this.

BY MR. LONGER:

Q: Did you also at one point want to get Preferred Health Care?

A: We did get Preferred Health Care.

Q: Had any other Members of the Board, prior to 1995, expressed a dislike for Blue Cross/Blue Shield in the same way that Mr. Craggs did?

A: Not that I know of.

Q: Do you know why it is that Blue Cross/Blue Shield was dropped years ago as an insurer for the Fund?

A: That's so many years ago I wouldn't remember.

[Comment] It is patently obvious that Sweeney is going out of his way not to help the plaintiff. After all, if he doesn't know why Blue Cross was dropped, who would? And who made the decision?

Q: And up until recently is it that Blue Cross and Blue Shield has not been an insurer of the Fund, to your knowledge?

A: To my knowledge—why haven't we had Blue Cross and Blue Shield? Because we were satisfied at the time with the self-insured plan. But then there came a time when we found out we could do away with our deductibles if we got Blue Cross and Blue Shield, if we got a PPO. Not only Blue Cross and Blue Shield, but any PPO. We could do away—we had a $500.00 family deductible and a $250.00 single person deductible, and by going with a PPO, we would do away with the deductible, and we thought we were doing something good for our members.

Q: Did you learn about the ability to do away with the deductibles at the time you discussed contracting Preferred Health Care as a PPO?

A: Yes.

Q: Was Preferred Health Care the first PPO ever contracted for?

A: I don't think so. I think we had an outfit called— oh, the guy's name is Lew and, he's from New York. It's a hospital PPO that we were dealing with. I don't know the name of it, though.

Q: It was out of New York at the time, you say?

A: Yes. Some care was for hospitals. We would use their network to get a discount from the hospitals.

Q: For hospitalization?

A: For hospitals.

Q: You recall it was a New York entity which the first PPO the Fund dealt with?

A: Yes.

Q: And that was in the 1990s or in the 1980s, or what's your recollection?

A: Probably the 80s.

[Comment] Where is the detail getting us? Why are we going so far back in time? On direct, we believe the jury asks itself, "What is the lawyer trying to tell us through the witness?" Vol. II, pp. 9–10. This is different from cross, where the assertions of counsel are usually clear, and where the jury votes on that

assertion and the answer it evokes. Vol. III, pp. 57–58. But what are we being told here?

Q: And in 1994 or thereabouts, did you discuss with Mr. Sussman or Tower Financial, using a different network?

A: Hospitalization? No.

Q: Did you discuss using a different one for the purpose of physicians' services?

A: Yes.

Q: Was that the first network that you discussed at anytime on behalf of the Fund with respect to physicians' services?

A: Personally? Just me, you mean?

Q: Okay. We'll start with you.

A: Personally, yeah.

Q: And what about with respect to the Fund?

A: I don't understand your question.

Q: I don't understand your answer.

A: Well, go ahead and state your question again, and I will give you an answer.

[Comment] That last is not so good for the examiner. When lawyers get cantankerous with witnesses, jurors usually side with the witness. One has to wonder at this point, under a cost-benefit analysis, whether this deposition should have been offered by the plaintiff. Or how was it that the PPO came into being with the union?

Q: The first time you spoke to Mr. Sussman about a physicians' services network was with respect to Preferred Health Care, right?

A: Wait a second. No. The first time—anytime I talked to Mr. Sussman about any business of this union, I told him we were looking into getting a PPO, because he's in the insurance business. He said he had a friend of his who did this, Roger Halverson. He said this was a friend of his, and afterwards, I found out it wasn't a friend of his. But Roger Halverson met with the Union Trustees, just the Union Trustees, to explain what a PPO was and explain to us how we could do away with these deductibles by having a PPO. Mr. Sussman was present at that meeting. Other than that—

Q: And was Mr. Halverson discussing Preferred Health Care?

A: Yes.

Q: He was not discussing the New York entity's PPO?

A: No.

Q: But I thought you had indicated that you were already familiar with that entity's ability to do away with the deductible?

A: I wasn't familiar—with the New York thing. It was a hospital PPO that I had nothing to do with. I know we had it. Where it came from, how we had it—we've had it for quite a few years, but I can't go back that far in my memory and remember how we got it.

Q: Now, the PPO that Mr. Halverson was discussing was a network for physicians' services; is that fair to say?

A: And hospitals, yes.

Q: Physicians and hospitals?

A: Right.

Q: All right. And that is the first discussion about a physician and hospital PPO that you're aware of that was presented to the public?

A: That I'm aware of, yes.

Q: And ultimately the Fund agreed to purchase or to contract with that PPO; is that correct?

A: Right, Preferred Care.

[Comment] How interested do you think the jurors are about the intricacies of the ancient insurance policies of the union?

Q: And was Mr. Sussman of Tower Financial, a broker in that contract with Preferred Care?

A: I don't <u>believe</u> so.

Q: Do you <u>believe</u> that Mr. Halverson was the only person?

A: I <u>believe</u> that Mr. Sussman got ahold of Mr. Halverson, and whatever commission there was or anything, they agreed to split it. Now, I don't even know that for a fact.

[Comment] Why is the testimony offered? Indeed, this testimony should have been objected to. A witness can only testify as to what he knows. And the point was, or should have been, important to the plaintiff, as the plaintiff should have made the argument that he gave up the commission he earned on Preferred Care to make another with Blue Cross.

Q: Do you <u>know</u> if Mr. Sussman provided any services in connection with engaging Preferred Health Care as a PPO for the Fund?

A: No.

[Comment] The last answer also should have been objected to, or, if demanded by the defendant, not read. If the witness did not know, his answer was not material. But, as read, it sounds as though the plaintiff did nothing to earn a commission. But the real problem is that this testimony is being offered by the plaintiff—and it sure doesn't help him very much.

Q: Do you recall attending any sessions at all, where Preferred Care was discussed as a potential PPO?

A: I told you, yeah, the one where he showed up with Halverson at our office in Philadelphia.

Q: This was one meeting that you do recall?

A: Yes.

Q: Who was present at that meeting?

A: The 11 Union Trustees, Roger Halverson and Leonard Sussman.

MR. LONGER: We're skipping to Page 43, Line 21, through Page 44, Line 20.

BY MR. LONGER:

Q: Did the Fund issue a Broker of Record letter to anyone with respect to that PPO contract with Preferred Health Care?

A: I don't know.

Q: Do you know if the Fund is paying commissions on that?

A: Our Fund?

Q: Yes.

A: No. We wouldn't pay anybody commissions.

[Comment] Does the testimony help the plaintiff? He is suing, of course, because of failure to pay commissions, but he is suing Blue Cross because it interfered with his economic relationship with the union, presumably to get commissions. This last answer by the head of the union drives a stake through the heart of the plaintiff's position.

Q: The commissions would come out of the insuring entity; is that fair to say?

A: I don't know how it's done.

Q: You would not expect to pay any commission to a salesman for the sale of an insurance contract to the Fund; is that right?

A: No. We wouldn't expect to pay anything.

Q: If the commission was to issue, would you expect that commission to issue from the insuring entity?

A: I don't know. I don't know how it works.

[Comment] Again, none of this helps the plaintiff. Why is he offering it? This witness is simply on the other side.

MR. LONGER: Now, we're skipping to Page 50, Line 15 through Page 53, Line 2.

BY MR. LONGER:

Q: When was the first time that you ever recall meeting with Ms. Hardy?

A: She came to my office.

Q: Was anyone else present at that meeting?

A: No. She just came and sat down and talked to me.

Q: When do you recall that meeting taking place?

A: She just walked in, rang the bell, and then my partner came back and told me there was a lady out here who wants to talk to you. I said, "Well, send her back." And that's the first time I ever met her.

Q: What did she talk to you about at that meeting?

A: Well, obviously, she's coming to my office. She wants to talk about Blue Cross.

Q: She was trying to sell Blue Cross coverage to the Fund or to the Local?

A: No. The Local gets its insurance from the Fund.

Q: And she was trying to sell Blue Cross/Blue Shield?

A: I don't know what she was trying. I told you before, I don't know whether she was trying to sell it or not. She came in and she was telling me what Blue Cross was.

[Comment] *The examiner should have hit him for this. Of course she was there to sell insurance. She was not simply doing a survey—but the examiner lets him get away with it.*

Q: After the meeting with Ms. Hardy, that we have been discussing, what did you do with the information that she gave you?

A: Nothing.

Q: When was the next time you met Ms. Hardy?

A: The next time I met Ms. Hardy. I don't know when the next time was.

Q: Do you recall there ever being a meeting between yourself, Mr. Sussman and Ms. Hardy?

A: Yes.

Q: Do you recall who set up that meeting?

A: Sussman.

[Comment] *Now, that's an important admission, but the examiner does not pursue it. It is important because Sussman claims that he was key in facilitating the deal—and the defendant denies not only that, but that Sussman did anything at all.*

Q: Did you talk to Mr. Sussman in advance of that meeting?

A: No.

Q: Ms. Hardy and Mr. Sussman appeared at your door, like before and—

A: Yeah.

Q: —entered. Do you recall what the substance of that meeting was?

A: No.

Q: Do you know if the two of them were trying to sell Blue Cross/Blue Shield as a network offered by Blue Cross/Blue Shield to the public?

[Comment] Now, watch the next answer.

A: Were they trying to sell it?

[Comment] That is a dead giveaway that the witness is in trouble. When the witness on cross repeats the answer, it is like a boxer going into a clinch.

Q: Yes.
A: I don't know what they were trying to do.

[Comment] Really, can you imagine that. The poor man simply had no idea why they were there. Now, that is truly incredible, but the examiner does not pursue it.

Q: What did you talk about? You don't have any recollection at all?

A: If I told you what I was talking about, I'd be lying to you. You know, we're going back now. I do a lot of business during the day.

[Comment] Well, well. It's a pretty good bet that they were talking insurance, don't you think? But, again, the examiner does not pursue it.

MR. LONGER: We're skipping now to Page 53, Line 22 through Page 55, Line 3.

BY MR. LONGER:

Q: In 1994, do you recall ever telling Mr. Sussman that there would be no activity on obtaining a new PPO, because you were satisfied with the Preferred Health Care Network that had already been in place?

A: Whether we were satisfied with it or not, I don't know. We said there wasn't going to be any discussion, because we had just got this company and we wanted to see how it worked, not whether we were satisfied or not, because it was a brand new thing for us.

Q: You wanted to see how it worked out in terms of providing services; is that what you mean?

A: Savings.

Q: And what was your experience with Preferred Health Care, were you obtaining any savings at all?

A: I don't know.

Q: <u>Would</u> Mr. Maresca <u>know</u>?

A: <u>Probably</u>.

[Comment] We are, by the way the question was phrased, asking for mind reading. He might have asked if it was part of Maresca's job to know. It would amount to the same thing, but the question would be unobjectionable.

Q: Did he explain to you at anytime that the Fund was not making savings with Preferred Health Care?

A: Did who say this?

Q: Mr. Maresca.

A: No.

Q: Did he ever explain to—

A: No. No, he didn't.

Q: Okay. I'll just say it again. I don't want to have a broken up record here. Did Mr. Maresca ever explain to you or any other Trustees that Preferred Health Care was not providing any savings to the Fund?
A: No.

[Comment] What is all this about? Does it help or hurt anyone? How? What does it matter?

MR. LONGER: Now, we're going to skip ahead to Page 55, Line 24 through Page 56, Line 11.

BY MR. LONGER:

Q: At the first meeting that you had with Ms. Hardy—

A: Ms. Hardy.

Q: I'm sorry. Ms. Hardy and Mr. Sussman, was there any discussion at all about Tower Financial claiming Mr. Sussman and Blue Cross/Blue Shield working together to sell you a PPO?

A: No.

Q: There was no discussion or you don't remember?

[Comment] Another non-event. Remember, this testimony is offered by the plaintiff. What are the jurors to make of it? They have been told by the plaintiff's counsel that this man was the friend of the plaintiff.

A: I don't remember.

MR. LONGER: Now, we're skipping to Page 68, Line 10 through Page 70, Line 2. Bear with us, this is the last one.

BY MR. LONGER:

Q: Also Exhibit 4. Did you have any understanding in any discussion that you had with Mr. Sussman, where Ms. Hardy was present, that Mr. Sussman was seeking to sell the Fund insurance using Blue Cross/Blue Shield as a preferred provider network?

A: Did I have any knowledge of that?

[Comment] Another repetition of the question and therefore another tip-off that he knows he is where he does not want to be.

Q: Did you have any understanding that that's what he was doing?

A: Well, I would say yeah. He was trying to—he was trying to get in someplace where he didn't belong, because he was told he couldn't do it.

[Comment] Finally! He admits that the plaintiff was selling something. But will anyone understand that given his aggressive attitude toward Sussman? What is the jury to make of this

overt hostility to the plaintiff in testimony offered by the plaintiff?

> Q: That's after the meeting with Mr. Maresca at the Viennese Restaurant?

> A: I don't know when it was. I don't know when it was. I can't remember dates like I told you, I don't keep a calendar. If I had a calendar, I would bring it here.

> Q: But is it fair to say that he was trying to sell insurance to the Fund?

> A: He can't sell insurance. He can't sell. He can't sell insurance to the Fund, he can't.

[Comment] Four times! Well, that is certainly emphatic enough.

> Q: Let me ask it a slightly different way. Did you have an understanding that Mr. Sussman was attempting to make a sale of insurance to the Fund using Blue Cross/Blue Shield as a preferred provider network?

> A: Did I have an understanding he was trying to sell Blue Cross insurance?

[Comment] Again, he repeats the answer. A telltale sign of a witness in trouble, like a golfer with his head up or a lawyer with his head down, or a cross-examiner repeating a bad answer as he struggles to formulate a new question.

> Q: Yes, sir.

> A: I would think he was.

[Comment] Finally, the examiner has scored. Notice that this answer is very different from the earlier offerings.

> Q: And would you think he was doing that with the expectation of making money as a result of that sale?

> A: I think he tries to make money at everything he does.

MR. LONGER: Thank you, Mr. Sweeney.

[Comment] The examiner struck gold—but he quits. Does the jury understand? He should have pressed further. If, as the witness has said, the fund does not pay, then who does? Why, Blue Cross/Blue Shield, of course, that's who!

THE COURT: We'll break for the day. Remember, please don't discuss this case with each other or anybody else. We'll see you tomorrow morning at 9:30, and we'll pick up there.

ANALYSIS OF THE DESIGNATED TESTIMONY

Mr. Sweeney remembers very little that is helpful to the plaintiff. He confirms that the union welfare fund originally wanted to switch from self-insurance to a preferred provider plan to avoid deductibles. He further admits that Sussman came to him along with Ms. Hardy, and then he finally admits that Sussman was trying to sell the union on Blue Cross in order to earn money. It is easy to tell that Sweeney is not happy being a witness. He surely cannot be happy with the fact that Sussman's claim rests upon a theory that Sussman was a friend of Sweeney's and that as a result Sussman persuaded Sweeney to listen to Blue Cross/Blue Shield and to contract with them. Sweeney, like any union official, wants the members to believe that he is always and only interested in insurance plans that work for them, irrespective of whether a friend is recommending the plan.

One problem for Sweeney is that years ago the welfare fund had dropped Blue Cross/Blue Shield. If the deal is so great, why wasn't the fund using the Blues earlier? This is something that no one wants to talk about in this case. But surely Sussman's lawyer knows that Sweeney must feel in an awkward position.

Given human nature, the best that Sussman is going to do is to have Sweeney confirm the fact that Sussman brought Hardy to him, that Sussman was involved for profit, and that Sweeney doesn't remember much else.

The last answer Sweeney gives, indicating that Sussman tries to make money at everything he does, can be interpreted two ways. One is somewhat favorable, a reference to a small business owner who seeks to make a living. Another is unflattering, a reference to greed. But the question is, has the examiner gone far enough in the deposition? Should he now bring out that there is nothing wrong in the plaintiff receiving a fee from the insurance company if he is representing them and brings them a new client? Because the direct examiner gets to pick who reads the answer, the direct examiner gets to control the way in which the answer is read. That could be crucial in this case.

This leads to a question: Who should read deposition testimony? In this case, Sussman's counsel read the questions and someone else read the answers. Another approach is for the counsel to read both questions and answers. The shorter the testimony, the better it is for counsel to do the reading himself. That is because there is less chance of error, and not much need to worry about monotony. As the testimony becomes longer, as in Sweeney's case, sharing the work between the lawyer and a person who reads Sweeney's lines does help to make the testimony seem more convincing and perhaps less contrived in the reading.

One interesting question is whether the defendants could have stopped the reading of the deposition testimony. Sweeney will be at the trial. He will testify. Although he is outside the subpoena power of the court, he will voluntarily appear. Had he voluntarily been present before his deposition was read, defense counsel could have objected on the ground that Sweeney was available. Sweeney, as you will see, is not cooperative toward the plaintiff. Had he surprised the plaintiff by showing up, the examination by plaintiff's counsel might have been difficult, notwithstanding the availability of the deposition testimony for impeachment.

In fact, by presenting the deposition testimony without any cross-examination at the time, plaintiff's counsel is able to use Sweeney to corroborate Sussman on some aspects of the plaintiff's case. Remember that Sussman is not suing the Ironworkers, and he is not suing Sweeney. He does not claim that they cheated him. He is suing the Blues, and it is they and Ms. Hardy whom he claims cheated him. However, all in all, this deposition could have been put aside by the plaintiff, who did not need it for his case. Perhaps counsel felt that having no Sweeney was worse than presenting this Sweeney. Well, that is a value judgment—but we do not agree.

Chapter Six

The First of "The Blues" Witnesses: Brian Sullivan

TEXT OF THE EXAMINATION

[Jury enters.]

- - - -

THE COURT: Call your witness.

MR. LONGER: Brian Sullivan.

THE CRIER: State your full name and spell your last name, please.

THE WITNESS: Brian Sullivan, S-U-L-L-I-V-A-N.

BRIAN SULLIVAN, WITNESS, after having been first duly sworn, was examined and testified as follows:

- - - -

MR. LONGER: For the record, we are calling Mr. Sullivan as of cross.

[Comment] In most jurisdictions, an adverse party can be examined on direct as though under cross-examination. Here, the witness, who is an employee of the defendant, is treated as its agent and cross is allowed. Indeed, the counsel for Blue Cross does not even object. We think it might have been wise to object, however. A mere employee is not necessarily adverse, and, as we shall shortly see, Sullivan does not and does not even try to hurt the plaintiff. Moreover, the leeway given to plaintiff's counsel by allowing him to examine by cross-examination is used very effectively by plaintiff's counsel. Watch.

- - - -

BY MR. LONGER:

Q: Good morning, Mr. Sullivan.

A: Good morning.

Q: We have met before, correct?

A: Correct.

Q: You were at my office for a deposition on October 25th, 1995; is that correct?

A: Yes.

Q: And you gave testimony that day under oath; is that correct?

A: Correct.

Q: You're an employee of Independence Blue Cross, right?

A: Yes.

[Comment] All of this is to remind the witness that counsel has the wherewithal to punish the witness if he deviates from his prior testimony.

Q: You work for Pennsylvania Blue Shield also?

A: Yes.

Q: Do you write policies for both Independence Blue Cross and Pennsylvania Blue Shield simultaneously?

A: Yes.

Q: You're a senior broker specialist; is that correct?

A: Correct.

Q: That's the title of your position?

A: Yes.

Q: And that is a position within the brokerage firm of Independence Blue Cross; is that correct?

A: Correct.

Q: And you've been in that position since April, 1992; is that correct?

A: Correct.

Q: And your job is to bring in new sales accounts through brokers; is that right?

A: Yes.

Q: And you work mostly with primary brokers; is that correct?

A: Correct.

Q: Primary brokers is a term of art within the company; isn't that true?

A: Excuse me?

Q: Primary brokers is something that Blue Cross calls particular brokers; isn't it?

A: Yes.

[Comment] All of this is crisp and leading. The witness is under control and the attorney is showing power. Now in a safe area, he opens the examination for a refreshing moment, giving the witness a chance to explain.

Q: Would you explain to the Jury what a primary broker is?

A: A primary broker is an agency or broker firm that we have appointed as individual to have other sub-producers, other brokers in the community, to place their business through, and then it comes to us. We pay all of our compensation to that primary broker and the primary broker then pays the commissions to the sub-producing brokers. It helps eliminate us receiving hundreds upon hundreds of calls into our department, that can filter through the primary first and then come to us.

Q: Now, a primary broker signs a document, right, an agreement—

A: A contract.

[Comment] Far from adverse, Sullivan is helping, with both hands.

Q: In 1995, did Tower Financial Planning Associates have a contract to be a primary broker with Blue Cross/ Blue Shield?

A: Not to the best of my knowledge.

Q: To the best of your knowledge, in 1995, Tower would not know what the terms of your contract were; is that fair to say?

[Comment] That is a tough question, because it requires a bit of mind reading.

A: Could you restate that, please?

Q: Doesn't it stand to reason that since Tower was not a primary broker, it would not know the terms of a primary broker contract that you offered in 1995?

A: I don't believe I can answer that with a yes or no without an explanation to you.

[Comment] The witness is not comfortable with the speculation which has now gone into major mind reading, but counsel insists.

Q: Why don't we get an answer and then you can explain.

A: Yes.

Q: Yes, Tower would know the terms?

[Comment] Counsel does not like the answer, and repeats it. So he gets the answer again.

A: I would believe so, since they worked through a primary broker, and the primary broker and the sub-producing broker had a contract that they signed.

[Comment] Ouch! Asked for a guess, the witness did so against counsel's wishes. Whatever the point counsel wanted to

make with this testimony, it was not made, because counsel had nothing to confront the witness with when the witness did not give the desired answer—nothing physical and no rule or law of probability. See Vol. III, pp. 57–60. So he got an answer that he did not want, and has to change focus.

Q: In 1995, did Tower have an agreement as a sub-producing broker, do you know?

A: To the best of my knowledge, they did.

Q: And who was that with?

A: Philadelphia Benefits.

Q: On April 7th, 1995, you met with Mr. Sussman to visit Mr. Sweeney at the Ironworkers Local 399; is that correct?

A: That's correct.

Q: And Mr. Sweeney is the co-chairman of the Board of Trustees for the Ironworkers; is that correct?

A: Yes.

Q: And you understood him to be the Head of the Ironworkers, didn't you?

A: My perception was that he was.

[Comment] This fellow, as one may see, is far from adverse, and now the examiner is making solid points.

Q: Now, you understood when you met with Mr. Sussman on April 7th that he was a broker, right?

A: Yes.

Q: And generally speaking, do brokers sell policies, because of people that they know and people that they meet?

A: Yes.

Q: And it's the connections that they have which allow them to sell more and more business?

A: In one way, yes.

Q: In one way, connections is the name of the game in selling insurance; is that right?

A: In one way.

[Comment] That is an excellent exposition – argument by counsel. The word "connection" might have been replaced by the less coarse "relationships," but then again the jury might not have gotten it as well. In any case, counsel is not only making hay with the witness, he is doing his opening right through him. See Vol. III, pp. 1–2, 7–8.

Q: Now, I would like you to look at Exhibit P-30, which is the black binder and there are tabs, Philadelphia Benefits, is that one of the principals there of a gentleman by the name of Mr. Eric Raymond?

A: Yes.

Q: Do you know if Mr. Raymond ever showed Mr. Sussman a primary broker contract?

A: Not to the best of my knowledge.

[Comment] Now, how would he know that?

Q: He did not to the best of your knowledge? You're not aware of it?

A: I'm not aware of him looking at the contract.

[Comment] Again, counsel has fished and come up dry. He has nothing with which to confront the witness.

Q: Now, Exhibit 30 is your planner, your calendar for the year 1995; is that correct?

A: Yes.

Q: And this document on Page IBC-312, reflects both a conversation that you had with Mr. Sussman and the fact that you were going to meet with him on April 7th, 1995; is that correct?

A: Yes.

Q: And among the things that it tells you, aside from the directions of where to meet Mr. Sussman at the Woodcrest Shopping Center, is that he was looking, you have, "a percent of savings there"; is that right?

A: Correct.

Q: And he told you that he wanted a percentage of the savings; is that correct?

A: Correct.

[Comment] Some adverse witness! Now the question is whether counsel should have used Sullivan before the Sweeney deposition and, indeed, given what Sullivan has to say, whether Sweeney should have been used at all.

Q: And you also have a note "Preferred Care PPO cross only." That is a note, that reflects that Preferred Care provided physicians' services; is that correct?

A: Correct.

Q: And then there is a note below that which says, "Percent of Ironworkers." Do you see that?

A: Yes.

Q: And that was telling you that Mr. Sussman wanted a percentage commission—or a contract that you had previously been talking about with respect to the Ironworkers; is that correct?

A: No.

[Comment] Not a good answer for the examiner. Now, watch the next question.

Q: What does your note there tell you?

[Comment] That is a completely nonleading question. The witness can answer as he wills. Now, watch the answer.

A: That is one percent of claims as a primary broker override, <u>that he was requesting</u>.

[Comment] This is wonderful for the plaintiff, but it is not clear. Does counsel clarify it? Sullivan gives him that Sussman wanted a commission, but the word is not used, nor is it clear who Sussman wanted the commission from. Moreover, the 1 percent override is a critical amount that needs clarification.

Q: <u>I see. Fine.</u> On April 7th you met with Mr. Sussman at the Woodcrest Shopping Center, right?

[Comment] It may be "fine" for the examiner and he may "see," but do the jurors understand the important admission that has just been elicited? The examiner, however, changes the subject. So far we only have Sussman "requesting"—did Sullivan agree to the request? This entire subject deserved to be mined and refined.

A: Yes.

Q: And you drove down together from that shopping center to the Local 39 office, correct?

A: Yes.

Q: And did Mr. Sussman say to you in that car drive that he was responsible for bringing Preferred Care to the Ironworkers?

A: Yes.

[Comment] Is this self-proclamation hearsay? Does the next question call for hearsay?

Q: And did Mr. Sussman tell you that he had met earlier with the Ironworkers and Ms. Hardy?

A: No.

Q: <u>He did not tell you that</u>?

A: No.

[Comment] Counsel does not like the last answer, and, not knowing what to do about it, repeats it. A sure sign of a cross-examiner in difficulty. Vol. III, pp. 59–60.

Q: To your knowledge, you believed that he had a meeting with Ms. Hardy scheduled and canceled; is that what you're saying?

A: Can I give an explanation of it? You use the word canceled, it was—

Q: Scheduled.

A: Mr. Sussman explained to me that there was an appointment set by himself and Ms. Hardy, and Ms. Hardy did not make the appointment.

Q: And it's your testimony that Mr. Sussman was only concerned about the broken appointment; is that right?

A: In reference to Ms. Hardy yes.

[Comment] One wonders if much of this testimony about what Sussman said, and what Sussman's position was, and what "concerned" Sussman could have been excluded as hearsay and speculation, respectively. So far, however, the witness has given much to the plaintiff. Now counsel asks for more than the man is likely to give, particularly as it is against a co-employee.

Q: He didn't tell you that he thought he couldn't trust Ms. Hardy?

A: He stated to me that Eric Raymond asked him to call me and deal with me since I work with the broker community and go on the call with him.

[Comment] They are passing like ships in the night. The answer is totally unresponsive—because the witness will not do what the examiner wants—that is, cast aspersions upon his colleague Hardy. Nevertheless, counsel tries again.

Q: And he didn't tell you or did he tell you that he felt he couldn't trust Ms. Hardy after having spoken to Mr. Raymond?

A: I don't recall the words "could not trust her," being said.

[Comment] Sullivan does not want to denigrate his co-Blues employees. We still wonder why there is no objection to Sussman's statement about Sussman's musings about Hardy's trustworthiness on hearsay grounds and also on speculation and also on plain materiality, if it comes to that.

Q: In words or substance, he was trying to convey to you that <u>he felt</u> that <u>he couldn't trust her</u>; is that right?

[Comment] Picking up on the witness's hiding behind nonrecollection of exact words, counsel cleverly rephrases the question—a question that we suggest should have been objected to.

A: I wouldn't get that perception from the conversation. I got the perception that he wanted to work with me because of the broken appointment and Eric Raymond directed him in my direction. What he conveyed to me was that she had broken the appointment and he was upset about that broken appointment, and in talking to Eric Raymond, Eric directed him to my attention to go on the call since I work with brokers.

[Comment] The witness is getting closer, but still no cigar. Sullivan will give that Hardy broke an appointment, but not that she is dishonest. Still no objections, and this emboldens the examiner to do it again.

Q: Did <u>he tell you</u> that <u>he felt</u> that Ms. Hardy was going <u>behind his back</u>?

A: In <u>that</u> conversation, no.

[Comment] Oh, ho! Notice the "that conversation." But counsel does not follow up the invitation to seek another conversation and, unfortunately, the point gets lost. For our purposes, the point is that when you enter a subject, close it. Do not prematurely go into another. See Vol. III, pp. 61–62.

Q: Now, the two of you spoke about going with an option using Blair Mill, correct?

A: And Blue Cross, both.

Q: And Blair Mill is a PPO, which is a subsidiary of Blue Cross/Blue Shield; is that right?

A: Blair Mill is a third-party administrator and offers many different types of plan designs, but it is owned by Blue Cross.

Q: Is it also owned by Blue Shield?

A: Not as of today.

Q: In 1995?

A: Yes.

Q: So, in the relevant time period that we are talking about, it was owned by Blue Cross and Blue Shield?

A: Yes.

Q: And Mr. Sussman brought you to meet Mr. Sweeney because he wanted to get them to contract with either Blue Cross or Blair Mill; isn't that correct?

[Comment] Notice how counsel has Sullivan read Sussman's mind by the use of "he wanted. . . ." There being no objection, Sullivan buys it.

A: He wanted me to explain the opportunity that we could bring to the table for networks because they were having difficulties.

Q: Right. With respect to with Blue Cross or a Blair Mill alternative, correct?

A: Correct.

Q: And he thought that he could get a commission with your assistance; isn't that correct?

A: Yes.

[Comment] Again, excellent. At least as to Sussman's intent and purpose, although we still do not fathom how counsel was allowed to use phrases like "he thought." Nonetheless, he did. Yet it is but half a loaf. Did Sullivan agree to give him a com-

mission? That is the real issue: not what Sussman wants, but what he was promised and by whom, and from whom. But then again, perhaps no one has such answers. We still have not heard about that because counsel has not asked him.

Q: Now, you met with Mr. Sweeney that day; is that correct?

A: Yes.

Q: And you talked about the networks that we had just discussed, right?

A: We discussed networks, correct.

Q: And you talked about locations, that Ironworkers had members all throughout the region here?

A: Yes.

Q: And you talked about the capabilities of Independence Blue Cross to service the Fund, right?

A: Yes.

Q: And did Mr. Sweeney tell you that he was familiar with Blue Cross/Blue Shield?

A: Yes.

Q: And did Mr. Sweeney tell you that the Fund was interested in going with the Blues?

A: Yes.

Q: After the meeting, did you provide the network directories to Mr. Sussman?

A: Yes.

Q: And Mr. Sweeney wanted to know who the doctors were that were in those directories, didn't he?

A: Yes.

Q: And that's why you gave the information to Mr. Sussman, right?

A: Yes.

Q: So that he could then take it to Mr. Sweeney, right?

A: Yes.

Q: And to your knowledge, Mr. Sussman provided that material to Mr. Sweeney?

A: To the best of my knowledge.

[Comment] What knowledge?

Q: And that was a service that the two of you provided to the Ironworkers Fund in connection with <u>trying to sell</u> Independence Blue Cross or Blair Mill?

A: Yes.

[Comment] Well done! So much for the defense that Sussman had done nothing! But, again, why not make the point clear by closing it? "Would it be true to claim to this jury that Mr. Sussman did nothing to aid Blue Cross to get the insurance contract from the union?" Or even, "Did you hear the opening when counsel promised to prove that Mr. Sussman had done nothing . . . ?"

Q: Now, you had spoken to Ms. Hardy about your meeting with Mr. Sussman and Mr. Sweeney; isn't that right?

A: Yes.

Q: And this is after the meeting, obviously?

A: Correct.

Q: And she was following your efforts to quote Blair Mill to the Ironworkers, wasn't she?

A: It was my understanding that after our meeting, we would stay in contact with each other and let everybody know what was coming along in the sense of trying to quote the Ironworkers.

Q: So, Ms. Hardy knew that Mr. Sussman was still

trying to sell Blue Cross to the Fund after that broken appointment that you had discussed earlier, right?

A: Yes.

Q: And this was after April 7th, 1995, correct?

A: Correct.

[Comment] Counsel is doing an excellent job. He is truly hammering the defendant's theory that Sussman is a leech who did nothing—but will the jury get the point in the here and now? If not, if counsel's purpose is not to argue now but to save it for summation, we think this is a mistake. Vol. III, pp. 220, 221, 225, 226, 228; Vol. IV, pp. 27–28.

Q: Now, I'd like you to flip to the next exhibit, which is Plaintiff's Exhibit Number-31, and would you tell the jurors what this document is?

A: That's my sophisticated way to retrieve my voice mail. I receive many voice mails everyday and I retrieve my voice mails and write them on a steno pad.

Q: It's a steno pad, correct?

A: Correct.

Q: And on April 12, 1995, you got a phone call from Leonard Sussman; is that what page IBC-299.1 is?

A: Yes.

Q: Page 2 of that document indicates that you got a phone call from Mr. Sussman on April 13th of 1995; isn't that correct?

A: Yes.

Q: That's a second phone call?

A: Yes.

Q: Next page, that's a phone call from Mr. Sussman on the 24th of April, correct?

A: Correct.

Q: Next page, that's a phone call from Mr. Sussman from the 25th of April, correct?

A: Correct.

Q: That's the fourth phone call—

A: Yes.

Q: —in your log. Next page, we have a fifth phone call on 4/28/95, correct?

A: Correct.

[Comment] Isn't that wonderful? And he keeps at it!

Q: And we could keep doing this. You have a phone call—on the 1st of May, you have a phone call on the 10th of May. You have a phone call on the 2nd of June. You have a phone call on the 7th of June. You have a phone call on the 6th of July. You have a phone call on the 7th of August. You have a phone call on the 8th of August. You have a phone call on the 15th of August, right?

A: Correct.

Q: Now, if I did my math right, I just counted out phone calls up until the 13th of August, you could agree with me or not, if you care to count.

A: Would you like—I don't know that number to be factual. I didn't count it.

Q: Well, why don't you count them?

A: [Witness complies.] Are you going all the way to August 31st?

Q: No. But if we did, we would have had 16?

A: I come up with 18.

Q: Eighteen. All right. You would say Mr. Sussman was persistent, wasn't he?

A: In calling me, yes.

Q: He was interested in pursuing a contract with Blue Cross and Blue Shield using your services; wouldn't you say that is correct?

A: He was pursuing, yes.

[Comment] The point must not slip-slide away. You do not want to argue that Sussman was using Sullivan, you want to argue that Sullivan was using Sussman. The many calls of the plaintiff were not as an interfering meddler. He was doing it for the insurance company that had agreed to pay him for assisting it. And he sure was working at it. Counsel is painting a much different picture than the do-nothing Sussman presented by the defense.

Q: And during one of those phone calls in August, did Mr. Sussman tell you that he was concerned that the Ironworkers were going to use their consultants to go directly to Independence Blue Cross?

A: Yes.

Q: And he was concerned that his commission was in jeopardy; isn't that correct?

A: Yes.

[Comment] We speculate that this last might have been objected to as both hearsay and conclusory as to Sussman's thinking. For his part, plaintiff's counsel still has not dealt with the question: what commission? We still have not heard about an actual deal between Sullivan and Sussman, or Sussman and the union, or anyone for that matter.

Q: And Mr. Sussman had told you about a meeting between Ms. Hardy and Mr. Maresca in New York at the end of July; is that correct?

A: He told me that the Ironworkers had met, but not about Ms. Hardy's meeting, no.

Q: But you <u>understood</u> that he <u>knew</u> that there was a meeting with the consultants and Independence Blue Cross?

A: He had a <u>concern</u> that Mr. Maresca was going to come directly to Blue Cross.

Q: And so he <u>wanted</u> to immediately or as quickly as possible, set up another meeting with Mr. Sweeney; is that right?

A: Yes.

[Comment] Again, these questions, focusing as they do on Sussman's knowledge and concerns, are potentially objectionable.

Q: And so on August 21st, 1995, the two of you again went and met Mr. Sweeney; is that correct?

A: Yes.

Q: And if we go back now to Exhibit-30, we see an entry on Page 315 of that document, Monday the 21st of 1995, "Woodcrest Shopping, Exit 32, 295, Leonard Sussman," correct?

A: Correct.

Q: And that's your note reflecting that you met with Mr. Sussman on the 21st to meet with Mr. Sweeney; is that right?

A: Yes.

Q: Now, just prior to that meeting on the 21st, you met with Ms. Hardy; is that right?

A: Prior to August 21st.

Q: Prior to that August 21st meeting with Mr. Sussman, you met with Ms. Hardy; is that right?

A: No, I did not.

Q: You do not recall talking to Ms. Hardy; is that what you're saying?

A: I had a meeting after the 21st with Ms. Hardy.

Q: But you didn't tell her before then that Mr. Sussman was still trying to broker a deal with the Ironworkers?

A: I don't recall any conversations with Ms. Hardy about what was going on <u>prior</u>.

[Comment] Whatever counsel's point, it seems to be lost in the befores and afters. Unfortunately, counsel moves on without the benefit of the Sullivan-Hardy conversations after the 21st.

Q: Then on August 1st—I'm sorry. On August 21st, you went to Mr. Sweeney's office?

A: Yes.

Q: By now, you knew that a request for a proposal by the Segal Company was outstanding; is that right?

A: From Mr. Sussman, yes.

Q: And the two of you, Mr. Sussman and yourself, when you spoke to Mr. Sweeney, focused only on the Blair Mill alternative and not Independence Blue Cross; is that correct?

A: Yes.

Q: And you tried to present an alternative to Independence Blue Cross; is that fair to say?

A: Yes.

Q: And you were doing that because you understood what was going on with Ms. Hardy was taking the place for the Independence Blue Cross and you can only offer the Blair Mill alternative, right?

A: I did so because Mr. Sussman requested me to explain Blair Mill.

[Comment] He is simply not going to hit Ms. Hardy. No matter what the lawyer does, he will not get that answer. But . . . so what? When the attorney makes an assertion, and the witness

makes a denial, the jury votes. They vote on every Q&A during cross. Didn't you? It does not matter what the witness says, it only matters what the jurors believe. That is why most of the so-called commandments of cross, bottomed on a fear of witness answers (always lead; just "yes" and "no," etc.), are plain wrong. See Vol. III, pp. 23–28, 217–219.

Q: Now, did Mr. Sweeney at that time tell you that it was too late?

A: No.

Q: Did he have any interest at all in the Blair Mill alternative?

A: My perception was he wasn't interested really in what we were talking about.

Q: He had told you to call Mr. Maresca, did he not?

A: No.

Q: Did Mr. Sussman ask you to speak to Mr. Maresca?

A: Yes.

Q: And did you try to reach Mr. Maresca?

A: Yes.

Q: Did you try to write a letter to Mr. Maresca?

A: No.

Q: Did Mr. Sussman ask you to write a letter?

A: No.

Q: He only asked you to give a phone call?

A: Yes.

Q: You were here yesterday, when you heard Mr. Sussman's testimony?

A: Yes.

Q: Do you <u>think</u> he was just <u>mistaken</u> between a phone call and a letter?

A: I heard what he said.

[Comment] This question was totally impermissible, unless the witness has studied mind reading.

Q: Now, Mr. Maresca was the firm's consultant; isn't that right?

A: At this point, I know that, yes.

[Comment] Counsel really means the union's consultant.

Q: You did not know that then?

A: No.

Q: Did you <u>understand</u> that Mr. Maresca had <u>advised</u> the Ironworkers to go with Blue Cross and not use a broker?

A: At that point, I did not.

[Comment] This is not permissible either, unless the witness had personal knowledge. See Fed. R. Evid., for example. But there was no objection.

Q: We talked about you coming to my office—

A: Uh-huh.

Q: —to testify?

A: Yes.

Q: And we talked about you testifying under oath?

A: Yes.

Q: And at that deposition, do you recall me asking what is your understanding—

MR. SONNENFELD: May I ask you what page and line, please?

MR. LONGER: Certainly, I apologize. Page 87, Line 2.

BY MR. LONGER:

Q: Do you recall me asking, what is your—

MR. LONGER: May I approach, Your Honor?

THE COURT: Sure.

MR. LONGER: I'm already a step up.

BY MR. LONGER:

[Comment] Watch this. The illegality of the question and answer is highlighted by the deposition testimony that the defense counsel has been specifically directed to, but still no objection.

Q: "What is your understanding of the advice that Mr. Maresca provided to the Ironworkers?" Do you recall me asking you that question?

A: Yes.

Q: And your answer was: "<u>Based on Mr. Sussman's comments to me</u>, was that Mr. Maresca advised the Ironworkers that he would go to Blue Cross on their behalf and not use a broker."

A: That's what is stated there. I'm referring to the meeting of the 21st when I was giving my answer. At that meeting, I did not recall at that time that they had been in contract with us. That's what—understood your question to be, is that they went with the Blues at that time. <u>Mr. Sussman explained to me</u> that they were issuing proposals directly, but at that point had no knowledge that they had agreed to go with Blue Cross. That's what I'm referring to.

[Comment] What Sussman says to Sullivan is hearsay when offered by Sussman, and this whole line of questioning is premised on Sussman's own proclamation about what someone else—Maresca—did outside of Sussman's presence, which compounds the problem.

Q: My point is that you understood from Mr. Sussman that they were not going to use a broker?

A: <u>That was his belief.</u>

[Comment] Again. He got to do it again. Not only does he say what Sussman said, he says what Sussman actually believed.

Q: Based on what <u>Mr. Maresca</u> was telling the Iron-workers?

A: Based on what Mr. Sussman informed me of, yes.

[Comment] So now he has Sussman saying what Maresca said to the whole Ironworkers as related by Sussman to Sullivan, and still no objection. So counsel gets to do it again, and this time, he tucks in the commission.

Q: <u>And the point of all that was that they could avoid a commission to Mr. Sussman; isn't that right?</u>

[Comment] Now counsel is asking the witness to explain what was in the minds of numerous people. And so he does.

A: From what Mr. Sussman explained to me, Mr. Maresca said they could go direct and not use a broker. He could do it directly for them. He was their consultant on their pension fund and they were going to do the health insurance, also.

Q: And he could avoid a commission to the broker; isn't that right?

A: Mr. Sussman shared to me that that was his statement, Mr. Sussman's statement, to avoid not paying a commission.

[Comment] Well, perhaps there was no objection because one can argue that all this hearsay actually helps the defendant. Why? Because it shows that it was Maresca, the agent of the union, who got the union to avoid the payment of Sussman's commission. But right now it sure looks as though Sussman is getting the short end . . . and juries do not like that. Let us see if this is made clear in the next examination by the defense.

Q: Now, you get paid a salary and a commission; isn't that right?

A: Yes.

Q: And with respect to the Ironworkers, you wanted to get a sale, didn't you?

A: Correct.

Q: And you would have liked <u>your broker</u> to have gotten the sale; isn't that right?

A: Yes.

[Comment] Plaintiff's counsel is getting away with larceny. What does what Sullivan likes *have to do with anything? And notice, Sussman has now become the Blues "broker." But then counsel goes to the well again, and gets a slightly different answer.*

Q: And Mr. Sussman was <u>your broker</u>, wasn't he?

A: Mr. Sussman was <u>the broker</u>.

[Comment] Excellent, these last four questions nail the point — except Sullivan will not buy the "your" broker a second time, and answers "the" broker. Counsel goes further, but unfortunately does not close the point.

Q: And he was the one who connected you to the Ironworkers, correct?

A: He introduced me to Mr. Sweeney.

[Comment] See, no closure. Why not nail it down? "Sussman was representing your company in this regard?" "When you say 'the broker,' you mean the broker on the Blue Cross/Union deal, right?"

Q: Now, in 1992, are you aware of the Ironworkers ever asking for a quote from Independence Blue Cross?

A: Not to the best of my knowledge.

Q: In 1993, are you aware of the Ironworkers ever asking for a quote from Independence Blue Cross or Pennsylvania Blue Shield?

A: Not to the best of my knowledge.

Q: How about into 1994?

A: Not to the best of my knowledge.

Q: In 1995, they did ask for a quote, correct?

A: Correct.

Q: And in 1995, you knew that Mr. Sussman was
<u>actively</u> involved with you trying to get business <u>to</u> the
Ironworkers, correct?

A: Again, I can answer that but I would have to
explain, because you're using the word "actively," and I'm
not—I can't fully agree with the word "actively."

*[Comment] Poor Sullivan is struggling, 18 telephone calls and
some meetings later, to do something for Blue Cross—this
adverse witness. But why does counsel say business to the
Ironworkers?*

Q: All right. You knew that Mr. Sussman was involved
in trying to get business <u>to</u> the Ironworkers, in 1995, correct?

A: Correct.

Q: And you knew that Mr. Sussman was trying to
work with Ms. Hardy in 1995, correct?

A: I knew that she had an appointment that she
broke.

*[Comment] He always hides behind the broken appointment
in an effort not to hit Hardy any harder than that, but he has
not answered the question. Unfortunately, the examiner did not
repeat it. See Vol. III, pp. 51–53.*

Q: Now, after all of the activities that you and Mr.
Sussman engaged in with Mr. Sweeney, and all the phone
calls and the transfer of information to Mr. Sussman, you
felt that you had performed a service to the Ironworkers
on behalf of Blue Cross and Blue Shield; is that fair to
say?

A: My delivering directories was a service, yes.

Q: You wrote a memo to your boss <u>asking to get a commission</u> because of <u>that</u>; is that right?

A: Correct.

[Comment] That last is not clear. What counsel means is that Sullivan sought a commission for himself *based on what* Sussman *did. Watch. But will the jury get it? Watch that too.*

Q: And the memo—I have it here—it's Exhibit Number-32, is talking about—well, let me just ask you this. This is a memorandum which you prepared; is that correct?

A: Correct.

Q: And you prepared it in the regular course of your business; is that fair to say?

A: I write memos, yes.

Q: And you prepared it on or about October 13th, 1995?

A: Yes.

Q: And in this memo, you wrote to your boss asking to get a commission, correct?

A: Correct.

Q: And the memo is talking about the April of 1995 time period; is that correct?

A: I would have to recall. It was during the time that I was meeting with Mr. Sweeney.

Q: And in this document, yet, say, "My concern here was that Jay had directed that if the case was sold by my broker, that a split would have to be made with the Health and Welfare Department." In that first line, the broker is referring to Mr. Sussman; is that correct?

A: Correct.

Q: And then in the next line, you say, "I must say that my broker did start the group up again in looking at Blue Cross." Do you see that?

A: Yes.

[Comment] We suggest that this memo should have been used when Sullivan quibbled about whose broker Sussman was. When you enter a point, close it. The same memo could have been used again for the excellent point that Sullivan, who did little, wanted a commission in part for what Sussman did. But back to the point of just who Sullivan is writing on behalf of.

Q: Now, at the time that you wrote this memo, you believed that to be the case, didn't you?

A: Based on information that Mr. Sussman had given me and what I knew at that time yes.

Q: You felt that Mr. Sussman got Blue Cross looking—I'm sorry, got the Ironworkers looking into Blue Cross, right?

A: With the information at that point I had, I believed that he got me in front of the Ironworkers.

[Comment] He might then have asked, "And you thought he deserved to be compensated for that by Blue Cross?"

Q: And what you understood was that the Ironworkers were going forward with a contract with Blue Cross, that Ms. Hardy had worked out; is that right?

A: At that point, yes.

Q: And that proposal ultimately ended up in a contract with Blue Cross and the Ironworkers, correct?

A: I have never seen the contract, but they did come with us, yes.

MR. LONGER: Thank you, Mr. Sullivan. I have no more questions.

ANALYSIS OF THE DIRECT EXAMINATION

The first thing counsel does is to indicate that the witness is being called "on cross." This is an indication that the witness is employed by the adverse party and thus counsel may examine the witness by asking leading questions. We have already noted our concern that this was not challenged. If it had been, successfully, the direct would have been far more difficult.

The examiner elicits the title "senior broker specialist," which strongly suggests that the witness is a senior official dealing with brokers. The examiner next elicits the fact that the witness's job is to bring in new sales accounts "through brokers" and that he deals mostly with brokers. Counsel leads until he gets to the concept of "primary broker." Once the witness acknowledges familiarity with the concept, counsel asks the witness to explain it. The explanation really is not as important as the point that Tower and Sussman were not primary brokers in 1994 or 1995 and thus did not know the terms of the typical arrangement that the insurer had with these brokers.

When the witness indicates that a "yes" or "no" will not provide an adequate answer, note that the examiner does not insist on simply a one-word answer. This is correct. See Vol. III, pp. 24–25. He permits an explanation, but in this instance the explanation hurts the plaintiff's case. Counsel should deal with this. In this situation, the rules and laws of probability would provide some help. It is almost a certainty that, if the witness did not show Sussman a primary broker policy, he would have no personal knowledge of whether anyone else did. Thus, the following questions would have made sense.

Q: You never showed Mr. Sussman a copy of the primary broker policy?

Q: You never summarized for him what the primary broker policy said?

Q: As far as you know, Mr. Sussman never had a primary broker policy with any Blue Cross or Blue Shield?

Q: As far as you know, Mr. Sussman never had a primary broker policy with any health insurer?

The examiner must know that the witness's primary loyalty is to his employer. He is bound to want to avoid saying anything negative about his colleague, Ms. Hardy. So, he naturally resists agreeing that Mr. Sussman had told him negative things about Ms. Hardy. The questions that could have been asked with little risk are these:

Q: You knew that Mr. Sussman was supposed to meet with Ms. Hardy?

Q: Ms. Hardy still worked for Blue Cross when you met with Mr. Sussman?

Q: It was Mr. Sussman who sought you out?

Q: So, you knew for some reason Mr. Sussman wanted to meet with you rather than Ms. Hardy?

As you finish reading this direct examination, you must have the feeling that another shoe is yet to drop. Sullivan's answers sound like he is saying that in October 1995, he thought he was entitled to a commission, but if he has the opportunity he is going to say that he learned something afterward that changed his mind. Remember, he works for Blue Cross. He won't even have a salary, let alone a commission, if he is fired. If the examiner knows that on cross-examination the witness is going to make a point, the examiner might well choose to deal with it first. That does not happen here, so the cross-examiner gets the first shot.

Without reading the cross-examination, can you guess the explanation for Sullivan's change of position regarding the commission? Our guess is that, when we read the transcript, we will find Sullivan saying that based on what he now knows, he believes that neither he nor Sussman was entitled to a commission. It is possible that the direct examiner could have dealt with this almost certain change of view by providing an explanation through questions before the jury even heard the witness's new view of the world. Imagine the following questions, for example:

Q: You wrote that October 13, 1995, memorandum because you believed you were entitled to a commission?

Q: And you believed on October 13, 1995, when you put your words in writing for your boss, that your broker, Mr. Sussman, was entitled to a commission?

Q: You didn't withdraw your memorandum and your request for a commission later in October 1995?

Q: You didn't withdraw your memorandum and your request for a commission in November 1995?

Q: You didn't withdraw your memorandum and your request for a commission in December 1995?

Q: It was only after Mr. Sussman sued Blue Cross, the company that pays your salary and your commissions, that you changed your mind and decided that neither you nor Mr. Sussman was entitled to a commission?

Q: You changed your mind after Mr. Sussman sued, to protect your job?

You know that the witness will vehemently deny that he changed his mind to protect his job. Nevertheless, if the questions are asked in this series, no matter how Sullivan answers, what will the jury believe? See Vol. III, pp. 177–184, 217–219.

TEXT OF THE CROSS-EXAMINATION

THE COURT: Cross-examine.

MR. SONNENFELD: May I proceed; Your Honor?

[Comment] Now, although this is styled cross, is it? Sullivan knows that the next lawyer represents his employer.

THE WITNESS: Your Honor, may I ask for water, please?

BY MR. SONNENFELD:

Q: Mr. Sullivan, you were asked by Mr. Longer a number of questions about Plaintiff's Exhibit Number-32, which Mr. Longer blew up to life-size proportions, and that was your memo to Mr. Poor, October 13th, 1995, correct?

A: Correct.

Q: And Mr. Poor was at that time your boss?

A: Yes.

Q: And in the memo you said that my broker, meaning Mr. Sussman, started the group up again in looking at Blue Cross?

A: I stated that, yes.

Q: You believed that to be true at that time; is that correct, sir?

A: Yes.

Q: What was the source of that statement?

A: The information that I'd gotten from Mr. Sussman at that point, and just my involvement that I had with Mr. Sweeney at that time.

Q: And based on what you know today, do you consider that statement to be true?

A: What I know today?

Q: Yes, sir.

A: No.

[Comment] Sullivan has just swept off the table everything he had put on it on direct.

Q: Why is that, sir?

A: Because I learned over time that the way the Ironworkers came to us and all that, I really didn't have any activity that warranted a commission.

[Comment] That was, obviously, not the answer counsel sought. The reformation he wanted was not on Sullivan's claim for a commission, but on the entitlement of Sussman's claim for a commission.

Q: And did you, in fact, receive from your employer, Independence Blue Cross, any commission in respect to the Ironworkers' contract with Blue Cross?

A: No.

Q: Do you think <u>you</u> were treated fairly by your employer?

A: Yes, I was.

[Comment] Do you think this Q&A will matter to a jury? After all, the man works there — what else is he to say? "No, I think my boss is a rotten . . . ."

Q: Now, let's step back, the term "broker of record letter" that's been used in this case, first of all, is there a difference between a broker and an agent?

[Comment] Nice use of transition questions. See Vol. II, p. 18.

A: Yes.

Q: Can you tell us what the difference is?

A: An agent is employed by a company and represents a company, and a broker is an independent individual that represents a client, a group.

Q: Now, was Mr. Sussman an agent of Independence Blue Cross?

A: No.

Q: Was he, then, a broker as you have used the term?

A: Yes.

[Comment] Technically, this examination is well done. Will the jury see the meaning of the defense? If Sussman was not the agent of Blue Cross, he was the agent of the union. Isn't that the

point? But counsel must ask it. The jury must not be left to its own conclusions. Once the point is made, then they must be told that if Sussman is the agent of the union, it is the union that should pay him.

Q: Now, what does the term broker of record mean?

A: The term broker of record means given by a group on behalf of an individual at this point a broker, to represent them to a company and receive information and compensation.

[Comment] Is that answer clear? If not, more questions should be asked, e.g., "If Sussman represented the union, as a broker, would he need a letter signed by them before Blue Cross would send him a percentage of the premium received from the union as a commission?"

Q: And what does the term "broker of record letter" mean?

A: It's the actual document that we receive that spells out, naming the individual, the entity, the broker and their ability to represent them to the company.

Q: Now, does Independence Blue Cross have a policy with respect to broker of record letters?

A: Yes.

Q: Can you tell us what that policy is?

A: That any case brought in by a non-employee, meaning a broker, must provide a broker of record letter in order to receive compensation or information.

Q: And what is the reason for that policy?

A: Twofold. One, to have authorization to pay commissions on behalf of a group to a broker, and secondly, to be able to release information on behalf of a group to a broker.

Q: And is that policy set forth in any writing?

A: Yes.

[Comment] We think counsel is making points, but he might consider using the documents to authenticate the testimony right here.

Q: And if you would look, please, in the blue notebook before you, if you would turn to Exhibit-22 and Exhibit-23, perhaps start with 22, and tell us what that is?

A: That is a broker checklist that we asked for on submission of new business from a broker.

Q: Does that broker checklist set forth the policy with respect to broker of record letters?

A: Yes, it does, in Section 2 of the letter.

Q: <u>Could</u> you read that?

[Comment] We bet he "could." The examiner is better off saying, "Please read it to his Honor and the jury." But what is being read is the checklist, not the policy on compensation.

A: It's stated as a broker of record letter. It says—the first item is, "Letter is on company letterhead. If letter is not on company letterhead, an explanation is required by the account. Broker is clearly identified. Information matches producing broker information on group enrollment form. Letter is signed by the owner or an officer of the company."

[Comment] Do you think this is clear?

Q: Would you turn please to the next exhibit, Exhibit Number-23. And these, for the record, are Defendant's exhibits. What is that?

A: That is the guidelines for submitting the business to Blue Cross on behalf of a broker.

Q: And do those guidelines contain any provisions with respect to the broker of record letters?

A: Item Number 2, Broker of Record Letter.

Q: Could you read that, please?

A: "Letter on company letterhead. If the letter is not on letterhead, an explanation by the account is required. The broker is clearly identified. Information matches producing broker information on the group enrollment form, signed by the owner or officer of the company."

Q: Now, were those policies with respect to broker of record letters in effect back in 1994 and 1995, during the time of events in question in this case?

A: Yes.

[Comment] Will a jury be able to follow this? And where does this take us on the issues about compensation and commission? But now counsel hits the point, and does it very well indeed.

Q: And in your experience as a broker specialist with Independence Blue Cross for the past several years, are you aware of any insurance in which a broker has received a commission from Independence Blue Cross, without having submitted a broker of record letter from the group?

A: Not to the best of my knowledge.

Q: And in your experience with Independence Blue Cross, have you ever encountered any situation in which a Health and Welfare Fund, a union Health and Welfare Fund, used a broker?

A: Not to the best of my knowledge.

[Comment] Very good. The point is made.

Q: Now, you testified about a meeting that you had on April the 7th, 1995, that Mr. Sussman arranged for you and Mr. Sweeney; is that correct?

A: Yes.

Q: And at the time of that meeting, were you aware of whether or not Ms. Hardy of Independence Blue Cross had ever met with Mr. Sweeney previously?

A: No.

Q: You were not aware?

A: Not to my knowledge, no.

Q: And have you, yourself, ever met Mr. Sweeney before?

A: No.

Q: Or any of the Trustees of the Ironworkers Fund?

A: No.

[Comment] Very good. The point is made, but counsel has a problem: we think this last line of questioning does not help the examiner. Indeed, he seemed surprised by the first answer.

Q: And had you ever met or spoken to Mr. Sussman before that meeting?

A: Not to the best of my knowledge.

Q: And I believe that you told us that in getting that meeting, you met Mr. Sussman at the Woodcrest Shopping Center in New Jersey?

A: Yes.

Q: And then drove down to the meeting in Mr. Sussman's car?

A: Yes.

Q: And in that car ride, was there any discussion of broker of record letters?

A: Yes.

Q: And can you tell us that discussion?

[Comment] "In substance, what did he say to you and what did you say to him about the need for a broker of record letter?" is the better way. See Vol. II, pp. 210–214.

A: Mr. Sussman had stated that he was a broker of record for the group currently, and he wanted to make sure that he was broker of record on the account with us. And I had stated to him that in order for that to occur, he would have to get a broker of record letter from the group.

Q: And did Mr. Sussman indicate to you, one way or another, whether he thought he would be able to get a broker of record letter from the group?

A: I don't recall him saying anything having to do with that.

Q: One way or the other?

A: No.

[Comment] Again, counsel seems surprised by the answer and he should not be, for this witness is one he undoubtedly had access to. But one thing is sure. This union was not going to pay Sussman anything. So . . . "Were you in court when Mr. Sweeney's deposition was read and he testified that Mr. Sussman was not entitled to any broker of record letter and the union would not pay anything?"

Q: But there is no question in your mind that you told him in that car ride, that to get a commission, he would have to have a broker of record letter from the group?

A: I stated that he needed to get a broker of record letter from the group in order for <u>us to</u>—for him to put the business through the Broker Relations Department and be compensated.

[Comment] A little slip. But the examination is excellent. The examiner himself likes it—see the next two words.

Q: <u>Thank you</u>. Now, how long did the meeting last with Mr. Sweeney on April 7th, 1995, and Mr. Sussman?

A: Less than an hour.

Q: And was there any discussion of Mr. Sussman's compensation or commission at that meeting with Mr. Sweeney?

A: No.

[Comment] Counsel is done with the point, and so he moves on.

Q: And I'd like to ask you to turn, if you could, to—we'll go back to the black notebook, the Plaintiff's Exhibits. You were shown on your direct examination by Mr. Longer, Plaintiff's Exhibit-30.

A: Yes.

Q: If you would turn to Page 312.1, I believe that is the very last page in that tab?

A: Yes.

Q: That is your notes on your calendar for April 7th, 1995; is it not?

A: Yes.

Q: At that meeting, can you tell us as best you can, what you recall discussing with Mr. Sussman and Mr. Sweeney?

A: We discussed the activities that Mr. Sweeney perceived the union workers having and the networks they were currently using, primarily Preferred Care. We spoke about the discounts that we would be able to provide to the Health and Welfare Fund. We also discussed the networks that we would use, and at that time he had given me a copy of his card that he carries that listed the networks that they are currently using now, and I took that with me. We also then spoke about what I would need from Mr. Sweeney in order to give him actual numbers, actual proposals, in order to have the Fund take a look at us and whether we are the right solution for them.

Q: And what information did you tell Mr. Sweeney and Mr. Sussman at that meeting on April 7th, 1995, you would need in order to give a quote?

A: Well, in my book, I wrote "they" at the top.

Q: You're referring to Plaintiff's Exhibit-30, Page 312.1?

A: Yes. And what they would owe me would be a census of the group, claims experience, and I'd asked for at least 12 months of claims experience that they currently had. And that would let us [get] started in being able to look at the programs.

Q: And did Mr. Sussman ever provide that information to you?

A: No.

Q: And did anyone ever provide that information to you?

A: No.

[Comment] Well, the point is made that Sussman did not follow through. But, in drawing out all this detail, it certainly seems that Sussman, who had previously met with Sweeney and Hardy, and now with Sweeney and Sullivan, was far more active than counsel made him seem in the opening.

Q: And following that meeting, did Mr. Sussman ever provide you with any information concerning the Fund?

A: No.

Q: And did you ever present a quote to Mr. Sussman for the Fund?

A: No.

Q: And did you ever present any quote to the Fund?

A: No.

[Comment] Does this point help, or does it obscure the point about the need for union approval of a commission?

Q: And now, at this meeting on April 7th, 1995, was there any discussion of what we have referred to as Blair Mill?

A: On April 7th, yes.

Q: And Blair Mill is what is called a third-party administrator; is that correct?

A: Yes.

Q: That administers for groups who are self-insured, administers their claims and charges a fee on top of the claims, is that right?

A: Yes.

Q: At anytime did you ever tell Mr. Sussman that if the Ironworkers went with Blair Mill he could get a commission without the necessity of a broker of record letter?

A: No.

[Comment] We see that we are back on the point about the right to a commission, without union approval, and away from how much was done by Sussman. This is a wise choice.

Q: So, you next met with Mr. Sussman and Mr. Sweeney on August the 21st; is that correct?

A: Correct.

Q: That is some four months later?

A: Yes.

Q: Did you have any communications with Mr. Sweeney or someone from the Ironworkers in between those two meetings?

A: No.

Q: So, it would be correct to say that those two meetings, April 7th, and August 21st, are the only times that you ever met with, or to your knowledge, spoke to anyone from the Ironworkers Fund?

A: Yes.

Q: And the meeting on August 21st, again, did you meet Mr. Sussman in his car at the Woodcrest Shopping Center?

A: Yes.

Q: He then drove you down to that meeting?

A: Yes.

Q: How long did that meeting take place?

A: Wasn't long at all. Thirty minutes at the most.

Q: And at anytime, did you ever tell Mr. Sweeney to avoid using Sussman or Tower?

A: No.

Q: And to the best of your knowledge, at anytime, did anyone on behalf of the Blue Cross or Blue Shield ever tell Mr. Sweeney or anyone at the Ironworkers not to use Mr. Sussman or Tower?

A: No.

[Comment] The last questions are on the tortious interference claim of the plaintiff, but it is doubtful that anyone knows this at the moment. "Are you aware that Mr. Sussman claims that Blue Cross interfered with his contract or business relationship with the union?" And then off you go. "Did you . . ." "Did anyone . . ." And so forth.

MR. SONNENFELD: If you'll bear with me one second, Your Honor.

THE COURT: Sure.

[Short pause.]

MR. SONNENFELD: I have nothing further.

THE COURT: Thank you.

ANALYSIS OF THE CROSS-EXAMINATION

Well, Mr. Sullivan did not surprise us. He loyally supports the arguments made by Blue Cross. He claims that he told

Sussman that Sussman needed a broker of record letter to receive a commission and that he was unaware of any broker receiving a commission without one. He also tries to minimize Sussman's role in Blue Cross's obtaining the Ironworkers account.

This cross-examination, when juxtaposed against the direct examination, demonstrates that whoever gets to a point first has an enormous advantage. There is nothing in the cross-examination that could not have been anticipated and worked into the direct examination in a manner that would have permitted the direct examiner to take the steam out of each point the cross-examiner tries to make.

The rules and laws of probability tell us a lot about Sullivan's changed testimony. Is it plausible that Sullivan would have shown up to meet with Sweeney and have focused on Blair Mill exclusively if Sullivan did not know that Sussman wanted a commission? Is it likely that Sussman knew anything about Blair Mill before Sullivan told him about it? Is it possible that Sullivan had less knowledge about what Sussman had done concerning the Ironworkers when he wrote his October 13, 1995, memorandum than at the time of trial? In short, is the changed testimony plausible? If not, it is fair game on direct and need not await redirect examination.

Look back at the direct examination so that you do not confuse what was actually asked with what we suggest could have been asked. Consider how the cross-examination might have gone had the direct examiner confronted the witness with his changed testimony. Recall that the direct examiner had the chance to treat Sullivan as an adverse witness. We suggest that the examinations of this witness reflect something of a view that there is "our case" and "their case." The facts, however, belong to both sides, and the facts—those things the jury will believe—can be used by a direct examiner before the cross-examiner has a chance to speak.

Sullivan is an example of a witness who can be used to corroborate Sussman and then impeached with respect to his changed testimony in a way that makes Blue Cross look bad. He is extremely important to the plaintiff's case.

TEXT OF THE REDIRECT EXAMINATION

THE COURT: Redirect, counsel?

BY MR. LONGER:

Q: Mr. Sullivan, when Mr. Sonnenfeld asked you in that first car drive going down to visit with Mr. Sussman to visit with Mr. Sweeney, you had mentioned to Mr. Sussman a broker of record letter being <u>needed</u>; do you recall that testimony?

A: Yes.

[Comment] Not a good question and answer for the plaintiff.

Q: And isn't it true, sir, that Mr. Sussman was looking for a way to <u>avoid</u> a broker of record letter and he had told that to you and that is why you were going down to meet with Mr. Sweeney?

A: No.

[Comment] Not a good question for the plaintiff. It sure implies, in this tortious interference claim, that Sussman was looking to get around his client—the union. Actually, the answer helps the plaintiff more than the question.

Q: You're saying that under oath, sir?

[Comment] That last is worthless and objectionable. Lawyers use this when there is nothing else.

A: Mr. Sussman never, that I recall, ever said to me that he was trying to avoid getting a broker of record letter. I can't do business without a broker of record letter.

[Comment] Bang! Counsel got shot.

Q: You can't do—

MR. LONGER: Thank you. I have no further questions.

[Comment] He knows it, and decides to stop.

MR. SONNENFELD: I have nothing further, Your Honor.

[Comment] Very wise, in our view.

THE COURT: Thank you. You may step down. Sir, you're excused.

ANALYSIS OF THE REDIRECT EXAMINATION

The examiner wants desperately to show that Sullivan is not being truthful about the broker of record letter. But asking the witness whether he is making his statement under oath is not a demonstration that the statement is implausible. As you already know, we believe that the implausibility of the statement can be demonstrated by asking a series of questions about Blair Mill and why Sullivan focused his attention solely on that entity, and combining those questions with questions about the October 13, 1995, memorandum he wrote to his own boss. It is doubtful that he could explain Blair Mill without reference to a commission for Sussman. However, this "argument" should have been made the first time around, not on redirect examination. The abrupt ending of that examination signaled a failure, not a success.

Chapter Seven

The Alleged Villain: Helen Hardy

TEXT OF THE DIRECT EXAMINATION

THE COURT: Call your next witness.

MR. LONGER: Thank you, Your Honor, we call to the stand, Helen Hardy.

THE CRIER: Place your right hand on the Bible. State your name and spell your last name.

THE WITNESS: Helen Hardy, H-A-R-D-Y.

HELEN HARDY, WITNESS, after having been first duly sworn, was examined and testified as follows:

[Comment] This, next to the plaintiff himself, will be the most important witness in the case. Counsel is wise to call her after Sullivan—although more might have been done with Sullivan to set the stage for her. Then, too, Sweeney's deposition has not been especially helpful either. Far from it. Nonetheless, it will now come down to whether or not the jurors believe that Hardy did something to cheat the plaintiff, and plaintiff's counsel will have to examine her as on cross, even though he calls her on direct. The decision as to whether to call her must have been a difficult one. But in our view, he made the correct one and most particularly in putting Sullivan on before her. Just imagine how much more difficult the examination of Hardy would be if Sullivan had not been heard. See Vol. II, pp. 215–220.

With Ms. Hardy, unlike the problem facing the cross-examination of Sussman, counsel will have to attack her credibility, even as he uses the other two techniques of cross, limiting and hitchhiking.

BY MR. LONGER:

Q: Good morning, Ms. Hardy.

A: Good morning.

Q: We have met before at my offices, correct?

A: Yes, we have.

Q: And you came to my office for a deposition on January 6th, 1995, correct?

A: I don't recall the exact date, but I was there.

Q: Fair enough. You're an employee of Independence Blue Cross and Pennsylvania Blue Shield?

A: Yes, I am.

Q: And you're a sales director of the Union Health and Welfare Fund Department; is that correct?

A: That's correct.

Q: And you started with the company in 1969; is that right?

A: Yes.

Q: And that was 27 years ago thereabouts?

A: Almost 28.

Q: And your current positions is sales director and you have been in that position since 1992, correct?

A: That's correct—about—what, 1992.

Q: And prior to that, you were the manager of the department?

A: That's correct.

Q: And how long were you the manager of the department?

A: Probably for—oh, maybe, about four years, five years.

Q: So, beginning 1988 or 1987?

[Comment] This long pedigree is not especially helpful if he wishes to discredit her. It is enough that she is the sales director.

A: Yes.

Q: Now, in your position as manager, starting in 1987, is it true that the Ironworkers District Council Health and Welfare Fund was not a client, of Independence Blue Cross or Pennsylvania Blue Shield?

A: That's correct.

[Comment] Excellent, we start out without a client.

Q: And is it also true that your company was interested in obtaining that Welfare Fund as a client?

A: Yes.

Q: And is it also true that you did try to procure, to get, their business?

A: Yes.

Q: And beginning in 1988, you are not successful doing that while you are in the management position that you were in, correct?

A: That's correct.

Q: And that continued for a period of time; isn't that correct?

A: Uh-huh. That's correct.

[Comment] Superb! The client is not only a desirable one, but one that the witness herself had tried unsuccessfully to enlist. The questions are short and crisp and counsel is arguing right through her to the jury. Vol. III, pp. 1–2, 7–8. One suggestion: Instead of a period of time, counsel might give the number of years.

Q: Now, in 1992, you helped prepare a prospect listing regarding this Health and Welfare Fund, did you not?

A: Yes.

Q: I draw your attention, if you will, to my book, the black binder, Exhibit Number-18. Now, the Ironworkers were an account that you were actively pursuing, correct?

A: Yes.

Q: You were interested in getting the Ironworkers?

A: Yes, we were interested.

Q: They were a big account to Blue Cross/Blue Shield, right?

A: Yes.

Q: It would be a feather in your cap to get it, right?

A: I would feel good about it.

[Comment] Notice the use of the rule of probabilities — using questions in sequence to force answers. See Vol. III, pp. 177–184. "Interested" — because "big account" and when "big" was adopted, "feather in your cap" could not be resisted.

Q: In 1992, you prepared this prospect listing. And would you tell the Jury what a prospect listing is?

A: Well, what we do is take an analysis of those accounts that we do not have, and we create what we call a prospect list. And from that, we have all of those accounts that do not have Blue Cross at that time, and periodically we review the information about each of those accounts and strategize ways that we might be able to obtain them.

[Comment] Notice, this same leading question evokes far more than a yes or no answer, which all helps the examiner.

Q: Right. And you were responsible for preparing this particular document; is that correct?

A: Yes, that's correct.

Q: And it indicates that the administrator of the Fund was a gentleman by the name of Nick Craggs; is that correct?

A: That's correct.

Q: And it indicates that you were the marketing director, right?

A: That's correct.

Q: And it also has a line there that says "status," does it not?

A: Yes, it does.

Q: And that line reads, "Total lack of interest"?

A: That is correct.

Q: And it's true, is it not, that there was a total lack of interest in Blue Cross/Blue Shield by the Ironworkers in 1992?

A: According to the information that we had, that's correct.

Q: And that didn't change in 1993, did it?

A: Not to my knowledge.

[Comment] This is as good as it gets. Simply wonderful. Counsel has superbly shown the utter frustration of the company with this prospective client — until, of course, the plaintiff enters the scene.

Q: And through 1992 and 1993, you were trying to meet Mr. Craggs to get the Ironworkers' business, right?

A: No.

Q: No?

A: That is not correct.

Q: You never met with Mr. Craggs to talk about getting business with Blue Cross/Blue Shield?

A: No, I did not.

Q: Do you recall telling me that you found him to be an obstacle to you getting business with Blue Cross/Blue Shield?

A: Yes, I did.

Q: And you felt that you had to talk to Mr. Craggs to get business with Blue Cross/Blue Shield; did you not?

A: No, I did not.

[Comment] She has made a few denials, but no matter. The main point has been maintained. She could not get the business, and she wanted it.

Q: Now, in early 1994, you spoke to a friend of yours by the name of George Walton; is that right?

A: That's correct.

Q: And Mr. Walton was your connection to Mr. Sweeney; is that fair to say?

A: Yes, that's correct.

Q: And you met with Mr. Sweeney in early 1994, right?

A: That's correct.

Q: And you found after having met with him, that there was a total lack of interest in 1994?

A: No.

Q: Is that right?

A: No.

Q: Did you get anywhere with Mr. Sweeney at the end of your meeting with him?

A: Yes.

Q: Where did you get, Ms. Hardy?

[Comment] He opens it all up to her.

A: I felt that it was a very positive meeting. I met my objective which was to begin to build a relationship with Mr. Sweeney, so I did meet my objective, yes.

[Comment] She has hurt the examiner, or so she may believe. But what the witness believes does not matter. What the jurors do *believe is all that matters. Now watch him make his point,* and do it without leading. *Indeed, more effectively because he did not lead. See Vol. III, pp. 26–27, 219.*

Q: Now, did Mr. Sweeney ask you to come back and give him any information at that meeting?

A: I don't recall that he did at that meeting.

Q: Did he ask you to give any directories to him?

A: No.

Q: Did he offer to give you any information about the Ironworkers at your meeting?

A: Not other than what we discussed while we were talking about the Fund.

Q: <u>This was a very positive meeting</u>. Did he offer to give you any Zip Code listings to show you where the Welfare Fund members were distributed through the area?

A: No.

[Comment] Counsel has earned the right to the sarcasm in the preceding question.

Q: Do you recall when that meeting was?

A: No, I honestly do not.

Q: You just know it was early 1994?

A: Somewhere in—right. I don't recall the exact—I don't remember the exact date.

Q: The next thing that happened between you and the Ironworkers, after that meeting with Mr. Sweeney, <u>that</u>

<u>very positive meeting that you had with him</u>, was when you got a phone call out of the blue from Mr. Sussman; isn't that right?

A: That's correct.

[Comment] No one is likely to believe that there was a satisfactory meeting for this salesperson, and if not, the jury is likely not to have liked her answers. Now the stage is set for the entry of the plaintiff.

Q: And Mr. Sussman called you in either May or June of 1994, right?

A: That is correct.

Q: Now, if you would, I ask you to turn to Plaintiff's Exhibit Number-17. Now, these are like Mr. Sullivan's very sophisticated note pads, right?

A: That's correct.

Q: And these indicate conversations that you may have had <u>relevant</u> to this case; is that right?

A: Uh-huh.

THE COURT: Is that a yes or no?

THE WITNESS: Yes.

MR. LONGER: Thank you, Your Honor.

[Comment] The question is technically not proper, for she is not the judge of relevancy. But counsel got away with it.

BY MR. LONGER:

Q: Now, go to the third page IBC-466. This is dated May 31st, 1994; is that correct?

A: Yes.

Q: And does that place in time for you when Mr. Sussman called you about the Ironworkers?

A: I believe he had called me just maybe several weeks before that date.

Q: And you made a note two weeks later; is that what you're saying?

A: No. This note had to do with a conversation that I had with John Hime, who is an employee of Blair Mill Administrators, and it was in discussion with or about the Ironworkers and Mr. Sussman.

Q: Now, this note indicates that Mr. Sussman is a broker, does it not?

A: Yes.

Q: And you understood Mr. Sussman to be a broker of insurance; isn't that right?

A: That's correct.

Q: And you understood that you were going to set up an appointment to meet with Mr. Sussman and Mr. Sweeney in about May or early June of 1994, correct?

A: Yes, that's correct.

Q: And did you meet with Mr. Sussman to go to meet with Mr. Sweeney at the Woodcrest Shopping Center?

A: Yes, I did.

Q: And before that—I'm sorry. In advance of that, you had a telephone call with him to set up that meeting?

A: Yes, that's correct.

Q: And during that telephone call, he told you that he wanted to be a broker on a contract between the Ironworkers and Blue Cross/Blue Shield; isn't that right?

A: I do not recall that that was <u>exactly</u> what he said.

[Comment] Notice her use of the word "exactly" to avoid any answer. But she is obviously ducking, and has surely not hurt the examiner, who simply puts another assertion right through her to the jurors.

Q: He told you that he could get you a favorable audience with Mr. Sweeney, that you would not have otherwise had; isn't that fair to say?

A: I do not recall <u>exactly</u> what was said during that conversation on the phone.

[Comment] She does it again, but to no avail. Now counsel puts it to her. Is she totally blank about the conversation?

Q: Do you recall that conversation <u>at all</u>?

A: While we were in the car driving over, we had a very lengthy conversation.

[Comment] She changes the subject. She moves from the telephone conversation in the question to a conversation in a car that she would rather talk about. But notice: He does not appeal to the judge or move to strike. He disciplines her himself. See Vol. III, pp. 49–53.

Q: I'm talking about the <u>telephone call</u> setting up that meeting?

A: No.

[Comment] Her answer may not now be understood. The "no" means that she does not recall the telephone call "at all," but the jurors may not get it. But it is not pursued. Once a witness does not recall, anything may be suggested as having been said. It is the doctrine of fencing off. Counsel goes ahead to do it.

Q: And during that <u>telephone</u> call, he told you that he was the broker with Preferred Care; isn't that right?

A: No, he did not.

Q: And he mentioned to you this arrangement with Preferred Care, did he not?

A: No.

[Comment] These are two denials about a call that she has just said she does not remember at all.

Q: Then the two of you—but he did talk about getting the two of you together?

A: That's correct.

[Comment] She does recall that.

Q: And you did meet?

A: Yes.

Q: You met at the Woodcrest Shopping Center?

A: Yes.

Q: And during the car ride down to meet with Mr. Sweeney, the two of you spoke about Mr. Sussman's arrangement between Preferred Care and the Ironworkers; did you not?

A: No, we did not.

Q: You didn't discuss about him having a contract with Preferred Care?

A: No.

Q: You didn't talk about him receiving commissions from Preferred Care?

A: No.

Q: You didn't talk about his arrangement with Mr. Halverson; is that what you're saying?

A: Yes. That's what I'm saying.

[Comment] Three times he repeated the same question and received four unwanted answers, without reprisal by him. The sign of a cross-examiner in trouble—and make no mistake, this is a cross.

Q: Now, he told you that he knew Mr. Sweeney, did he not?

A: Yes, he did.

Q: He told you that he [was] a good friend of Mr. Sweeney, did he not?

A: Yes, he did.

Q: He told you that [he] could get you a favorable audience with Mr. Sweeney, didn't he?

A: Yes.

Q: One that you would not have been able to have otherwise, right?

A: I do not believe that's right.

[Comment] She says no. But if she was doing as well without, why bother with the plaintiff?

Q: He told you he was introducing you because he thought his relationship with Sweeney was good enough to get a contract between the Ironworkers and Blue Cross/Blue Shield?

A: Yes, he thought that.

Q: And he thought that he could convince Bob Sweeney to contract between you and the Ironworkers, didn't he?

A: Yes.

Q: And when you met with Mr Sweeney—and Mr. Sweeney was willing to meet with you, right?

A: Yes.

Q: And that was not that far beyond when you had just met with Mr. Sweeney; is that right?

A: That's correct.

[Comment] Excellent. These are valuable conclusions, and ones she must give under the rules of law and probability. Vol. III, pp. 177–184.

Q: Now, you didn't meet with Mr. Sweeney every other month, did you?

A: No, I did not.

Q: Prior to 1994, had you ever met with Mr. Sweeney?

A: No.

Q: When Mr. Sweeney was the co-chairman of the Board of Trustees for the Ironworkers, right?

A: That's correct.

Q: And you understood that going down there, right?

A: Yes, I did.

Q: He was an important person to speak to in terms of getting an account with the—Ironworkers; was he not?

A: Yes, he was.

Q: And you thought that going with Mr. Sussman would—that meeting with Mr. Sussman would be advantageous because Mr. Sussman was a friend of Mr. Sweeney's, correct?

A: Yes.

[Comment] OK. Now we know for certain, because she has admitted it, that she believed the plaintiff represented added value to Blue Cross.

Q: Now, at that meeting you talked about the extent of the listings of your doctors, did you not?

A: Yes, we did.

Q: And you talked about pricing and discounts, did you not?

A: Yes, we did.

Q: And Mr. Sweeney talked about getting experience under the Ironworkers' belt with a contract with Preferred Care, did he not?

A: I believe he did, yes.

Q: And he was not immediately willing to talk more about Blue Cross/Blue Shield; is that fair to say?

A: That's fair, yes.

Q: But he was interested in getting more information, was he not?

A: I do not recall that he was, no.

[Comment] Not a good answer. But watch the examiner. He makes her change that answer.

Q: After the meeting, the meeting resolved itself, however, with you understanding that Mr. Sussman was going to provide information to Mr. Sweeney?

A: Yes, I believe that is correct.

Q: And he was going to give information about your discounts, right?

A: Yes.

Q: And he was going to give information about prices per procedure, correct?

A: We discussed that, yes.

Q: Now, that is already more, than you had heard from Mr. Sweeney in your prior meeting in 1994; isn't that fair to say?

A: Yes.

[Comment] Excellent. Counsel has pushed her far. Now he tries to get further, as he has a right to. But she won't cooperate. Watch.

Q: And certainly, this was a more positive meeting than yours, right?

A: I want to answer and then can I explain something? I would say yes, but the information or the statements were from Mr. Sussman, not necessarily from Mr. Sweeney. So, in terms of Mr. Sussman wanting to proceed, yes, it was more positive.

Q: And Mr. —

MR. SONNENFELD: <u>Wait. Wait. She is not done</u> [with] her answer.

MR. LONGER: Excuse me?

MR. SONNENFELD: I saw her lips <u>about to burst</u> <u>open</u>.

[Comment] Counsel for Blue Cross is encouraging the witness's outpourings. But we suggest she is not helping him.

THE WITNESS: What I was going to say is, I was not sure and really didn't positively get that sense from Mr. Sweeney. But I would say it was positive because Mr. Sussman certainly wanted to proceed.

[Comment] She thinks she has hurt counsel, but is she believable? Do the jurors believe that her meeting alone was just as positive as the one with Sussman?

BY MR. LONGER:

Q: And Mr. Sweeney was willing to listen to what Mr. Sussman had to say, correct?

A: I don't know that.

[Comment] She has tried to muddy the waters. Counsel could nail the point because the information was accepted by Sweeney, but counsel elects to change topics.

Q: Now, after that meeting—well, how long did that meeting last?

A: I would say maybe a half hour to 45 minutes, something like that. Less than an hour.

Q: Now, after that meeting, you wrote a letter to Mr. Sussman; is that right?

A: Yes, I did.

Q: And that is the letter that was dated June 3rd, 1994. It's Exhibit P-8; is that right?

A: Yes.

Q: P-8.

A: Yes. That's correct.

Q: Now, this is a letter that says: "This is to confirm that 85 percent of the doctors located in Pennsylvania are contracting with Pennsylvania Blue Shield under the U.C.R. Program. Because the listing of doctors is so extensive, we do not have a copy readily available, however, I have requested a copy for you and it should be ready by later next week." This listing was what we had just discussed you talking to Mr. Sweeney and Mr. Sussman about at that meeting, correct?

A: The number of doctors that were part of Blue Shield, is that's correct.

Q: And you agree that, either at the meeting or right thereafter, to give that information to Mr. Sussman, and that is what this letter is reflecting, right?

A: That is correct.

Q: And you say after that, "It was a pleasure meeting with you and Bob Sweeney, I look forward to continuing our dialogue so that we can hopefully meet objectives which are beneficial to all of us." Correct?

A: Absolutely.

Q: And, when you said that, "it would be beneficial to all of us," you were thinking from Blue Cross/Blue Shield's perspective that you were going to make some money on this deal, right?

A: No, that's not correct.

[Comment] *Now, that is some answer. What could "beneficial" mean to Blue Cross, if not that? Let's see how counsel deals with it.*

Q: Would you agree that something that is beneficial to Blue Cross/Blue Shield is a contract with the Ironworkers?

A: That is correct.

Q: And that Blue Cross/Blue Shield makes money off of contracts with anyone it sells to?

A: Not with all.

Q: Well, you might take less sometimes, but the thinking is that you're going to make money when you sell a contract, right?

A: I cannot say that, no.

[Comment] Her answers are not what he wants, but they can't hurt him unless they are believed. Now, he nails the point.

Q: You don't think that selling a contract is beneficial to the company?

A: Selling a contract is beneficial to our company in most cases.

[Comment] Bang! He got her—but he does not close the point. He might have said "and you certainly intended to try to make money on this one?" Instead, he changes the topic. Nonetheless, he did get the point made, although not as fully as he might have.

Q: Now, when you were saying that, you understood that Mr. Sussman would have had to have made a commission to benefit; isn't that right?

A: Yes.

Q: And that's what he does for—that's how he makes a living as a broker, he gets commissions, correct?

A: That's my understanding.

Q: And to have a beneficial relationship with him, he would have to have a commission from Blue Cross/Blue Shield, right?

A: Yes.

[Comment] So far, so good. As a matter of fact, very good. At that point, he might have gone back to the letter with its benefits to "all," including Sussman. But counsel goes too fast and she turns the discussion.

Q: And you considered Mr. Sussman to be a broker with respect to the Ironworkers; isn't that right?

A: No.

Q: Well, in—never?

A: He told me that he was a broker, but I did not have any documentation authorizing him in that position.

[Comment] Now, a little late, he goes back to the letter.

Q: This letter doesn't talk about a broker of record letter, does it?

A: No, it does not.

Q: Now, prior to your meeting with Mr. Sweeney, do you believe that you spoke to Mr. Sussman about a broker of record letter?

A: Yes.

[Comment] Not a good question and certainly not a good answer.

Q: And do you believe that Mr. Sussman <u>would</u> have dealt with you <u>if he knew</u> he couldn't have gotten a broker of record letter?

A: Would you repeat that question?

[Comment] The question is impossible, unless she is a qualified mind reader. But there is no objection, and the next question is no better.

Q: Why <u>would</u> Mr. Sussman have met with you <u>if</u> he couldn't have gotten a broker of record letter?

A: I don't know.

Q: It doesn't make any sense, does it?

A: No.

[Comment] Amazingly enough, because there was no objection, counsel obtained a very damaging answer with this last. But then he goes out of control and gets hurt.

Q: You didn't talk about a broker of record letter in your meetings with him prior to meeting with Mr. Sweeney, did you?

A: Yes, I did.

Q: You want them to believe that?

A: Yes.

[Comment] The "them" must refer to the jurors. Again, no objection.

Q: All right. Now, some days go by. And if you would, turn to Page 19—Exhibit-19, I'm sorry. And on June 6th, you write a letter to Mr. Sussman, "Enclosed is the Pennsylvania Blue Shield listing of participating physicians for the Philadelphia five-County area. Although this is not the listing for the entire State of Pennsylvania, it should provide you with a good idea of the extensiveness of our physician network statewide. If you have any questions, please call." Now, to your knowledge, did Mr. Sussman provide that information, of the listing to Mr. Sweeney?

A: I do not know.

Q: Did Mr. Sussman provide to you any information about the Ironworkers, after this meeting in June of 1994?

A: Yes, but I would like to explain. Mr. Sussman provided me with a list of some procedures, and he wanted to know what the allowance or payment would be by Pennsylvania Blue Shield. I do not know for sure that they were actually procedures from the Ironworkers. But there were procedures and they were with regard to him providing additional information to the Ironworkers.

Q: If you would, turn to Exhibit-11.

[Witness complies.]

Q: Did Mr. Sussman provide you with this document, after the meeting with Mr. Sweeney?

A: I do not recall who gave me this list of Zip Codes.

Q: This is a listing of Zip Codes, by the way, correct?

A: That's correct.

Q: And isn't it true that Mr. Sussman gave it to you?

A: I do not remember.

[Comment] Counsel has scored again. She would do better to concede the point.

Q: Now, Mr. Sussman also gave to you the codes that—the procedures that you had just described in Plaintiff's Exhibit Number-10, didn't he?

A: I do not recall receiving these—

Q: Now, these are procedures—

A: —these procedures, check vouchers. I do not recall receiving these, what I'm looking at.

Q: You don't recall Mr. Sussman giving you procedures for a Steven Michael Sweeney—I'm sorry—for a Lauren Sweeney with the insured Steven Michael Sweeney; is that what you're saying?

A: That is correct. I don't remember seeing that.

[Comment] These answers, which are not even denials, are more hurtful to Blue Cross than admissions would be.

Q: He didn't ask you to reprice these things under Blue Cross/Blue Shield? You don't remember that?

A: I remember talking about it. I do not remember receiving this.

Q: Do you recall after meeting with Mr. Sweeney in June of 1994, telling Mr. Sussman that that was the best meeting that you had ever had with the Ironworkers?

A: No, I don't recall saying that.

Q: You may have, you just don't recall saying that?

A: I do not recall saying that it was the best meeting that I had ever had with Mr. Sweeney.

[Comment] She has not answered, notice. And she has no intention of doing so. See the following.

Q: I was referring to the Ironworkers.

A: No. I do not recall saying that with regard to the Ironworkers.

Q: Now, if you would, turn to page—to Exhibit Number-17, again, and if you would, turn to the page which is Numbered 467 in the lower right-hand corner. You have a note that says that, "Ironworkers on hold at Tuesday meeting." You have a listing that says, "Len Sussman," do you see that?

A: Yes, I do.

Q: Did you understand that there was going to be a period of time then when you were going to wait for the Preferred Care contract to continue with the Welfare Fund before you would come back?

A: Yes.

Q: And then you continued to talk to Mr. Sussman, did you not? On the next page, 468, July 13th, you spoke to Mr. Sussman; is that right?

A: Yes.

Q: And you were talking about the Ironworkers?

A: I don't know.

[Comment] Of course she does. She had no other business with the man. But in this instance counsel does not nail the point.

He might have asked, "Did you have any other business with Sussman other than the Ironworkers' contract?", for example.

Q: And then, if you would, turn to Page 470. That's a September 22nd, 1994 date; do you see that?

A: Yes, I do.

Q: It says: "Called Len Sussman, re: compensation." You spoke to Mr. Sussman and you initiated a phone call on September 22nd, 1994; is that correct?

A: I negotiated that phone call in response to a question that Mr. Sussman asked me about compensation.

Q: And what you told him was that he could expect to receive 1 to 3 percent of the total premiums billed; isn't that right?

A: No.

[Comment] She has made a critical denial. Counsel now confronts her with the deposition. This is the correct way to do it. Notice, it is a public — not a private — confrontation. Vol. III, pp. 73–76.

Q: In your deposition, Ms. Hardy, I asked you about this document. Do you recall me asking you what the 1 to 3 percent of meant?

A: Yes, I do.

Q: And do you recall telling me —

MR. SONNENFELD: Could I ask for a page and a line?

MR. LONGER: Page 94, Line 2.

BY MR. LONGER:

Q: The next page dated — I'm sorry. And do you recall telling me that 1 to 3 percent of meant total premiums billed?

A: That's correct.

MR. SONNENFELD: Wait. I object. I think it's out of context, if you look at the preceding—

THE COURT: Well, you'll have a chance to question her on this.

MR. SONNENFELD: Thank you.

BY MR. LONGER:

[Comment] It is not clear what anyone is talking about. But the jurors may surmise that there was some such talk of a 1 to 3 percent commission. So he makes it clear.

Q: Now, you were talking to Mr. Sussman about compensation because the two of you expected to proceed with this account; isn't that true?

A: Yes.

Q: And Mr. Sussman was, obviously, interested in receiving a commission; is that true?

A: Yes.

[Comment] Good for him. He has now gotten her to contradict her denial. Remember: "And what you told him was that he could expect to receive 1 to 3 percent of the total premiums billed; isn't that correct?" And she replied, "No." We think he should have gone back to the original question at this point, to close the point.

Q: Did you talk about a broker of record letter in that conversation?

A: Yes.

Q: Is that reflected in your notes?

A: No.

[Comment] Excellent. Now he must nail the point, if he can.

Q: It wasn't significant enough for you to write it in your notes; is that fair to say?

A: No, that is not fair to say.

Q: Well, it's correct, though, that it is not in your notes, right? You didn't think it was that important to write it down, right?

A: I would—I'll answer, but I have to give more information.

Q: Well, why don't you answer first and then you can give more. You didn't write it down, right? It wasn't significant enough, right?

MR. SONNENFELD: Well, there are two questions. You didn't write it down and it wasn't significant enough. I don't know which one he wants answered.

THE COURT: Well, start with the first one.

BY MR. LONGER:

Q: You didn't write it down, correct?

A: Correct.

Q: You didn't think it significant enough to write it down, correct?

A: That is not correct. May I now explain? This is note—it was not only relative to the Ironworkers. There was another customer that Mr. Sussman had spoken with me about, and this note also referred to that customer because I have information written there about the other customer, which was one that Blue Cross already had, it was the cement mason, and I had also had conversations with a Pat Finley.

Q: But you were talking about compensation to Mr. Sussman with respect to the Ironworkers, weren't you?

A: I cannot say that I was talking about <u>only</u> compensation with regard to the Ironworkers in this note.

[Comment] She has tried to avoid the thrust by adding another insured. But counsel skillfully brings her back to the Ironworkers. Watch.

Q: But it would have applied to <u>both</u> accounts, right?

A: That is correct.

[Comment] Good for him. He picked up that it was both and that means the Ironworkers were included, and there is no mention of a letter for either, in spite of the Blue Cross policy.

Q: And the nature of how Blue Cross/Blue Shield pays compensation, the 1 to 3 percentage that you're talking about, would have applied to <u>either</u> the Ironworkers <u>or</u> the cement masons, right?

A: That is correct.

[Comment] Excellent. Whatever diversion she may have intended has been funneled back into the case with the last question and its answer. But now he should close the point, that is, that she wrote nothing about the necessity of a letter for either. Instead, he moves to another subject.

Q: Did you ever meet with Mr. Sussman and Mr. Sweeney again after that June meeting?

A: I do not recall that, no.

Q: Now, yesterday you were here and you heard Mr. Sussman give his testimony, did you not?

A: Yes, I did.

Q: And you heard him say that he met on March 1 with you, and March 31 with you, right?

A: Yes, I did.

Q: Now, you recall setting up an appointment with Mr. Sussman in 1995; isn't that right?

A: Yes.

Q: And you, because of some calendaring issue, canceled that appointment or didn't appear at the appointment, right?

A: I did not cancel the meeting, and I did not appear without—if it was a tentative meeting and I had on my calendar it was tentative, I expected Mr. Sussman to call me and confirm that the meeting was going to go on and he did not do that. So, I did not attend, because I did not know that it was still on.

Q: And you don't remember ever following up and meeting with Mr. Sussman and Mr. Sweeney again in 1995?

A: No, I do not.

Q: You never met with Mr. Sussman or Mr. Sweeney—sorry. You never met with Mr. Sussman and Mr. Sweeney again after your June 1994 meeting?

A: I do not recall that, no.

[Comment] His point is that, having had the access that Sussman provided, she dumped the man. Well, if that is the point, why not put it to her directly?

Q: Ms. Hardy, if you would turn to Exhibit Number-13.

[Witness complies.]

Q: This is a letter written <u>to you by Mr. Maresca</u>, dated July 31, 1995, correct?

A: That's correct.

Q: And this is a letter which is a request for a proposal; is that correct?

A: Yes.

Q: And prior to receiving this letter, had you spoken to Mr. Sussman about—in 1995, had you spoken to Mr. Sussman about his activity in providing a proposal to Blue Cross—I'm sorry, to the Ironworkers?

A: No.

Q: Did you understand Mr. Sussman to still be related as a broker to the Ironworkers when you received this letter?

A: No.

Q: At the meeting on July 26th, that's referred to in this letter, did you understand Mr. Sussman to be the broker that you were dealing with, with the Ironworkers?

A: No.

[Comment] Counsel is now in a critical area: discussions between Maresca and Hardy about Sussman and whether Sussman was to receive a commission. This is critical because of the claim of interference that counsel has put into the complaint.

Q: Let me say that again. Do you recall, at that meeting, asking Mr. Maresca what about the broker, Mr. Sussman, at the July 26th meeting?

A: No.

Q: Prior to that meeting, had you received a phone call from Mr. Maresca to set it up?

A: Yes.

Q: Did <u>you ask</u> Mr. Maresca, at that meeting, what about Mr. Sussman, what about his commission, what about him being a broker?

A: The meeting <u>or the phone call</u>?

[Comment] She has given him an opening, so he takes it and gets the answer.

Q: The phone call?

A: <u>Yes</u>. I believe I did do that <u>I asked him</u>.

Q: You were concerned, going into the July 26th meeting that there was a broker involved on this contract, were you not?

A: Yes.

Q: And that broker was Mr. Sussman, right?

[Comment] So far, so good. He is but one step away.

A: I'd like to answer and then make a comment. Yes, but it—was not documented.

Q: I know. That's why we're here today, right?

A: That is correct.

[Comment] Counsel's admission of no documentation, in our view, does nothing for him.

Q: Now, that's because Blue Cross/Blue Shield has a company policy, right?

A: Yes.

Q: It's only Blue Cross/Blue Shield's policy, correct?

A: I do not believe that is correct.

Q: It's not the case with Preferred Care, is it?

A: I don't know.

[Comment] He is out of control on this, for he has nothing to confront her with. Moreover, he has diverted himself from his point, which is that she brought the subject of Sussman's entitlement up to the union's consultant. This is a critical part of his claim that she interfered in plaintiff's relationship with the union. But can the jurors follow this now? Look at the next question, which commingles dates.

Q: Now, you didn't have any meetings, according to your testimony, with Mr. Sussman all the way back to June of 1994 and yet, at this conversation that you had with Mr. Maresca, setting up a July 26th meeting, you still were concerned about Mr. Sussman's relation as a broker in this contract, right?

A: Yes.

Q: And Mr. Maresca and you talked about Mr. Sussman, right?

A: Again, I would like to answer and make a comment. I would say yes, but we didn't talk about Mr.

Sussman, we talked about a broker being involved with this customer.

Q: And the broker that you were talking about was Mr. Sussman, right?

A: He was—he is a broker that is correct.

Q: And you were talking to the consultant of the Ironworkers Fund, right?

A: That's correct.

Q: And you were talking about the broker that may be involved in this account, right?

A: Yes.

[Comment] He is certainly making her agree with his assertions, however reluctant she may be. And yet, this is a dangerous area for him to enter, because Maresca, the union consultant, will say that he said to Hardy that there would be no commission for Sussman because the union would not authorize or pay it, not the other way around.

Q: And you were talking about whether or not there would be a commission to a broker, right? You were talking about there not being a broker of record letter, any written document about a broker, right? Let me say it a different way: The only significance about a broker of record letter would be whether or not the broker would receive the commission, right?

A: No.

Q: You were talking to Mr. Maresca about a broker of record letter, because you knew that by not paying a commission, the price to the Ironworkers would be reduced, right?

[Comment] That is not such a good question for him. It makes it clear that the men and women of the union pay the commission, not the company from its profits.

A: Repeat that, please?

Q: You knew when you were talking to the consultant of the Ironworkers about not having a broker involved, because you believed that it would <u>reduce the price of this contract</u>, right?

[Comment] A little better. But still, where is he going? We would think he would want to make the point that it was more valuable to Blue Cross to avoid a commission, rather than more economical to the union, for he wants Sussman's end to come from Blue Cross's profit margin.

A: I'm sorry. You have to repeat that again. I'm—I want to make sure I answer it correctly.

Q: You were talking to Mr. Maresca about there not being a broker of record letter because you knew that if there was none, there would be no commissions to a broker and you could have a less—a smaller price on the contract between the Ironworkers and Blue Cross/Blue Shield?

A: Yes.

[Comment] Now he finally asked it the way he wants to and he got her to admit it! But we still believe it should have been more profit to Blue Cross rather than a "smaller price," for that, as you will see, is what he argues later. Now for the final thrust.

Q: And you were trying to avoid that price, right?

A: No.

Q: You wanted this account, didn't you, Ms. Hardy?

A: Yes, I did.

Q: If you could get it at a lesser price, you would get it, right?

A: I'd like to answer and then make a comment after.

Q: You have been doing that so keep going.

[Comment] He wisely understands that it is wrong to limit witnesses to "yes" and "no" answers. Vol. III, pp. 24–25.

A: Well, okay, but, it does not matter to me or to Independence Blue Cross whether a broker is involved or not. That is the customer's decision. In this case it would be the Fund's decision as to whether or not they wanted a broker to do work for them with regard to setting up a program, and load the rate.

[Comment] Happily for him, she leads him to a better subject, for him.

Q: The policy of Blue Cross/Blue Shield, is that it pays brokers' commissions as percentages of premium dollars for what the customer pays you; is that correct?

A: Yes.

Q: And what was it that you were talking to the Ironworkers about them paying you? Do you recall the numbers, the dollars that were involved?

A: You mean the whole—the cost of the account, the potential bottom line?

Q: Yes.

A: Probably was going to be somewhere around 6 to 7 million dollars.

Q: And you pay percentages on that amount?

A: With caps, correct. That's correct.

Q: And the percentages are 1 to 3 percent, right?

A: Loaded, yes.

Q: And that's what you had talked to Mr. Sussman about on September 22nd, 1994, correct?

A: Yes.

[Comment] Excellent! Counsel is scoring and he does so with the force of his questions, not by limiting the witness's answers.

He now has 1 to 3 percent on $6 to 7 million, and we are off the more difficult bottom-line question of whether it comes from the union in the form of higher premiums or from Blue Cross in the form of less profit.

Q: But you didn't talk about caps to him on September 22nd, 1994, did you?

A: I don't recall.

[Comment] He has her now. And he knows it. Watch!

Q: Is it fair to say that Mr. Sussman would have expected a pretty big payday on September 22nd, 1994?

A: Yes.

[Comment] Wow! That is some answer. One might be tempted to end the examination right now, or right after valuing the contract, but counsel goes on.

Q: Now, I'd like to go back to that meeting that you had with Mr. Maresca in July of '95. Maybe it was the conversation that you had before that. But after that conversation, you didn't have any expectation that Mr. Sussman would be involved; is that right?

A: Yes.

[Comment] Notice, he edits out how she knew that Sussman was out. He does not want to hear that it was Maresca who told her.

Q: And you didn't care about whether or not Mr. Sussman was involved or not after that conversation, right?

A: Yes.

Q: He could do whatever he wanted and you were in and he was out, that's how you felt, right?

A: No.

Q: You could have cared less about him, right?

A: No.

[Comment] The examiner knows he will get a no. That really does not matter. What matters is that counsel also knows that the answer will not hurt him unless it is believed. He also knows something else. If he is reluctant to say what he wants the jurors to conclude, he must not expect them to say it for him. Vol. I, pp. 23–24.

Q: Well, now, do you recall doing your deposition and me asking you on Page 148, Line 6, "Did you care what his status," referring to Mr. Sussman, "was at the July 26th, 1995 meeting"?

A: Yes, I did.

Q: Do you remember your answer being, no?

A: May I read that?

Q: I'm pointing to it right here.

A: I did answer no there, yes.

[Comment] On a cost-benefit analysis, the result of this confrontation is not clear.

Q: And then did you deal with Mr. Sussman with respect to the Ironworkers after that?

A: No, I did not.

Q: <u>You</u> did get the sale on his contract, did you not?

A: Yes, <u>we</u> did.

[Comment] She has changed the "you" to "we." He lets it pass, although he could have punished her: "You got a commission, right?"

Q: And as a result of that sale—let me back up one second. You responded to that request for a proposal, or at least Blue Cross/Blue Shield did?

A: Yes, we did.

Q: And that is Plaintiff's Exhibit Number-28; is that right?

A: Yes, that's correct.

Q: And that's a big document, right?

A: Yes.

Q: And the person that responded to this request for a proposal is a gentleman by the name of Ken—you're going to have to help me out here.

A: Olejniczak.

Q: Now, Mr. Maresca referred to him as Kenny O. Is that how a lot of people referred to Mr. Olejniczak?

A: Yes.

Q: For ease of reference, you mind if I call him Mr. O?

A: No.

Q: Now, Mr. O was the person who responded to Mr. Maresca's request for a proposal; isn't that right?

A: That's right.

Q: You turned this account over to Mr. O, right?

A: Yes.

Q: And for the most part, it was Mr. O that dealt with Segal Company in terms of preparing the information necessary to prepare the proposal, right?

A: Not for the most part. We did it jointly.

Q: Mr. O was the one who dealt with Mr. Maresca's company primarily, correct?

A: No.

[Comment] These last questions and answers are not among the best moments of the examination. They seem to go nowhere. Time is capital in the courtroom. You spend it at your peril. Jurors can only be held for so long once you leave the highway

*of the case for its back alleys. But now we are taken right back
to the center of the case.*

Q: Now, the next page, Exhibit Number-29, that's the
contract that you ultimately entered into that we just discussed a moment ago, right?

A: Yes.

Q: And as a result of this contract you received a commission, did you not?

A: Yes, I do.

Q: And you received a commission for doing this contract, right?

A: Yes.

Q: And you have another commission called a retention commission; is that right?

A: That's correct.

Q: And the retention commission is going to continue
for you for as long as this contract is in effect; is that
right?

A: Yes, that's right.

Q: And it's paid on a monthly basis; isn't that right?

A: Yes.

Q: And you expect to receive that retention commission for a long time; is that right?

A: Yes.

Q: And you expect it to go on for how many years?

A: I guess until I retire, hopefully.

*[Comment] Well done. But then he goes a mite too far, in our
view. Watch.*

Q: You want this contract to stay in effect—how old
are you, Ms. Hardy?

A: How old am I?

Q: I don't mean to embarrass you.

A: 8/8, I'll be 50. In a couple of weeks.

Q: You expect to retire at that age?

A: I don't know.

Q: Well, another 15 years?

A: Hopefully, 55.

Q: I see. But you expect this contract to continue in effect after you retire?

A: Yes.

Q: And will you still receive a commission after you retire?

A: No.

[Comment] It was enough that she would get a yearly commission. Counsel may have gone too far, especially with a female witness.

Q: Were you aware of Mr. Sussman entering into a contract with the Ironworkers with Preferred Care?

A: No, I was not.

Q: Didn't Mr. Sussman tell you that he had brokered a contract with Preferred Care and Mr. Halverson?

A: Not initially.

[Comment] She tries to duck on timing. He pursues.

Q: But you knew that he would—he did mention it to you?

A: He mentioned to me that there was another PPO involved and that it was Preferred Care, but we did not have a long discussion or much discussion about his involvement with that.

Q: But he told you he was receiving commissions on that contract, did he not?

A: I don't recall that specifically, no.

Q: Did he tell you that he was sharing his commission with Mr. Halverson?

A: I don't recall that.

Q: Have you ever offered to share your commission with Mr. Sussman?

A: My personal commission?

Q: Yes.

A: No.

Q: Mr. Sussman was your connection to Mr. Sweeney, wasn't he?

A: No.

Q: Mr. Sussman got you into a favorable meeting with Mr. Sweeney; isn't that right?

A: It was a favorable meeting.

Q: And Mr. Sussman helped you out, right?

A: He helped to further things along.

[Comment] Good for the examiner. She has changed her answer from what she said earlier that it was no more a positive meeting with Sussman and Sweeney than when she met with Sweeney alone.

Q: And you would use <u>anything</u> you could to get that contract, including Mr. Sussman's help, right?

[Comment] That is some question! Counsel has been emboldened by the failure to object earlier.

A: Would you repeat that?

Q: You would do anything you could including using Mr. Sussman's help to get you that contract, right?

A: Again, I'll answer and make a comment after that. Yes. I just have difficulty the way that you said that. It's not that I would do anything. I don't—

Q: I know it's a difficult question.

[Comment] You bet it is a difficult question. Does "anything" include anything? Counsel seems to know he has gone too far.

A: I do things properly, and it does not matter to me who is involved, whether it is a broker or consultant. I just want to do things according to the proper requirements that we have. And as long as that happens, that's fine, but I would not do anything.

[Comment] He got what he deserved with that answer, given that question.

Q: Now, you want to follow company policies, that's what you're saying?

A: That is correct. And—

[Comment] She gets cut off. Counsel, for good reason, wants to get out of the swamp he has marched into.

Q: Now, I'd like you to turn to Exhibit Number-26. This is a letter that you received in the ordinary course of business, isn't it?

A: Yes.

Q: And this is a letter that you would refer to as—I'm sorry. This is something that you have in your files?

A: Yes.

Q: And it's a letter dated January 29, 1996, from Mr. Maresca to you, right?

A: Yes.

Q: And it says, "In the letter received from Ken Olejniczak dated January 23rd, 1996, the indicated retention charge of 10.3 percent is the same as was originally quoted." Your retention charge with the Ironworkers is the amount that you charge them for the cost of administering their program; is that right?

A: That is correct.

Q: That is where Blue Cross/Blue Shield makes money from this contract, right?

A: Again, I'll answer and make a comment. Yes, as long as it does not end up costing us more than the 10.3 percent. There are times that it might cost us more than we charge the customer.

Q: And there are times when it might cost you a lot less, right?

A: That is correct.

Q: And you can make a big profit when it costs you a lot less, right?

A: I could not say that.

[Comment] Ah, yes. She really could, if he pursues it. Watch the laws of probability: "The lower you get in cost from 10.3 percent, the more you make, right?"

Q: Now, you have had a year's experience under this contract—year and a half, isn't that right? It's been renewed?

A: Yes, that's correct.

Q: And the reason I say that it's a January 1, 1996 contract. The year 1996 has passed and we are now into 1997, correct?

A: That is correct.

Q: And do you recall how much profit you made in 1996 on your retention charge?

A: No, I do not.

Q: Do you recall what your retention charges were?

A: Yes.

Q: What were they?

A: 10.3 percent.

Q: Do you recall the amount that that added up to, that 10.3 percent?

A: No, I do not.

Q: Yesterday, Mr. Craggs spoke about their seeing approximately 6 million dollars in benefits paid. Is that a fair estimate of what the number is?

A: Yes, that's probably about what it is.

Q: So, the retention charge would have been 10.3 percent times 6 million, right?

A: The calculation—I'm not positive if the calculation is times that or if it is the reciprocal and it's divided, but it's close enough.

Q: So, it would have been about $600,000?

A: That's correct.

[Comment] Excellent point. He has lots of money flowing now.

THE COURT: Let's take a short recess.

THE CRIER: Everyone remain seated while the Jury leaves.

[Jury exits.]

- - - -

[Short recess.]

- - - -

[Jury enters.]

- - - -

[Back on the record in open court.]

- - - -

MR. LONGER: May I proceed, Your Honor?

THE COURT: Yes, please.

MR. LONGER: Ladies and gentlemen, I mean no disrespect by taking my jacket off, but it's getting hot.

BY MR. LONGER:

Q: We were talking about a lot of money before the break, Ms. Hardy. And this letter, Exhibit Number-26, talks about what Mr. Maresca thinks about your 10.3 percent retention charge. He says in the next paragraph, "As I discussed with you, this amount is excessive for this group. We would suggest that you consider reducing that percentage to 9 percent." Did you ever talk to Mr. Maresca about his thinking that you were being excessive with the union workers here, the Ironworkers?

A: Yes.

Q: And did he tell you that he was—you were <u>gouging</u> the Ironworkers?

A: I don't recall that word.

[Comment] He got a break on that one. She might have said no, and, as you will see, Maresca is a defense witness.

Q: But you were charging 10.3 percent and he wanted it down in terms of—dollar terms, at least $100,000, right?

A: Uh-huh. Yes.

Q: Now, that's the money that you're getting. Did you ever think of sharing that with Mr. Sussman?

[Comment] This is what he really wants—a fee from Blue Cross based on a performance by Sussman after a promise of a benefit to him by Blue Cross. This, however, is not the suit that he has brought.

A: That's not the money that I am getting.

Q: That's the money that your company is getting, right?

A: To administer the program, yes, that's correct.

Q: And the company's profit is built into administering the program, right?

A: We are a non-profit organization.

[Comment] She has neatly turned the point. Let's see how counsel handles it.

Q: But there is nothing stopping you from paying Mr. Sussman a commission, right?

A: No.

Q: It's just your company policy that is stopping you, right?

A: That is correct.

[Comment] He leaves the point that he was making, that the company seeks funds beyond its costs, and he goes on to the commission point. He might have done better with the point he abandoned. For example, the company may be nonprofit, but it has to pay for services it receives. It pays her and it pays its president, and so forth. In any event, counsel has concluded an excellent interrogation; ending with the notion that nothing stops Blue Cross from paying a commission, except Blue Cross itself, is an excellent point to end on. Unfortunately, that is not what he has sued Blue Cross for failing to do.

MR. LONGER: I have no further questions. Thank you.

THE COURT: Thank you.

MR. SONNENFELD: Your Honor, I have no questions of Ms. Hardy <u>at this time</u>.

[Comment] This is a critical decision by the defense. The choices are between doing nothing now, doing a limited examination based on the "direct," or doing the entire examination

that counsel will later do on his own case now, right in the plaintiff's case. Had Hardy been called earlier, for us the choice would be easy. We would do our entire examination and argument right through her early in the plaintiff's case. See Vol. III, pp. 330–334.

In this instance, however, she is the last *witness to be called in the plaintiff's case. Under these circumstances, we are in agreement with the defense in withholding the majority of the interrogation until it can be integrated into the organization of the defense. One point we think should have been made: The examiner did not go into the Maresca/Hardy conversation in which Maresca tells Hardy that the* union *wants Sussman out. "How did you learn that Mr. Sussman was not to get a commission?" "Did you suggest that to Maresca or did Maresca tell you that?" We suggest that, given the narrow issue of the complaint, and the fact that on "direct" the examiner kept indicating that any commission would have increased costs to the union, this point needed to be made as soon as possible.*

THE COURT: Thank you. Ms. Hardy, you may step down.

ANALYSIS OF THE DIRECT EXAMINATION

Note that plaintiff's counsel did not ask for permission to treat Ms. Hardy as an adverse witness. It is clear from the examination, though, that he is doing so. According to the plaintiffs, she is the villain in this piece, so her testimony is important.

The examination begins with a confrontation as to whether Ms. Hardy had tried or wanted to meet with Mr. Craggs to try to get the Ironworkers' business. This is a confrontation which, surprisingly, Ms. Hardy won. The examiner did not use the kind of simple logic that could have compelled either the answers he wanted or answers that the jury would not have believed. Almost certainly, he could have asked whether Ms. Hardy thought that the administrator of the welfare fund might have had some voice in the choice of health care plans and insurers, and whether she thought that if the administrator were interested, Blue Cross/Blue Shield might get a better hearing. If she said "yes," her answers would have been believable. If she said "no," her answers probably would not have been believable, because she had no reason to believe before she met with Mr. Sweeney that Mr. Craggs, the administrator, was not an important player in the health insurer selection process.

But is this the right place to begin? Surely, the jury now understands that, although there are 22 trustees and it might technically be true that Mr. Sweeney cannot pick a health insurer by himself, Mr. Sweeney is the person who can virtually make the decision that counts. So, with hindsight, Ms. Hardy knows that Mr. Craggs is not the decision maker; that role belongs to Sweeney. The examiner knows this too; therefore, why get distracted with Craggs early in the examination?

Remember that, in his opening statement, plaintiff's counsel attacked Ms. Hardy. He identified her as the principal person responsible for cheating Mr. Sussman. By making her a plaintiff's witness, plaintiff's counsel has first crack at her testimony. This is a witness that the jury expects to be attacked, and the jury is not going to want to wait long to see whether plaintiff's counsel can deliver what he promised.

It seems pretty clear that Ms. Hardy and Blue Cross had wanted the Ironworkers' business, and had wanted it for some time, but had had no luck in getting it until Sussman got in the picture. In fact, it appears that Blue Cross may have given up on trying to get the business before Sussman contacted it.

The use of chronology has some force at the beginning of this examination. Counsel demonstrates that Blue Cross first tried to get the Ironworkers' account in 1988, and that in 1992 Ms. Hardy developed a "prospect list" but concluded in a memorandum to her company that there was a "total lack of interest" on the part of the Ironworkers. It might have been more powerful to ask whether, prior to Sussman's getting involved, Ms. Hardy ever wrote any other memorandum suggesting that things had changed or that the Ironworkers were showing signs of interest. The questions about Ms. Hardy's contact with Mr. Sussman in 1994 are somewhat confusing. The undeniable fact is that before Sussman was on the scene, Ms. Hardy's only written communication to her company was that there was no interest on the part of the Ironworkers in Blue Cross.

Ms. Hardy denies that she and Sussman talked about the Preferred Care account, either when they first spoke on the phone or in the car on the way to meet Sweeney. Is it possible that this is so? The rules and laws of probability suggest otherwise.

Consider, for example, the following questions:

Q: In the car with Mr. Sussman, you must have wanted to know what coverage the Ironworkers had so you could know how to pitch your company as superior?

Q: Surely, while you were in the car, you must have wanted to know whether the Ironworkers were happy or unhappy with their current health care policy?

Q: Surely Mr. Sussman told you that he could provide you with information about the Ironworkers' current policy because he was the broker on that policy?

Q: You were interested, were you not, in why Mr. Sussman believed he could deliver the Ironworkers as a Blue Cross account when your company had failed to do so since 1988?

For us, this is the art. The questions argue the plaintiff's theory of the case. When the witness is compelled either to answer "yes" and confirm the theory or to answer "no" and undermine her own credibility, plaintiff's counsel could not be in a better position. Counsel is effective in using the rules and laws of probability at several points, as we observe in the transcript. One of the best moments is when he pushes Ms. Hardy to deny that her reference (in a letter to Sussman, plaintiff's Exhibit 8) to obtaining an agreement "beneficial to all" was intended to suggest that she hoped Blue Cross/Blue Shield would make a profit. We have suggested that a jury will not find this credible. Counsel might have followed up with additional questions:

> Q: You wanted the Ironworkers' business?

> Q: You used Mr. Sussman's help in an effort to obtain that business?

> Q: Blue Cross/Blue Shield did not want the Ironworkers' business in order to take a loss?

> Q: Blue Cross/Blue Shield wanted the business to make money?

> Q: When you created your prospect list in 1992 for Blue Cross/Blue Shield, you looked at prospects that would produce profits for the company?

> Q: No one at Blue Cross/Blue Shield rewarded you for losing money?

> Q: No one at Blue Cross/Blue Shield was seeking new business that would result in losses?

Is a denial by Ms. Hardy to any of these statements likely to enhance her credibility? We don't think so.

We have trouble with questions of any witness like "you want them to believe that." It is an obvious but weak way to indicate the examiner's belief that the witness is not being candid. If the examiner thinks she is lying about the broker of record conversation, rather than asking this kind of question, the examiner might use the rules and laws of probability to persuade the jury that the answers ring false.

The witness denies remembering whether she received ZIP Code information and medical information regarding Mr. Sweeney's grandson from Mr. Sussman. Because she has no memory, she cannot deny that she received them from Mr. Sussman. Whenever a witness says, "I don't remember," the door is open for the examiner to clarify:

> Q: Since you don't remember, you cannot deny that Mr. Sussman gave them to you?

Q: Since you don't remember if or how you got them, you cannot say whether any conversation took place when they were delivered?

Q: Since you don't remember if or how you got them, you cannot say why they were delivered?

Q: What you can say, however, is that if you got them from Mr. Sussman, you must have known that he was providing them to you in connection with seeking the Ironworkers' account?

The examiner's use of the deposition to impeach the witness serves as a reminder that the best way to use a prior statement is to combine within the four corners of a question the witness's current answer with the witness's prior statement, to cite the page and line of the question and answer, and to read it so that there can be no interruption or objection. Ms. Hardy flat-out denied that she told Sussman that he could expect a 1 to 3 percent commission on the total premiums billed. In her deposition, she testified that this was the arrangement. Thus, the confrontation with the witness should be sharp and clear:

Q: Ms. Hardy, you just denied that the 1 to 3 percent was of total premiums billed, but isn't it true that in your deposition, taken on [date], at page __, lines ___, you were asked this question and gave this answer: _____.

This puts the contradiction in its starkest form before the jury. It avoids the interruption by opposing counsel regarding page or line. And it makes clear that these are the precise words used by the witness under oath on a prior occasion.

Finally, after much of the examination, counsel asks Ms. Hardy whether she received a commission on the Ironworkers' contract. This is not something that counsel opened on, and it is not something that he thought should be brought out early in the examination. For us, the fact that she received a commission could be very important. It shows a motive for forgetting, a motive for cheating Sussman, and a motive for wanting to win the case. Moreover, it is evidence that everyone—Hardy, Sullivan, Sussman, and Blue Cross/Blue Shield—had a profit motive for acting as they did. This is something that, in our judgment, should have been a centerpiece of the plaintiff's case. It should have been a key part of the opening statement, and it should have been developed early in the examination of both Sullivan and Hardy. Hardy's commission—especially the retention part—makes Sussman's claim for a commission on renewals seem like standard practice in the industry, not greed.

The examiner ends by pointing out that Hardy expects to receive a commission on the Ironworkers contract until she retires and that there was nothing to stop Blue Cross/Blue Shield from paying a commission to Sussman other than the broker of record policy to which she testified.

Getting to the commission is important, but so is the amount. If it is a large commission, greed is more readily inferred. If it is small, greed may not be as obvious. At some point, the jury will learn about the magnitude of the commission. Remember that the lawyer who elicits the information first has the chance to cast his or her light on it. Plaintiff's counsel had the chance to go first, but did not embrace it as to the amount of the commission.

Look back on this examination, and consider that Ms. Hardy even denied that Blue Cross/Blue Shield was out to make a profit on the Ironworkers contract. Put her commission together with Blue Cross/Blue Shield's desire to make a profit, and her motive to use Mr. Sussman to meet with and persuade Mr. Sweeney becomes a lot clearer.

The examination ends strong, stronger than it began. The witness's memory problems and her attempt to downplay the financial interest she and Blue Cross/Blue Shield had in the Ironworkers contract might have been even more effective for the plaintiffs had the order of the examination been changed so that her commission and her interest in testifying were elicited up front. Then, each memory lapse could be accompanied by a question as to whether the failure to remember is a result of her not wanting to put her commission at risk in this case.

One of the nicest parts of the examination was the way in which plaintiff's counsel managed to get Ms. Hardy to concede that she was concerned about "a broker" (and that only could mean Sussman) when she spoke with Maresca. This demonstrated that she always thought Sussman had to be dealt with somehow, and that his presence was not an isolated occurrence that had passed from her mind.

DEFENDANTS' DECISION NOT TO EXAMINE THE WITNESS

The plaintiffs made Ms. Hardy the focal point of their attack in their opening statement. Her direct examination was in large part an assault on her memory and credibility. Yet, for the first time in this trial, defense counsel has no questions "at this time." We have indicated our agreement that, because Ms. Hardy was the last plaintiff's witness, the decision to defer most of her examination—rather than to try to put on the defendant's entire case—is sound.

There is a risk here, however. The failure to ask any questions after Ms. Hardy has admitted that she wants a commission, based on the Ironworkers contract, for the rest of her working life leaves the plaintiff in a very powerful position. Moreover, the suggestion is planted that the commission she is receiving is large. If this is not so, it might have been preferable to make this and a couple of other points, particularly on noninterference, while clearly indicating to the jury that the bulk of the defendants' examination of Ms. Hardy will await the presentation of the defense case.

As we shall see, the defendants call Ms. Hardy later, on their own case. In most cases, later is almost always too late. The calling of an adverse witness leaves the one calling the witness open to a full examination—the equivalent of having all the linebackers in the backfield before the play is fully formed. Defense counsel should seize the opportunity to put his case in the midst of the plaintiff's case. See Vol. III, pp. 330–334.

Defense counsel is stuck with the memoranda that Ms. Hardy made and the fact that Sussman did get the ball rolling

with Sweeney. He cannot avoid the fact that Ms. Hardy discussed a commission with Sussman. In addition to eliciting evidence about the amount of the commission, defense counsel
might have chosen to plant the seeds of the defense, with the
details reserved for the defense case. He could, for example,
have made some simple points that might have cast a reasonable light on her overall approach to Sussman:

Q: When Mr. Sussman called you and identified himself as a broker, whom did you believe he represented?

A: The Ironworkers.

Q: Why did you think he called?

A: I figured that someone at the Ironworkers might
have expressed some interest in Blue Cross/Blue Shield.

Q: And when Mr. Sussman and you discussed a commission, whom did you think Mr. Sussman was representing?

A: The Ironworkers.

Q: Did you do anything to prevent the Ironworkers from
using Mr. Sussman as a broker?

A: No.

Q: Who did?

A: Mr. Maresca told me that there would be no broker.

Q: Who chose Mr. Maresca to represent the Ironworkers?

A: The Ironworkers did. Mr. Sweeney and his people
did.

Q: Did you have any choice between dealing with Mr.
Sussman and Mr. Maresca?

A: No.

Q: Did you have any authority to choose the Ironworkers' representative?

A: No.

Q: Why did you discuss Mr. Sussman with Mr. Maresca?

A: I wanted to be sure that Mr. Sussman was not overlooked.

Q: Was he overlooked?

A: Absolutely not. Mr. Maresca made it clear to me that the Ironworkers did not want to use a broker.

Q: Had the Ironworkers chosen Mr. Sweeney as their broker, would he have received a commission?

A: Yes.

Q: What sort of commission?

A: One to three percent.

Q: Just as you had discussed with Mr. Sussman and recorded in your notes?

A: Yes.

Q: Did the Ironworkers want Mr. Sweeney as their broker?

A: According to Mr. Maresca, they did not.

Q: When you first dealt with Mr. Sussman, did you know about Mr. Maresca and the Segal Company?

A: No.

Q: Did you know when you first dealt with Mr. Sussman that he had no authority to speak for the Ironworkers?

A: No.

Q: Would you have talked to him about a commission if he had told you he had no broker authority?

A: No.

This line of examination makes an argument that it was Sussman who assumed authority he did not have, and it was the Ironworkers—not Blue Cross/Blue Shield—who made it clear that he could not serve as a broker.

We cannot emphasize enough that it is far better for these points to be made *earlier* and then *again* later, rather than just later.

Chapter Eight

Concluding the Plaintiff's Case and Motions

CONCLUDING MATTERS

MR. LONGER: Your Honor, I have one or two matters that I think I have—two points to raise, Your Honor, and I'm going to conclude my case. One is I would like to read into the record an interrogatory answer by these Defendants, and number two, is that this morning the parties were able to agree to a stipulation of undisputed facts and we'd like to read that into the record, as well.

THE COURT: Very well. These are—an interrogatory answer is basically an admission, which means that you can take it as fact. And the same with stipulations. A stipulation means that both parties agree that these are the facts, and they are, therefore, facts for you to consider in the case. So, unlike any other statements of counsel, these are evidence.

[Comment] This instruction is, of course, correct, but hardly understandable to a lay jury, which might simply have been told that these are the statements of the defendant company. The problem is compounded by counsel's reading superfluous legal jargon.

MR. LONGER: "Interrogatory Number 6: State whether you have a policy or practice, that a physical document is required to establish a broker of record relationship before you'll recognize the broker of record relationship. If so, identify every broker of record to whom you have paid a commission pursuant to such a policy or practice, the documents establishing the broker of record relationship and the company policy, if written. In addition, identify whether you have ever paid a commission to a person or entity as a broker of record lacking such documentation."

The response is: "Defendants object to this Interrogatory on the grounds that it is overly broad and to the extent that it seeks information that is irrelevant and/or not reasonably calculated to lead to the discovery of relevant information. It is further objected to this Interrogatory, on the grounds that the terms 'policy or practice,' and 'broker of record relationship,' are vague and ambiguous."

[Comment] So far, this preliminary mumbo-jumbo need not have been read. One wonders if the jurors are still there. Why in the world would this first part be relevant to the jurors?

"Subject to and without waiving the foregoing objection, the Defendants respond as follows: A broker of record letter is not required in order for Defendants to quote a contract for a prospective client, relative to Defendants by a broker. However, a broker cannot receive a commission when and if the sale to the prospective client is consummated unless the broker provides defendants with a broker of record letter. If two brokers are involved in bringing the same prospective client to the Defendants, the broker who approaches Defendants second must receive authorization from the prospective client before Defendants will quote the contract or the second broker. It is Defendant's policy and practice never to pay a Commission to a person or an entity without first obtaining a broker of record letter."

[Comment] What was that? Who's on first? Is a letter required or not? As Yul Brynner said, "Is a puzzlement." It is clear that counsel is putting things in the record to use later, much later, because one can only imagine what the poor jurors are doing by the end of this reading. But there is more to come.

The stipulation of undisputed facts dated today, reads as follows: "Defendants, Independence Blue Cross and

Pennsylvania Blue Shield, and Tower Financial Planning
Associates Incorporated, Tower, hereby stipulate and
agree to the following undisputed facts. Number one, on
or about the last week of May or the first week of June
1994, Helen Hardy, of I.B.C., and Leonard Sussman of
Tower, met with Robert Sweeney of the Ironworkers
Union Local Number 399, the local of the—I'm sorry, at
the Local's offices in New Jersey to discuss health bene-
fits coverage for the Ironworkers Philadelphia Vicinity
Health and Welfare Fund. Number 2: On April 7th, 1995,
a meeting among Mr. Sussman, Mr. Sweeney and Brian
Sullivan of I.B.C., occurred at the Local's offices in New
Jersey. Number 3: On June 23, 1995, the Board of
Trustees of the Fund met in New Jersey and authorized
the Investment Committee of the Fund to meet with the
Segal Company (Segal, the Fund's consultants to review a
Preferred Provider Organization (P.P.O.) Program and
report the fundings at the September, 1995 meeting.
Number 4: On July 26th, 1995, Ms. Hardy and other
I.B.C. representatives met with representatives of the
Fund and Segal at the offices of I.B.C. in Philadelphia.
Number 5: On July 31, 1995, Segal requested that I.B.C.
provide a proposal for introducing a managed care P.P.O.
for the Fund. Number 6: On August 17, 1995, I.B.C. pro-
vided Segal with the requested proposal. Number 7: On
August 21, 1995, a meeting among Messrs. Sussman,
Sweeney and Sullivan occurred at the local's offices in
New Jersey."

I should put a sic in there because it says "in
occurred." "Number 8: On September 5, 1995, the
Investment Committee of the Fund met, along with representatives of Segal and I.B.C. to review the August 24,
1995 memorandum prepared by Segal, analyzing the
I.B.C. proposal. It was agreed to approve the concept of a
voluntary P.P.O. and a hospitalization program through
I.B.C. and to recommend implementation of the program
to the Board of Trustees of the Fund at the meeting

scheduled for September 2, 1995. Number 9: On September 22, 1995, the Board of Trustees of the Fund met in Philadelphia and approved the implementation of the I.B.C. proposal with an effective target date of January 1, 1996."

With that, Your Honor, the Plaintiff rests its case.

THE COURT: Thank you.

*[**Comment**] It is clear that counsel has no hope of the jurors' following any of this. Then why is he doing it? To make his record so that he can explain it all in summation. Ah, but will it matter by then? See Vol. IV, pp. 27–29. And, as you will see for yourself, in this very case, the summations could not have mattered much. But that is for later. The point is this: When speaking to people, any people — and that includes jurors — speak to them. To fail to do that is to risk being misunderstood, or worse. If the stipulated facts were important to the plaintiff's case, we suggest they should have been integrated into the opening and / or into the examination of witnesses.*

MR. SONNENFELD; Your Honor, just so the record is clear, I.B.C., as used in the stipulation, referred to Independence Blue Cross. I think someone reading the record might not have understood that, so we wanted to make that clear.

THE COURT: Very well. And we'll deal with your exhibits when the Jury leaves.

MR. LONGER: Very well.

THE COURT: Are there any objections to any of the exhibits, for that matter?

MR. SONNENFELD: No objections to any of the exhibits that he has introduced in this case.

THE COURT: Thank you.

MR. SONNENFELD: I would like to get a list.

THE COURT: We can do that on the break. Thank you. The Plaintiff has rested. Now, once again, I want you to ask you to please don't discuss the case with each other or anybody else because, obviously, you only heard half the case and you haven't received the instruction on the law and you haven't heard the arguments of counsel. So, have a nice lunch and I'll see you at—well, I was going to say 2:00, which gives you an hour and a half. But I'll make it 2:15. I want to clean up a couple of things with counsel before we start and there's no sense in just sitting in the little room if you don't have to. So, I'll see you at 2:15. Thank you.

- - - -

[Jury exits.]

DEFENDANTS' MOTION

[Comment] This is the time when the defendant moves for a dismissal—a nonsuit, as it is often termed—on the ground that no reasonable juror could find for the other side. It is not often granted, of course, because it requires the judge to predict what a juror could do. Sometimes it can be valuable, though. In our judgment, this is such a case. In our view, the plaintiff is really not suing for interference with a prospective contractual relationship between the plaintiff and the union, but rather for breach of an agreement by Blue Cross for Blue Cross to pay him a commission for work done for Blue Cross. But that is not what the complaint alleges, and so the defendant has a real chance to dump this case, if he can persuade the judge accordingly. Let us watch the way he handles it.

[Discussion on the record.]

- - - -

MR. SONNENFELD: If I may proceed, Your Honor, at this time the Defense moves for a compulsory nonsuit. I have a memorandum of law which I would like to hand up. If I may, I'll hand the Court the original, and certainly have a copy for Mr. Longer. Your Honor, as the Court knows, this is an action on a two-count Complaint. Count

1 alleges intentional interference with the prospective
contractual relationship; Count 2 alleges negligent interference with a prospective contractual relationship. So,
therefore, Count 1 alleges an intentional tort, Count 2
alleges a negligent tort.

There are four elements to the intentional tort in
Count 1 of tortious interference a prospective contractual
relationship. I would submit on the evidence in the
Plaintiff's case, none of those four elements have been
established. Under the Thompson Cole Case, the four elements are to show a prospective relationship, an improper interference, lack of absence of privilege and damage
resulting. In here, you look at the first element, a
prospective relationship, the Ironworkers clearly didn't
want Mr. Sussman or Tower as their broker and there
was no prospective relationship. The mere fact that Mr.
Sussman had at some time in the past been a broker for
the Ironworkers for another contract for Preferred Care is
irrelevant. We heard Mr. Craggs and we've heard from
the evidence, the Ironworkers simply didn't want
Sussman or Tower, there was no prospective relationship.

*[Comment] We do not understand how Blue Cross interfered
with a relationship because it would not pay a commission. We
suppose that would be a breach of their contract if they had one
with the plaintiff. "He claims we owed him a commission—but
he isn't suing us for that." That's what we suggest might be
said.*

There has to be something more than a hope or a
glimmer of something in the future. Every salesman has
that hope. You remember the famous Arthur Miller play,
The Death of a Salesman, how the salesman lives on a
smile and a shoeshine. Every salesman has the hope of
making a sale. <u>We all know what life insurance salesmen
are like. They are like chewing gum that gets stuck on
your shoe</u>, they call you up on the phone and you can't get
rid of them. That was Mr. Sussman, always calling and
hoping some day to get his foot in the door. And here you

have the Ironworkers who don't want him, and Blue Cross is caught in the middle. But it's clear that there was no prospective relationship.

[Comment] We suggest that this unkind argument is counterproductive. It even contradicts counsel's argument that Sussman was doing nothing. It sure does nothing to point out that Sussman has brought the wrong kind of lawsuit. The point, if one agrees with us, is slip slipping away, as we used to sing.

You then need an intentional or improper interference. Where is the interference? Mr. Sussman admits that he is not aware of anyone from Independence Blue Cross or Pennsylvania Blue Shield ever telling the Ironworkers not to deal with Sussman or Tower. No evidence of that. Or anything, the evidence is to the contrary. Ms. Hardy went out of her way to try to make sure, whether or not the Ironworkers wanted—it is their call, whether or not they wanted Sussman involved. And she asked Maresca, who is this Ironworker's consultant of 40 years, and was told no.

[Comment] What he might have said was "everyone, including Sussman, knew we would not pay him a commission unless authorized in writing by the union. Everyone, including Sussman, says the union would not authorize it. No one, including Sussman, says that we told the union to refuse. So . . . where's the beef against Blue Cross?"

The third element is that they acted without justification or improperly. Well, here, what else was Blue Cross to do in this situation? You had a situation where for some time Ms. Hardy has had contacts with the Ironworkers and Mr. Sweeney. She has met with him already on her own. She has a single meeting with him that Mr. Sussman sets up in late May or early June of 1994, and gets no further than the meeting she had on her own. He then sets up a meeting. He expresses the salesman optimism and Mr. Sweeney doesn't take it any

further than the previous meeting Ms. Hardy had with
him. That's in May or June of 1994. And then, a year
later, a year later, more than a year later, Ms. Hardy is
contacted by Mr. Maresca on behalf of the Ironworkers to
set up the meeting that took place on July 26th, 1995.
And she asked what about Mr. Sussman and she's told he
is not involved. What more could Blue Cross do? Can they
say, "Gee, Ironworkers, we don't want to have anything to
do with you. Take your 2,500 members and go somewhere
else because unless you hire Mr. Sussman as your broker"—they're really caught in the middle here. They're in
a very difficult position. Clearly, whatever they did, they
did with justification and privilege, as those terms are
used as one of the elements of the tort of intentional
interference with a contractual relationship. And then
beyond that, you have the fact, and I think it goes to both
the prospective relationship of the account and the lack of
privilege, is there was no broker of record letter. There's
nothing to evidence that the Ironworkers Fund wanted
Mr. Sussman or Tower to be their broker. And the evidence that came out repeatedly shows that he was told to
get a broker of record letter. Ms. Hardy tells him that in
the meeting of May or June of 1994. Mr. Sussman admits
he knew that from the New Jersey Ironworkers and New
Jersey Blues, when he dealt with them in November of
'94, and was told by them he needed a broker of record
letter to get a commission. And then he has the same conversation with Mr. Sullivan, when he tries to go around
Ms. Hardy's back in April of 1995. So, it is no mystery,
there is nothing unique about a broker of record letter.

*[Comment] We suggest he has now shifted the argument closer
to the real point. We suggest that he is scoring on that point,
but we fear that it has been buried in the prior material. And
now, unfortunately, he shifts away from the point to another:
the do-nothing argument which the judge, on the record, cannot
possibly use to dismiss the case.*

I think the problem Mr. Sussman wound up in is he
was in unfamiliar territory to himself to give himself
credit. I mean, he admits his experience is primarily life,
not health, primarily small groups, not a group of this
size, and never before dealt with a Health and Welfare
Fund. He was operating in a different field. And he had
no prior experience with Independence Blue Cross. He
never had been to their offices. He never placed anybody
with them, you know, there are two and a half million
people with Independence Blue Cross in this area, and he
never placed any of those two and a half million people.
So, he was just operating on something that he was out of
his customary practice and did nothing to confer benefits,
which also goes, I think, to the absence of privilege. It is
clear that, at the most, he set up three meetings of a half
hour to hour in length and never produced the kinds of
information that would be necessary for Independence
Blue Cross to submit a proposal, and indeed Mr. Sussman
admitted that he never submitted a proposal and never
submitted to the Ironworkers a contract on behalf of Blue
Cross. So, I think none of those first three elements have
been established.

*[Comment] Now, he returns to what we believe is — or should
be — one of his main points.*

And fourth, finally is the issue of damage. In order to
get damages, you have to show them with some degree of
specificity, some degree of certainty. Here there never was
any agreement as to what the commission would be that
Mr. Sussman or Tower would get, even if they got a broker of record letter.

*[Comment] Finally, we get to the heart of the problem, which
looks, at least to us, to be a failure of proof that there was a contract between Blue Cross and the plaintiff, or the plaintiff and
anyone, even assuming the plaintiff had brought a suit for
breach of contract. He might better sue on a quantum meruit
theory, and that against Blue Cross directly, upon whom he*

probably did confer a benefit, rather than this interference theo-
ry, but he did not.

When Mr. Sussman dealt with Preferred Care, he had
a written contract with them that spelled out what his
commission was. He admits that he had no such contract
with Independence Blue Cross. Instead, you have conversations with ranges of commission, but nothing agreed
upon. And to suggest that he gets some extraordinary
amount of money for setting up two or three meetings
that didn't go anywhere, it's not the degree of certainty
that you need to prove damages under our law. So, I think
that would dispose of the first count.

*[Comment] Very good. But Count I does not allege breach of
contract, and the meeting did get somewhere, eventually.*

The second count is even easier to dispose of. And
this, I would like to direct the Court's attention to the
case on point. The second count alleges the tort of negligent interference with a prospective contractual relationship.

Here, I would submit, Your Honor, there is no such
tort in Pennsylvania. That tort simply doesn't exist and
in so stating, I rely upon the Superior Court's decision in,
I believe, it's *Akins versus the Baltimore and Ohio
Railroad,* a decision by Judge Olszewski, from Wilkes
Barre, on Superior Court. And also, I guess this is a case
that is the leading case in Pennsylvania, and held that
there's no recognized tort in Pennsylvania of negligent
interference with a prospective contractual relationship.
And the Court said that negligent harm, economic advantage alone is too remote for recovery under a negligence
theory and the Court held the allowance of a cause of
action for negligent interference with economic advantage
would create an undue burden upon industrial freedom of
action. So, we would submit that there is no such tort. I
would like to hand up, if I could, the Superior Court's
decision, which I think is controlling on this Court. And I

think it would be error to submit that second count to the Jury, regardless of what the evidence showed. But even looking at the evidence, you know, where is the negligence?

What did Blue Cross do negligently? The thing that always racks my brain is, I think about this, is if the same thing happened tomorrow, what would you do differently? How would you protect yourself if Mr. Sussman starts to pester them tomorrow on behalf of some other union? What would you do differently? Where was the negligence? Where was the lack of care?

[Comment] We agree, but the real issue is, where is the tort? Where was the duty, if not in contract? And that, of course, is not alleged by the plaintiff.

And I guess the only lack of care probably, is not getting an indemnity from the Ironworkers, if Mr. Sussman bothers you, to be able to say that he is your problem. But in those jurisdictions that have recognized the tort of negligent interference with a prospective contractual relationship, and Pennsylvania [is] not one of those jurisdictions, those jurisdictions have required some kind of a special relationship between the Plaintiff and the Defendants, some kind of a relationship of trust and fiduciary relationship. Here there was a zero relationship between Blue Cross and Mr. Sussman. He called Ms. Hardy up out of the blue, had no contract with Blue Cross, no prior dealings with Blue Cross, no subsequent dealings with Blue Cross, never been to their office, no relationship that would justify even in those jurisdictions that recognize the tort, imposing that special relationship upon the facts of this case.

So for these reasons, Your Honor, we would respectfully request that the Court grant our motion for compulsory nonsuit as to both counts.

THE COURT: Thank you. Counsel?

MR. LONGER: May I proceed?

THE COURT: Yes.

[Comment] And now in response, counsel wields an arcane rule, put aside as ancient nonsense in most jurisdictions, that if a defendant offers any evidence on the plaintiff's case, it may no longer move for dismissal at the close of that case. Nonetheless, he skillfully causes great concern with it.

MR. LONGER: Thank you. At the end of the day yesterday, we had a discussion where I know I said to you, you got me paranoid now because you started talking about the rules and you said Mr. Sonnenfeld would bring up that motion and you'll read the rule and you'll tell me where it is. And what we have here is a procedural issue, which, I believe, estops them from even presenting this motion to Your Honor.

Yesterday, Mr. Craggs, who is the Fund Administrator, appeared here pursuant to a subpoena. He was, in my mind, a hostile witness. He was certainly unwilling to appear here without a subpoena. Mr. Sweeney told me—

MR. SONNENFELD: Well, I think whatever Mr. Sweeney told—

MR. LONGER: Mr. Sweeney was unwilling to appear here is as polite as I'll put this. And that's why we read his transcript into the record. But, be that as it may, Mr. Craggs took the stand, and Your Honor will recall that Ms. Bennett began a cross-examination, to which I objected as being beyond the scope of the direct examination and Your Honor sustained that objection and Ms. Bennett's request, and over my objection, she presented Mr. Craggs in the Defense's case in chief, during my presentation.

The Defendants presented evidence, Your Honor, supporting their defense in my case in chief, over my objection. And I read the rule last night, Your Honor, and the rule makes it pretty clear, that wherever the defendant upon the trial of a cause in any Court of Common Pleas of this Commonwealth, shall offer no evidence, it shall be lawful for the Judge presiding at the trial to order a judgment of nonsuit to be entered. That's not the case here.

They presented evidence, and they should be estopped from even presenting this motion. Their defense is already of record. Now, I think that that is the law in Pennsylvania. I think it is binding, so I think that as far as the procedure goes, the motion is baseless and should be denied.

[Comment] The procedural point made, counsel goes to the substance of the motion.

Now, substantively, I'd be happy to address several of the points which Mr. Sonnenfeld raised, and I'll begin with the intentional prospective contract claim. There are four elements of prospective relationship. Clearly there is a big factual dispute here between how *many* meetings took place between Ms. Hardy, Mr. Sweeney, and Mr. Sussman. There is a big factual dispute as to what his expectations were. Especially, as you heard Ms. Hardy today discuss, even in September, she is talking to him about the commission that he can expect to receive. The next year, in 1995, when she is talking to Mr. Maresca about a contract that she is expecting to have a request for proposal, she is asking Mr. Maresca, what about Mr. Sussman? Mr. Sussman would have every expectation, just like Ms. Hardy had every expectation, that this was going forward, and it is more than a mere hope of a salesman. We're not talking about Willy Loman here. We are talking about—we are talking about Mr. Sussman who got these two parties together.

[Comment] Hope of a contract, and a commission from where?

Now, the second element was that the Defendants interfered with the relationship. And what we've heard, is that Ms. Hardy, and she's denying it, but I think it raises a question of fact as to what she was doing with Mr. Maresca talking about Mr. Sussman's right to a commission. And what she was doing about this company's policy to exclude brokers who don't have the letter, but get them into the process of getting to the point where they could contract? I think the evidence yesterday was very clear. Mr. Sussman got these people to the point where Ms. Hardy could just sort of take over and kick him out. And in a way, that talks about the third element, too, which is this privilege element. The privilege element, I think, is like Jello. I don't know how to describe it, because the case law out there makes it like Jello.

The case law says, well, something wasn't right. It's—the business world is up in the air, <u>and what is right or not in the business world is what a Jury has to decide</u>. And I think that it's pretty clear in the case law that is cited, even in Mr. Sonnenfeld's brief to Your Honor which was just presented.

[Comment] This is really his best argument. And it is an emotional, not a legal or even a rational one: Sussman, who brought a benefit upon both union and company, got nothing. And that just ain't fair.

Lastly, damages. We're talking about a very unique cause of action in Pennsylvania. Intentional interference with a prospective contract. You don't have the contract, it's prospective. What are the damages in a prospective contract? One that hasn't yet been fully negotiated, one that hasn't yet been memorialized, one that isn't in existence yet.

[Comment] Negotiated with whom? To be contracted with whom? Interfered with by whom?

Mr. Sussman had every expectation to negotiate either one of two things. He had talked to Ms. Hardy about his Preferred Care formula of computing his commission. And we have Ms. Hardy saying today that she discussed with Mr. Sussman, a 1 to 3 percent commission based on just the premiums billed. So, I think one way or another, this Jury is going to be able to calculate that figure. They are either going to look at the 6 million dollar figure and they are going to say, 1 percent, they are going to look at the 1—or 3 percent. I mean it could be 60,000, or it could be 180,000.

Yesterday, Mr. Sussman talked about gross billings of—what was it—17 million. And we talked about the arithmetics at 17 million. Or we have the Preferred Care formula, based on the $600,000 figure, which would have been 20 percent of the 600, or $120,000. That's what Mr. Sussman <u>would</u> have been willing and <u>hoping</u> to negotiate a point to receiving.

[Comment] The "would" and the "hoping" are telltales of a legal weakness in the plaintiff's case.

So, I think that we have established all four elements and that gets us to the negligent interference with a prospective contract. Mr. Sonnenfeld is presenting to Your Honor a motion for summary judgment. Again, he is reasserting his preliminary objections. He's claiming that the cause of action does not exist in Pennsylvania. At the preliminary objection stage of this case, that issue was raised, it was briefed. The motion was denied. The reason the motion was denied is because the tort, which we all agree is the relevant case, the Superior Court—

MR. SONNENFELD: There was no opinion, so I don't think anybody knows the reason why it was denied. We just simply got an order.

THE COURT: Who denied it?

MR. LONGER: You're testing our memory.

MR. SONNENFELD: We didn't have argument. It was just—

MR. LONGER: It wasn't Judge Ackerman.

MR. SONNENFELD: I can find out.

THE COURT: It's not that important.

MR. LONGER: I can tell you, Your Honor, if you have the file, that it was denied July 8th, 1996.

THE COURT: I have it. Don't worry about it.

MR. LONGER: At any rate, the reason that it was denied is because the *Akins* case, says that—and I'm referring to 501 A 2nd, 277, and specifically at 278, a cause of action exists in this situation only if the tortious interference was intentional or parties in a special relationship to one another. What it is referring to is the negligence theory.

This was an issue dealing with economic loss doctrine, and it came up in a negligent interference, a contract context. And what the Court was saying is, ruling on a negligent interference with prospective contract, it says: "A cause of action exists where there is a special relationship."

Then, what you have to do is find out what a special relationship is. And the Court there cites to the petition of S.C. Loveland, Incorporated, which is at 70 F. Supp. 86, and it also refers to Prosser, the *Handbook of the Law of Torts,* Section 130. And what you find is that a special relationship exists where the interfering party knows of the prospective contract. Ms. Hardy knew Mr. Sussman was involved. For her to say she didn't know Mr. Sussman was involved, is baloney. So, a special relationship is exactly what's going on here, because these parties were working this case together until she found out a way to get him cut. And that's essentially the law in Pennsylvania, according to *Akins.*

And I'll quote to Your Honor from the *Loveland* case. First of all, the Court made a factual finding in the *Loveland* case, that there was no allegation of proof that Loveland knew of a contract. So, the Court made a factual finding in *Loveland,* that the defendant party knew of the contract. Here, there is no doubt that Ms. Hardy knew what Mr. Sussman was doing. And the Court in *Loveland* says, the law has consistently recognized that negligence, as opposed to intentional conduct, which results in interference with the contract right of another, is no basis for a cause of action where the negligent party has no belief or knowledge of the existence of such contract right. She knew about it. There is a negligence cause of action.

[Comment] Interesting. The plaintiff invited Blue Cross into the deal in hopes Blue Cross would pay him for his services. He did perform for Blue Cross. Now he complains about interference by Blue Cross with his prospective contract with the union simply because he was not paid. It might be different if he had any evidence that Blue Cross told the union not to give him a broker letter. But, as far as we can see, he has none.

THE COURT: Thank you.

MR. SONNENFELD: May I respond, very briefly?

THE COURT: Very briefly.

[Comment] For sure the judge has had enough.

MR. SONNENFELD: In the *Loveland* case that Mr. Longer cited, the Court again refused to find a cause of action and threw the case out. In the *Loveland* case, unlike this case, the tort that was alleged was intentional interference with a contract, not a prospective contract. Here, we are talking about a prospective contract. There was no contract to know about. So, again, would submit that under the law, as set forth by Judge Olshevsky, and consistent with the *Loveland* case, no Pennsylvania Court, Eastern District, Third Circuit or Superior Court has recognized this tort of negligence interference with a prospective contractual relationship. And I think there is certainly no claim of a special relationship here. There is no contract between Mr. Sussman and the Ironworkers to have known or acted in disregard of. So, I think it would be just error to permit that count to go to the Jury.

[Comment] On the procedural rule, counsel makes a good point. He was simply being polite.

As far as whether the rule—first of all, we simply appended to accommodate Mr. Craggs's schedule yesterday, and what was put in through him was simply the documents, the Minutes of the meetings of the Ironworkers, which are then the basis of what Mr. Longer stipulated to, and he himself put in anyway stipulating to that chronology. So, I think it would really elevate form over substance on that basis alone to deny the motion for compulsory nonsuit, especially as to the second count.

THE COURT: Thank you. Now, if I could trouble you, because I'm going to take it under advisement until after lunch, could I borrow your copy of *Loveland*?

MR. SONNENFELD: We would also like to give you a couple Third Circuit cases.

THE COURT: Yes. If you have any cases you want to give me.

MR. LONGER: Your Honor, what I'd like to do, since I wasn't anticipating, I just want to present to Your Honor, my brief, my memorandum, in opposition to the preliminary objections which gives you my points on the law.

- - - -

[Luncheon recess.]

BRIEF COMMENTS ON THE MOTION

We claim no expertise on Pennsylvania law or on the tort of interference with prospective contractual relationships, but our gut instinct is that the defendants' legal arguments were stronger than the equities upon which they relied. With the benefit of hindsight, our clear preference (as our comments along the way indicate) would be for a claim against breach of implied contract between Sussman and Blue Cross. Such a claim would have been based on an implicit understanding that Sussman was a middleman who expected a percentage from Blue Cross if he could connect them with the Ironworkers.

The beauty of this case is that it demonstrates most powerfully that juries are not legal scholars. They, and more than a few judges too, are not concerned with the niceties of tort law and the distinctions that Prosser and torts experts draw between various torts. Most of all, they are concerned with justice and fairness. If they conclude that Blue Cross used Sussman and breached an implied agreement, they will find for Sussman and make the tort law fit the case.

Of course, some judge or appellate tribunal might have the last word on the law. Our focus is on the trial, however, and it is clear to us that the arguments made by defense counsel must persuade the judge because the jury will not rely on technicalities. The judge indicates he is taking the issues under advisement, and the trial will resume without a ruling being made.

One aspect of the argument is notable. Plaintiff's counsel claims that the defendants cannot raise this motion at this time, because they offered evidence in the form of going beyond the scope of the direct of Craggs and thus cannot claim that the plaintiff's case is insufficient to withstand a motion. Even if the trial judge thought that this was the law, if he concluded that at the end of the defense case plaintiff's case still would be lacking, it would not be surprising for him to find any procedural mistake harmless and to grant the motion. The plaintiff's argument serves as a reminder, however, that in some instances the decision to offer evidence may have procedural implications for the court independent of the probative value of the evidence, depending on the law of the jurisdiction.

Chapter Nine

The Defendants' First Witness: Mr. Maresca

TEXT OF THE DIRECT EXAMINATION

[Comment] What happened to the ruling on the motions heard before lunch? The judge is still considering them. He will deny them later.

The first witness is just as important a decision for the defense's case as it was for the plaintiff on his case. It seems to us that the choice comes down to either Maresca or Sweeney; Hardy, most vulnerable to cross, must be last. This analysis, of course, repudiates the notion of recency over primacy, summation over opening. We completely agree with the defendant's counsel in putting Hardy last and are inclined to agree with calling Maresca first. Why? Because Maresca first makes it more difficult to cross Sweeney, who comes after. And, once heard, Maresca and Sweeney make the cross of Hardy harder, and she is the one who needs the most protection. Among all the considerations that go into the selection of the order of proofs, a decision that most lawyers make last, the protection of the advocates' central theme and key witness is paramount. This subject, the order of witnesses, is the most sophisticated in the lexicon of trial exposition. For those interested in a full discussion of the subject, with attendant problems, and underlying analysis, we can only refer to Vol. II, pp. 215–220.

[Jury enters.]

- - - -

THE COURT: Okay. Defense, call your first witness.

MR. SONNENFELD: May I proceed, Your Honor?

THE COURT: Please.

MR. SONNENFELD: Defense calls Mr. Maresca.

THE CRIER: Place your right hand on the Bible. State your name and spell your last name.

THE WITNESS: Charles Maresca, M-A-R-E-S-C-A.

- - - -

CHARLES MARESCA, WITNESS, after having been first duly sworn, was examined and testified as follows:

MR. SONNENFELD: May I proceed, Your Honor?

THE COURT: Please.

BY MR. SONNENFELD:

Q: Can you hear me all right, Mr. Maresca?

A: Yes, I can.

Q: Please keep your voice up, because we want the Jury to be able to hear you. For the record, please state your full name.

A: Charles Maresca.

Q: Where do you live?

A: Pearl River, New York.

Q: Where are you employed, sir?

A: Segal Company.

Q: Where is your company located?

A: 1 Park Avenue, New York City.

Q: What is your position with the Segal Company?

A: Senior Vice-President.

Q: How long have you been with the Segal Company?

A: Forty-two years.

Q: And how old are you, sir

A: Sixty-two.

Q: Can you tell us, please, your educational background?

A: I have a Bachelor's and Master's degree in Business Administration from the City College of New York.

[Comment] Counsel, as does his adversary, has a practice of beginning many, if not most, of his questions with "and." As we noted earlier, this usually unconscious mannerism among many examiners is merely a verbal pausing for a mental breath—but it is distracting and should be curtailed. All one needs to do is pause the extra second, quietly, until the next words of the actual question are formed, or to be more precise, until the next answer is heard in one's inner ear, which automatically triggers the next question. See Vol. II, pp. 14–16. In any event, "and"s should not be used.

Q: <u>And</u> can you tell us, please, what the Segal Company is?

A: Segal Company are consulting actuaries. What we do is establish pension and health funds on a basis of, in my particular area, multi-employer, on the basis of contributions that are negotiated by a union in conjunction with either an employer's association [or] group of employers.

Q: What are your duties and responsibilities as [a] Senior Vice-President at the Segal Company?

A: I serve as a liaison in terms of the clients and the company.

Q: <u>And</u> is one of the clients for whom you serve as a liaison, the Ironworkers District Council of Philadelphia and Vicinity Health Fund?

A: It is.

Q: <u>And</u> for how long have you been involved with that Fund?

A: I, myself, since 1958.

Q: <u>And</u> for how long has the Segal Company been involved with that Fund?

A: Since the Fund's inception, which, I believe, is 1951.

Q: <u>And</u> since, how long have you been the primary contact between the Segal Company and that Fund?

A: For more than 30 years.

[Comment] Very good, as far as it goes. We, the authors, know, although the jury perhaps does not, that the Segal Company is the preeminent company in the field, handling thousands of such funds, many much larger than this one.

Q: Now, is the Ironworkers fund what is known as a Taft-Hartley Act Fund?

A: It is.

Q: Can you tell us what you mean by that term?

A: The Taft-Hartley Fund is a fund that is jointly administered by an equal number of employers and union representatives.

Q: <u>And</u> is the Taft-Hartley Act an act of the Federal Congress, the law of the Federal Congress?

A: Yes, it is.

Q: <u>And</u> is your primary area of responsibility at the Segal Company, working with Taft-Hartley Act Funds?

A: It is.

Q: <u>And</u> how is the Segal Company compensated by the Ironworkers?

A: Compensation is a fee that is negotiated annually with the Board of Trustees.

Q: It's a flat fee?

A: It's a flat fee.

Q: Is that fee approved by the Board of Trustees?

A: It is.

Q: Does the Segal Company receive a percentage of insurance placed by the Fund?

A: Sorry, I don't follow your question.

Q: Does it receive any percentage commission on insurance paid by the Fund?

A: No.

Q: Can you describe for me the kinds of services that the Segal Company provides to the Ironworkers Fund?

[Comment] The "can you" is our old friend, the call for help from the witness, and here comes the outpouring of information, much of it of no value to the controversy.

A: What we do is, first of all, attend all of the Trustees meetings. We provide them with advice in terms of the costs of the benefits that are being provided by the Fund, and whether or not they are within the framework of what has been negotiated to sustain a plan of benefits. In this particular area, the construction area, they have fallen on hard times. Most construction trade funds had to curtail benefit programs because of a downturn in employment in most of the areas, particularly here on the East Coast. What we do for a Fund is to monitor on a monthly basis their cash flow and advise the Trustees, in this particular case on a quarterly basis, that they have regular quarterly meetings, of what position the Fund is in with regard to finances.

Q: Now, are you familiar with the decision of the Ironworkers Fund to enter into a contract effective January 1, 1996, with Independence Blue Cross and Pennsylvania Blue Shield?

A: I am.

Q: And were you personally involved in that decision?

A: I was.

Q: And can you tell us the nature of your personal involvement?

A: What we did was contact Blue Cross and provide them with a request for proposal to submit a presentation for underwriting surgical/medical hospitalization benefits for the Fund.

Q: You contacted Independence Blue Cross on behalf of the Fund?

[Comment] Notice how nicely the examiner loops this question into the last answer. See Vol. II, pp. 17–18.

A: I did.

Q: <u>And</u> was that the result of an action by the Board of Trustees?

A: It was.

Q: If I could ask you in the blue notebook before you, to please turn to Exhibit-25.

A: [Witness complies.]

Q: Do you have that before you, sir?

A: Yes, I do.

Q: Can you tell us what that document is?

A: That's the Minutes of a meeting of the Board of Trustees which was held on June 23rd, 1995.

Q: <u>And</u> did you prepare those Minutes?

A: I did.

Q: <u>And</u> if you look, please, at Page 4 of those minutes?

A: Yes.

Q: Is that the resolution that you testified about, at which the Board authorized the Investment Committee of the Fund to direct you to investigate placing insurance <u>with Blue Cross</u>?

A: <u>That's correct</u>. <u>Not with Blue Cross</u>, that the motion that was passed was to authorize the Committee to meet with the consultants, to review consideration of a preferred provider organization.

[Comment] It seems to us there is a slip here. Maresca wants to be the one who selects Blue Cross to talk to, but counsel has the resolution directing Maresca to Blue Cross.

Q: <u>And</u> as a result of that resolution, what did you do?

A: What we did in terms of the geographical needs of the Fund, and you'll have to understand it's a Fund that covers a Tri-State Area, Eastern Pennsylvania, Southern New Jersey and Delaware, what we had to do was contact a provider that could establish a network that would cover the geographical area where the membership was located.

Q: <u>And</u> what provider did you contact?

A: We contacted Blue Cross.

Q: <u>And</u> did you contact any provider other than Independence Blue Cross?

A: We did not.

[Comment] Well, Maresca did go to Blue Cross and only to Blue Cross.

Q: Why was that, sir'?

A: We had P.P.O.'s in place through Multi-Plan and subsequently I find out from Preferred Care. They did not have the capability of providing a network of physicians that satisfied the geographic dispersion of the membership of the Council.

Q: Was it <u>your decision</u> to contact Blue Cross?

A: Yes, it was.

[Comment] We are getting the impression that none of this was influenced by anyone other than the witness — not Sweeney, not Sussman, not even Hardy, or so it seems.

Q: Now, who did you call at Blue Cross?

A: I called Ms. Helen Hardy.

Q: <u>And</u> as a result of that phone call, did you set up a meeting with Ms. Hardy?

A: I did.

Q: <u>And</u> where did that meeting take place?

A: At the offices of Blue Cross here in Philadelphia.

[Comment] Nice crisp examination. Short answers to looping questions. But are we to believe that Sussman played no role? Has Maresca come to this decision to use the Blues all by himself, in spite of the Sweeney-Sussman-Hardy meeting?

Q: <u>And</u> if you would turn, please, to Exhibit-8 in the blue notebook, Exhibit-8, is a copy of a letter that you sent to Ms. Hardy on July 31st, 1996, is it not?

A: That's correct.

Q: <u>And</u> the first paragraph references a meeting on July 26th?

A: Correct.

Q: That's the meeting that you attended?

A: That's correct.

Q: <u>And</u> can you tell us what you recall happening at that meeting?

A: The initial meeting that I had with the—there were several representatives from Blue Cross at the meeting, was an exploratory meeting to see if they could put together a network with affiliated Blue Cross plans in the Tri-State Area covered by the District Council to satisfy the needs in terms of the membership of the Council with regard to a network of physicians and hospitals.

Q: <u>And</u> how long did that meeting take place?

A: Several hours.

[Comment] *Counsel continues to adopt the "and" before many questions, which we suggest should be dropped. We will stop noting the practice at this point, although he does not.*

Q: Who do you recall attended that meeting—with you on behalf of the Segal Company?

A: One of my associates, a fellow by the name of John Cassaro, was in attendance at that meeting.

Q: Who do you recall attended that meeting on behalf of Independence Blue Cross?

A: Well, there was Ms. Hardy and Kenneth can't pronounce his last name.

Q: Kenny O. The jurors know him by that. He works for Ms. Hardy?

A: Yeah. It was a Mr. Young, I believe, was in attendance at the meeting.

Q: And who attended the meeting, if you recall, on behalf of the Ironworkers Fund?

A: There was Mr. Sweeney, who was the business manager of the Camden Local of the Union, Mr. Rabino, the business manager of the Trenton Local of the council.

Q: Following that meeting, then, you sent to Ms. Hardy the July 31st letter, 1996, that we have identified as Exhibit-8; is that, correct, sir?

A: That's correct.

Q: Is this letter what you call a request for proposal?

A: It is.

[Comment] *It seems as though, according to Maresca, this meeting was the genesis of the deal, but we are puzzled. Are we expected to believe that none of this was stimulated by the earlier Sussman-Sweeney-Hardy meeting?*

Q: And I see you enclosed with that letter certain information, did you not?

A: I did.

Q: What information did you send with the letter?

A: We sent them a copy of the plan of benefits that was in effect for the council, which up until this point in time, was all provided, on a self-insured, a self-funded basis. We provided them with a demographic distribution of the covered membership in the Tri-State Area. And we also gave them copies of the last two years of claims experience so that they would be in a position to determine what kind of activity they were going to have with regard to this particular Fund, which had a direct effect on what it is that they would be charging as administrative overhead.

Q: And why did you send this information to Blue Cross?

A: To get a meaningful proposal in terms of what it is that they could provide to satisfy the needs of the membership.

Q: Was this information that you considered necessary for Blue Cross to prepare a proposal?

A: Of course. I don't understand how they could commit to anything if they didn't understand what they were committing to.

Q: Without this information they couldn't submit a proposal?

A: Not a meaningful proposal, no.

Q: And did you, in response to this request for a proposal, in fact, receive a proposal from Independence Blue Cross?

A: I did.

[Comment] Again, it is a beautifully executed examination. But, again, is the message that we are intended to receive and believe that Mr. Maresca and Ms. Hardy simply did all this by themselves, with no help from Sussman? Not even by an earlier introduction?

Q: And if you would turn, please, to Tab 11, Exhibit-11, do you recognize that, sir?

A: Yes. That's the proposal that was submitted in response to our request.

Q: And that proposal is, I guess, roughly an inch or so thick; is that correct?

A: Yeah.

Q: And if you would look, please, at the second page — actually, the third page. That's a letter, dated December 17, 1995, addressed to you?

A: That's correct.

Q: From Kenny O?

A: Kenny O, right.

Q: And that was the proposal, correct?

A: Yes.

Q: Can you tell us what you did, then, with the proposal, once you received it sometime on or after April 17th, 1995?

A: Well, what we do is turn it over to a Department of Benefit Analysts in the company who analyze the proposal and summarize its salient points.

Q: And was that done in this instance?

A: Yes, it was.

Q: And did you receive back from your analysts an analysis of the Independence Blue Cross proposal?

A: I did.

Q: And you were not at that time considering any alternative carrier or provider, were you?

A: We were not.

Q: So, it wasn't a question of comparing against Brand "X" or whatever?

A: No, it was not.

[Comment] Again, his technical skills are great. It is clear that he is arguing through the witness in ways that he could not do if his questions were written down. See Vol. II, pp. 8–9, 12–15. But, though the message is clear enough that Sussman was not part of this, we are again forced to ask two questions. The first is: Are the jurors likely to believe that Sussman played no role in getting Hardy in the door? The second, just as important, if not more so, is: If any commission due Sussman is to be paid by the union, and if the insurance company did not, in fact, tell the union not to pay it—both as Blue Cross claims—then just why is it so all-fired important for Blue Cross to insist that Sussman did nothing and is entitled to nothing? In our view, when the weakness of the first point is coupled with the seeming incongruity of Blue Cross needing to put it forth, the portents do not bode well for Blue Cross.

Q: And once you got the analysis back, did you then send the analysis in written form to the Investment Committee of the Ironworkers Fund?

A: I sent a memorandum summarizing the proposal in memo form to the Investment Committee.

Q: Could you please turn to Defendant's Exhibit Number-12, Tab 12 of the blue notebook. Do you recognize that, sir?

A: Yes, I do.

Q: And can you tell us what that is?

A: That's a memorandum from myself to the Investment Committee summarizing the proposal that was submitted by Blue Cross for providing the benefit program.

Q: And can you tell us who were the members of the Investment Committee of the Ironworkers Fund?

A: There were three union representatives, Sweeney, Rabino and Jordan, and three management representatives, Reith, Samango and Hake.

Q: And are Mr. Sweeney and Mr. Reith here in the courtroom today, by the way?

A: They are.

Q: Point them out, please.

A: Sitting right over there.

Q: Mr. Sweeney and Mr. Reith, are they the two co-chairs of the Fund, sir?

A: They are.

Q: Mr. Sweeney being the union co-chair and Mr. Reith being the management co-chair?

A: That's correct.

Q: And they serve on the Investment part of the Committee?

A: They do.

Q: And you submitted your memorandum which is dated August 24th, 1995; is that correct, sir?

A: That's correct.

Q: Did you then meet with the Investment Committee of the Fund?

A: We did.

Q: And would you turn, please, to Defendant's Exhibit-13; do you have that before you, sir?

A: Yes, I do.

Q: Is Defendant's Exhibit-1 the Minutes of the Investment Committee meeting which you met with the Fund concerning your analysis of the Independence Blue Cross proposal?

A: It is.

Q: What was the date of that meeting?

A: September 5th, 1995.

Q: And I assume that you prepared these Minutes?

A: I did.

Q: And what was the conclusion of that meeting?

A: The recommendation was that we enter into an arrangement with the Blue Cross plans, that would be involved in establishing the network. Bear in mind there are five different Blue Cross plans that were going to be involved in administering this program, or centrally administered to Independence Blue Cross here in Philadelphia. They would handle the processing of all of the claims and then remit to the other area of Blue Cross plans whatever their share of claims expense was.

Q: And the recommendation of the Investment Committee was made to the full Board of Trustees, was it not?

A: Yes. The Investment Committee cannot act on their own. They can recommend, which they did, at a subsequent full meeting of the Board of Trustees.

[Comment] We suppose that the purpose of this tortuous history of the process of selecting Blue Cross is meant to persuade us that not only Sussman, but Sweeney as well did not dictate or even influence the selection. But we are left with the same two questions about Sweeney. Are the jurors likely to believe that Sweeney, whom Hardy was so anxious to see, and to influence, and to see again and again, even to the point of talking commissions with Sussman before he brought her in to see Sweeney, is the same Sweeny that had no role or influence in the selection?

Q: <u>And</u> if you would turn, please, to Exhibit-14. Do you recognize that as the Minutes of the September 22nd, 1995 meeting of the Board of Trustees?

A: I do.

Q: That's Exhibit-14?

A: Uh-huh.

Q: <u>And</u> if you look at the fourth page, is that the resolution of the full Board to approve and implement the Independence Blue Cross proposal with an effective target date of January 1st, 1996?

A: It is.

Q: <u>And</u>, again, you prepared these Minutes?

A: Yes, I did.

Q: <u>And</u> following this meeting, did you and the Segal Company then work with Blue Cross to finalize the arrangements with the Ironworkers Fund?

A: We did.

Q: <u>And can</u> you tell us <u>about</u> what you did?

[Comment] A cry for help from the witness. At this point, the insecurity of the examiner is, in our opinion, revealed not only by the inveterate use of his "and"s, but in his direct call for help from the witness.

A: We met with representatives of Blue Cross in New York in our office. There were certain benefits that did not coincide with what it is that the Fund was provided. What we did was attempt to resolve the differences so that the program of benefits was the same as what was previously in effect. By the way, when this was implemented on January 1st, understand that it was implemented on a dual-choice basis. The member had the option of opting in to the network plan or continuing to be covered by the plan or benefits previously in effect.

[Comment] Counsel is now ready to bring Sussman onto the stage. Notice, he does so after the union has decided to use Blue Cross, but we know that Sussman had made at the very least a cameo appearance earlier.

Q: Now, are you familiar with Leonard Sussman?

A: I am.

Q: And had you met him at anytime before today?

A: Yes, once.

Q: And when was that, sir?

A: It was in 1995. I had dinner out in Cherry Hill, New Jersey, I believe.

Q: At the Viennese Restaurant?

A: I believe that was the name of the restaurant, yes.

Q: And who was present at that meeting or that dinner?

A: Well, it was Mr. Sweeney and one of his associates, myself and one of my associates, and there were several individuals from a money managing firm. I don't recall who else.

Q: Was that the Viennese Restaurant?

A: Yes.

Q: And was that dinner more of a social occasion than a business occasion?

A: Yes.

Q: During the course of that dinner, did Mr. Sussman introduce himself to you?

A: It wasn't during the course of the dinner, it was at the bar prior to the dinner.

Q: And did Mr. Sussman introduce himself to you?

A: Yes, he did.

Q: Did he say anything to you?

A: He mentioned about the possibility of an arrangement with Blue Cross, where commissions would be payable.

Q: To him?

A: I assumed to him, right.

Q: And what did you say to him?

A: Well, what we told him was that there weren't going to be any commissions involved in this particular instance, that what we were placing in terms of coverage through a Blue Cross network was part of the services that we rendered from which was contained in our consulting arrangement with the Board of Trustees. So, no commissions were going to be paid. You should bear in mind, that commissions, if they are paid, they are paid out of dollars that the Fund has to pay to the carrier who is going to pay the commissions.

Q: Why is that, sir?

[Comment] Very good so far. But here is a missed opportunity. Instead of "Why is that, sir?", it might have been "Why would any commission come from the working men and women's benefit fund?"

A: Well, the carrier is not going to pay commissions out of their own—you're going to pay for it if you direct the commissions are paid.

Q: Now, as far as you're aware, did Mr. Sussman have anything to do with the decision of the Fund to enter into the contract with Independence Blue Cross and Pennsylvania Blue Shield?

A: Not to my knowledge, no.

[Comment] Of course he does not know everything and so could be cross-examined on meetings he was not present at. But, again, given the last question and answer, it was the union that

decided not to pay any commission.

Q: <u>As far as you're aware</u>, did Mr. Sussman broker that contract?

A: He did not.

Q: <u>As far as you're aware</u>, did that contract result from any introduction that Sussman made to Mr. Sweeney for Ms. Hardy of Independence Blue Cross?

A: <u>Not that I'm aware of, no</u>.

[Comment] Technically good. Nevertheless, given what we have heard up to now, we are aware of a lot more contact between Sussman and both the union and Blue Cross than apparently this witness is. Is this a good message to deliver, albeit that it was well delivered? Again, why, if Blue Cross did nothing to counsel against a commission, is Blue Cross arguing so hard that Sussman is not entitled to one? Why not, given the complaint, simply focus us on the fact that it was the union, totally on its own, that decided not to give Sussman a commission? If that is true, the complaint charging interference by Blue Cross must be dismissed.

Q: By the way, you were familiar with Independence Blue Cross before getting involved with these negotiations for the Ironworkers, were you not?

A: Oh, yes.

Q: Do you represent other union health and welfare funds in the Philadelphia area?

A: The company does, yes.

Q: Can you tell us what other funds the company represents in the Philadelphia area?

A: Several Teamster groups, several construction trade groups.

Q: Do these other groups have relationships with Independence Blue Cross?

A: Some of them do.

Q: So, Independence Blue Cross was no stranger to you?

A: Absolutely not.

[Comment] Well enough done, but why here, unless it was that counsel recognized that he should get off the point that he just made.

Q: Now, are you familiar with the term broker of record?

A: I am.

Q: Can you tell us what you understand that term to mean?

A: Broker of record is normally what—how it is defined, it's a person who places business through a particular insurance company and is directed by the Trustees to receive commissions for the brokering of the business.

Q: What is a broker of record letter?

A: It's a letter that is submitted by—usually by a Board of Trustees, directing the carrier to pay commissions to a stipulated agent on the basis of a scale that is agreed to by the carrier and the Trustees.

Q: Is that a common practice, for an insurer to require a broker of record letter to pay?

A: In the jointly trustee[d] multi-employer area, it was a very common practice years ago. In today's business world, commissions are not generally paid to consulting advisors. They are paid by a flat fee that is negotiated annually.

Q: But the concept of a broker of record letter is not unique to Blue Cross?

A: No, it's not.

Q: It's a common practice?

A: It's a common practice in the insurance industry.

[Comment] Now comes the question that goes to the heart of the whole case. Indeed, given the theory of the complaint, it is the only real question in the case.

Q: Now, as far as you're aware, did anyone from Independence Blue Cross or Pennsylvania Blue Shield ever direct any representative of the Ironworkers Fund not to do business with Tower Financial, Mr. Sussman's company, or with Mr. Sussman?

A: Not to my knowledge, no.

[Comment] Well done. Aimed right at the legal claim of tortious interference. Indeed, this is the entire case as brought by the plaintiff.

Q: Did anyone from Independence Blue Cross or Pennsylvania Blue Shield ever suggest to you as the consultant for the Ironworkers Fund, that the Fund should not do business with Tower or Mr. Sussman?

A: That subject was never brought up with me.

Q: And specifically, did Ms. Hardy ever suggest to you that it would be cheaper for the Fund to cut out Mr. Sussman and Tower and not pay them a commission?

A: Did she suggest that?

Q: Yes, sir.

A: Absolutely not.

[Comment] Again, well done. If the witness is believed, it is the total end of the plaintiff's case. But will the jurors understand? How about this: "Do you understand, that this plaintiff alleges that Blue Cross attempted to interfere with a prospective relationship between the union and Sussman?" "Yes." "Now, did anyone from Blue Cross ever say to you, in any way . . . ?" In any event, and in our view unfortunately, instead of nailing the point and the plaintiff, the examiner lurches away to a more, if not most, unhappy subject.

Q: One final point, did you ever accuse Independence Blue Cross of <u>gouging</u> on its administrative fee?

A: <u>Gouging</u>?

Q: <u>Yes, sir</u>.

A: I don't think that is the proper word. What we suggested was that their administrative fee was a little high. We are still in the process of negotiating that fee with them, and to date, I haven't heard from them, but I expect that I will.

[Comment] Why is this in the case? Why is counsel introducing this subject? Notice, too, that he has selected a highly prejudicial term. It may be that he was bringing it out before the plaintiff did, but in our judgment the plaintiff would not be likely to be able to do it.

Q: And just so we understand the arrangement, the arrangement between Blue Cross and the Ironworkers is what is called a cost-plus arrangement?

A: That is correct.

Q: Where Blue Cross, because of its bargaining power, is able to get certain discounts from hospitals and other providers, pays the medical bills and then charges the Fund an administrative fee for processing the claims and so forth?

A: It's a percentage of the claims that are paid.

Q: So that, in essence, the Fund is self-insured but with Blue Cross administering the plan?

A: That's right. What Blue Cross effectively has done is deliver a network that is a feasible one for the Tri-State Area covered by the Council and they deliver that network and process claims that go through the network system for a fee.

[Comment] What has all this to do with the plaintiff's case? Well, Blue Cross may be proud of this, and what comes after,

*but it does not seem to be on point—at least to us. We suggest
the same is true for the rest of what follows. Counsel, in our
view, is simply too defensive about Blue Cross's costs. After all,
Blue Cross is not being sued for charging too much. It is being
sued for telling the union not to give Sussman a commission.*

Q: And are you familiar with the services that
Independence Blue Cross and Pennsylvania Blue Shield
provide in return for that administrative fee?

A: Yes. They process all of the claims that are submitted through the network.

Q: And there are approximately 2,500 members of the
11 locals, making up the Ironworkers Fund?

A: That's correct.

Q: Do you have any idea the number of claims per
year?

A: Offhand, I would not know. That would have been
in the request for the proposal.

Q: In the thousands?

A: Yeah.

MR. SONNENFELD: Excuse me one second.

- - - -

[Short pause.]

- - - -

MR. SONNENFELD: I have nothing further.

ANALYSIS OF THE DIRECT EXAMINATION

The point of the direct examination is clear, and the examiner makes it well. It was Mr. Maresca who selected Blue Cross
once the welfare fund decided that it wanted to consider a different form of insurance; it was Maresca who contacted Blue
Cross; and it was the Segal Company that did the analysis. Mr.
Sussman did nothing.

Moreover, Maresca testifies that the use of commissions for brokers or advisors who help unions and welfare funds on insurance coverage has been replaced by a flat-fee contract such as the one that Segal has with the Ironworkers. The point is that the Sussman claim is not typical; it is unusual.

On the points that Maresca makes, he is virtually untouchable. It must be true that his company is familiar with Blue Cross/Blue Shield and that, once Segal was brought into the picture, they advised the Ironworkers on the details of the Blue Cross/Blue Shield contract. It also must be true that Sussman had nothing to do with the contract *once Segal was in the picture*.

As far as Segal knows, Sussman did not have any role in inducing the Ironworkers to go with Blue Cross/Blue Shield. It is doubtful that any cross-examination will be able to demonstrate that what Maresca has said is incorrect or that he sought to exaggerate the Segal role.

The problem for Blue Cross/Blue Shield, of course, is that Sussman did not claim any role with respect to the *details* of the contract. Nor did Sussman deny that the Ironworkers sought the help of Segal and that Segal provided it. Indeed, nothing that Maresca has said is actually inconsistent with what Sussman said. Maresca did not deal with Sussman, and Sussman did not deal with Maresca. So, the Maresca testimony may not be that harmful, particularly as the jury must know that it knows more about what Sussman did than apparently Maresca does.

To the extent that the defense is arguing that Sussman is seeking a windfall and that he really did not do much, Maresca is helpful. Maresca demonstrates that Segal negotiated the contract and did the detail work, although not the contract. Although Sussman never claimed otherwise, Maresca undoubtedly reinforces one part of the central theme of the defense, namely, that Sussman does not deserve a lot of money for the little that he did. But, a possible error here is that counsel seems to be arguing that the plaintiff did *nothing*. While that may or may not be true in respect to the fund, that certainly cannot be said by counsel for Blue Cross, which Sussman almost certainly helped, at least initially.

There is one line of defense that is not pursued with Maresca: that it was Sussman who created confusion as to whom he represented, and Sussman who caused his own problem by failing to make clear to the union and to Blue Cross who was to pay his commission. In thinking about whether this point could have been effectively made, consider the following hypothetical examination:

Q: Are you familiar with brokers of insurance?

A: Yes, I am.

Q: Are you familiar with commissions on insurance contracts?

A: Yes.

Q: Do some people earn commissions paid by an insurer like Blue Cross/Blue Shield?

A: Yes.

Q: Do others earn commissions paid by insureds like the Ironworkers?

A: Yes.

Q: What determines who pays a commission?

A: It is determined by agreement between the broker and the party he represents.

Q: How important is it that the broker know whom he represents?

A: Very important, because the broker has a responsibility to whomever he represents.

Q: Now, let me ask you a question based on your experience. If a broker contacted an insurer like Blue Cross/Blue Shield and said he was doing so on behalf of a union welfare fund, who would Blue Cross/Blue Shield think the broker is representing?

A: In my opinion, the fund.

Q: Now, if a broker contacted a union welfare fund and said that he wanted to bring a Blue Cross/Blue Shield representative by, who would the Ironworkers think the broker's client is?

A: Blue Cross/Blue Shield, in my opinion.

Q: If a broker failed to clarify, to both an insurer and a union welfare fund, who he represented, would that be ethical in your experience?

A: No, it would not.

Q: How important is it for the broker to have a clear understanding with a client as to their agreement?

A: It is essential for the broker to do his job.

Q: In your experience, when do a broker and a client agree on the fee or commission arrangement that will govern their relationship?

A: At the very beginning, since there will be no deal if they cannot agree.

Q: If Mr. Sussman misled Blue Cross/Blue Shield into thinking he was the Ironworkers' broker and misled the Ironworkers into thinking he was working for Blue Cross/Blue Shield, did he act properly?

A: No, he did not.

Q: In your experience, can a broker be cheated out of a commission if he never had any agreement from a client to pay a commission?

A: No, he cannot.

This argument does not, of course, address the legal issue that Sussman raises, which is tortious interference. But, to the extent that the jury believes that Sussman got cheated somehow, it may suggest that Sussman was trying to have it both ways and should not be rewarded for his conduct.

In any event, because Maresca is put into the scene late, he is left open for cross-examination about the facts he does not and could not know about. He also is open to questions about the preferred provider plan that Sussman obtained for the welfare fund for which Sussman receives commissions. We turn to that examination.

TEXT OF THE CROSS-EXAMINATION

THE COURT: Cross-examine.

MR. LONGER: Thank you, Your Honor.

[Comment] The interesting question is how to cross-examine the witness. Going after his credibility would be an error, and he has little affirmative evidence with which to help the plaintiff. It would seem that the third approach, that of limiting, would be the way to go. That is, point out all the meetings and activities that the witness has no knowledge of because they were outside of his presence and before his involvement. See Vol. III, pp. 16–20.

BY MR. LONGER:

Q: You are the consultant with this Fund, correct?

A: That's correct.

Q: And you're responsible for talking to them about their health benefit insurance?

A: Among other things, yes.

Q: And they act through you to do their health benefit insurance, right?

A: I don't quite follow. They act through me?

Q: They come to you and say "Mr. Maresca, please tell us what to do about insurance," right?

A: That's correct.

Q: And that's what the Board does, because the Board wants your insight into how to arrange insurance?

A: That's correct.

Q: Mr. Maresca—

MR. LONGER: May I approach, Your Honor?

THE COURT: Certainly.

BY MR. LONGER:

Q: I'm going to show you Plaintiff's Exhibit Number-5. That's a contract dated August 1, 1994, between the Ironworkers Fund and Preferred Care, is it not?

A: That's what it is, yes.

Q: The Ironworkers' Board didn't come to you seeking your advice on that contract, did they?

A: No.

Q: This was a contract that Mr. Sussman receives a commission on, isn't it?

A: I have no idea.

[Comment] Excellent. Sussman was already earning commission. But the witness denies knowledge, so counsel punishes him.

Q: The Board entered into this contract and it's effective, isn't it?

A: If the Board entered into it and it is signed by the Board of Trustees. You know, I never saw that contract and you showed it to me a few weeks back when you took the deposition.

Q: And you're their consultant. It's important for you to give your advice on insurance, but they didn't seek your advice on this?

A: Apparently not.

Q: Do you know if Mr. Sweeney was responsible for getting this contract—

A: Do I know if he was?

Q: —into place?

A: No, I do not know that. No.

Q: <u>And you didn't find out about this until</u> the lawsuit; is that right?

A: That's correct.

[Comment] We learn that there is much the witness does not know. Counsel has also tucked some knowledge into the witness with the last question.

Q: Now, have you ever sold insurance?

A: Excuse me?

Q: Have you ever brokered D&O insurance for the Board of Trustees?

A: Yes, we do.

Q: When you do that, you get a commission on that?

A: Yes, we do.

[Comment] Excellent. Everybody gets a commission but poor old Sussman.

Q: Now, Mr. Sonnenfeld asked you if you ever get commissions on insurance for the Health and Welfare Fund and you answered no, didn't you?

A: That's correct.

Q: So that was wrong, you should correct it to say you do get commissions for selling D&O insurance, right?

A: Well, we don't sell the insurance. We place it.

Q: Fair enough. And D&O insurance, just so the Jury knows—

A: It's errors and omissions insurance. It's fiduciary coverage.

Q: And that's in case they breach their fiduciary duties, right?

A: That's correct.

Q: Now, Mr. Sonnenfeld asked you to take a look at Exhibit Number-7, of the Defendant's Exhibit, which is the blue notebook. These are Minutes of the Board of Trustees that were held on June 23rd, 1995, correct?

A: That's correct.

Q: And you were present at that meeting; isn't that correct?

A: That's correct.

Q: And it was at that meeting, on Page 4 of the Minutes, that the Board adopted authorizing the Committee to meet with consultants, Segal Company?

A: That's correct.

Q: To consider a P.P.O., right?

A: Correct. P.P.O. that they were talking about was.

Q: And the *that* they were talking about was Blue Cross/Blue Shield, wasn't it?

A: At that time, nothing was discussed with regard to a particular P.P.O.

Q: Are you sure about that?

A: I'm pretty sure. I was there. What happened subsequent to that meeting was a discussion concerning contacting Blue Cross.

Q: Do you recall anything about that meeting on June 23rd?

A: Do I recall anything about it?

Q: I strike that question. Do you know who sponsored that motion?

A: No, I don't.

Q: Do you recall who had discussions in that—during that motion proceeding?

A: It was probably discussed the day before at an Executive Committee meeting.

Q: I'm asking you do you remember the substance of any of the conversation during that meeting?

A: No, I do not.

Q: So, you don't know or you don't recall, whether or not Blue Cross/Blue Shield was discussed at that meeting?

A: No, I don't.

Q: Did Mr. Sweeney propose that motion?

A: I have no idea who proposed the motion.

Q: Was that motion presented by the Union Trustees?

A: I don't recall that.

[Comment] This line, largely nonleading, sounds more like a direct examination, but seems to go nowhere. But the suggestion that Sweeney proposed the motion resonates against the earlier meetings between Sweeney, Hardy, and Sussman.

Q: Now, you only considered Blue Cross/Blue Shield as the P.P.O.; is that right?

A: That's correct.

Q: Do you know a gentleman by the name of Al Crowell?

A: Do I know him? Yes.

Q: He's an attorney in North Jersey?

A: He is.

Q: And he represents the Ironworkers up in North Jersey, right?

A: Yes, he does.

Q: And in 1994, they investigated Blue Cross/Blue Shield, did they not?

A: I believe they did.

Q: And they used you as the consultant, right?

A: No, not at that time.

Q: Didn't they ask you to do some competitive bidding?

A: Not in 1994, no.

Q: Was it 1995?

A: I believe it was.

Q: I had the year wrong. In 1995, the Ironworkers Fund up in North Jersey asked you to do some investigation into insurance, right?

A: That's correct.

Q: And they told you, we want you to do competitive; isn't that right?

A: That's correct.

Q: And they felt that was important because they didn't want to violate their fiduciary duties by considering only one carrier?

A: I'm not sure that was the case at all, but you have a different set of circumstances in the law in Northern New Jersey. You have a concentrated membership in a particular area. The fact is that here in Philadelphia, it was our considered judgment that given the geographic dispersion of the membership of this Council that Blue Cross was the most suitable vehicle for providing benefits meaningful to the entire membership.

Q: You didn't do any competitive bidding?

A: That's right, we did not.

Q: You only considered Blue Cross?

A: That's correct.

Q: That's because the Union Trustees were telling you to go with Blue Cross/Blue Shield; isn't that right?

A: That is not correct. Nobody tells us what to do.

[Comment] Again, we seem to go to no destination, in terms of the case. Counsel need not attack the witness's credibility. He should use the doctrine of limiting. See Vol. III, pp. 16–20. But he does not and he gets seriously hurt.

Q: I just want to be clear. You said you were not aware that the Fund was considering Blue Cross/Blue Shield until some time after June 23rd, 1995?

A: That's correct.

Q: You met Mr. Sussman at the restaurant in New Jersey in May of 1995?

A: That's correct.

Q: And he was telling you that he was going after Blue Cross/Blue Shield to put Blue Cross/Blue Shield together with the Ironworkers?

A: He mentioned that he was trying to broker a relationship with Blue Cross—

Q: And that was—

MR. SONNENFELD: Wait. Let him finish his answer.

THE WITNESS: —and we told him if an arrangement was brokered with Blue Cross, there would be no commissions.

[Comment] Bang! The witness volunteers an answer and hurts the examiner, but counsel never should have gone near the subject.

BY MR. LONGER:

Q: Well, you didn't—

MR. SONNENFELD: Let him finish his answer.

THE WITNESS: Nothing had been decided at that juncture in May as to where we were going at all with this plan.

BY MR. LONGER:

Q: You didn't want to see Mr. Sussman involved in this at all, did you?

A: Mr. Sussman had no relationship with this Fund, as far as I was concerned.

Q: You didn't want to see him involved at all; isn't that right?

A: If you want to put it that way, fine. He had no relationship with the Fund.

[Comment] Again, counsel is taking blows he need not take. To the extent that the union or its agents did not want Sussman, the case against Blue Cross for tortious interference is wounded, if not terminated. Sussman is not seeking anything from the fund. Counsel should confront the witness with this. Unfortunately, he does not use the doctrine of limiting to show what Sussman did for Blue Cross that the witness knows nothing of and which entitles — or so the plaintiff says — the plaintiff to money from Blue Cross. This witness has been hurting the plaintiff more on cross than he did on direct. What should counsel do? Well, for example: "I gather you are unaware of earlier meetings that Mr. Sussman had, first with Mr. Sweeney alone and then with Mr. Sweeney and Ms. Hardy." Once this line is pursued, counsel can put into his questions other aspects of the earlier activity, including conversations between Sussman and Hardy about a 1 to 3 percent commission. Unfortunately, counsel does not pick this area where, using the doctrine of limiting, he can score points. Instead he returns to areas he should not, and concludes the examination with additional injury to his own case.

Q: And Ms. Hardy called you prior to your meeting on July 26th, 1995, to talk about Mr. Sussman's relationship?

A: Ms. Hardy never called me to talk about Mr. Sussman.

Q: She never called you?

A: No. I initiated the first call with Ms. Hardy.

Q: And let me ask you this. Did you ever discuss Mr. Sussman with Ms. Hardy?

A: I did not.

MR. LONGER: Well, I have no further questions, Mr. Maresca.

ANALYSIS OF THE CROSS-EXAMINATION

We made the point repeatedly above that Maresca is vulnerable for what he does not know. He cannot possibly testify that Sussman did not open the door to the Ironworkers for Blue Cross. He cannot possibly refute Sussman's testimony concerning his conversations with Ms. Hardy. It is not difficult to imagine how Maresca could have been examined to score points for the plaintiff.

Q: You have no personal knowledge of what Mr. Sussman and Ms. Hardy discussed concerning the Ironworkers in 1994?

Q: You have no personal knowledge whether Mr. Sussman and Ms. Hardy met with Mr. Sweeney in 1994 to talk about Blue Cross handling the Ironworkers' account?

Q: You don't know whether Ms. Hardy promised Mr. Sussman a commission if she landed the Ironworkers' account?

Q: There was nothing to prevent Blue Cross/Blue Shield from promising a commission to Mr. Sussman?

Q: There was nothing to prevent Blue Cross/Blue Shield from paying a commission to Mr. Sussman?

Q: You understand that the plaintiff is not suing the fund for anything, only Blue Cross, because of its broken promises and its efforts to prevent a commission here?

Q: Blue Cross/Blue Shield could have paid a commission to Mr. Sussman from the profit Blue Cross/Blue Shield made on the Ironworkers?

Q: Blue Cross/Blue Shield would not have made any profit on the Ironworkers if there had been no contract?

Q: Ms. Hardy received a commission on the contract?

Q: She would have received no commission if there were no contract?

Q: She will get another commission every year the contract is renewed?

Q: There would be no renewal had there never been a contract?

Q: You don't work for Blue Cross/Blue Shield?

Q: You weren't working for Blue Cross/Blue Shield from 1992 to 1995?

Q: You have no personal knowledge of how much Blue Cross/Blue Shield valued the Ironworkers' account in 1994?

Q: You don't know how important the Ironworkers' account was to Blue Cross/Blue Shield in 1994?

Q: You have no personal knowledge of how important the Ironworkers' account was to Ms. Hardy in 1994?

Q: You don't know how valuable Blue Cross thought Mr. Sussman's contacts with the Ironworkers were in 1994?

Q: You have no knowledge how valuable Ms. Hardy thought Mr. Sussman's contacts with the Ironworkers were in 1994?

Q: You simply have no personal knowledge whether Ms. Hardy promised Mr. Sussman commission on any Ironworkers' contract with Blue Cross?

The fact that Mr. Maresca had no knowledge of any of these things makes them safe territory for a cross-examiner. This cross-examination would have focused the jury on the time before Mr. Maresca was involved in negotiations with Blue Cross/Blue Shield and invoked the doctrine of limiting.

There is no doubt that the cross-examination demonstrates that Maresca and the Segal Company are potential rivals for the Ironworkers' business and that Maresca did not want to see Sussman involved in the health care contracting. The examination succeeds in making the point. The problem is that the plaintiff does not claim that Blue Cross chose Maresca or that Maresca did not do all he was asked to do. The plaintiff focuses on the wrong time period in examining Maresca.

Perhaps more importantly, the cross-examination succeeds in pointing out a contradiction. Ms. Hardy said that she talked with Maresca about Sussman; Maresca denies this. Because there is no reason to believe that Maresca has any reason to distort his testimony on this point, the examiner could have developed it more fully and driven it home to the jury more effectively.

For us, the question is not whether the cross-examiner made the points that he sought out to make. We think he did. For us, the question is whether he made all the points that he should have made. We think he did not.

TEXT OF THE REDIRECT EXAMINATION

MR. SONNENFELD: Briefly.

[Comment] We wonder if counsel needed to open the door to another cross. He seems well ahead, at least with this witness, and a redirect will invite a recross.

BY MR. SONNENFELD:

Q: Does the Segal Company receive any commission with respect to the January 1st, 1996 contract between Independence Blue Cross and Pennsylvania Blue Shield?

A: We do not.

Q: And as far as you're aware, did Mr. Sussman do <u>any</u> work in connection with that contract that would entitle him to receive a commission?

A: <u>I never saw any work</u> that he may have done.

MR. SONNENFELD: Thank you, sir.

THE COURT: Thank you. You may step down. You're excused.

[Witness excused.]

- - - -

THE COURT: Let's take a short recess, and then we'll call the next witness.

THE CRIER: Everyone remain seated while the Jury leaves the room.

- - - -

[Jury exits.]

ANALYSIS OF THE REDIRECT EXAMINATION

The point of the redirect examination is that Mr. Sussman did not earn a commission. However, it is clear from Maresca's answer that he knows he cannot adequately demonstrate the point, because he was not present when Sussman did whatever he did. Given the cross, we think there was no benefit to the redirect, and, given the hazy last answer, some harm may have been done. We wonder whether the direct examiner would have dared a redirect if the cross-examination we suggested had been done. This redirect examination did open the door to another round of cross-examination intended to clarify all the things that Maresca does not know and highlight that any opinion about whether Mr. Sussman is entitled to a commission is based largely on ignorance of what Sussman might have done, but the opportunity was not taken. The cross-examiner did not get up again. We believe he decided that he had enough of Mr. Maresca.

Chapter Ten

The Trustee Witnesses

MR. SWEENEY: THE UNION CHAIR

[Comment] We recall having had his deposition read in the plaintiff's case, where it was not especially helpful to the plaintiff. Now he comes forward to testify in person, this time for the defendant.

Text of the Direct Examination

[Jury enters.]

- - - -

THE COURT: Call your next witness.

MR. SONNENFELD: Your Honor, for my next witness, I call Mr. Sweeney.

THE CRIER: Place your right hand on the Bible. State your name and spell your last name.

THE WITNESS: Robert C. Sweeney, S-W-E-E-N-E-Y.

ROBERT C. SWEENEY, WITNESS, after having been first duly sworn, was examined and testified as follows:

- - - -

BY MR. SONNENFELD:

Q: Good afternoon, Mr. Sweeney.

A: Good afternoon.

Q: Could you tell us by who you're employed, sir?

[Comment] That same old "could" that plaintiff's counsel used. "By whom are you employed, sir?"

A: Ironworkers Local 399, Camden, New Jersey.

Q : What is your position?

A: I'm the President and Business Manager.

Q: Where is your office located?

A: 409 Crown Pointe Road, Westville, New Jersey.

Q: Where do you live, sir?

A: 142 Greenville Road, Cherry Hill, New Jersey.

Q: How old are you?

A: Sixty-five.

Q: How long have you been an ironworker?

A: Forty-four years.

Q: You've been an ironworker for 44 years?

A: Yes.

Q: Since we have been hearing about ironworkers for three days, maybe you ought to tell us what an ironworker does?

[Comment] Nicely done. Good repetition. Nice lead into the next question. We are going to have a feel for the witness as a human being, what he does and has done.

A: We are what is called a mixed local. We do foundation work for large buildings and bridges. We do rigging work, moving machinery and large vessels, and stuff as rigging. And weld structural steel work, high buildings, bridges and stuff like that.

Q: How long have you been President and Business Manager of your local?

A: Twenty-six years.

Q: And do you also hold a position with the Ironworkers District Council Philadelphia and Vicinity Health Benefit Fund?

A: Yes, I do.

Q: What position do you hold with that?

A: I'm a Trustee.

Q: How long have you been a Trustee of that Fund?

A: In excess of 20 years.

Q: And how many locals are in Fund?

A: Eleven.

Q: And are you an officer of the Fund, as well? Are you co-chair?

A: Yes, I'm co-chairman.

Q: How long have you been co-chairman?

A: Probably close to 20 years.

Q: And for the past several years, who has been the— you're the union co-chair?

A: Yes, I am.

Q: Has there been a management co-chair?

A: Yes, there has.

Q: Who is that?

A: Jack Reith.

Q: Who is sitting here in court today?

A: Yes.

Q: Now, do you also serve on the Investment Committee of the Fund?

A: Yes, I do.

Q: Would you tell us what the Investment Committee does?

[Comment] Very nicely done. See how each question loops into the last answer. Notice also that counsel is in total control of the examination.

A: Between regular meetings of the Trustees, we have quarterly meetings at different places around our District

Council. And if something comes up, that has—that is pretty important and has to do with some of the business of the Fund, we call together the Investment Committee instead of trying to get all people together. The Investment Committee is only six people.

Q: Now, are you familiar with the decision of the Fund to enter into a contract with Independence Blue Cross and Pennsylvania Blue Shield effective January 1st, 1996?

A: Yes, I am.

Q: And can you tell us how that contract came about?

[Comment] Not so good, this last question; although the technical answer would be a simple "yes," that is not the intent of the question. It is instead an abrogation of counsel's job to elicit testimony and to argue through the witness to the jury, because it calls for the witness to give a long narrative—which he then does. This may seem easier for the examiner, but makes it harder for the jurors to assimilate the information that pours out. See Vol. II, pp. 7–11.

A: Well, in the first place we were trying to keep up with inflation with our health fund. Our health fund was starting to bleed, and it was going from a lot of money down to small money. And what we were trying to do is stop the bleeding. And we were also trying to do away with the deductibles that our members had. Our members had a $500.00 family deductible and a $250.00 single deductible, and we wanted to do away with that. We started talking about getting a P.P.O. Now, we had several meetings with Mr. Maresca, with the representatives of Blue Cross, and we decided that's what we were going to do.

Q: Who was responsible for negotiating the contract on behalf of the Fund with Independence Blue Cross and Pennsylvania Blue Shield?

A: Mr. Maresca.

Q: And on whose advice did the Fund rely in entering into the contract with Independence Blue Cross and Pennsylvania Blue Shield?

A: Mr. Maresca.

Q: How long have you known Mr. Maresca?

A: Twenty-five years.

Q: And that's in your capacity as a Trustee of the Fund and President of your Local?

A: Yeah. Most of that time.

[Comment] This was much better. After the last long Sweeney eruption, counsel has taken it piece by piece.

Q: Now, do you know Leonard Sussman?

A: Yes, I do.

Q: He's seated here at the counsel table here?

A: Yes, he is.

Q: How long have you known Mr. Sussman?

A: Approximately, 15, 16 years.

Q: Is he a friend of yours?

A: He was.

Q: Is he no longer a friend?

A: No.

Q: Why is that, sir?

[Comment] What a question! Lord only knows what the witness can do to the plaintiff now. Counsel for plaintiff would be wise to object. He does not, and gets lucky because Sweeney, who now has Sussman helpless before him, doesn't want to hit him.

A: Well, do I have to answer that?

Q: If it makes you uncomfortable—

A: Well, I introduced him to some friends of mine, I told them what a nice guy he was and he ended up suing them.

[Comment] Still no objection. No motion to strike. So the examiner keeps on going.

Q: Who was that, sir?

A: The Ironworkers District Council of Northern New Jersey.

[Comment] Again, no objection. So . . .

Q: What did he sue them over?

MR. LONGER: Your Honor, I object. You've already ruled on this.

[Comment] Finally, an objection, although the ground is somewhat interesting. But the examiner believes he will lose the objection, and so he backs off.

MR. SONNENFELD: <u>I'll withdraw the question</u> and move on.

[Comment] The ruling is now predictable.

THE COURT: Sustained.

MR. LONGER: And I'm going to ask you to strike this—or tell the Jury to disregard this.

[Comment] Counsel really has to move to strike, or else the answers will be in the record. Counsel might have been more specific as to which questions and answers. As for the information given by the question, any chance that the jurors may forget about it has been diminished. Indeed, the judge is about to repeat that Sussman has sued a union.

THE COURT: Yes. Disregard the information about the suit. That really has nothing to do with this whatsoever.

MR. LONGER: Thank you, Your Honor.

[Comment] The lesson in all this for both sides is simple: If you ask a question and the other party objects, let the judge rule rather than retreat. At the worst, the chances are never far from 50/50 on the ruling. If you are objecting to the question and the judge sustains the objection, and you need to move to strike, do so specifically, and, most important, do so if you can, at sidebar.

BY MR. SONNENFELD:

Q: Did Mr. Sussman, in your view, have anything to do with the decision of the Ironworkers to enter into the contract with Independence Blue Cross and Pennsylvania Blue Shield effective January 1st, 1996?

A: No.

[Comment] We are back to the defense that Sussman did nothing.

Q: Now, do you know Helen Hardy?

A: Yes, I do.

Q: And can you point her out in the courtroom?

A: The lady over there in the white dress.

Q: And you understand her to be employed by Independence Blue Cross?

A: Yes, I do.

Q: Had you in the past met with her?

A: Yes, I have.

Q: At your office and—

A: Yes.

Q: In New Jersey?

A: Yes.

Q: And have you ever met with her along with Mr. Sussman?

A: Yes, I have.

Q: On how many occasions?

A: One.

[Comment] Very nice. Clear. Crisp. Counsel is nailing the points.

Q: And did your meeting with Ms. Hardy alone take place before or after the occasion when you met with her with Mr. Sussman?

A: The first time—

MR. LONGER: Objection. Foundation. I don't believe he testified to having a meeting with her separately.

MR. SONNENFELD: He did.

THE COURT: Overruled.

THE WITNESS: She came into my office, unannounced. I didn't know who she was and I didn't know what she was doing there. My partner sits out front, he says there's a lady in here to see you. She came back and introduced herself and told me she represented Blue Cross. That was the first time I ever met the lady.

[Comment] This is offered, obviously, in explanation as to why the first meeting, with Hardy alone, was not as wonderful as the second, with Hardy and Sussman. The most interesting aspect of the answer is that the witness has obviously been prepared and is very willing to do the task. The object of this, of course, is to minimize the usefulness of Sussman.

BY MR. SONNENFELD:

Q: And how long did that meeting last, that first time?

A: Fifteen minutes.

Q: And did anything come of that meeting?

A: No.

[Comment] The implication is clear. If only she had made an appointment, it would have been different. See . . . who needed Sussman? But will the jury buy this? And the fundamental question still abides: If Blue Cross is taking the position that it had nothing to do with the union's decision not to give Sussman a commission, why is it so important to Blue Cross to contend that Sussman was not entitled to one from the union because he did nothing for Blue Cross?

Q: And you then met with her along with Mr. Sussman?

A: Yes.

Q: And how did that meeting come about?

A: I believe he called and said that he was coming in with her, or she called and said—I don't know which one of them initiated it, but they said could you see us and I said yes, I can.

Q: How long did that meeting last?

A: Twenty-five minutes, half hour.

Q: And in your view, did anything come of that meeting that you had with Mr. Sussman and Ms. Hardy?

A: No.

[Comment] Sussman's meeting is a total loss, apparently.

Q: As a result of that meeting, did you direct Mr. Craggs, the plan manager, to provide any information to Ms. Hardy?

A: No.

Q: And as a result of that meeting, did you direct Mr. Craggs to meet with Ms. Hardy?

A: No.

Q: Was Mr. Sussman, in your view, responsible for Ms. Hardy having access to you?

A: No.

Q: And—

A: My door is open. Anybody wants to talk to me, they can come in and talk to me.

[Comment] Of course, as long as you have an appointment. Being a friend does not help at all!

Q: That includes Ms. Hardy?

A: That includes anybody. I get money managers that come in. I get people that want to come in and sell different things, especially in the financial. And everybody that comes in and rings the bell, I'll talk to.

[Comment] Very well. The point is carefully nailed down. Well done. Whether it stays down is something else. We must remember that the words of a witness are only one thing. Whether they are believed is quite another. The obvious efforts of the witness to hurt Sussman may have the opposite effect. Now counsel begins to jump around a little.

Q: Now, at some point in time, did Mr. Sussman ask you for a broker of record letter from the Fund?

A: Yes.

Q: And what did you say to him?

A: I said I can't do that. That's not—I'm one vote out of 22. And for anybody to give a broker of record letter that would have to be from all 22 Trustees, they have to agree to it before anybody can do it. I'm not authorized to do anything like that.

[Comment] Rather jarring in its change of topic without any transition, such as "I would now like to discuss the issue of commissions with you." For example, see Vol. II, p. 18.

Q: At any point in time, did Ms. Hardy call you on the telephone and ask you what role, if any, you wanted Mr. Sussman to have with respect to the negotiations with Blue Cross?

A: Yes.

Q: What did you tell her?

A: I told her he wasn't involved in it.

Q: And did you tell Mr. Sussman whether he was involved?

A: I told him he wasn't involved in it.

Q: Was not involved?

A: Yes.

[Comment] Now, again, the subject abruptly changes without a transition.

Q: And at anytime did either Ms. Hardy or anyone for Independence Blue Cross suggest to the Fund that they should avoid doing business with Mr. Sussman or with his company, Tower?

A: No.

Q: At anytime did Ms. Hardy or anyone from Blue Cross suggest that it would be cheaper for the Fund to cut Mr. Sussman out?

A: No.

[Comment] Will the jurors understand—then and there—why counsel asks these questions? What he might have done is, "I want to direct your attention to plaintiff's claim that Blue Cross interfered with the fund's relationship with the plaintiff."

Q: Incidentally, has the membership of the locals in the Fund been satisfied with the arrangements with Blue Cross?

A: Yes, they have.

[Comment] If the last point is an important one, it deserves more than this.

Q: If you'll excuse me, one second. One final point. In your view, did Mr. Sussman broker the contract between Blue Cross and the Fund?

A: No.

Q: Did Mr. Sussman ever present the Fund a contract on behalf of Blue Cross?

A: No.

Q: Did Mr. Sussman ever present the Fund a bid or a proposal on behalf of Blue Cross?

A: No.

Q: Did Mr. Sussman ever present the Fund any analysis of Blue Cross for the Fund?

A: No.

Q: And did you ever receive any writing from Mr. Sussman concerning Independent Blue Cross?

A: Not that I know of.

Q: Nothing prepared by him analyzing Blue Cross as to benefit claims or anything else?

A: No.

Q: And again, on whom did the Fund rely in this decision to go with Blue Cross?

A: Maresca.

Q: And the Segal Company?

A: And the Segal Company.

[Comment] The ending is well done. Crisp and clean with counsel in command, arguing his opening or his closing right through the witness. But we suggest finishing with a question as to whether Blue Cross did anything that interfered with the Ironworkers' relationship with Sussman.

MR. SONNENFELD: Thank you, sir.

THE COURT: Cross-examine.

Analysis of the Direct Examination

This a short, clean direct examination that makes a few points and makes them clearly. First, the direct examiner establishes that Mr. Sweeney has been president of his local for many years, but co-chair of the welfare fund for only a few. Second, he establishes that Mr. Sweeney has known Mr. Maresca for 25 years, or almost a decade longer than he has known Mr. Sussman. Third, Mr. Sweeney leaves no doubt that he and Mr. Sussman were once friends, but they are friends no longer. Finally, and most importantly, Mr. Sweeney unequivocally states that, in his opinion, Sussman did not broker the contract between the Ironworkers and Blue Cross/Blue Shield. Sweeney gives Maresca and the Segal Company all the credit.

Plaintiff's counsel was slow to object to Sweeney's giving the reason for his falling-out with Sussman and permitting reference to another suit by Sussman. This reference may have been more damaging than previous references because it highlights a suit between Sussman and another union (a union that used Sussman at Sweeney's behest), rather than a dispute between Sussman and Blue Cross/Blue Shield companies, and might have been worse for all the opposing counsel knew. During the opening statements, the judge sustained an objection to a reference to the New Jersey suit, yet plaintiff's counsel was slow to object during Sweeney's direct examination.

As short and clean as this examination is, there are aspects of the case that Sweeney is not asked about, and about which he is almost certainly vulnerable. He is not asked, for example, about the health insurance contract that Sussman did broker for the welfare fund, a contract for which Sussman had no broker of record letter, and the fact that Sussman was giving up fees by urging Blue Cross upon the fund. He is not asked whether it is possible that he gave Sussman the hospital bills relating to his grandson so that Sussman could get Blue Cross/Blue Shield to make a comparison of the Blue Cross/Blue Shield costs as compared to the actual costs for the grandson. He is not asked about whether he believed that, when Sussman sought to bring Blue Cross/Blue Shield and the

Ironworkers together, he thought Sussman was trying for a commission. You will recall the deposition testimony used as part of the plaintiff's case in which Sweeney said that Sussman was always looking to make money.

The most important question to be asked with respect to Sweeney is what his role is in supporting the defense theory. Did Sussman contend that Sweeney promised him anything? Did Sussman contend that Sweeney cheated him? Did Sussman contend that Sweeney did not use Maresca and the Segal Company to negotiate with Blue Cross/Blue Shield? The answer to all these questions is no.

Thus, the importance of Sweeney must be to corroborate the defense claim that Sussman's presence in 1994 and again in 1995 had no bearing on the ultimate success that Blue Cross/Blue Shield had in securing the Ironworkers contract. Sweeney may well believe that, especially as he seems satisfied with the contract and angry at Sussman because of his lawsuit against another union. In any event, he is hardly likely to admit that friends can be influential in the award of contracts, or even in getting people "access," as they say today. But will the jury accept this defense claim, that Sussman did not position Blue Cross/Blue Shield to make the deal and that Sussman's friendship with Sweeney did not open the door that Blue Cross/Blue Shield could not otherwise open? That is the question that will decide the case in the end.

Text of the Cross-Examination

MR. LONGER: Thank you, Your Honor.

BY MR. LONGER:

Q: Mr. Sweeney, you are not friends with Mr. Sussman anymore?

A: That's right.

Q: You are not going to try and help him out, right?

A: I'm not going to try and hurt him either. <u>I'm here to tell you the truth</u>.

[Comment] The witness has volunteered, but counsel has wisely chosen not to move to strike. See Vol. III, pp. 49–53. The witness's gratuitous eruption is the hallmark of one who has a mission, and has not hurt the cross-examiner.

Q: The meeting with Ms. Hardy, that Mr. Sussman was not there?

A: Yes.

Q: You say it lasted 15 minutes?

A: Fifteen, 20 minutes. You know, we're talking about a couple of years ago. It's pretty hard to remember an exact timeframe.

Q: Ms. Hardy said it was early 1994. Would you describe that as a positive meeting?

A: No. She just came in and introduced herself. It wasn't positive. It was nothing really.

[Comment] That is good stuff for the examiner. After all, Hardy testified that it was a "positive meeting."

Q: Do you think that you gave her any reason to believe that it should have been a very positive meeting?

A: No.

[Comment] Notice that the questions are not leading; given the answers, the answers are more effective for the cross-examiner because of it. See Vol. III, pp. 13–15. However, how likely is it that the jury understands that counsel is showing that Hardy's testimony conflicts with Sweeney? What should he do? "Now, Ms. Hardy has told us repeatedly that the meeting was, in her view, a positive one. Am I correct that you have just sworn to us that not only was it not positive, but that it was nothing?"

Q: The meeting that took place with Ms. Hardy in your office with Mr. Sussman—

A: Yes.

Q: —after that meeting, did you direct Mr. Craggs to give any information to Mr. Sussman?

A: No.

[Comment] Unfortunately, counsel is jumping around a bit, which can be jarring. And he is selecting an area where he cannot control the witness.

Q: Do you know if Mr. Sussman gave him any information after that meeting?

A: If Mr. Sussman gave who information after that meeting?

Q: Did Mr. Craggs give Mr. Sussman any information about the Ironworkers after your meeting with Ms. Hardy and Mr. Sussman?

A: I really don't know.

Q: Did Mr. Sussman ever give you any information about Blue Cross/Blue Shield after that meeting?

A: No.

[Comment] None of the last questions is leading. And none of the last answers help the examiner, although not because of the form of the question, but rather because the answers do not help and the examiner has nothing to confront the witness with.

Q: This morning, Ms. Hardy—and I believe it's stipulated, the meeting took place in May or June of 1994. Do you recall getting any directories or listings of doctors from Mr. Sussman after your meeting in June of 1994?

A: Do I recall any? No, I don't.

Q: You never talked to him about directories of Blue Cross/Blue Shield and the extent of Blue Cross/Blue Shield's doctors?

A: Could I explain something? Mr. Sussman and I were friends. We used to go to lunch quite a bit and we might have talked about a lot of things. But no, as I told you before, it didn't make any difference what I said to Mr. Sussman, <u>because I'm one vote out of 22</u>.

[Comment] That answer, which was volunteered, did not help the witness or Blue Cross. We suggest the jury has a real sense that if Sweeney is anything, he is not just one vote out of 22.

Q: You're one vote out of 22. You have no influence over the other Trustees?

A: Absolutely not.

Q: You are the co-chairman of the Board of Directors and you have no influence over any other Trustees in that position?

A: No. No.

[Comment] Excellent. He used the Rules and Laws of Probability to make his point. See Vol. III, pp. 177–180. Notice also that he does not care about the answer, for no answer can hurt him unless it is believed, and that last answer will likely not be believed. See Vol. III, pp. 180–183.

Q: Let me show you Exhibit Number—Defendant's Exhibit Number-7. And I'm sorry, I don't want to approach. In the blue notebook there, Exhibit D-7.

A: I don't see any Ds.

Q: Oh, right here. The June 23rd note. June 23, 1995, meeting of the Board of Trustees. And these are the Minutes, correct?

A: Right.

Q: You're present at that meeting, right?

A: Yes.

Q: Page 4 of the document?

A: Yes.

Q: Do you see that first full paragraph, "After discussion, motion was made, seconded and unanimously

adopted authorizing the Committee to meet with the consultants to review consideration of a P.P.O. (Preferred
Provider Organization) program and to report their findings at the September 1995 meeting"?

A: Yes, I do.

Q: Did you have anything to do with that motion?

A: Absolutely not. I'm the Chairman. I'm running the
meeting. I can accept the motion from somebody on the
floor, but I can't make a motion from the podium.

Q: Do you recall who made the motion?

A: I have no idea.

Q: Did you ask anyone to make that motion?

A: No.

Q: You had nothing to do with Blue Cross/Blue Shield;
is that right?

A: I don't think I said that.

*[Comment] Sweeney has reached his limit. The "nothing to do
with" is just too much.*

Q: I'm sorry. You had nothing to do with that motion?

A: No, I accepted it. I had something to do with it. I
was the Chairman and I was running the meeting and I
accepted the motion and hold a vote on it.

*[Comment] Pretty good job. Not likely the jurors are going to
believe that the motion sprang from Zeus's brow. Yet a few questions, like "This motion suddenly appeared at the meeting you
chaired after Sussman met with you?," might help. The purpose
of cross—as the purpose of direct, as the purpose of opening—is
to argue your case to the jury; in cross it goes right through the
witness. See Vol. III, pp. 1–2.*

Q: Plaintiff's Exhibit Number-5, it's in the black notebook. This is the contract with Preferred Care, is it not?

A: Yes, it is.

Q: Did Mr. Sussman have anything to do with this contract?

A: Yes, he did.

Q: Did he bring Mr. Halverson to you?

A: Yes, he did.

Q: And together, do you know that the two of them <u>are making a commission</u> on this contract?

A: At the time, I didn't. But subsequently, <u>I found out that they do</u>. At the time that it was being brokered, I didn't know anything about a commission. My understanding, at that time, was that there was a level of the commission that somebody would get, but that the provider would pay it. In other words, P.P.O. was going to pay Mr. Halverson, and that's my understanding.

[Comment] Might be a good time to point out that all that is being asked in this case is for the provider, Blue Cross, to pay Sussman's commission.

Q: Now, you are having lunches with Mr. Sussman in the 1994 time period, weren't you?

A: Yes.

Q: Didn't Mr. Sussman tell you, "This is what I'm doing, Bob, I'm putting the P.P.O. in. I'm going to get a commission"?

A: No, he didn't tell me that.

Q: He's your friend, he's dealing in a contract with your organization, the Ironworkers District Council Health and Welfare Fund and he's not telling you that he's going to make a commission on this?

A: If I tell him to make a commission, I'm taking money out of my Fund that I don't have any reason to take out. No, I didn't say it was okay for anybody to get any commission.

Q: Your company isn't paying Preferred Care a dime in commissions, right?

A: I have no idea what we're paying Preferred Care. I don't have any—I never knew there was any commissions involved until this stuff came up.

Q: You didn't have to pay a commission, the Ironworkers didn't have to pay commission on this contract?

A: I don't know whether they did or not. You're telling me they didn't. I don't know that.

[Comment] But he already testified that the provider was in fact paying a commission, that is, Preferred Care. But the issue slips away.

Q: Mr. Sussman didn't tell you that you could do this without having to fork out a dime for him?

A: Now you're going back to 1994.

Q: I am.

A: And I don't know what Mr. Sussman told me in 1994.

Q: You don't remember?

A: No.

Q: You don't remember a thing he told you in 1994?

A: No. I don't remember what you're talking about.

Q: Mr. Sussman was responsible for bringing Mr. Halverson and you together so that you could contract on this agreement, right?

A: That's right.

Q: And you didn't think it was necessary to use your consultants on that?

A: Could I elaborate on that?

Q: Why don't you answer?

A: I just said yeah. Now, what happened with Preferred Care was something that should have never happened. We were panicking because we had to do something about the way the Fund was going. Now, instead of getting the consultants and the management Trustees together, which we always do, we just rushed into something. Whether we should have got into it or not, I don't know, but it <u>worked out successfully for us</u>.

Q: This <u>was a successful contract</u>?

A: Yes.

Q: <u>Mr. Sussman got you involved in a successful contract</u>?

A: Mr. Sussman introduced me to Mr. Halverson.

Q: <u>And he got you into a successful contract</u>?

A: Yes.

[Comment] Excellent. Counsel asks a question, the witness does not answer that one, but another. So counsel, seeking no help, simply repeats the question word for word. Right on. See Vol. III, pp. 51–53.

Q: And together the two of them are making a commission; isn't that right?

A: I don't know. You're telling me that. I never seen any checks or anything where he says here is what I'm making.

[Comment] Again we forget about the earlier testimony, when he says he has "subsequently found out" that commissions are being paid.

Q: Is the Blue Cross/Blue Shield contract a successful contract?

A: Very successful.

Q: And didn't Mr. Sussman bring Ms. Hardy in to meet with you, and say, "Bob, listen to me. I'm going to put you with Blue Cross/Blue Shield because it's better than Preferred Care?"

A: No, he didn't say that.

Q: He never said that?

A: No.

Q: That's a lie?

[Comment] That is an improper question, asking a witness to term another statement a lie. And Sweeney deals with it very well indeed.

A: He never said it. I don't know whether it's a lie or not. You're asking me if he said it and I'm saying no.

[Comment] And now counsel improperly refers to the jurors, the "they," "them," and "they're" in the next three questions and answers.

Q: And you want them to believe you too, right?

A: I don't know why they wouldn't believe me. I'm not up here lying to them.

Q: Well, they're going to decide, Mr. Sweeney.

[Comment] This last is not only improper, but also rather nasty. The witness has, to be sure, been rather unpleasant, but counsel should not make such a personal attack or challenge.

MR. LONGER: Thank you very much. I have no further questions.

Analysis of the Cross-Examination

If you are the cross-examiner, you know as matter of logic certain things about Mr. Sweeney. He will maintain that at all times his only concern was about his union members, and there is no evidence to contradict him on this point. He will not attack Blue Cross/Blue Shield because they have the contract with his welfare fund, and he wants that contract to look like it was a good idea, not a bad one. He won't attack Mr. Maresca or the Segal Company, because of their longstanding ties and also because they negotiated for the fund the contract that Mr. Sweeney wants to defend. You also know that Mr. Sweeney is angry at Mr. Sussman because Sussman sued another union after Sweeney recommended him to that union, and also because it is Sussman's suit that has made Sweeney a witness in this case. Mr. Sweeney obviously prefers not being a witness.

If you know all these things as the cross-examiner, then we believe you have to attempt to undertake a cross-examination that will demonstrate to the jury facts that cannot be denied because they are obviously true, and that if denied hurt the witness and the party relying on the witness more than if they are admitted. The key to examining a witness like Sweeney is to identify those facts that the jury will believe based upon their own experience and upon common sense.

In our judgment, the cross-examiner did make some points by using the rules and law of probability. Sweeney claims that he is simply one of 22 trustees and has no unusual influence. We doubt that any juror will believe that. The point could be made more powerfully. We offer some additional suggestions:

Q: Mr. Sweeney, when Ms. Hardy came to see you for the first time, she came to see you personally, not to see Mr. Craggs?

Q: Ms. Hardy did see you personally?

Q: You know that Ms. Hardy chose you as the man to see because she thought you had some influence over the trustees of the welfare fund?

Q: As far as you know, Ms. Hardy did not seek to contact any other trustee before seeing you?

Q: As far as you know, Ms. Hardy had no reason to be encouraged by her meeting with you?

Q: As far as you know, after that meeting with you, Ms. Hardy did not seek to contact any other trustee of the welfare fund?

Q: Ms. Hardy apparently thought you were the man to see regarding a contract with the Ironworkers?

Q: After Ms. Hardy selected you as the man to see, Mr. Sussman contacted you and sought to arrange a meeting with you, him, and Ms. Hardy?

Q: At the time Mr. Sussman contacted you, the two of you were friends?

Q: In fact, the two of you had been friends for about 15 or so years when he contacted you about meeting with him and Ms. Hardy?

Q: Before contacting you to arrange that meeting, Mr. Sussman had introduced you to Mr. Halverson?

Q: The meeting with Halverson led to a contract between the Ironworkers and Preferred Care?

Q: As far as you knew, Mr. Sussman had not sought to introduce Mr. Halverson to other trustees of the welfare fund?

Q: Mr. Sussman sought to arrange a meeting between you, him, and Ms. Hardy, no one else?

Q: Mr. Sussman knew you were co-chair of the trustees?

Q: Mr. Sussman knew there were other trustees?

Q: Mr. Sussman did not request that other trustees attend the meeting with you, him, and Ms. Hardy?

Q: As far as you know, Sussman wanted to meet with you and only you among the trustees?

Q: Now, you understood that Mr. Sussman asked for this meeting because he thought you had considerable influence over the trustees, didn't you?

Q: You understood at the meeting that Mr. Sussman was trying to get you interested in Blue Cross/Blue Shield?

Q: When Mr. Sussman sought the meeting with you, him, and Ms. Hardy, he wanted it at your office?

Q: That's where the meeting was held?

Q: You understood that Mr. Sussman wanted to meet at your office because this was a business meeting, not a social occasion?

Q: After Mr. Sussman and Ms. Hardy met with you, approximately a year later the trustees of the welfare fund voted to have the investment committee study a preferred provider option?

Q: That option led to the Blue Cross contract?

Q: As far as you know, the only contacts between any health insurer and the Ironworkers in the year before you agreed to the Blue Cross contract were the two meetings—the one Ms. Hardy had with you, and the other that Ms. Hardy and Mr. Sussman had with you?

Q: As far as you know, no other trustee had been contacted by Blue Cross or any other preferred provider in the year before you signed the Blue Cross contract?

Q: You yourself had become interested in considering a preferred provider because of concern about deductibles and other matters?

Q: And, in fact, you told others about your interest in considering a preferred provider?

Q: The fact is, Mr. Sweeney, it was your interest and your influence with the trustees that caused them to approve the investigation by the investment committee that led to the Blue Cross contract?

For us, this is an argument made through the order and logic of questions. It does not matter whether Sweeney admits or denies the premise of the last question. The jury will make up its mind about whether Sweeney had influence, and about whether both Sussman and Hardy believed that Sweeney had sufficient influence to be a key player.

Let us turn now to the question of commissions. Sweeney, in our judgment, is in the position of wanting the jury to believe that he could care less who gets a commission, or whether anyone does, so long as his union members are protected. This judgment leads us to suggest a cross-examination that makes this very point:

Q: Now, Mr. Sussman introduced you to Mr. Halverson?

Q: Eventually, Mr. Halverson worked with the Ironworkers to develop the contract with Preferred Care?

Q: That has been a successful contract?

Q: When that contract was negotiated, your concern was making sure your union members had adequate coverage and that they did not pay too much?

Q: Your responsibility was to the union, not to the insurance company?

Q: You weren't worried whether the insurance company was making money or losing money, as long as the contract protected your members?

Q: You did not take time to investigate how the insurance company might compensate Mr. Halverson or anyone else?

Q: You knew the Preferred Care contract was being brokered?

Q: The details of the insurance company's dealing with the broker or brokers was not your concern?

Q: If the insurance company paid commissions, that was its business, not yours?

Q: As far as you know, the welfare fund did not pay any commissions to anyone?

Q: But you did not know whether the insurance company paid any commissions?

Q: The reason you did not know was that you did not care as long as the contract was a good one for the union members?

Q: Now, when Ms. Hardy first contacted you about Blue Cross/Blue Shield, she did not tell you that she would receive a commission if she could land a contract?

Q: You did not ask her about her salary or her commissions?

Q: You were not interested in how Blue Cross/Blue Shield paid its employees?

Q: When Mr. Sussman and Ms. Hardy came to see you, you understood that Mr. Sussman was in the brokerage business?

Q: Mr. Sussman did not tell you he was volunteering to contribute time and services to Blue Cross/Blue Shield?

Q: As you said in your deposition, you assumed Mr. Sussman was interested in working with Blue Cross/Blue Shield and the Ironworkers to earn something?

Q: But as long as the Ironworkers were not paying a fee, it was not your concern?

Q: Once Mr. Maresca and the Segal Company were negotiating a contract with Blue Cross/Blue Shield, they did not tell you that Ms. Hardy would receive a commission on the deal?

Q: You did not ask whether she would, because that was Blue Cross/Blue Shield's business, not yours?

Q: In fact, as you sit here today, you don't know what the exact terms of Ms. Hardy's contract with Blue Cross/ Blue Shield are?

Q: That's not your concern, right?

Q: It's Blue Cross/Blue Shield's concern?

Q: If Ms. Hardy had promised Mr. Sussman a portion

of her commission to work with her in getting the Ironworkers interested in Blue Cross/Blue Shield, that would be her concern, not yours?

Q: You have no personal knowledge of what Ms. Hardy said to Mr. Sussman?

Q: As between Ms. Hardy, or Mr. Sussman, or someone at Blue Cross/Blue Shield, you don't know, as the co-chair of the welfare fund, and you don't care which of them Blue Cross/Blue Shield pays a commission?

Q: You care about the health coverage for your members?

Q: You care about what you pay for that coverage?

Q: But it is not your business how Blue Cross/Blue Shield spends any profit it earns?

Q: It's not your business whether Blue Cross/Blue Shield agrees to pay commissions to brokers?

Q: Mr. Sussman came to you at some point to request a broker of record letter?

Q: He did not ask the Ironworkers to pay a commission?

Q: He did not seek to change the terms of whatever deal Mr. Maresca would negotiate?

Q: He told you that Blue Cross/Blue Shield would not pay his commission without the letter?

Q: You have no idea when Blue Cross/Blue Shield first told Mr. Sussman he needed that letter?

Q: You have no knowledge whether Blue Cross/Blue Shield promised Mr. Sussman a commission for his services?

Q: You don't know whether Blue Cross misled him into thinking they would pay him a commission?

Q: If Blue Cross/Blue Shield decided to pay Mr. Sussman a commission out of its profits on the Ironworkers contract, that would be Blue Cross/Blue Shield's decision, not yours?

Q: If Blue Cross/Blue Shield told Mr. Sussman he would have a commission and then cheated him, that's none of your doing?

Q: Even though you and Mr. Sussman are no longer friends, you would not want to see a man cheated by an insurance company, would you?

As for Sweeney's testimony that his friendship with Mr. Sussman had nothing to do with the ultimate contract the Ironworkers made with Blue Cross/Blue Shield, questions about friendship might have elicited different answers:

Q: As president of the Ironworkers, you meet a lot of people?

Q: Some of these people are strangers when you meet them?

Q: Sometimes you meet people once and never see them again?

Q: Other people become friends?

Q: Mr. Craggs, who worked for you, he became a friend?

Q: When you say someone is a friend, you mean that's a person who has a special relationship with you?

Q: Not everyone you meet becomes your friend?

Q: Your friends trust you?

Q: You trust your friends?

Q: You care about your friends?

Q: If a friend calls you up and wants to talk, you treat that call differently from that of a stranger?

Q: When Ms. Hardy first came to see you, she was a stranger?

Q: You did not know her?

Q: You had no reason to believe that you would ever see her again?

Q: You were polite, but she was not a friend?

Q: You had no history with her?

Q: You had no information about her other than what she might have told you at your meeting?

Q: Mr. Sussman, on the other hand, had been your friend for approximately 15 years when he came to see you with Ms. Hardy?

Q: At that time, you had no reason to believe your friendship would end?

Q: You treated Mr. Sussman with the respect you give friends?

Q: You listened to Mr. Sussman the way you listen to a friend?

Q: You knew that Ms. Hardy understood Mr. Sussman was your friend?

Q: You did nothing to embarrass Mr. Sussman in front of Ms. Hardy?

Q: You paid attention when your friend spoke?

Q: At that time, you understood that your friend, Mr. Sussman, was suggesting that Blue Cross/Blue Shield would be of benefit to the Ironworkers?

Q: You, of course, were interested in things that could benefit your union?

Q: So you listened to your friend, Mr. Sussman, to learn how Blue Cross/Blue Shield could assist you?

Q: You heard what he said?

Q: You heard him say that Blue Cross/Blue Shield could deal with the deductible problem?

Q: You heard him say that Blue Cross/Blue Shield could provide a larger pool of doctors?

Q: You were concerned about deductibles for your members?

Q: You wanted a wide variety of doctors available for your members?

Q: You wanted to do what you could to help your members?

Q: And you listened to Mr. Sussman on behalf of your members?

The plain fact is that friends treat friends differently from the way they treat strangers. Sweeney admitted that Sussman was his friend, and it will be difficult for Sweeney to look like the kind of person most witnesses want to look like if he is insistent that he treated his friend like a stranger. The power of a cross-examination is often derived from putting a witness in the impossible position of conceding something he does not want to concede or insisting upon something that he cannot bear to say.

The defense now has the opportunity to redirect. But should he take it? We think that he has not been hurt on cross and so should not. But he does do a short redirect.

Text of the Redirect Examination

BY MR. SONNENFELD:

Q: Mr. Sweeney, a few brief questions. Did you ever ask Mr. Sussman to investigate Independence Blue Cross on behalf of the Fund?

A: No.

Q: And before Mr. Sussman brought Ms. Hardy to you, had you heard of Independence Blue Cross?

A: Yes.

Q: Before Mr. Sussman brought Mr. Halverson to you, had you ever heard of the company called Preferred Care?

A: No, I hadn't.

Q: And was Mr. Sussman in any way responsible for bringing the Fund and Blue Cross together?

A: No.

MR. SONNENFELD: Thank you, sir.

[Comment] Did this last interrogation help Blue Cross? Do you believe that Sussman was "in any way" responsible for bringing the parties together? If you do, the jurors likely do as well, and then Sweeney must be disbelieved by you and by them.

THE COURT: Counsel.

MR. LONGER: I have no further questions.

THE COURT: Thank you, Mr. Sweeney.

THE MANAGEMENT TRUSTEE

Text of the Direct Examination

MR. SONNENFELD: Your Honor, our next witness is Mr. Reith. With Your Honor's permission, Ms. Bennett will conduct the examination of Mr. Reith.

THE COURT: Sure.

THE CRIER: State your name and spell your last name.

THE WITNESS: John Reith, R-E-I-T-H.

JOHN REITH, WITNESS, after having been first duly sworn, was examined and testified as follows:

BY MS. BENNETT:

Q: Good afternoon, Mr. Reith.

A: Good afternoon.

Q: Are you currently employed, Mr. Reith?

A: Yes, I am.

Q: And who is your employer?

A: General Building Contractors Association.

Q: Are you also affiliated with the Ironworkers District Council Philadelphia and Vicinity Health and Welfare Fund?

A: Yes, I am.

Q: What is your position with the Fund?

A: Trustee and co-chairman.

Q: And are you co-chairman from the union side or the management side?

A: The management side.

Q: And are you also a member of the Investment Committee of the Fund?

A: Yes, I am.

Q: Are you familiar with a decision by the Fund to enter into a contract with Independence Blue Cross and Pennsylvania Blue Shield?

A: Yes, I am.

Q: And were you involved at all? Did you have any role in the implementation of that contract?

A: No. Other than listening to the presentation and voting along with the other Trustees.

Q: If you could, tell me a little bit about that and how the contract came to be and how it was that the idea was initiated?

[Comment] Notice the "and"s. The last question is a pure invitation to the witness to take over the examination.

A: At one of the meetings, I'm not exactly sure which meeting, because I attend so many meetings and, in fact, a discussion to engage Blue Cross was also going on with another trust fund that I'm sitting on, so a lot of this was going on at the same time. But, it was mentioned, I believe, by Mr. Maresca, that we should take some action and make some changes in what we were doing and engage a P.P.O. with a broader network, and my assumption was what that would probably be Blue Cross.

Q: <u>And</u> when you say, "a meeting," do you mean a Board of Trustees meeting <u>or</u> just an informal meeting?

[Comment] Excellent. She leads by giving alternatives. See Vol. II, pp. 19–20.

A: It first came out of a full Board of Trustees meeting and progressed from there.

Q: After the full Board of Trustees meeting what was decided at the Board of Trustees meeting that eventually made this idea progress?

A: It was decided that we should explore it, we should look into it.

Q: <u>And</u> is that what, in fact, occurred?

A: Yes, it was.

[Comment] But then she returns to the "and"s and to the "could"s, seeking help in the form of narratives from the witness. Remember, the actual answer to a "could you" question is "yes."

Q: <u>And could</u> you tell me the next step in the process of what happened, to the best of your recollection?

A: Representatives of Blue Cross were invited to an Investment Committee meeting where they gave us a presentation and we were in favor of their presentation, and recommended that we proceed with this at the next—the recommendation was then made that the next full Board meeting, that we proceed with, going ahead with the proposition made by Blue Cross. We instructed

Mr. Maresca to work out the details, the fee and so forth, and take it from there.

Q: <u>And</u> when you said that Independence Blue Cross was invited to one of your meetings, in that regard, could you please turn to Exhibit-13 in the blue notebook.

A: [Witness complies.]

Q: <u>Could</u> you take a look at that document and tell me what it is?

A: It's a meeting of the Investment Committee held on September 5th.

Q: <u>And</u> where was the meeting held?

A: At the GVC office.

Q: That was your office?

A: Yes.

Q: Was that the meeting that you said you referred to when you said Independence Blue Cross was invited?

A: Yes.

Q: <u>And</u> did the Segal Company, in fact, continue to negotiate the contract with Blue Cross after the Board of Trustees decided to implement?

A: Yes, they did.

Q: <u>And</u> was a contract eventually entered into?

A: Yes, it was.

[Comment] All well and good. And it was good, in the sense that she got what she wanted, and clearly at that. But how does it fit into the case? To know, we have to "step back."

Q: Stepping back to these meetings that you recall where the idea to go with Independence Blue Cross and Pennsylvania Blue Shield was initiated, was this something that was pushed or forced by the Union Trustees or anybody from the Union?

A: No.

Q: Was this something that the Management Trustees wanted, as well?

A: Yes.

Q: And you are the—

A: We felt that it was the prudent thing to do.

[Comment] Well done! And now management is about to nullify Sussman.

Q: Mr. Reith, had you heard of Leonard Sussman or Tower Financial Planning before this lawsuit?

A: No.

Q: In your view, did Leonard Sussman or Tower Financial have anything at all to do with the contract with Independence Blue Cross?

A: Not to <u>my</u> knowledge.

[Comment] Very good, technically. But . . . what about what he does not know, that we by now know! By the way, do you, the reader, believe that Sussman had nothing to do with getting this contract with Blue Cross? What is the benefit of having a witness of limited knowledge truthfully answer only within these confines, if everyone knows that less than the entire truth is being presented?

Q: To your knowledge, did anybody from Independence Blue Cross speak with anybody at the Fund and tell them to <u>avoid</u> doing business with Leonard Sussman?

A: No.

[Comment] Now, that is not only a different point, but it also addresses the charge in the complaint.

Q: Did Leonard Sussman or Tower Financial do anything to help Independence Blue Cross gain access to the Ironworkers Fund?

A: No. As I say, I never heard of him.

Q: You just said you never heard of Tower Financial. Had you ever heard of Independence Blue Cross before you entered into the contract with them?

A: Yes.

Q: Okay. And where did you hear of them from?

A: Well, as I say, I serve as a Trustee on many other trust funds and on at least two of the other ones, we utilize the services of Blue Cross.

Q: And are those trust fund also union funds?

A: Yes.

Q: Union Health and Welfare Funds?

A: Yes.

Q: And do you know which ones they are, just off the top of your head?

A: Yeah. The Operating Engineers Local 542 in Philadelphia. And Carpenters Local 600 in Bethlehem, Pennsylvania.

MS. BENNETT: Thank you very much.

Analysis of the Direct Examination

This is one of those examinations that looks on its face as though it supports the defense, but which, upon careful analysis, may actually do more to undermine it. Reith never heard of Sussman, which means that Sussman was able to introduce Mr. Halverson to Sweeney and to obtain a commission on the Preferred Care account without any knowledge of the co-chair of the welfare fund. So much for Mr. Sweeney's lack of influence.

If Reith had never heard of Sussman, he would have no idea of what relationship Sussman had with Sweeney and thus cannot deny that Sussman might have been influential in interesting Sweeney in Blue Cross/Blue Shield. Moreover,

Reith apparently did not propose Blue Cross/Blue Shield as an
insurer for the Ironworkers even though he was familiar with
Blue Cross/Blue Shield. That raises the interesting and important question of who it was who decided that suddenly the
trustees should look into a preferred provider organization in
September 1995. Reith says that management as well as the
union supported the motion, but it is apparent that he hasn't a
clue as to what forces resulted in the making of the motion.

In short, Reith has no information that responds to the
essential allegations of the plaintiff's case. He is wide open for
cross-examination, particularly one of limitation. See Vol. III,
pp. 16–19. The next question is whether the cross-examiner
will deliver.

Text of the Cross-Examination

THE COURT: Cross-examine.

BY MR. LONGER:

Q: Mr. Reith, we met before in Mr. Sonnenfeld's office
when I took your deposition, December 16, 1996; do you
recall that?

A: Yes, I do.

MR. LONGER: Your Honor, may I approach?

THE COURT: Yes.

BY MR. LONGER:

Q: I have one question for you, Mr. Reith. Do you
recall me asking you, do you have any knowledge—

MR. SONNENFELD: May I have a page?

MR. LONGER: I'm sorry, I do this all the time. Page
40, lines 9 through 13.

BY MR. LONGER:

Q: "Do you have any knowledge of any actions of Ms.
Hardy prior to September of 1995 to—

MR. SONNENFELD: Your Honor—

MS. BENNETT: Your Honor, I object. He's showing—this witness is here to testify, I'm not sure—he hasn't asked him any questions yet.

THE COURT: Well, I guess he's going to ask him a question as a result of this answer.

BY MR. LONGER:

Q: "Do you have any knowledge of any actions of Ms. Hardy prior to September of 1995, to sell insurance to the Ironworkers District Council Fund?" Do you recall what your answer was?

A: "None at all."

MR. LONGER: I have no further questions. Thank you, Mr. Reith.

THE COURT: Redirect?

MS. BENNETT: No, Your Honor.

THE COURT: Thank you, sir, you may step down.

[Witness excused.]

Analysis of the Cross-Examination

Not only does the cross-examiner get interrupted, by failing to indicate the page and line of the deposition he is using (a problem we identified earlier), but he also asks impeachment questions before showing that there was anything to impeach. The objection was sound and more times than not would have been sustained.

The cross-examiner should take no solace in winning over the objection. The choice to use the deposition rather than having the witness admit the facts in front of the jury was not good advocacy. Either the witness will admit that he knew nothing about Ms. Hardy's efforts or he will deny it and be impeached. In either event, getting the witness to testify before the jury is better than referring to his deposition.

So there is reason to criticize the technique. But, more importantly, there is reason to criticize the substance. For the reasons stated in our analysis of the direct examination, Mr. Reith may well be a more valuable plaintiff's witness than a defense witness. He has the ability to establish that Sweeney, in fact, was calling the shots; that Sweeney had benefited from Sussman's brokering in the past; and that Sweeney had never told Reith and perhaps never told any other trustee. This, plus the facts that Reith had never suggested Blue Cross/Blue Shield and apparently did not know the background of the motion that led the investment committee to work with Maresca and the Segal Company were powerful points available to the plaintiffs. But these points were not made.

Too often in a case, one side calls a witness and the other side decides that the witness is "their" witness, not "our" witness. This is a mistake. Reith need never have been called to support the defense. Indeed, the best defense may be one that Reith knows nothing about, which is that Sussman misled both Sweeney and Hardy. However, this defense is inconsistent with Sussman's being simply irrelevant and having had no influence. Reith is a wonderful witness for the plaintiff because he proves that the management trustees were out of the loop when it came to health insurance and how decisions were made. Indeed, the one question in deposition that would have been useful on cross established that the management people had no idea about the meetings between Sweeney and Hardy, as well as Sweeney and Sussman, before the vote. Because it is a bare question and answer from a deposition, though, it is not likely that the jurors will get the point.

Plaintiff's counsel surely could have done more with this witness. Indeed, he might have been a witness in the plaintiff's case-in-chief. The defendants gain little from his testimony but do not pay the price that they might have paid for calling him.

The stage is now set for the return of Ms. Hardy to the witness stand.

Chapter Eleven

Ms. Hardy Returns

TEXT OF THE FIRST PART OF THE DIRECT EXAMINATION

THE COURT: Call your next witness.

MR. SONNENFELD: Should we go—

THE COURT: Yes, let's start.

MR. SONNENFELD: How late?

THE COURT: See how it goes.

MR. SONNENFELD: Ms. Hardy.

THE CRIER: For the record, state your name, please.

THE WITNESS: Helen Hardy.

THE CRIER: And you're still under oath.

BY MR. SONNENFELD:

Q: Now, Ms. Hardy, you are employed by Independence Blue Cross, as we know from your testimony when you were called in the Plaintiff's case. How long have you been employed with Independence Blue Cross?

A: Just about 28 years.

[Comment] Nice transition question. Brings us back to where we were and loops into testimony from many hours before. See Vol. II, pp. 17–18.

Q: And for how long have you been working with the Union Health and Welfare Funds?

A: Twenty-five years.

Q: And did you have a life before you were at Independence Blue Cross?

A: Yes.

Q: What were you before you were employed by Independence Blue Cross?

A: I was a nurse, licensed practical nurse.

Q: How did you come to be employed by Independence Blue Cross?

A: Do you want me to tell the story?

Q: Sure.

[Comment] Not such a good idea. The examiner has accepted her invitation to turn the examination over to her. Indeed, he himself invited it with his question. Here comes the outpouring. Better for the examiner to take it step by step, to be from Hoboken and make all the stops along the way. See Vol. II, pp. 7–11.

A: Well, I'm from the shore right outside of Atlantic City and I worked at Shore Memorial Hospital in the Intensive Care Unit. And one of our patients was a gentleman by the name of Tom Manley. Mr. Manley had had a heart attack and he was my patient and I found out that he worked at Independence Blue Cross. Well, at that time, it was called Blue Cross of the Greater Philadelphia Area. And I decided I wanted to come to the city, get out of the sticks of South Jersey and come up to the big city, and I came up here and had an interview at Jefferson Hospital and actually, I did get the job. And as it turned out, I was walking down the street, and although happy I got the job, I was disappointed that I was going to have to work weekends. I was young and decided that I would like to have more of my own time. But in any case, I walked down the street and I saw Blue Cross and I thought gee, I'll go see Tom Manley. In the Intensive Care Unit we tended to get fairly close to our patients. So, I walked in and asked if I could see Tom Manley, not having any idea that he was the President, and they kind of looked at me like who is this young lady <u>with this long blonde hair</u>. And, I went in and they called Mr. Manley, and said, "Helen—<u>at the time my name was Jacobs</u>—Helen Jacobs is here to see you." And <u>he was very happy to see me</u> and I went in and he said, "Why don't you work here." I said, "Gee, I'm a nurse, I can't type." And in those days, as a woman, you either would be a secretary, a school teacher, or a nurse.

MR. LONGER: Your Honor, I object to the narrative.

[Comment] It is a narrative and the objection is proper, although not necessarily helpful to the objector, particularly as to her use of the word "sticks" and assorted other observations about herself that are not likely to endear her to the jurors. Hearing the objection, the witness, who is now an advocate, answers him back.

THE WITNESS: It's a long story.

[Comment] The direct examiner wisely gets both his witness and himself out of there.

MR. SONNENFELD: Well, I'll move on.

BY MR. SONNENFELD:

Q: What was your initial position at Independence Blue Cross?

A: In the Marketing Department, although at that time, we called it enrollment, and I was what they called a junior representative, but I did deal with customers.

Q: <u>And</u> how long did you have that position?

A: Oh, I would say approximately one to one-and-a-half years.

Q: <u>And</u> what did you do after that?

A: After that, I did purely new business for maybe about a year, little over a year.

Q: <u>And</u> then what?

A: <u>And</u> then I moved into the Health and Welfare Fund area as a sales representative. Well, actually, it was sales and service and I had a book of business where I handled many of the units in health and welfare funds in the city.

Q: <u>And</u> do you yourself have a union background?

A: Yes.

[Comment] Putting aside this habit, notice how nicely he took the last testimony, piece by piece. Unfortunately, in our view, his next question, an open one, causes us to get more information than we can easily handle.

Q: <u>Can</u> you tell us?

A: Yes. Independence Blue Cross, their sales representatives have, probably from about 1972 until oh, maybe about five years ago, we were represented by the U.A.W. I think it was Local 757, I don't know if I have that local correct, but was a member of that and I also served on the Negotiating Committee a couple of times. I'm not a cardholder now, but I was then.

Q: And you have a union background in your family?

A: Yes. My dad is a carpenter and he's just recently retired.

Q: And your position now is you are the manager of the Union Department?

A: No, I'm the director.

Q: Director. And do you work with various union health and welfare funds?

A: I work with all of the health and welfare funds in the city and the surrounding counties, yes.

Q: <u>Can</u> you tell us what some of those funds are?

A: Oh, goodness. All of the buildings trades, so that would include the carpenters, the operating engineers, the electricians, the painters, the plasterers, all the building trades. The ironworkers, steamfitters, plumbers, all building trades, mason workers. And in addition to that Teamster Health and Welfare Funds, we have approximately five of them as well as the Teamster and Vicinity Funds. That means that it is Tri-State. The United Food and Commercial Workers, we have two of them, two funds. The bakery and confectionary workers. The transport workers. I'm sure I'm missing a few, but just all of them. There's only about two health and welfare funds that are not yet with Independence Blue Cross.

[Comment] Again, too much too soon. If counsel wants us to appreciate the scope of her work with unions, we suggest he should take it in slower and smaller bites.

Now, however, he makes a good point. Blue Cross itself has union leaders who sit on its Board.

Q: And are there union representatives on the Board of Trustees or Board of Directors at Independence Blue Cross?

A: Yes.

Q: Do you know how many there are?

A: I believe there are now four.

Q: Do you recall what unions are represented on the Board?

A: Yes. The President of the Carpenter's Union, Ed Correlle. He's on our Board. I'm trying to remember. This gentleman has a new title, he's with the International now. His name is Pat Finley, and he's with the cement masons. A gentleman by the name of Pat Gillespie who is the—again, I'm not sure of his title, but he's like a business manager of all of the building trades, the Building Trades Association for the unions.

Q: What is that, three, four? Three or four?

A: Three. Who did I miss?

Q: Well, we won't dwell on that.

A: I'm sorry. I don't remember.

[Comment] All very nice. Back and forth. Bit by bit. He could achieve the Wimbledon effect. See Vol. II, pp. 7, 8.

Q: We'll move on. Now, what is Independence Blue Cross?

A: Independence Blue Cross is a non-profit company that provides health benefits for individuals. We also provide those benefits through group contracts, whether it is an employer or an association or a health and welfare fund.

Q: And where is Independence Blue Cross located?

A: Today, it is at 1901 Market Street.

Q: In Philadelphia?

A: In Philadelphia.

Q: And where was it located when you came to work for the company?

A: It was at 13th and Chestnut in the Widener Building.

Q: 1334 Chestnut?

A: Correct.

Q: 1333?

A: I forgot that. 1333 Chestnut. Long time ago.

Q: Now, when you say Independence Blue Cross is a non-profit corporation, can you tell us what you mean by that?

[Comment] Very nice. Looping. He provides filler so we are oriented, and he gets us ready for the point that any award against Blue Cross will come from its subscribers.

A: We do not have any shareholders, nor do we make any profit. All of the monies that are taken in for these contracts, is used for the costs of administering the programs. Part of those monies that come in go to research. Part of the money goes to our community efforts. We have some programs that are available to folks who do not have insurance, our caring Foundation Program.

Q: You also have what you call the social mission?

A: I used the term community, but I meant the social mission.

Q: What do you mean by "the social mission"?

A: The social mission, primarily means that Independence Blue Cross will accept any individuals or cover any individuals when they make application. We don't turn anyone away. That is the primary social mission.

Q: And, in essence, who owns Independence Blue Cross?

A: The subscribers. Cardholders are called subscribers and, in fact, they are the owners.

Q: Now, can you tell us what Pennsylvania Blue Shield is?

A: Pennsylvania Blue Shield?

Q: Are you uncomfortable?

[Comment] Apparently, something is bothering her. As she begins her next answer, it seems to us that she has donned the mantle of advocate.

A: I just want to make sure you can hear me. I guess you can. Pennsylvania Blue Shield is also a non-profit company. They primarily provide coverage for the medical/surgical portion which would be doctor bills. Blue Cross, for the most part, is the hospital side; Blue Shield, the physicians' side. Now, recently that has been changed because there have been some mergers of plans within the state, so, we each now are doing—providing, making available coverage for all types of health care benefits.

Q: But, at the time of the events in question in this case, 1994 and 1995, that was the case?

A: They were separate, that's correct. And Pennsylvania Blue Shield also has available a vision program and dental programs.

Q: And where is Pennsylvania Blue Shield located?

A: They are in Camp Hill, in Harrisburg.

Q: Pennsylvania?

A: Harrisburg, Pennsylvania.

Q: Is Pennsylvania Blue Shield also a non-profit corporation?

A: Yes, it is.

Q: At the time of the event in question, Pennsylvania Blue Shield and Independence Blue Cross occasionally marketed joint programs?

A: Yes. In fact, Independence Blue Cross is the agent, the selling agent for Pennsylvania Blue Shield. They do not have individuals who go outside and market their products. We do it on their behalf, because generally, the product is purchased together, both Blue Cross and Blue Shield, so that it is a total package.

Q: Now, what year was it that you came to work for Independence Blue Cross?

A: October 6, 1969.

[Comment] Regard how nicely he has stepped back in as he goes back and forth with his questions. The examiner is not only clearly in command, but his messages to us are clear, or they were up until right now.

Q: And <u>can you tell us</u> how the company has changed since then?

[Comment] This invitation is immediately accepted, and we get told a lot all at once.

A: Oh, dramatically. We went from approximately 800 employees. Now, we probably have somewhere in the neighborhood of 3500, over 3000 employees. We have a new President—I'm saying new about five years, Fred DiBona, and he has done tremendous things for us and the community in terms of our having a lot more flexibility with regard to the products and the financial programs that we can make available to customers. Prior to that we were fairly rigid in the type of programs that we had available. So, you had maybe a three-choice menu, where today, you would have a choice of, oh, goodness, 10 to 15 to 20 different products designs and programs, P.P.O.s, HMOs, et cetera. So, he has done a lot for us and cleaned up a lot of the problem that we had had in the past with regard to the administration of claims.

Q: Now—

A: We're doing real good now.

[Comment] She thinks she is helping herself with the volunteered information, but is she? To be fair, isn't this what the examiner wanted?

Q: When you say you have more flexibility in products now, can you tell us what you mean by that?

[Comment] Here we go again.

A: Yes. In the past, our product was primarily Blue Cross, which I said is hospitalization. And we provided a program that would give coverage in the hospital and you could pick the number of days that you wanted and maybe a small co-payment. And on the physician side, there was a physician coverage which was either a fee schedule or what we called U.C.R., or 100 percent payment. Now, we are much more flexible, because there has been a lot of change also in the delivery of health care. We now have available our P.P.O., which is called Personal Choice.

Q: P.P.O. means what?

A: Preferred Provider Organization.

Q: And what is a Preferred Provider Organization?

A: Originally—I shouldn't say originally. There are some companies that offer preferred provider organizations or networks, and you or the customer could purchase that program and it would provide a network and discounts. And basically, that is it, there's not much managed care that goes on with just that kind of a contract. Our P.P.O., our Personal Choice product is one that has a network of both hospitals and doctors and it also includes the other types of benefits, like home health care agencies, skilled nursing facilities, et cetera. And what that does also, or what we do, is manage all of that care for the individuals. So, we go out and we contract with all of these providers and gain discounts that we then can pass onto our customers. We provide them with a book of all of the providers, and they look in the book, find each provider you want to go to, and you go to that provider. And if it is a doctor, you hand him five or ten bucks, depending on which program you have, and it's covered.

Q: Now, what other new programs do you have besides the Personal Choice P.P.O.?

A: The next one that we have is called Point of Service. In essence, that is the same type of a program as a P.P.O., except now you must select a primary care physician and any care that you might need would have to be referred by that physician. But you would also still have the opportunity to go out of network and make your own choice to any doctor or hospital that you want and then you then would be subject to a deductible and co-insurance.

Q: Does Blue Cross also have a health maintenance organization, an HMO?

A: Yes. The next one down on the continuum would be the HMO. Our HMO is called Keystone.

Q: Keystone Health Plan?

A: Keystone Health Plan East.

Q: What is an HMO?

A: That program requires that you select, the individuals in your family each select a primary care physician, and it is that physician who is responsible to refer your care throughout the course of any treatment that you might need. If it is a pure HMO, you do not have out-of-network benefits. So, it's a little bit more restrictive. But it's totally managed care, and it's something along with the P.P.O. as we provide it, that is important today to save money and just to, you know, meet the changes in the health care delivery system.

Q: Now, does Blue Cross also offer a traditional indemnity coverage, as well?

A: Yes, we do.

Q: What is that?

A: That would be our traditional program, similar to what I mentioned a few minutes ago, where you could purchase—where the customer would purchase Blue Cross and Blue Shield. So, it would be a Blue Cross program and a Blue Shield program and a major medical to wrap around to provide the coverage for the skilled nursing facilities or for private duty nurses, prescription drugs, and things like that. That program is what we would refer to as having total access. You don't have to go to a network, you can go to any hospital or doctor and you would receive the same benefits. And it's really not managed. We do a little bit of management in terms of the pre-certification, but, other than that, you would have or the individual would have the freedom of choice of provider.

[Comment] The witness is on a roll. But is counsel? She is offering lots of information in each answer, but would it go down better, and stay down better, if he took it piece by piece, using questions to break it up and to clarify? See Vol. II, pp. 9–11. Also, just what is the point of this education as to the services of Blue Cross? If it is that the program was advantageous to the union, then—putting aside the so what—why not make that clear through questions designed to show how the Blue Cross deal was superior to the one it replaced at Ironworkers?

Q: Now, is Independence Blue Cross the only health insurance company in this area that has what is called the social mission?

A: To my knowledge, yes.

Q: And you mentioned discounts. How does Blue Cross go about obtaining discounts from hospital providers?

[Comment] Why we need to know this detail is not clear to us, but here we go again.

A: One of the departments within our company is responsible for provider contracting. And they, in fact, visit—I shouldn't say visit. They, in fact, contract with the hospitals, all the hospitals in our area here, and they negotiate a discount. There are some of those discounts that are quite high. What we do, as far as passing that discount on to our customers, at the moment I'm talking about Philadelphia, the five county area, we'll guarantee our customers a 50 to 55 percent discount for hospital care, depending on which product you would buy. On the physician side, it's a little bit more—it's a little bit more involved. Because we do what is called credentialing of physicians. We actually have nurses who visit the doctor's office to be sure that they are meeting the criteria to be in our network. Even as simple assuring that their office hours will meet the needs of the community. You know, if they are 9:00 to 5:00, then most likely they are not going to be accepted into our network.

[Comment] Wow! That's a lot of stuff to get all at once.

Q: Now, you mentioned the five county area. Are there other Blue Cross plans located in other geographic areas?

A: Yes, there are.

Q: For example, there's a separate New Jersey Blue Cross Plan; is that correct?

A: Yes.

Q: There's one in Central Pennsylvania and one in Western Pennsylvania?

A: Yes.

Q: Are they all separate corporations?

A: Yes.

[Comment] We are now in a postgraduate course on this subject.

Q: Do you on occasion work in conjunction with them to provide coverage for large groups that spread over more than one state or more than one geographic area?

A: Yes, we do. We have a separate department within our marketing unit, that so-called National Accounts and they handle any national account except those health and welfare funds that are national accounts. Any health and welfare fund is under my responsibility, whether it is a local account or national where it would require us visiting another Blue Cross plan and asking for their input and their agreement to provide coverage for our customers.

[Comment] Counsel now takes a firmer hold.

Q: You mentioned negotiating discounts with hospitals. Does Blue Cross have contracts with the hospitals that reflect these discounts?

A: Yes, they do.

Q: Do you know how many hospitals in the five county area, Blue Cross has contracts with?

A: All of them. In addition, if I may, we do have contracts directly with hospitals that are located in South Jersey, and moving up a little bit, maybe towards Trenton, and also, now, we are extending a little bit into Lehigh County and some of the other counties of New Jersey.

Q: How many subscribers does Independence Blue Cross have?

A: I believe we are just about, and we might be now, at 2.8 million.

Q: And what do you mean by a subscriber?

A: A subscriber would be any individual who is covered under the plan. We might use the term a contract, that would be the individual who the identification card's name is on, but if there are 10 dependents, each one of those dependents would be considered a subscriber.

Q: And you mentioned in the last several years, changes to improve your service I think you said?

A: Correct.

[Comment] Notice how nicely this last portion goes. And why? Because counsel is using his questions as tools to carve testimony into small, digestible bits. See Vol. II, pp. 9–11.

Q: And <u>can you tell us</u> what changes have been made in recent years to improve your service?

[Comment] There is the telltale sign of a call for help from the witness.

A: Yes. We have tremendously enhanced our operating area with regard to how we pay claims. They are being paid much more—much faster than they had in the past, with much more accuracy. There are a number of—there's different criteria that we need to follow and there is something; called NMIS—I'm not going to remember what that acronym is—NMIS, I think, that is a standard that is set for us by the Blue Cross Association, and we do meet that. As a matter of fact, I think we are approximately 99 percent of meeting that standard, meaning that we pay claims accurately and timely.

Q: Have you received any other awards, recognitions?

A: Yes. Recently we received accreditation by the N.C.Q.A. That's an entity that provides—well, actually they come in and take a look at all of your operations, everything from the financial side to the programs that you have in effect, how you monitor them, how you direct them, and we have just recently received a three-year accreditation, which is not too easy to attain, so we are very proud of that.

Q: All right. Now, directing your attention to 1994—

[Comment] The "all right" signifies that the preliminaries are over, thankfully. The judge senses it too. But he has had enough for the day.

THE COURT: Since <u>we're going to get to the substance now</u>, why don't we break for the day?

[Comment] Translation: Up until now was just the appetizer, the main course is about to be served. Well, if so, is that a good use of time by the defense?

MR. SONNENFELD: Thank you, Your Honor.

THE COURT: I'll see you tomorrow morning and don't discuss the case.

THE CRIER: Everyone remain seated while the Jury leaves the room.

[Jury exits.]

ANALYSIS OF THE FIRST PART OF THE DIRECT EXAMINATION

You can tell from the way the judge talks to counsel that it is late in the day. The judge does not want to waste time, though, so the direct examination of Ms. Hardy begins. We all know she is the target of the plaintiff's attack. The jury knows it too. They must expect that an innocent person, someone who cheated no one, would be outraged at being made a villain and being called a cheater. They want to know whether she is going to defend herself. She can only do that effectively if her advocate makes her case to the jury through her testimony,

Is this direct examination the way you would want to end a day, to send a jury home? Is there one word of outrage, one sign of denial, one utterance of anger in this examination? We see none.

Yes, it is true that the direct examiner demonstrates, or has the witness do it herself, that Ms. Hardy belongs to a union and comes from a union family, and that Blue Cross/Blue Shield is an insurer that does business with any number of unions both in the Philadelphia area, outside the area, and around the country. But is this a case in which any of the jurors are likely never to have heard of Blue Cross/Blue Shield? Surely not. It is not necessary to demonstrate that Blue Cross/Blue Shield seems to have a virtual lock on much of the health care insurance in the area. The jury will likely assume that.

It may be worse than unnecessary, however. A large company with a virtual lock on the insurance market may not be a company that plays fair. That is what Sussman alleges.

To us, this portion of the direct examination is cumbersome. It provides the jury with more information about health insurance than it needs or wants to know. It will not recall and will not use this information in deciding the case, and even if it needed it, there is no chance that the jury could recall the volume of it offered in long monologues by this witness. It fails to provide any sense of outrage at being falsely accused. In short, this examination lacks human drama. It is stiff. It does not make Ms. Hardy credible.

The jury will recall that the plaintiff called Ms. Hardy as a witness. The plaintiff made an argument during "direct" examination of her as an adverse witness. She was hurt. Her counsel made no effort at the time to fight back. This is her first chance to speak to the defense theory of the case, and the day ends with a tutorial on health insurance plans.

Juries, like the rest of us, are most influenced by and remember best that which they hear first (primacy) and last (recency). See Vol. I, pp. 115–120. The first impression of any witness is important. Plaintiff's counsel has already created a first impression of Ms. Hardy. For that reason, we believe that what happens early in her examination is extremely important. Nothing much happens here, and that is a problem.

Because the jury is about to retire for the day, this examination afforded an opportunity to plant the seeds for a battle that will continue the next day. Counsel could have begun with a very different examination that might have included questions like the following:

Q: How long have you worked for Independence Blue Cross?

Q: How long have you worked with union health and welfare funds?

Q: Tell the jury how many times during your 28 years with Independence Blue Cross any broker has accused you of cheating him out of a commission?

Q: Tell the jury how many times during your 25 years with Independence Blue Cross working with union health and welfare funds any broker has accused you of cheating him out of a commission?

Q: Have you ever cheated any broker out of a commission in your life?

Q: How did you feel when you sat here and heard Mr. Sussman's lawyer allege that you and Blue Cross/Blue Shield cheated Mr. Sussman?

Q: Had you ever heard of Mr. Sussman before he called you out of the blue in 1994?

Q: Was Mr. Sussman seeking to talk about insurance for himself or another person or group?

Q: What prior knowledge did you have about Mr. Sussman when you received his call?

Q: What was your understanding as to who Mr. Sussman's client was when he called?

Q: What was your belief as to whether Mr. Sussman had been authorized by the Ironworkers to call you on their behalf?

Q: Did there come a time when you learned the truth about whether Mr. Sussman was authorized to speak to you on behalf of the Ironworkers?

Q: When was that?

Q: How did you feel when you learned that he had no authority to act on their behalf?

Q: What would you have done when Mr. Sussman called you if he had honestly told you that he had no authority to speak for the Ironworkers, but that he was looking to earn a commission from Blue Cross/Blue Shield?

Once these points are made, the examiner can go back over details. The order of the examination is not dictated by chronology. It is to be organized as an *argument*. It begins at its most effective point, not at its chronological beginning. See Vol. I, pp. 199–205; Vol. II, pp. 195–199; and Vol. III, pp. 348–351. The jurors wants to know whether Ms. Hardy is a cheater. They must feel that, if they were attacked, they would fight back. Thus far, there is no fight. The jury leaves for the day undoubtedly bored.

Chapter Twelve

The Ruling on Defendants' Motion

TEXT OF THE JUDGE'S RULING

THE COURT: On the motions for compulsory nonsuit, the plaintiff having waived the effect of the rule as to the negligence side of the case only, I'm going to grant the compulsory nonsuit on the negligence. What's the name of —

MR. LONGER: Negligent interference with prospective contracts, Your Honor.

THE COURT: And deny it as to the other count.

MR. LONGER: Thank you, Your Honor. Your Honor, I would just like to make a record that with respect to the Jury instructions, the parties are basically in agreement with respect to all of the instructions with one exception, Jury Instruction Number 6, which has a listing of several elements of the claim. In Element Number 1, there is a second sentence which says that Tower must demonstrate there was a reasonable likelihood or probability that the Ironworkers Fund would have entered into the contract with Tower Financial had it not been for the actions of Blue Cross/Blue Shield. I think that is confusing and I take exception to that. But with that note, I think that we are in agreement on the Jury instructions.

THE COURT: Very well. Okay.

[Comment] As we can see, the plaintiff still maintains that the suit is for Blue Cross having interfered with his ability to contract with the union. His theory, we suppose, is that Blue Cross in some way told the union not to give the broker of record letter to the plaintiff, but where is the evidence of that? It is no wonder that the plaintiff does not like the objected-to instruction.

MR. SONNENFELD: Should we hand them up to the Court?

THE COURT: Yes. I was going to say—

MR. SONNENFELD: Why don't we hand you a clean copy?

THE COURT: In fact, if you happen to have two clean copies Whitney [the official court reporter] will be happier.

MR. SONNENFELD: We also have a verdict form.

THE COURT: Do you have an agreed verdict form?

MR. LONGER: No, Your Honor.

THE COURT: That you don't have, okay. What do you have there? I have your copy. I assume you're not changing it?

MR. LONGER: The only thing that would change with respect to mine—

THE COURT: I can't find yours at the moment. Let's get the Jury in.

ANALYSIS OF THE JUDGE'S RULING

The judge has decided to grant the defendants' motion for a compulsory nonsuit and to eliminate the plaintiff's second count for negligent interference with prospective contractual relations. Given the law that the parties argued, the plaintiff cannot be totally surprised by the ruling.

The judge's ruling provides an important lesson. Lawyers in their opening arguments should promise to prove all of the elements of the causes of action or defenses they are relying upon (because in some jurisdictions failure to do so might result in a judgment against a party with the burden of proof as to a claim or defense), but it is neither necessary nor wise to spend time going through claims and defenses element by element. Some claims or defenses may be stricken, others may be dropped. The jury has not gone to law school. They want to know the essence of the case. In this case, it is unlikely that the jury's decision will change because the negligence count is included or excluded. Sussman has alleged that he was cheated, and if the jury finds that he was, it will strain to find a way to return a verdict for him. If they find that he was not cheated, he will lose.

If you look back and compare each side's opening argument, you will see that plaintiff's counsel decided—wisely, we think—not to stress elements of the two counts. Defendants' counsel argued about the law. Such arguments are likely to impress judges, not juries. The important thing is to choose a theme or theory of the case that will not change from beginning to end. As long as the theme or theory remains constant and supported by the evidence, the fact that one or more counts or defenses are dismissed or dropped will have little impact on the likely outcome of a case.

Indeed, in some cases parties may deliberately include a count or defense which they believe might be stricken before the case ends. Inclusion may serve two purposes. If the judge strikes one count, the judge might feel that the benefit of the doubt should be given to another count. Thus, by ruling in this case against the plaintiff on the negligence count, the trial judge might have felt impelled to permit the other count to go to the jury. Therefore, one strategic reason for including a legal theory that might fall is to make stronger legal theories more likely to withstand the judge's scrutiny.

The other reason for including a legal theory that may fall is that it may distract opposing counsel and lead to an opening argument that is devoted to a legal argument that will not be relevant when the case ends. If a lawyer makes a factual assertion in an opening argument and fails to prove the assertion, the lawyer's credibility may suffer when opposing counsel points out the failure of proof. However, the fact that a complaint or answer contains one or more legal claims that disappear as the case develops is unlikely to result in one lawyer being able to suggest to the jury that opposing counsel has not proved what was promised, as long as the evidence promised in the opening statement is delivered.

As long as a lawyer does not go into detail about the law in an opening, the judge is likely to regard the dismissal or dropping of a legal claim or defense as irrelevant for the jury's deliberations, unless the removal of a claim or defense requires the striking of evidence previously admitted. Even in that instance, the judge will usually find a limiting instruction to be all that is required and to permit argument about the evidence that has been stricken.

Chapter Thirteen

Ms. Hardy Continues and the Defense Rests

TEXT OF THE CONTINUED DIRECT EXAMINATION

[Back on the record in open court.]

- - - -

THE COURT: Let's re-call the witness.

- - - -

THE CRIER: Ms. Hardy, you are still under oath.

HELEN HARDY, WITNESS, previously sworn, testified as follows:

BY MR. SONNENFELD:

Q: Good morning, Ms. Hardy. When we broke yesterday afternoon, I asked you to direct your attention to 1994. In 1994, you recalled that you were contacted by Mr. Sussman, correct?

A: Yes.

Q: And prior to that, did you know Mr. Sussman?

A: No, I did not.

Q: You never had any dealings with him?

A: No.

Q: Now, before the contact, that you received a telephone call from Mr. Sussman some time in roughly May of 1994, had you already met with Mr. Sweeney of the Ironworkers Fund?

A: Yes, I did.

[Comment] He has brought us to the point where he wants us very nicely, through the use of his questions. Now, unfortunately, in our view, he again opens the sluice gates.

Q: <u>And how</u> did that meeting come about?

A: There was a gentleman by the name of Walton, George Walton, who is the administrator of another health and welfare fund, a Teamster fund, who I had known for many, many years. And I had a lot of dialogue with Mr. Walton about the Ironworkers because many years ago, he was the administrator. That was prior to Nick Craggs. So, we had always talked about it, and he kind of helped me to strategize as to how to approach them. He knew Bob Sweeney quite well, <u>and our hope</u>—I <u>shouldn't say the hope was</u>, but we thought that Mr. Craggs was going to be retiring and it seemed like that might be a good time, because <u>he was not very favorable of Blue Cross</u>, that we felt that that might be a good time to approach the Fund. And it just happened, that we kind of accelerated our conversations, my conversations with George Walton, and he suggested that I give Bob Sweeney a visit, and that's <u>what I did</u>.

[Comment] The question calls for a narrative, and the witness is happy enough to respond. Has she helped herself? Why was all this necessary? Why not simply bring out that there came a time when she reached out to Sweeney to see if he was interested in Blue Cross insurance?

Q: <u>And</u> you then met with Mr Sweeney; is that correct?

A: Correct.

Q: Had you ever before sought to meet with Mr. Sweeney?

A: No, I didn't.

Q: <u>And</u> did you have any trouble getting an appointment with Mr. Sweeney?

A: No.

Q: Have you ever had a problem getting an appointment with Mr. Sweeney?

A: No.

Q: You heard him testify about his open door yesterday?

A: That is correct.

[Comment] That is superb! He relates the testimony of the one to what the other has just said, by the use of questions. Everyone knows what he is saying through the witness.

Q: <u>And</u> you and Mr. Sweeney met by yourselves; is that correct?

A: That's correct.

Q: About how long did that meeting last?

A: I thought maybe about a half hour to 45 minutes. It could have been shorter. I don't remember exactly.

Q: <u>And how</u> did that meeting go?

[Comment] Counsel's habit of beginning many questions with "and" is obviously a sometime thing. Many of us suffer from the same nervous habit. But we should get rid of it, for it is distracting and, as previously noted, it is used primarily as a momentary breather for the examiner before the next question. With this last question, counsel has asked the witness to take over the examination. He calls for anything and everything she wants to say. Review the question and then watch her take off.

A: From my perspective, went well. He opened the door, let me in, smiled, and for me, as a salesperson, I thought that was pretty good. I had an opportunity to share with him information about the products that we had to offer at Blue Cross, the different benefits designs. Just talked briefly about what they had and basically the meeting concluded. I knew that they had an arrangement being self-administered. They did a lot out of their office up on Castor Avenue and I did not know that they would be ready to make a change. From my viewpoint, <u>it was a very positive meeting</u>. Again, because I had the opportunity to at least open the door and let him know what we had available, and really, mainly, who I was. I went through some of my background as far as working with the health and welfare funds for 25 years. I didn't want him to think that I, you know, just came off the street and was not sensitive to the union population or to health and welfare funds, because they are a little unique in how they operate and what their needs are. So, I just wanted to make sure that he knew that I was credible and that I had history. And we talked about a lot of individuals who we both knew. Obviously, they were in the building trades, so, I threw out quite a few names of folks who I have known through the building trades. And, you know, that kind of at least gave us a bond, if you will.

[Comment] Wow! That is some answer. She has become an advocate on the stand and, in fairness to her, that is what the examiner seems to want her to do.

Q: So, you met your objective?

A: I met my objective. I certainly understood that he was not ready to say, "Oh, here's the contract. Come back in." But—I met my objective.

[Comment] He is back in the saddle, but she is still pitching and advocating.

Q: Would that meeting have been roughly some time in the April of 1994 timeframe?

A: Somewhere around that. I don't remember exactly, but that's probably about right.

Q: And also in that timeframe, in April of 1994, did you meet with a Mr. Dougherty?

A: Yes, I did.

Q: And perhaps you could turn to Exhibit-13 of the blue notebook.

A: Okay.

Q: And Exhibit-18 is your handwritten notes, are they not?

A: Yes, that's correct.

Q: And they show a phone call with Mr. Dougherty on April 4th, 1994?

A: Right.

Q: Can you tell us about the phone call?

[Comment] This, as we have noted in respect to both counsel, is not a proper question, because it calls for a narrative, and a selective one, at that. Well, here she goes.

A: Yes. Actually, Mr. Dougherty called me. He is the Business Manager for one of the Locals that was mentioned or has been mentioned a number of times. There are actually 11 different Locals that are in the Health and Welfare Fund. And Joe Dougherty is the Business Manager, which is the same position that Mr. Sweeney was, in New Jersey, for this Local. I'm sorry, I don't remember what the Local number was. They are located up—somewhere up in the Northeast, like around Nabisco, up in that area.

Q: Just off the Boulevard?

A: Correct. And he was calling because the Health and Welfare Fund was in some financial—had some financial difficulty, and as a result they had to eliminate the benefits for their retirees. And in doing that, Mr. Dougherty, of course, having responsibility and concern about those retirees wanted to offer them something.

[Comment] The point of all this seems to be lost, and so he takes her to it.

Q: Did he ask to meet with you?

A: Yes.

Q: Did you then meet with him?

A: Yes, I did.

Q: And if you would go back to Exhibit 17—do you have Exhibit-17 in the blue notebook?

A: Yes.

Q: That's your calendar, is it not?

A: That's correct.

Q: Does that show that you met with Mr. Dougherty on April 26th, 1994?

A: I think it was the 25th—no, excuse me. The 23rd.

Q: April 23rd, 1994?

A: Right. Yes, at 2:30.

Q: You met with Mr. Dougherty?

A: Correct.

Q: Tell us <u>what happened</u> at that meeting?

[Comment] Here we go again. She is given unlimited discretion, and she not only uses it, she exceeds it.

A: The purpose of that meeting was to give him information about what we had available for retirees, and I showed him—or actually brought brochures and all the information about our bill-direct polices, both for Medicare eligible and non-Medicare eligible, because both segments were affected. He explained to me that what he was going to do was to bring in a few different carriers, and have a meeting for all the retirees, so they would not feel as though they were just left in the lurch, because the Welfare Fund could no longer provide their benefits.

So, what I did from that was go back to my office and I spoke to some of my staff, and as a matter of fact, Ken

Olejniezak, Kenny O., I had him and one of our support folks, Dori Colton, the two of them then attended that meeting where they actually discussed the benefit programs that were available directly to these retirees. U.S. Healthcare was also there and someone from AARP.

Q: <u>How long</u> did that meeting last on April 23rd?

A: Oh, goodness, I would say probably a good hour, hour and a half, because I also did take the opportunity then to tell—to talk just a little bit. I know that's not why he wanted me there, but I wanted to let him know that we also had products and benefits designs that could be available for the Health and Welfare Fund. And, again, probably very similar to my meeting with Mr. Sweeney, I let him know who I was and who I knew, just to kind of set a tone of credibility and history, that, again, I knew folks in the building trades.

[Comment] She is well beyond the scope of the question, which only called for the length of time of the meeting. Can anyone doubt that she, with counsel's consent, has become a kind of co-counsel on the stand?

Q: Now, if you would look again at Exhibit-13, your handwritten notes in the next tab, if you would turn to the third page, those are a set of notes dated May 31st, are they not?

A: That's correct.

Q: And from those notes, does it suggest to you that the meeting that you had with Mr. Sussman and Mr. Sweeney would have been a day or two before May 31st?

A: Yes.

[Comment] Suddenly, we have Sussman in the midst of all this. The point is, or we think should be, that she was doing all of this without Sussman.

Q: Now, the meeting with Mr. Sussman and Mr. Sweeney, where did you meet Mr. Sussman?

A: At the Woodcrest Shopping Center in New Jersey.

Q: And then did the two of you go from there together to Mr. Sweeney's office in Westville?

A: Yes, we did. Mr. Sussman drove.

Q: And <u>can you</u> tell us what you recall of the conversation you had with Mr. Sussman in the car on the way from the Woodcrest Shopping center to Mr. Sweeney's office in Westville?

[Comment] Here we go again. She takes off.

A: Sure. What I attempted to do, I wanted to let Mr. Sussman know who I was. We only had a conversation on the telephone and I <u>probably</u> shared a little bit with him, but again, I felt that it was important that he knew <u>my background</u>, that I have dealt with health and welfare funds for 25 years, that they are a bit unique, and just kind of wanted to make sure and find out <u>what he knew about health and welfare funds</u>. We also discussed <u>his position as broker</u> and I shared with him, <u>I don't recall in how much detail I went into</u>, but I <u>definitely</u> told him that a <u>broker of record letter</u> is required, it's our policy, and talked just a little bit about what his objective was with regard to having me there. What did he want me to talk about. I <u>felt</u> that <u>it was his meeting</u> and I just wanted to make sure that I didn't go into the meeting with Mr. Sweeney and start <u>babbling, which I have a tendency to do</u>—

[Comment] Counsel senses that this last, though perhaps entirely credible, is too much!

Q: Let me stop you right there. You just said that you talked about four different subjects riding in the car. One, health and welfare funds, why they are unique. Secondly, you said benefit designs or products. Third, broker of record letter, and fourth, Mr. Sussman's objective in the meeting.

A: Correct.

[Comment] Now, that is a good piece of work by counsel. He has us focused. What really matters are the third and fourth subjects, which is what the case is all about. Unfortunately, he begins with the first, which really matters not.

Q: What is unique about dealing with health and welfare funds?

A: Well, in terms of buying benefits, health care benefits, if you have a corporate client, or a client where it's not a union, if you are dealing with a customer—a law firm, or something like that, generally the meeting and the decision to buy is made by the benefits manager and certainly with the authorization from either the owner of the company or the President of the company or however they work it, but it's basically a one-on-one. And the way that I look at it, their objective is to do certain things for—maybe a little bit more with the company in mind. When you have a health and welfare fund the employers who employ the union members, who then are the participants of the health and welfare fund, they send contributions into the health and welfare fund. In fact, those contributions are the result of collective bargaining. So, when there is union bargaining going on, those monies are designated depending on what that amount is—I don't know, $4.00 an hour, it varies. So, those monies go into the health and welfare fund. It is then the Board of Trustees' responsibility to select benefits for the union members, who they refer to as participants in the health and welfare fund. And prior to 1947, which is when the Taft-Hartley Act went into place, it was really just done by the union or whoever was involved, and I don't know how much management was involved at that time. But the Act wanted to make sure that those monies that were being contributed were being used for the members or the participants or the union members in their best interest.

[Comment] Whew! That's enough information for a one-day class. Again, we see the defect in an examination that relies on the witness rather than the examiner. Vol. II, pp. 9–11. In any event, for our purposes in this case, why do we need this burden of material?

Q: And this was a subject you discussed with Mr. Sussman?

A: <u>I don't believe</u> I went into <u>that much detail</u>, but I certainly did go into the <u>detail</u> that there is a <u>Board of Trustees</u> and what is so important is that the decision makers are all of those Trustees. So, they're the ones—in fact, they even have what they call a fiduciary responsibility—that they are responsible to be sure that the funds, all those monies and the benefits and everything that is being done is being operated and handled in a prudent fashion.

[Comment] She has given a long, conflicting answer. If her point is that no one man, even Sweeney, controls the award, that it is the trustees as a body, why does she have to tell this to Sussman, who has already sold insurance to the fund?

Q: Now, as of this time, as of this meeting in May of 1994, in your experience, had you ever encountered a union health and welfare fund using a broker for its health insurance?

A: No.

[Comment] Well, hadn't the union already used Sussman?

Q: Now, you next say you discussed with Mr. Sussman, a broker of record letter. And we've heard from Mr. Sullivan the policy of Blue Cross to have a broker of record letter to receive a commission. Can you explain for us the reason for that policy, especially in the context of a union health and welfare fund?

[Comment] Now that "question" takes the gloves off and strikes blows with looping. See Vol. II, pp. 17–18. Well done!

A: Well, most important and this is for all of our customers, first in general, in order that we pay a commission, the commission is loaded into the rate, or if it is what is called a cost plus account, it is then loaded into an administrative charge. <u>So, in fact, the customer is really the one paying for it. It would not be prudent for us to do that unless we had proper documentation from the customer authorizing us to do that</u>. And with a health and welfare fund, as I said, they are under what's called the Taft-Hartley Act and they are responsible to send reports to the Federal Government—

MR. LONGER: Excuse me, Your Honor, I'm going to object to the lack of foundation. I don't know that she's an expert on the Taft-Hartley Act.

THE COURT: Sustained.

[Comment] Counsel knew he had to stop this, and he was lucky enough to do so. Actually, if she had stopped her answer after the last emphasized phrase, the point would have been clearer and not subject to objection. Counsel virtually tells her that in his next "question," but she doesn't get it. Watch.

BY MR. SONNENFELD:

Q: Why don't we move on from the Taft-Hartley Act.

A: It's important that—they do, and I know this for sure, they have to submit forms, ERISA forms, and on that form any commission or anything—any monies in and monies out, that has to do with the Fund, must be documented on that form.

Q: Now, is it correct to say that because the commission with a broker would be loaded into the rate and, therefore, paid only by the customer, to protect the customer, you want to make sure that that commission is authorized in advance?

A: That is correct.

[Comment] That is an excellent piece of work. And notice, it is the examiner who does it.

Q: And the purpose is not to cut off a broker, but to protect the customer?

A: Absolutely not.

Q: And, in fact, Blue Cross has a whole department that deals with brokers, does it not?

A: Yes, we do.

Q: That's Mr. Sullivan's department, correct?

A: Yes.

[Comment] Bang! Bang! Bang! To the lay ear it might sound as though the witness is doing great. But we know it is the lawyer using his questions as weapons and tools of his argument.

Q: Now, you also said you discussed in the car product or benefits designs. By benefits designs, you mean products; is that correct?

A: That is correct.

Q: Did Mr. Sussman have a familiarity with the products of Independence Blue Cross?

A: He did not seem to.

[Comment] That is just fine!

Q: And did you attempt to explain to him the products offered by Independence Blue Cross?

A: I did.

Q: Did he show any interest?

A: He did not seem to.

[Comment] It goes much better when the witness confines herself to the questions, although the question itself might have looped better: "Did he show any interest in the products of Blue Cross?"

Q: Now, fourth, you said that Mr. Sussman explained to you his objective in this meeting. What did he tell you was his objective in this meeting?

A: From my viewpoint, as I understood what Mr. Sussman wanted to do, was to provide or determine whether or not Blue Cross and Blue Shield, whether or not we had a network that would be broader than the network that the fund was currently using. And also, that that network that the discounts were greater than the discounts available through the networks they were currently using. He seemed to be focused on that.

[Comment] That answer seems to be different from the last. If not, it is not clear why not.

Q: And did he inquire whether Blue Cross would, in essence, rent the network?

A: I don't believe that he actually used that term. Based on what he was sharing with me, I wanted to be sure that he understood that we do not lease or rent out networks.

Q: Tell us what you mean by that, just so that is clear?

A: There are some PPOs that are made available, and those PPOs are networks of doctors. And I am not an expert on all the details, but basically what they do is contact doctors to get discounts and then they will rent that network of doctors to a company or whoever wants to buy them, and then the advantage of those discounts are passed on through that entity. But the claims processing is generally done by either that company or whoever is seeking that group.

Q: That's not something that Blue Cross would do?

A: That is correct.

Q: And you explained that to Mr. Sussman?

A: Yes.

Q: Now, <u>tell us about the meeting</u> itself. I think you testified that the meeting was about a half hour, 45 minutes. Tell us what you recall of the meeting between yourself and Mr. Sussman and Mr. Sweeney in Mr. Sweeney's office in late May of 1994.

[Comment] Again, the examiner turns the entire spigot controlling the information over to the witness. The witness answers at great length and her selection of words is not so good for Blue Cross.

A: To the best of my recollection, I remember that we talked mostly about the size of the networks and I did say that we do have networks that are—well, our network is certainly the largest, that is available to customers in our area. I don't recall that we really got into a discussion as to whether or not we would or would not lease the network. <u>I wanted to stay in the background</u>. I had asked Mr. Sussman—<u>it was his meeting</u>, and as I said earlier, <u>it wasn't my place to run the meeting</u>. So, I just wanted to make sure that any comments I made were appropriate to what it was that we could provide.

[Comment] Now, we may ask ourselves, if Sussman did nothing, why was it "his meeting"? And why was it desirable for her to "stay in the background"? It seems to us that none of this would be necessary if the simple defense is that Blue Cross did not tell the union to refuse the letter to the plaintiff and the union refused because it did not want the extra expense. Indeed, given what the case is about, and the nature of the testimony of this witness, we begin to wonder whether it would have been better to have made Maresca and Sweeney the only defense witnesses—testifying that the refusal to give the letter was made solely by the union to save the union money, without any input from Blue Cross. What happens to the plaintiff's case then?

Q: So, Mr. Sussman did most of the talking then?

A: Yes.

Q: Not you or Mr. Sweeney?

A: No.

Q: At this meeting with the three of you, was there any discussion of any specific products or benefits design packages?

A: Not in any detail other than me maybe mentioning Personal Choice, which was our P.P.O., but again, it seemed to be the concern for Mr. Sussman was more in the area of putting something in place of the network that they currently had and how could that be improved.

[Comment] This seems to confirm what Sussman has been saying about replacing the insurance he had brokered to the union with a better one.

Q: Now, did you consider that meeting to be any more positive or less positive than the meeting you had recently had by yourself with Mr. Sweeney?

A: No.

Q: And to the best of your recollection, is that the only meeting that you and Mr. Sussman ever had with Mr. Sweeney?

A: Yes.

[Comment] Here he is making his argument, and it is clear by reason of his questions. Whether or not he can sell the argument that the meeting Sussman arranged was no more positive than Hardy's earlier Sweeney meeting is a different issue.

Q: Now, after the meeting did you receive from Mr. Sussman a Zip Code listing of the members by Zip Code of the various unions?

A: I did receive one. I honestly don't recall if I received it directly from Mr. Sussman or if I had received it from John Heim at Blair Mill, but I know I did receive it, and whether it was direct or indirect, I did get it from Mr. Sussman.

Q: Was that Zip Code listing of any use to you in preparing a bid or proposal?

A: <u>No</u>, not for <u>that</u> purpose.

[Comment] We are again out to show that Sussman did no work. But . . . if not for that *purpose, then for* what *purpose?*

Q: And did you—I believe you were shown on your examination yesterday, by Mr. Longer, some medical bills for Mr. Sweeney's children. Did you ever receive those medical bills either from Mr. Sussman or Mr. Craggs or anyone else?

A: No. Not those <u>actual</u> bills.

Q: Did you ever reprice any of those bills at Mr. Sussman's request?

A: Not those <u>specific</u> bills, no.

[Comment] It was Sweeney's grandchildren, not children, but no matter. Notice, however, the use of the words "actual" and "specific" in the last two answers. Is there a careful dance going on here?

Q: Now, following the—did you receive any procedure codes, however?

A: Yes.

Q: And tell us what you mean by procedure codes?

A: Every procedure that a doctor performs has a code, and that's the way that we make payments. It's much easier for the computers. So, he sent me maybe about a half a page or so of procedure codes and he wanted to know what Blue Shield would have allowed for each one of those procedures. And I got that information for him. And obviously, that was so that he could compare whether or not our network and discounts would be greater than what they were currently receiving.

Q: And following the meeting, I believe, you also sent to Mr. Sussman some directories of physicians?

A: It was not directories. It was a listing, and I believe that that was the one <u>I had delivered to him. We had met at another diner, Sage Diner in New Jersey</u>. And I think that's where I delivered that listing.

[Comment] Well, that sounds *like a second Sussman / Hardy meeting.*

Q: And you heard Mr. Sussman testify that that is something that anybody could get by calling up Blue Cross and telling them to send it; is that correct?

[Comment] Look how nicely he knits prior testimony into his question to orient everyone in the courtroom.

A: Generally. I mean, these are computer listings. We have directories now that can easily go out to anyone, but generally, the computer any broker or any salesperson or, anyone who we would be working with, we would certainly provide that.

Q: Now, following this meeting you had in late May, 1994, with Mr. Sussman and Mr. Sweeney, did you have any meetings with Mr. Craggs?

A: No.

Q: Did you ever meet with Mr. Craggs at anytime from the time of the meeting with Mr. Sussman and Mr. Sweeney in May of 1994, up to July of 1996, when Mr. Maresca ultimately got involved?

A: No.

Q: '95, rather?

A: No.

Q: Did you ever receive from Mr. Craggs any information concerning the Ironworkers at anytime from the time of the meeting you had with Mr. Sussman and Mr. Sweeney in May of 1994, up until the summer of 1995?

A: No.

Q: And did you, then, in June 1994, a couple weeks after the meeting you and Mr. Sussman had with Mr. Sweeney after you had delivered these directories, receive any telephone calls from Mr. Sussman about the status of the situation with the Ironworkers?

A: Yes, I did.

[Comment] Oh? Sussman is active?

Q: I would like to direct your attention, please, to Exhibit-4. Would you look at that? Can you tell us what Exhibit-4 is? You may have a tab, if you turn all the way to the right side of the notebook in the front.

A: Yes, I have it.

Q: And can you tell us what Exhibit-4 is?

A: Yes. This is a note from the tablet that I keep in front of my telephone, and it says—the date is 6/16/94, and it says, "Len Sussman," and this is a conversation I had with Len when let me know—and it says, "on hold." And then I have another little note here that says, "Used Rubin, out and now in."

Q: And what did you understand as a result of that note?

A: Well, that we were not going to proceed with trying to put in a program for the Ironworkers.

Q: Why don't you turn, please, to the next exhibit, Exhibit-5. Do you recognize Exhibit-5?

A: Yes, I do.

Q: Can you tell us what that is?

A: Yes. This is a note from my little memos where it says, "Memo from Helen Hardy". What I did here was to document something and actually put it in my Ironworkers file. So, here it says, "Ironworkers"—and this date was 6/20/94—it says, "Per tel con on Friday, 6/17, with Len Sussman, the Ironworkers dead at this time."

Q: So that memorializes your conversation that you had with Mr. Sussman?

A: That's right.

[Comment] Very nice. His very question authenticates the writing. The answer, though legally necessary, is superfluous. And now he ably summarizes the point. Notice: he is not waiting for summation.

Q: So, therefore, it's fair to say that the meeting that you, Mr. Sussman and Mr. Sweeney had in May of 1994, didn't go anywhere?

A: Yes. That's correct.

[Comment] All of this is obviously meant to terminate Sussman's contribution. But, putting aside the question of whether the jurors will believe it, why is that so terribly important to Blue Cross if it did not interfere with Sussman's relationship with the union and did not counsel against a commission?

Q: Now, let's move on, if we could, to the spring of 1995. Did you some time in March of 1995, receive a telephone call from Mr. Sussman suggesting a second meeting between you and Mr. Sweeney?

[Comment] He begins with a transition question to reorient us, and then moves on. See Vol. II, p. 18.

A: Yes, I did.

Q: And did that meeting ever take place?

A: No, it did not.

[Comment] This leaves us with more questions than he seems willing to ask. Is the project dead? Why no meeting? What did she say to Sussman? Was a date made? Did she break it?

Q: Now, if I could direct your attention, please, to Exhibit-17, if you would look at the second page of Exhibit-17, that is your calendar, is it not, for March of 1995?

A: Yes, it is.

Q: And you have an entry there for March 31st?

A: Yes, I do.

Q: Would you please read that entry to us?

A: Well, it has an 8 o'clock meeting with Carolyn Rugg.

[Comment] She has not answered as he wishes. But he is not troubled. Watch him take command.

Q: She's another employee of Blue Cross, and has nothing to do with this case?

A: No. Right. It says, "Tentative, Len Sussman, Iron," meaning the Ironworkers.

Q: Did Mr. Sussman ever confirm that meeting with you?

A: No, he did not.

Q: Did that meeting ever take place?

A: Well, I was not—I did not attend. I don't know if it took place, but I did not attend. I was waiting for Mr. Sussman to confirm the meeting and I didn't hear from him, so I stayed in the office.

[Comment] Well, now we have the answer of why she did not attend. Apparently, she wanted a second invitation.

Q: And did you attend any meeting with Mr. Sussman and Mr. Sweeney at anytime in March of 1995?

A: No, I did not.

Q: Now, in April of 1995, did you have a meeting with a Mr. Fratalli?

A: Yes, I did.

Q: I would like to direct your attention to Exhibit-18. If you would look at the second to last page of Exhibit-18, can you tell us what that is?

A: Okay.

MR. LONGER: Excuse me. Where are you—

MR. SONNENFELD: Exhibit-18 of the Defendant's Exhibits in the blue notebook, we're looking at the second to the last page of that exhibit.

BY MR. SONNENFELD:

Q: That's a page dated April 24, 1995. Are those the handwritten notes of yours on that date?

A: Yes, they are.

Q: What do those notes pertain to?

[Comment] That is an open-ended question, of which one should be leery. See Vol. II, pp. 21–22. She accepts the invitation to soliloquize and begins to rattle on, so he stops her. Watch.

A: This is the book in front of my telephone, when I get calls. And this is a note that I made as a result of a telephone call which I received from Pat Finley. Pat Finley is, the—or at that time, was the administrator for the cement masons Health and Welfare Fund. Pat Finley is also a member of the Independence Blue Cross Board of Directors. So, for both reasons I know Pat very well. And Pat called me and told me or asked me if I would call Al Fratalli, who was just made or voted as the business manager for the rod setters Local 405. That's another one of the locals of the Ironworkers Fund, and I did that. I went and visited with Al—

Q: Now, if you would look, please at your calendar, Exhibit-17, the preceding exhibit, do you see an entry for April 16th, 1995?

A: Yes.

Q: And is that the—tell us what that entry is?

A: Yes. It says, "7:30, Ironworkers," and that was my meeting with Al Fratalli.

Q: Tell us <u>briefly</u> what happened at that meeting.

[Comment] Not such a good question. The torch passes and she can pick and choose and go on as long as she wants, although he does hope she will be "brief." Her initial "okay" is one of pleasure, for she is back in control again.

A: Okay. I met with Mr. Fratalli in the morning and we probably met for maybe an hour, hour and a half, something like that. As I had said earlier, Al was just made the business manager for that local, and he was a Trustee or was to be a Trustee on the Fund, and felt very strongly that he wanted to do something to change the benefits design for the participants, for the members. He knew that the members in his local were not happy with the current program, so he was very interested in making a change. So, I told him in detail about our Personal Choice program. He was familiar with that because of conversations with other administrators and union officials and so many of them have our program. So, I went into detail about what Personal Choice was, and we had a very good meeting, and that's it.

[Comment] The "that's it" signifies that she is done with her selection. Whether or not anyone in the jury box understood the point of all this is an open question.

Q: Now, moving on, in July of 1995, you met, did you not, with—or you receive, a phone call that resulted in a meeting with Mr. Maresca and others; isn't that correct?

A: That's correct.

Q: And if you look at your calendar, Exhibit-17, if you look at the entry for July 26th, that reflects that meeting, does it not?

A: Yes, it does.

Q: And that meeting took place at the offices of Independence Blue Cross here in Philadelphia at 19th and Market Streets?

A: That's correct, 11:00 a.m.

Q: And can you tell us who you recall attended that meeting?

A: That meeting included, from my staff, Ken Olejniczak and his manager who reports to me, Michael Young, and I believe I may have also had Dori Colton, who is our support person and our administrative guru. And Mr. Maresca was there, one of his associates, John—I don't recall John's last name, and Bob Sweeney was there and also a gentleman by the name of Morris Rabino, believe it's spelled R-A-B-I-N-O. Mr. Rabino is the Business Manager for another of the Locals, and that Local is in Trenton. Again, I don't recall the number of that Local. And to the best of my knowledge, I think is who was there.

Q: How long did that meeting last?

A: Actually, that one was a few hours. The purpose of that meeting was to discuss what we could do for the Fund.

Q: And at that meeting, did you understand that you were in competition with anyone else for providing what the Fund wanted?

A: No.

Q: And, in fact, is there any other health care provider in this area who could provide what the Fund wanted from Independence Blue Cross?

A: I don't believe so.

Q: You're the only game in town?

A: I think so.

Q: It's either that or self-insured?

A: Right.

[Comment] That was a nice exchange. He staked out his point and then made it himself.

Q: Now, following that meeting, you then received, did you not, a request for a proposal from Mr. Maresca?

A: Yes, I did. It was formalized.

Q: And if you would look, please, at Plaintiff's Exhibit-8. It's all the way at the beginning of the book. That's a letter dated July 31st, that you received from Mr. Maresca, isn't it?

A: Yes, it is.

Q: And that's the request for the proposal?

A: Yes.

Q: And along with that letter, Mr. Maresca enclosed— he states he was enclosing a copy of the plan currently in effect for the Ironworkers Fund, a demographic distribution of the active eligibles and a copy of the last two years' claim experience by line of coverage. Do you see those?

A: Yes.

Q: Had you ever previously received that information from Mr. Sussman or as a result of any of Mr. Sussman's efforts?

A: No, I didn't.

Q: Was that information necessary for you in order for you to prepare a proposal responsive to Mr. Maresca's request?

A: Yes.

[Comment] Well done. Perhaps a little more questioning as to the plaintiff's lack of contribution of necessary information might have been helpful.

Q: Now, following this meeting, some time following this meeting, and the receipt of the July 31st letter from

Mr. Maresca, did you have a telephone conversation with Mr. Sweeney concerning Mr. Sussman?

A: Prior to this?

Q: Following this?

A: Oh, following. Okay. Yes, I did.

Q: Would you turn, please, to what we have marked as Exhibit-9.

A: [Witness complies.]

Q: Could you identify Exhibit-9 for us?

A: Yes. It's another page from my book, by my phone, and it was August 7th, 1995, at 8:45 a.m., I had a conversation with Bob Sweeney—

Q: Why don't you read us the note?

A: Okay. The note says, "Bob Sweeney, Ironworkers. Talked to Len Sussman and advised him that he is not involved." Then I have Ken O. with a circle around it. I don't know why I did that.

[Comment] As a suggestion, it might be well to have the witness give her recollection, and then confirm that with a reading. In other words, the note is not the vehicle of testimony, but rather the footnote of the credibility of the testimony. At a minimum, this technique would have given two, if not more, whacks at this important point.

Q: And this is a phone call that you placed to Mr. Sweeney?

A: I don't recall if I placed that call to him or if he was returning my call.

Q: And who raised the subject of Mr. Sussman?

A: I did.

Q: Why did you raise the subject of Mr. Sussman?

A: Well, I had concern. I wanted to know what Mr. Sussman's position was with regard to the Health and Welfare Fund. I had had dialogue with him prior and had that one meeting, and I just wanted to know what his position was. Frankly, I just wanted to make sure that—I wanted to know, should I or should I not be dealing with Mr. Sussman, or should I only be dealing with Mr. Maresca.

[Comment] The answer, selected in these terms, has dulled the point, which seemed to be that Sussman had no role. Now counsel completely takes any such interpretation off the table.

Q: Either in that conversation or at any other time, did you ever suggest to Mr. Sweeney that the Ironworkers not use Mr. Sussman or Tower?

A: Absolutely not.

Q: Did you have any reason or interest in doing that?

A: Absolutely not.

Q: Can you explain why?

A: It makes absolutely no difference to Independence Blue Cross or to me whether the customer chooses a broker or a consultant or no one. They may just want to come directly and let us talk to them about their program. It does not matter, but it has to be the customer's decision. It would not be appropriate for me to say positive or negative as to whether or not the customer should or should not use again, a broker, consultant or anyone.

Q: Did you <u>feel you</u> were <u>in any way bargaining</u> over Mr. Sussman's commission?

A: Absolutely not. My <u>personal</u>—we call it incentive, rather than commission—but <u>my personal commission</u> is the same whether the business comes in through a broker, through a consultant or direct. It is absolutely not affected at all. It doesn't matter to me. I'll work with whoever the customer tells me to work with.

[Comment] Now, that is an interesting answer. She has trans-formed the discussion from a conversation — which did not take place, according to her — about Sussman's commission to her personal monetary interests. Perhaps the examiner's choice of words played a role.

Q: So, therefore, it's the Fund's call?

A: Absolutely.

Q: And you made no effort to influence them one way or the other?

A: There would be no reason for me to do that.

[Comment] What is not clear is that she is saying this because a "broker" would be paid by the union, not the insurance com-pany. This is a critical point, and one the jurors (indeed, all of us) need an education about because in our noninstitutional experience we are most familiar with the situation where we buy insurance sold to us by a broker who is paid a commission by the insurance company. To be sure, most of us at some level recognize that this is built into our rates, so we are in a sense paying the commission. But we really have no choice, because as individuals we must use a broker; we usually do not deal directly with the company. Not so here. It strikes us that this distinction should be made clearer, given the probable life expe-rience of the jurors.

Q: Now, what did Mr. Sweeney say to you in response to your inquiry?

A: He told me that Mr. Sussman was not involved.

Q: And did he tell you that he told Mr. Sussman that he was not involved?

A: Yes, he did.

[Comment] This last question was objectionable on hearsay grounds.

Q: Now, did you ever discuss Mr. Sussman's involve-ment with Mr. Maresca?

A: I don't believe that I did, although I know yesterday that came up and I re-read my deposition, and I just must have been confused as to which names were being used. I absolutely definitely talked with Bob Sweeney about it, because I was concerned, again, I don't remember speaking with Mr. Maresca and I don't know why I said it. In January, I was confused by the way the questions were being asked and the different names in there, so—

Q: So, the conversation you thought you had with Mr. Maresca, that is reflected in your notes was with Mr. Sweeney?

A: Absolutely. I know I talked—I know I talked to Mr. Sweeney, absolutely.

[Comment] Very nice. Counsel undoubtedly prepared her to volunteer the explanation of the inconsistency between her deposition and trial testimony on direct, before she could be accused on cross. See Vol. II, pp. 199–209. He expects her to be cross-examined on it, as indeed she will be.

Q: And had you, by the way, during this time period, had some discussions with Mr. Sweeney concerning another union, the cement masons?

A: Not with Mr. Sweeney.

Q: Excuse me, Mr. Sussman?

A: Yes, I did.

Q: Did that go anywhere?

A: No, it did not.

Q: They were already a client of Independence Blue Cross, weren't they?

A: Yes.

[Comment] We wonder how it benefits Blue Cross to introduce another potential deal between Sussman and Blue Cross—one

the jurors had not heard about earlier. Shouldn't Blue Cross's position simply be that the issue of commissions raised by this case is a Sweeney/Sussman issue, not a Sussman/Hardy issue?

Q: And now, Independence Blue Cross submitted a proposal to Mr. Maresca; is that correct?

A: Yes, we did.

Q: And if you would look at Exhibit-11, that is the proposal, it's about an inch thick?

A: Yes, it is.

Q: And that proposal was prepared under your direction, was it not?

A: That's correct.

Q: Had Mr. Sussman ever requested that Independence Blue Cross prepare a proposal for the Ironworkers?

A: No, he didn't.

Q: Had you ever submitted to Mr. Sussman a proposal for the Ironworkers on behalf of Independence Blue Cross?

A: No, I did not.

Q: And following submitting this proposal, did you then attend a meeting of the Investment Committee of the Ironworkers Fund?

A: Yes, I did.

Q: And if you turn to Exhibit-12, that is the meeting of the Investment Committee that took place at Mr. Reith's office on—excuse me, Exhibit-13. I gave you the wrong number. I'm sorry. That's the Minutes of the meeting of the Investment Committee that took place at Mr. Reith's office in Philadelphia on September 25th, 1995, correct?

A: Yes.

Q: And you attended that meeting and made a presentation to the—participated in making a presentation to the Investment Committee, correct?

A: Yes, I did.

Q: And it was at that meeting that the Investment Committee, acting on the analysis of Mr. Maresca, recommended to the full Board of the Fund, the Independence Blue Cross proposal?

A: Yes.

Q: And, thereafter, you went up to New York and met with Maresca at the Segal Company, did you not?

A: That's correct.

[Comment] He is getting a little leading, but he is getting away with it and the testimony is now, as the Muppets say, "moving right along."

Q: If you look at Exhibit-17, again, your calendar—

MR. LONGER: What page, Mr. Sonnenfeld?

BY MR. SONNENFELD:

Q: If you look at the entry for October 20th, 1995.

A: Yes.

Q: That entry reflects a meeting in New York at the Segal Company, does it not?

A: Yes.

Q: And you attended that meeting?

A: Yes, I did.

Q: With others from Independence Blue Cross and Mr. Maresca, and you continued your negotiations over the contract between Blue Cross and the Ironworkers?

A: Yes.

Q: And that contract then went into effect January 1st, 1996; is that correct?

A: That's correct.

Q: And if you turn, please, to Exhibit-15, that is a copy of the contract, is it not?

A: Yes, it is.

Q: And that contract is an annual contract, isn't it?

A: That's correct.

Q: And it's now renewed in the second year?

A: Yes, it is.

Q: There are no guarantees beyond that, are there?

A: No.

Q: You hope it will be renewed, but no one knows?

A: That's true.

[Comment] Excellent point — but will the jury get it? Do you? His point is that the plaintiff is suing for future as well as present commissions. It might have been prudent for the examiner to make that point alongside the one he did. For example, "Are you aware that this plaintiff is claiming as damages commissions not only for this initial contract but future contracts as well?" Now, unfortunately in our view, he directs the examination back to the Sweeney / Sussman / Hardy meeting and discussion.

Q: And that contract is for Personal Choice; isn't that correct?

A: That's correct. I'm sorry. It's Personal Choice in the Philadelphia area, but because it was a national account, the—it's the same benefits design, but it's called something different in New Jersey and in the Lehigh Valley area.

Q: Now, was this benefits design something you discussed with Mr. Sussman and Mr. Sweeney, when you met with the two of them?

A: Not in any <u>detail</u>, other than me making a comment that Personal Choice was available, but we did not talk in <u>detail</u> about it.

[Comment] Her answer does not seem to advance any issue helpful to Blue Cross, but does remind us that Sussman was there at the beginning of the deal.

Q: And this, I believe it's called, a cost plus contract—

A: That is correct.

Q: Meaning that Blue Cross processes the claims, pays the hospitals and the providers, charges that back to the Fund and then it adds on an administrative fee which we learned is about 10.3 percent?

A: That's correct.

Q: And that 10.3 percent is not profit, is it?

A: No, it's not.

[Comment] Well, some of it must be. But let's see, although why counsel wants to get into this is not clear to us. In any event, here we go.

Q: What does that 10.3 administrative fee cover?

A: The 10.3 percent includes—there's a number of components. I would like to add that the formula for the retention is filed with the Pennsylvania Insurance Department. We have to get their approval. It is consistent, as far as how we apply it to all of our customers. We cannot change it. But what it does, it allows us to have monies for paying the claims. An estimate, but because of the size of the account, I would guess that we probably pay in a year, in excess of 15,000 claims for the Ironworkers and that is including hospital claims, physicians' claims, private duty nurse claims, tests, everything. So, it includes all of that, the cost to do that, salaries, et cetera. It <u>also includes probably part of my salary</u> and the account executive who works with the account, at least on a weekly basis in order to help them, assist them with any problems that they might have.

Q: That's Kenny O.?

A: That's Kenny O. and Mike Young. It also includes a contribution to our community effort, which I talked a little bit about yesterday, our social mission. Some of our customers would like that to be removed, but the Pennsylvania Insurance Department won't allow that, that contribution has to be there. In addition, it includes the cost of managing the whole program. The efforts that we take to negotiate the discounts that we talked about, we have a whole department that does that. The nurses who visit the hospitals, to make sure that everything is being done properly. The interactions that we have directly with the customers. We have various programs and one is called the Connections Programs for diabetics and back surgeries, et cetera. So, there's a lot of activity—

[Comment] She had the bit in her teeth and would have gone on and on, but he wisely stops her.

Q: It also includes, does it not, the overhead for the people who negotiate the discounts with the hospitals and some portion of that?

A: Correct.

Q: Now, you were asked yesterday whether you receive a commission, as part of your salary or compensation from Independence Blue Cross in terms of this Ironworkers contract, and you told us your answer was yes.

A: Yes.

[Comment] He has led into his next point beautifully. And it is an important one.

Q: How much of a commission have you received as an employee of Independence Blue Cross with respect to the Ironworkers contract?

A: Our commission is broken into—and, in fact, again, I would just like to say that we call it incentive rather than a commission.

Q: How much is your incentive?

A: Okay. With the selling of the account, for the sales piece of it, for me personally, I probably received around $1800.00. Now, I don't recall the exact amount.

[Comment] So far, so good. She gets a pittance for doing all the work, and the plaintiff is suing for much, much more. Of course, she does get a salary. However, given the issue that plaintiff's counsel had made over her commission, the detail of the smallness of it had to be brought out. One wonders if this is a point that might have been made after the plaintiff finished with her on his case during cross. But now, she begins to suffocate the point in detail with a long volunteered answer.

Q: That's one time?

A: That's one time and that's it. We <u>then receive an incentive for retention</u>. And that's paid on a monthly basis and that's for the work that we do during the month, directly with the account, visiting or attending Trustee meetings, handling claims problems, talking about financial reports, et cetera. That amount is—I did the calculation and, again, it's not exact, but it is approximately $400 a year, which, I guess, is about $35.00 a month. I would like to add that I did look at my deposition and in the deposition I said about a hundred dollars a month, but I would have to calculate it, and I did do that, and in fact I was way off. One reason why I wouldn't know that right off the top of my head is because those checks that we receive, which is part of our total compensation, includes retention for all the accounts that I am responsible for and it doesn't have them listed. But it turns out to be about $35.00 a month.

[Comment] It may be seen that she is still representing herself on the stand. In any event, counsel is now ready to move his final argument right through the witness to the jury.

Unfortunately, he uses the witness's answers and opinions rather than his questions.

Q: Now, did Mr. Sussman perform any services which, in your view, would entitle him to receive a commission?

A: No.

[Comment] Aside from the objectionable calling for her opinion, we again enter, in our view, an alternative argument to the main point that any responsibility was the union's, and a point not likely to sell: that Sussman did nothing compensable by anyone.

Q: Tell us what you mean by that.

[Comment] Now she is fully deputized to argue the case from the stand. And with the baton passed to her, she takes off.

A: Well, there's a lot that is involved with regard to selling a customer. It's not just the introduction and meeting the customer, it includes an analysis of their current benefit program and discussing what their objectives are. I think Mr. Sweeney mentioned that they did want to eliminate some co-payments and have less out-of-pocket burden on the union member. So, that analysis needed to be done. An evaluation of what benefits programs or benefits designs that we might have to meet those needs, and it also would include a financial analysis of the contributions that the Fund receives from the employers and what those monies look like, and a determination as to whether or not they can afford or we can meet their contributions, whether or not there's enough money—or depending on how much money there is, how comprehensive their benefits program can be.

[Comment] Notice: she has impliedly conceded that Sussman did help sell the "customer."

Q: Did Mr. Sussman provide you with any access to Mr. Sweeney that you otherwise would not have had?

A: No.

Q: Did Mr. Sussman provide you with any information that was useful to you in preparing your proposal to the Ironworkers?

A: No.

[Comment] Now the examiner enters an area that makes the witness uncomfortable, and her answers become watery.

Q: Did you ever tell Mr. Sussman in words or in substance that he could expect a big payday from <u>Independence Blue Cross</u> as a result of the Ironworkers?

A: No, <u>I would not say that</u>.

[Comment] Does that sound like a clear denial to you?

Q: Those wouldn't be your words?

[Comment] And does that question make it any better?

A: Again, <u>it was not my decision</u>. That would be the customer's decision, so I would not be presumptuous. I know that he had a relationship with Mr. Sweeney, but that did not mean to me that that was a guarantee that he would be the broker of record. And if he was, fine.

[Comment] Again, the examiner has failed to be clear. What she is really saying is that the broker, if that is what the plaintiff is, is to be paid by the client, not the insurance company. But this is not made clear, principally because the question focused on a "payday from Blue Cross."

Q: And in your conversation, and meetings with Mr. Sussman, did he appear to you to understand the products and benefits designs that Blue Cross had to offer?

A: No, he didn't.

[Comment] One wonders if this testimony is necessary.

Q: Could he be capable of doing the analysis that Mr. Maresca and the Segal Company performed?

[Comment] This question could be objected to, calling as it does for her evaluation of Sussman's abilities, but counsel, probably wisely, does not object to this rather gratuitous attack.

A: <u>No</u>. He seemed disinterested when I wanted to talk with him about some of the things that we had, and again, he seemed to be focusing on just the network, the size of the network and the discounts.

[Comment] Now counsel concludes with the assertion by the plaintiff that the defendant interfered with the plaintiff's relationship with the union, which is an unfathomable claim. The real claim, of course, should be one for quantum meruit against the company for benefits conferred by the plaintiff on the company. In any event, given the issues posed by the complaint, counsel hits them well, and hard, and at the end.

Q: And did you ever intend to do anything to interfere with Mr. Sweeney's [sic] relationship, if any, with the Ironworkers?

A: Absolutely not.

Q: And did you ever at anytime suggest to the Ironworkers that they avoid doing business with Mr. Sussman or Tower?

A: No, that would be inappropriate and I would not do that.

MR. SONNENFELD: I have nothing further, Your Honor.

[Comment] As a suggestion, counsel might have used some additional questions to remind us that Sweeney in court was adamant that the union objected to any commission, e.g., "Were you in court when Mr. Sweeney testified . . . ?"

THE COURT: Thank you. Let's take a short recess.

[Jury exits.]

- - - -

[Short recess.]

ANALYSIS OF THE DIRECT EXAMINATION

The direct examination picks up steam on this new day. However, the thrust of the examination is to make a point that, in our view, the examiner cannot sell: namely, that Ms. Hardy did not need Sussman's help to get the Ironworkers account.

The direct examiner elicits from the witness the fact that she had already met with Mr. Sweeney before Sussman called her, and that she had friends in the labor movement who had advised her to contact Mr. Sweeney. The examination cleverly suggests that Mr. Craggs (who, we recall, had some unkind things to say about "the Blues") was himself a problem and regarded as such by other labor people. Thus, Ms. Hardy appears to be locked in on Sweeney before Sussman and she ever met.

Ms. Hardy testifies that she arranged a meeting with Mr. Sweeney and had no problem doing it. She also describes her purpose in having the meeting and claims that she was able to discuss a range of Blue Cross/Blue Shield products with Mr. Sweeney and that she accomplished her goal. Not only did she meet with Mr. Sweeney at the suggestion of another labor leader, but she also received a telephone call from another union welfare fund leader, Mr. Dougherty, who asked for her help with health insurance for retirees. Ms. Hardy describes a lengthy meeting in which she and two others from Blue Cross/Blue Shield made a pitch, as did other health care organizations. The testimony subtly demonstrates that she did not need Mr. Sussman to make a presentation to a union welfare fund.

The problem here is that Blue Cross lost the Ironworkers account 20 years earlier, and we know that Ms. Hardy wrote a memorandum indicating that there was no interest among the Ironworkers in Blue Cross. All of her testimony about a successful meeting with Mr. Sweeney cannot demonstrate that the Ironworkers had any interest in talking with her. Remember that Sweeney testified that he met with her to be polite.

The testimony relates a conversation between Ms. Hardy and Mr. Sussman in his car on the way to meet Mr. Sweeney.

This conversation is especially important because Ms. Hardy indicates that her telephone conversation with Sussman had been short and that this was her first opportunity for detailed discussions. Her recollection as to what was discussed is, however, a two-edged sword. Ms. Hardy clearly recognizes that Sussman is a broker who is going to the meeting in order to do business, and she explicitly says that she recognized that it was "his" meeting, not hers. Also, Ms. Hardy's testimony about the Taft-Hartley Act and the responsibility of trustees of a welfare fund to act for the members is somewhat odd, because she sought out Mr. Sweeney herself for an initial meeting, not the entire board of trustees. She agreed to attend a meeting with Sussman and Sweeney, not the entire board. Thus, it seems strange to think of her suggesting in the car on the way to the meeting that she was concerned about the board of trustees as opposed to one trustee, Sweeney.

Ms. Hardy is asked whether it is usual for a welfare fund to use a broker, and she indicates that it is not. But which way does this cut? If something is unusual, does an experienced professional ignore it or inquire about it? The rules of probability suggest to us that some inquiry would be made. Thus, the direct examiner might set Ms. Hardy up for a cross-examination that would suggest that she must have ascertained that Mr. Sweeney had a unique relationship with Sussman, since she knew that use of a broker was unusual.

Ms. Hardy also concedes that Mr. Sussman did almost all the talking at the meeting with Sweeney. This is pretty good evidence that Sussman thought his relationship with Sweeney was more important than anything Ms. Hardy had to offer. Although Ms. Hardy suggests that Sussman did not know much about health insurance, her testimony indicates that Sussman had a plan in approaching Sweeney and believed that one key was expanding the pool of doctors and hospitals for union members.

The examiner does a good job of minimizing Ms. Hardy's repricing of the Ironworkers' medical expenses and providing directories of physicians to Sussman. The impression is that the repricing was a modest effort, and the directories were something that virtually anyone could have received upon request. But the effort is to minimize Sussman's importance in the case, an effort that is likely to fail.

To make the point that the meeting Sussman arranged for himself and Hardy with Sweeney was unsuccessful, the direct examiner asks Hardy about two notes she made of telephone conversations. These notes, written before there was any contract with the Ironworkers, are strong corroborative evidence that, at the time, Hardy believed that the Ironworkers were not going to use Blue Cross/Blue Shield as their insurer. This may not be a point that the direct examiner should be emphasizing, however, as it suggests that something must have happened between the time she took her notes and a year later, when things changed. The next thing that happened, according to her testimony, is a telephone conversation from Sussman. This hardly looks good for the defense.

The meeting that Ms. Hardy had with Al Fratalli seems potentially important. It occurs several months before the Ironworkers are in heavy negotiations with Blue Cross/Blue Shield. It does not involve Sussman. Fratalli's union is a local Ironworkers' union, but the potential importance of this meeting is not developed. Nor is the absence of Sussman mentioned. The potential argument that might have been made is not made strongly.

The examination moves to the negotiations between Blue Cross/Blue Shield and Maresca on behalf of the Ironworkers in July of 1995. During the period in which the negotiations were taking place, Hardy admits that she raised the subject of Sussman with Sweeney. She claims that she wanted to make sure that she should be dealing with Maresca and not Sussman, but the fact that she made the call undoubtedly is evidence that she was concerned that Sussman had been involved or was involved. That concern is not entirely consistent with the defense claim that she had no reason to believe that Sussman was a player at the time of the negotiations.

Hardy claims that she simply erred in testifying that she had a conversation with Maresca about Sussman. She seems to recognize that, if she did, it might look as though she were bargaining with Maresca to exclude any commission for Sussman. She claims that the questions that were asked of her in her deposition were confusing. The problem is that she testified under oath before this very jury that she spoke with Maresca about Sussman. The direct examiner could try to make the point that review of her deposition confused her, or he could try to have her admit that maybe she did have a conversation to assure that Sussman was not involved. Later, she will claim that it did not matter to her whether she spoke to Sweeney, Maresca, or both about Sussman. But, if it does not matter, it is a mistake to offer an explanation that requires the jury to believe that the witness was confused not only during her deposition but also during her earlier testimony in this case.

The part of the examination that focuses on the contract negotiations makes a point that is really not in dispute. The plaintiff does not contend that, once Maresca and the Segal Company began negotiating with Blue Cross/Blue Shield, Sussman remained part of the negotiations. Rather, it contends that Sussman laid the groundwork, was led to believe he would have a commission, and was cut out of the process.

In our judgment, the questions that are asked about Ms. Hardy's commissions ought to have been asked earlier. The jury wants to know whether she has sufficient incentive to cheat Sussman for personal gain. If, in fact, her commission is inconsequential, the motive to cheat is not great. Moreover, the lower the commission, the more her testimony amounts to an attack on the personal credibility of plaintiff's counsel. Plaintiff's counsel has suggested that Hardy had a profit motive and implied that she would be earning a large amount of money for the rest of her career as a result of the Ironworkers contract. If this proves to be exaggeration, it not only undermines the motive theory of the plaintiff, but it strikes a strong blow at the integrity of the plaintiff's argument. Having her go through the entire chronology of events before getting to the profit motive is a mistake, in our judgment. Perhaps even more significant, the paltriness of her commission makes Sussman's demand for hundreds of thousands of dollars grotesque.

The direct examination ends with Hardy testifying that Sussman did nothing to earn a commission. This is consistent with the opening argument made by defense counsel. The theme is that Sussman did not deserve a commission. However, that theme is difficult for the defense to make because Blue Cross/Blue Shield did nothing to keep the Ironworkers interested in Blue Cross/Blue Shield after Hardy's private meeting with Sweeney. Sussman apparently kept at it, even as Hardy described events. Moreover, Hardy cannot have personal knowledge of what Sussman was doing. The jury will conclude that within approximately a year of Sussman's being involved, the Ironworkers, whom Blue Cross/Blue Shield had been trying to contract with for years, was in serious negotiations with Blue Cross/Blue Shield. Surely he was a factor. The real defense is that Sussman was representing the union and, in any event, his suit for tortious interference is a sham. There was no interference. He sues for this because without an agreement with Blue Cross, he cannot sue for breach of contract, which is his real claim.

TEXT OF THE CROSS-EXAMINATION

[Comment] Now the stage is set for one of the critical moments of the trial: the cross of the main defense witness.

[Jury enters.]

[Back on the record.]

MR. LONGER: May I proceed, Your Honor?

THE COURT: Yes.

BY MR. LONGER:

Q: Ms. Hardy, Mr. Sonnenfeld started out by asking you some questions about a meeting that you had with Mr. Fratalli, about the retirees' benefits.

A: No, it was not Mr. Fratalli. It was Mr. Dougherty.

Q: That's right. But then you had a meeting, did you not, with the Ironworkers, you said, about retiree benefits?

A: With Mr. Dougherty for his local members, that is correct.

[Comment] Not such a good start. She is right and he is wrong. Better to begin with a victory, no matter how minor, than a defeat, no matter how minor.

Q: Did you go to a meeting to get business from the Ironworkers?

A: Yes.

Q: Did you end up with the retirees contract?

A: They were individual retirees contracts. I don't know how many, but, yes we did.

Q: In 1994, did you get some contracts for retirees benefits?

A: Yes, we did.

Q: In 1994, do you know if someone else got retirees benefits?

A: Yes, they did.

Q: Do you know if Mr. Sussman got retirees benefits?

A: No, I don't know.

Q: Do you know if U.S. Healthcare provides retirees benefits to Ironworkers?

A: Yes, I believe he mentioned that.

Q: Do you know that Mr. Sussman has a contract with U.S. Healthcare for retirees benefits for the Ironworkers?

A: No, I did not know that.

Q: Do you know that Mr. Sussman gets commissions on those contracts with the Ironworkers retirees?

A: I did not know that.

Q: Do you know that Mr. Sussman didn't need a broker of record letter to get those commissions from U.S. Healthcare?

A: No, I didn't know that.

Q: Would it surprise you that he would need a broker of record letter or didn't need a broker of record letter?

A: If it was a group contract, yes, it would surprise me.

[Comment] He is making some good points, suggesting that the broker of record letter is not a necessity, but self-imposed by the Blues. But . . . does he want us to believe that this requirement was created out of whole cloth by the defendant just to deprive Sussman of a commission?

Q: Now, the next thing you said was that you went to a meeting with Mr. Sussman—and let's start again. The objective—no, I'll start again. You spent some time in the past couple of days, I take it, reviewing your deposition transcript; is that right?

A: Yes.

Q: This contract here?

A: Yes.

Q: —this is the contract between the Ironworkers and Blue Cross/Blue Shield; is it not? This is Exhibit Number-29.

A: I'm sure that it is.

Q: In the black binder.

A: I can't see from there, but . . .

Q: Is this essentially a contract to lease Blue Cross/Blue Shield's networks?

A: No, it is not.

Q: Could you describe the way that the networks are used by the Ironworkers here? Aren't they using you as a third party administrator?

A: No, they are not.

[Comment] The cross-examiner has not been winning. Remember, the jury votes on every question and answer. The cross-examiner now throws the entire examination open to the witness.

Q: Tell the Jury what they are doing with this contract?

A: That contract provides that the Ironworkers gives us applications for each one of the members, for each one of the Ironworkers, who opted for the Blue Cross program, opposed to their self-administered program, and we load that information into our system, the name, address, dependent information. We assign an identification number. We send them identification cards, Independence Blue Cross identification cards, or those who are New Jersey, they receive a New Jersey identification card. They use that card to access health benefits. If they are sick they go to the doctor, they hand the doctor the card. The doctor in turn sends the bill to—well, actually, it is done electronically. It is not quite that simple.

Q: The doctor sends the bill to you?

A: To us, that is correct.

Q: And you reprice the bill correct?

A: We do not reprice it. We pay according to our contract.

Q: According to the price?

A: That's correct.

[Comment] We suggest that we now know more about the inner workings of Blue Cross than we need to, or want to.

Q: And the Ironworkers pay you the costs of those services, plus your retention charge, right?

A: Generally, in essence, yes.

Q: And by paying you the cost of your services, and the retention charge, they're, in essence, leasing your P.P.O. network, aren't they?

A: I disagree with that.

[Comment] Well, so what. We are now fighting in the back alleys of the case instead of on its boulevards.

Q: Now, when Mr. Sussman spoke to you in 1994, that was his idea, wasn't it?

A: To lease? That was my understanding of what he wanted to do, yes, to lease the network.

Q: And you just disagreed that that is what is going on here?

A: We are not leasing our network. What—if I may, when a network—

MR. SONNENFELD: Wait. I think Mr.—

MR. LONGER: Mr. Sonnenfeld, you can ask her on your own examination.

MR. SONNENFELD: Your Honor, I think Mr. Longer cut Ms. Hardy off.

THE COURT: Well, let her explain her answer and then continue.

MR. SONNENFELD: Thank you, Your Honor.

THE WITNESS: A network that is leased, generally the claims are paid by the customer or a third party administrator. And it's generally done out of the monies that are in an account that is the customer's. That's not the case with any accounts at Independence Blue Cross. We do not lease networks.

BY MR. LONGER:

Q: Now, let's switch gears here. Exhibit Number-9.

[Comment] We see the examiner is fixed or fixated on the point. But it is a so-what point—it is time to move on.

A: Which book, please?

Q: In the blue book. Mr. Sonnenfeld asked you some questions about that. It's a handwritten note that you wrote—you say it's August 7th, 1995.

A: Yes.

Q: Now, yesterday we talked about a conversation that you had with Mr. Maresca; do you recall saying that?

A: Yes, I do.

Q: And we put a date on that as preceding the July 26th, 1995 meeting in New York, at the Segal Company, didn't we?

MR. SONNENFELD: If I could just interject. I have no objection as to what the record reflects. Mr. Longer is holding exhibits up in front of the Jury, and I think it's fine for the Jury to see it, but I think if we're going to do that, then I think it ought to be reflected in the record.

THE COURT: Very well.

MR. LONGER: I have no problem with that, Your Honor, if I could have had it bigger, I would have made, it bigger. I had no—

MR. SONNENFELD: Juror Number 5 has her hand up, Your Honor.

THE COURT: Yes, ma'am.

JUROR NO. 5: All of us can't see that. Some can and some can't, in terms of reading, so I think that's not fair.

MR. SONNENFELD: That's why I wanted it on the record of what was happening.

THE COURT: Why don't we just pass it around?

[Jury views document.]

[Comment] All in all, not a good moment for the plaintiff, particularly when the juror said, "That's not fair."

BY MR. LONGER:

Q: Now the 8 representing August is obliterated by the black line around the document; is that fair to say?

A: That's correct.

Q: And that's an August 1995 document, right?

A: Yes.

Q: And the meeting that we talked about yesterday, was a July 1995 meeting, right?

A: Correct.

Q: It was July 26th, 1995?

A: That's correct.

Q: And you spoke to Mr. Maresca before that meeting, didn't you?

A: Yes, I did.

[Comment] Now the examiner walks into the contradiction that the witness has already explained away, and will do so again.

Q: And it was at that meeting, that we talked about yesterday, that you said you spoke to Mr. Maresca about Mr. Sussman's commission, right?

A: I did say that.

Q: And now you're telling this Jury, the Ladies and Gentlemen of this Jury, that that whole testimony was wrong, right?

A: I believe that—well, I'll answer and then I'd like to explain. What you just said was right. As I think I said just a few minutes ago, when I was being examined by Mr. Sonnenfeld, when I went—my recollection is that I spoke only with Mr. Sweeney with regard to the status of Mr. Sussman. I realize, and I did say that I went back last night and read my deposition, because Mr. Longer did point out that during my deposition, I said that I spoke with Mr. Maresca about Mr. Sonnenfeld. And the deposition—excuse me. I'm doing the same thing. Mr. Sussman. Everybody is getting the names mixed up, which is, I guess, what happened to me during the deposition. That was wrong. I spoke with Mr. Sweeney, but I would like to add what difference does it make? My concern was whether or not Mr. Sussman was involved, so whether I spoke with Mr. Sweeney, Mr. Maresca, both of them, what difference does it make? I just—wanted to know whether or not this gentleman was to be part of this program and I was told no. It's the customer's decision, not mine. I didn't care. I could work with him. I said I'd be very happy to work with him. That's not my decision.

Q: Are you through?

[Comment] Notice, he wisely has not tried to stop her. See Vol. III, pp. 49–54.

A: Yes, I am.

Q: Now, the reason you spoke to Mr. Maresca about Mr. Sussman before this July meeting, is because—

MR. SONNENFELD: Objection. He's misstating her testimony. She said she didn't speak to Mr. Maresca about Mr. Sussman before the July 26th meeting.

THE COURT: Sustained.

MR. SONNENFELD: Thank you, Your Honor.

BY MR. LONGER:

Q: Ms. Hardy—

A: Yes.

Q: —during your deposition on January 6th, 1997, where you were confusing Mr. Maresca and Mr. Sweeney, do you recall me asking you whether the reason you were talking to Mr. Maresca—

MR. SONNENFELD: Excuse me.

THE COURT: Let him finish his question.

BY MR. LONGER:

Q: —was because of Mr. Sussman's involvement?

MR. SONNENFELD: I object. If he wants to confront her with the deposition, he should read—

THE COURT: Well, it is cross-examination. I'll let him.

MR. LONGER: Thank you, Your Honor.

THE WITNESS: Would you repeat your question, please?

BY MR. LONGER:

Q: Do you recall when we were talking at the deposition, that I asked you whether the reason that you were speaking to Mr. Maresca was because of Mr. Sussman's involvement?

A: I remember you asking me that. I remember how I answered and I have just told you that I answered incorrectly. I did not speak with Mr. Maresca about Mr. Sussman.

Q: And let me ask you this: If we substituted Maresca for Sweeney, your answer would be correct?

A: Which answer?

[Comment] Who's on first. No, he is playing third. What's on first.

Q: In the line of questioning dealing with your conversation with Mr. Maresca before the July 26th, 1995 meeting?

MR. SONNENFELD: Well, I object, because I think Ms. Hardy has said the conversation with Mr. Sweeney was on August 7th, 1995, which was after the July 26th meeting. It's a misleading question.

THE COURT: Sustained.

MR. SONNENFELD: Thank you, Your Honor.

BY MR. LONGER:

[Comment] Actually, the point is a critical one for the plaintiff. It goes to whether or not she in any way told the union to drop Sussman. So counsel is trying to begin by showing she at least had a conversation about Sussman with union representatives.

Q: Ms. Hardy, you spoke to Mr. Sweeney about a conversation you had with Mr. Maresca, did you not?

A: No, I did not.

Q: Were you somehow confusing Mr. Sweeney with Mr. Maresca at your deposition; is that what you're saying?

A: The way that you were asking me the questions, yes, that's correct.

[Comment] See, it was all his fault. But he presses on and on.

Q: Let me ask you to explain this line of questioning, then, and maybe you can explain to these people how you confused Mr. Maresca in the question and answer.

MR. LONGER: And, Mr. Sonnenfeld, for your benefit, I am going to direct you to Page 115. Here we are, Ms. Hardy, Line 3. We'll start there.

BY MR. LONGER:

Q: "Did you discuss with Mr. Maresca, when he called you, whether or not Mr. Sussman could be involved?" And your answer was: "I believe I did, yes." Is that right?

A: That's what it says.

Q: And then I said: "What was the substance of your conversation with Mr. Maresca about Mr. Sussman?" And you said, "I don't recall exactly, other than he would have talked with Mr. Sweeney."

A: That's what it says.

Q: So, you were confusing Mr. Sweeney with Mr. Sweeney; is that what you're saying?

A: Apparently, I was. If—the way that you were asking all of the questions during that—there was many other questions that you asked me about my conversation with Mr. Sweeney about Mr. Sussman <u>where I did say that I had discussed—because I had concern</u>—again, all these conversations were only <u>in concern about Mr. Sussman's status</u>. Whether it was Mr. Sweeney or Mr. Maresca, to me doesn't make a difference. <u>I just wanted to know whether or not I should deal with the man</u>. I was very happy to do that.

[Comment] These answers are actually very helpful to the examiner. Why? Because they show her initiating conversations about Sussman's status. And that initiation goes to the heart of the plaintiff's interference claim. Unfortunately, the cross-examiner does not seize the moment, so we go back to unclarity.

Q: And then let's skip a couple of lines. "What do you recall being informed about Mr. Sussman?" I asked you. And you said "Nothing, other than he would talk to Bob Sweeney." So, you're confusing Mr. Sweeney again—

MR. SONNENFELD: Excuse me, I object. He hasn't accurately read the answer. The answer was, "I don't recall exactly other than he would have talked with Mr. Sweeney—" So, I think if we're going to refer to the deposition, it ought to be quoted accurately.

[Comment] The failure to be complete has given the adversary an opening. Now everyone is confused. But apparently, not enough.

BY MR. LONGER:

Q: Okay. Two questions, I'm asking you about a conversation with Mr. Maresca and you're confusing Mr. Maresca with Mr. Sweeney and you're confusing Mr. Sweeney with Mr. Sweeney, right?

A: The way that you're asking those questions, right.

[Comment] Unfortunately, we have drifted far away from the opportunity for cross which she has offered with her volunteered "concerns" about Sussman and whether she should "deal" with him, which she raised with the union.

Q: All right. And then you said to the Ladies and Gentlemen of this Jury, that you had only one meeting with Mr. Sussman and Mr. Sweeney; is that correct?

A: That is correct.

Q: And you talked about your calendar and your calendar shows on March 19th, 1995, a meeting with Mr. Sussman, correct?

MR. SONNENFELD: Ms. Hardy is turning to it. It is Exhibit-17.

MR. LONGER: I'm sorry.

BY MR. LONGER:

Q: Exhibit-17, second page.

A: I got it.

Q: Now, since we're handing out calendars, I'm going to ask you to turn to Exhibit-7 in the black book, also.

MR. SONNENFELD: Could I ask what is being shown to the Jury, just so it is on the record.

MR. LONGER: Yes. For the record, I'm showing the jurors the pages which are date stamped TF-9 and TF-10 from Exhibit Number-7 of the Plaintiff's notebook. Do you need help?

THE WITNESS: I'm sorry. Give me those numbers again, please.

MR. LONGER: TF-9 and TF-10.

THE COURT: You can pass that around.

[Jury views exhibits.]

BY MR. LONGER:

Q: Ms. Hardy, isn't it a fact that the tentative meeting that you did not appear at—

MR. SONNENFELD: I just want to make clear that this calendar is Mr. Sussman's calendar.

MR. LONGER: They have both calendars, Mr. Sonnenfeld.

MR. SONNENFELD: Have you passed Ms. Hardy's, as well?

MR. LONGER: They have both calendars.

MR. SONNENFELD: Thank you.

[Comment] Well, counsel should really know and not have to ask about what has entered the jury box. Indeed, he must monitor the entry before the penetration.

BY MR. LONGER:

Q: You had originally scheduled a meeting with Mr. Sussman and Mr. Sweeney on Monday, March 27th; isn't that true?

A: Mr. Sussman scheduled that meeting, yes, that is true.

Q: And that's the one that you didn't appear at; isn't that true?

A: That meeting was canceled, I believe, by Mr. Sweeney.

Q: And you're saying that you didn't have a meeting on March 31st?

A: The meeting was to be rescheduled for March 31st, and that's why I put tentative in my calendar. Mr.

Sussman was going to call me and confirm that it would take place and he never called me, so I did not go.

Q: You're saying that you only had one meeting with Mr. Sussman and Mr. Sweeney?

A: Absolutely, that's what I'm saying.

[Comment] So . . . what is he going to do about it? Back to who's on first, but it is now "I don't care" that usually plays second.

Q: Now, in your deposition, when you were confusing Mr. Maresca for Mr. Sweeney or maybe Mr. Sweeney with Mr. Sweeney, do you recall me asking you—

MR. SONNENFELD: Your Honor, I object. Because this is now—it's an argumentative question.

THE COURT: Well, what's the page number?

MR. LONGER: Page 116, Line 11.

THE COURT: Go ahead. Overruled.

BY MR. LONGER:

[Comment] Finally, he takes her back to her answer about her "concerns." Now the cross-examiner begins to score.

Q: <u>About your concern about Mr. Sussman's commission</u> and his <u>involvement</u>, do you recall me asking you that?

[Comment] Notice, he has changed her earlier answer about concern about "status" to concern about "Sussman's commission" and involvement.

A: I'm sorry. Would you please repeat that whole question?

Q: The discussions <u>that we had</u>, about a conversation over Mr. Sussman's <u>commissions</u> and your concerns about Mr. Sussman's involvement, with either Mr. Maresca or Mr. Sweeney, because <u>it's confusing</u>—

[Comment] Notice, "commissions" are now part of the deposition, apparently. But that was not read to anyone, if it is there. In any event, she buys into it.

A: <u>Right</u>.

Q: —do you recall talking about Mr. Sussman's <u>involvement</u>?

A: <u>Yes</u>.

Q: And do you recall that you were speaking to him because of conversations that you had with Mr. Sussman?

A: Yes.

Q: And do you recall speaking to Mr. Sweeney or Mr. Maresca, because of this confusion, about meetings, plural?

A: I don't know in terms of—I mean, there are ahs and oohs in there. I don't know if I said meeting or meetings. There was one meeting. I may have said meetings or maybe the reporter who was taking that deposition thought I put an S on it.

Q: Ms. Hardy—

A: That was not my intention to define one or two meetings.

Q: —you went to a meeting with Mr. Sussman and Mr. Sweeney in March of 1995, didn't you?

A: No, I did not.

Q: <u>You're under oath</u>. You tell this Jury you didn't go to a meeting in March of 1995?

A: I did not attend a meeting in March of '95 with Mr. Sussman and Mr. Sweeney, under oath.

[Comment] The "under oath" business did not help him, particularly as she emphatically repeated her denial.

Q: But in your testimony, of January 6th, 1997, you referred to meetings; isn't that correct?

A: Yes.

[Comment] Now the other lawyer gets involved, but the judge is not, at this late stage, going to settle disputes as to what the testimony has been.

MR. SONNENFELD: Your Honor, I object, because it is misleading, because Ms. Hardy has testified that she had met separately with Mr. Sussman alone in, the diner, so, there was—

THE COURT: I think the Jury's recollection will control.

[Comment] An entirely predictable ruling which both sides expect.

MR. SONNENFELD: Thank you, Your Honor.

MR. LONGER: Thank you.

BY MR. LONGER:

Q: Now, Mr. Sussman told you that he already had a contract with the Ironworkers and Preferred Care, did he not?

A: I do not recall him telling me that, that he had a contract.

Q: Mr. Sussman told you that he was getting commissions, though, from the Ironworkers, based on the contracts with Preferred Care?

A: No, he did not tell me that.

MR. LONGER: Mr. Sonnenfeld, I'm looking for the exhibit that talks about John Heim.

MR. SONNENFELD: Exhibit-13, Page 3.

MR. LONGER: Exhibit-13, Page—

MR. SONNENFELD: It's the May 31st, 1994 notes.

THE COURT: For the record, we are publishing this to the Jury.

[Jury views exhibits.]

MR. LONGER: Your Honor, should I allow some time?

THE COURT: Yes.

[Short pause.]

[Back on the record.]

BY MR. LONGER:

Q: Ms. Hardy, this is a note of one or two things. It's either your notes of a conversation that you had with John Heim, or it's a conversation—notes of a conversation that you had with John Heim and Mr. Sussman; is that correct?

A: It would have been only me, because this is from my telephone report, so I could not have had a conversation with both of them. This conversation was with John Heim.

Q: This only was with John?

A: To the best of my understanding, my note, yes, and I say that because at the end it says, that—well, first it starts with John Heim and then at the end it talks about John has a list of the participants' Zip Codes, which we had mentioned earlier. I didn't remember if we received them from Mr. Sussman or from Mr. Heim.

Q: And in the right-hand side of the page, it says "Fee, 25 percent of 25 percent discounts," correct?

A: Correct.

Q: And Mr. Heim told you about Mr. Sussman's arrangements with Preferred Care?

A: I cannot say that he actually told me about Mr.—that it was Mr. Sussman—that he was getting a commission. But that commission paid while someone had or leased a network program generally was in terms of a percentage of the discount. The piece that I did not know, and what I'm saying that Mr. Sussman did not tell me, is that he, in fact, was receiving commissions. He talked to me about a commission being based on the percentage of the discounts, but not specifically that he was already getting them. I didn't know that. I didn't ask. Frankly, it was none of my business.

[Comment] Now counsel confronts her with her deposition, and does so as we recommend. See Vol. III, pp. 73–84. No private showing. The jury hears the inconsistency with the witness.

Q: Do you recall me asking you at your deposition, Page 67, Line 6, with reference to this document, "Did you and Mr. Sussman discuss his fee as being 25 percent of the 25 percent discounts?" Do you recall me asking you that question?

A: If that is what's written in there, yes.

Q: Do you recall that your answer was? "He" being Mr. Sussman, "told me, and again this may have been two conversations, like right-back-to-back and I just wrote it all on one page, but whether it was this day or another day, I know that he did tell me that he had other customers, other clients that he had entered into or worked to enter an arrangement with another P.P.O., Preferred, and here it's, Preferred Health, and that generally their compensation or their commission was a percentage of the discounts. So, he must have told me," he being Mr Sussman, "25 percent of the 25 percent discounts that they would obtain from this Preferred Health." Do you recall giving that answer?

A: Yes.

[Comment] In our view, he has her. Now he drives the point home.

Q: And that is Mr. Sussman telling you about Preferred Health, Preferred Care, right?

A: That is correct. But it still isn't telling me that Mr. Sussman himself was getting that commission. I absolutely agree that he shared with me that that was the way that the commission was calculated, but I didn't understand or didn't ask because again, I didn't—it didn't matter whether or not he was already getting a commission.

[Comment] Now she avoids the point of the question, by raising the issue of whether the commission was a "shared" commission. But counsel skillfully keeps after her.

Q: Mr. Sussman had a discussion with you about <u>his commission</u> with Preferred Health and that is what this note is all about. You knew—

A: <u>Yes</u>, but not in—

Q: You knew what Mr. Sussman was doing with Preferred Care, Preferred Health didn't you?

A: Yes. But not in terms of the Ironworkers.

[Comment] We think he made the point and that the jury saw that he had established that she knew that Sussman was getting a commission on Preferred Care. Indeed, in our view, she saw it too, and shifted the topic to the Ironworkers.

Q: And that was prior—do you know that he has another arrangement with the Preferred Health?

A: He told me he had several customers and this is how they generally calculated their commissions, but I didn't know that it was specific to the Ironworkers.

[Comment] Up until now, counsel is trying to make the point that the plaintiff, who was getting a commission from the prior provider, would hardly want to replace that provider with one that would give him nothing. But he gets it as a volunteer answer.

Q: But you were going—and he called you specifically about the Ironworkers, didn't he?

A: Yes. Because I was under the impression he wanted a commission from Blue Cross. He wanted our commission.

Q: Why would he be talking about Preferred Health for every customer under the sun when he was calling you about the Ironworkers?

A: Repeat that, please?

[Comment] So now he does. And he lays the point out.

Q: He is telling you, isn't he, that, "Helen, let's go meet with Bob Sweeney. I want to get you in to see the Ironworkers, because I have an agreement with Preferred Care where I'm getting this kind of a commission and I think I can get you in to see the Ironworkers and get a good favorable audience with Bob Sweeney." Isn't that what happened?

A: No. May I tell you my reading on it?

THE COURT: Let's just answer the question <u>so we can get done.</u>

[Comment] It may be seen that the Court itself is tired of her volunteering.

MR. LONGER: Thank you, Your Honor.

BY MR. LONGER:

Q: Now, yesterday, we were talking about this contract going on, the contract with the Ironworkers and Blue Cross and Blue Shield, going on for a long period of time, weren't we?

A: That was our hope, yes.

[Comment] See how nicely he loops back to the earlier examination.

Q: That it would have a life of its own, it would just keep continuing and renewing itself annually, right?

A: If we met their needs.

Q: And today, Mr. Sonnenfeld asked you a question about that contract and today you don't feel as confident about that contract any more, do you?

A: I don't think that's true.

Q: This contract will continue on and on and on; is that right?

A: I don't have the ability to cancel that contract, but absolutely, my hope is—I know that this customer is satisfied, and so today, my expectation is it would continue, but I can't guarantee that. That is absolutely my expectation and it is no different than it was yesterday.

Q: Okay, so, it's the same. You have every expectation that it will continue on and on?

A: Sure, I certainly hope so.

[Comment] See how nicely he brings her back to his point. One thing is certain: no examiner can do this with written-down questions.

Q: And you get that commission on every year that it is renewed?

A: That is correct.

Q: And when you were talking to Mr. Sussman about commissions, <u>he had every expectation that his commission</u> would be renewed every year that this contract continued, right?

A: <u>I would imagine</u>, yes.

[Comment] That last is great! She has bought into Sussman's "expectation." We think an objection might have been made. She has also bought into his expectation about not just a commission, but a perpetual commission, and to do so she has used her imagination. *We think an objection and a motion to strike would be needed here.*

Q: And you were talking to Mr. Sussman on September 22nd, 1994, about <u>his commissions being 1 to 3 percent</u> of the amount billed, right?

A: I gave Mr. Sussman, at that point, what I understood our commission payment to be. And it was between 1 and 3 percent. I don't know all the details and I shared that with him as well, that that would have to be explored.

[Comment] Again, an excellent question, which built on the last answer. She now has her company paying Sussman, based on what her company, not the union, was willing to pay. This is, of course, contrary to the entire defense that the money comes from the union . . . although not the narrow allegation of interference in the complaint. Might be a good place to stop, now that she herself does not remember.

Q: And let me ask you this: With respect to your retention charges, Blue Cross/Blue Shield does make a profit on this contract, doesn't it?

A: I cannot say that.

Q: You wouldn't disclose your discounts to the Ironworkers; is that right?

A: We give our customers an average. We guarantee an average discount. We don't give them the discount per each admission.

Q: And Mr. Craggs can't determine the precise discount because he doesn't have that information; is that right?

A: Not on a hospital basis, but he does get that information overall. It is a 6 percent guaranteed discount on all claims that are incurred in the Philadelphia five-county area.

Q: And in good years, Blue Cross/Blue Shield is going to profit from this contract, isn't it?

A: It would depend on the types of admissions, so I cannot say that. I don't know.

MR. LONGER: I have no further questions. Thank you.

THE COURT: Thank you.

ANALYSIS OF THE CROSS-EXAMINATION

The cross-examination fails to make clear points, in our judgment, until the very end, and then it goes on a hair too long. Part of the problem is that the examiner seems to feel some need to consider the points made on direct in the order that they were made. This is not only unnecessary, but plays into the hands of the direct examiner.

The examination of Ms. Hardy ought to be based upon lines of examination that should not change much as a result of the direct examination. Some of the things she said on direct examination actually bolster logical lines of cross-examination that were available. Consider, for instance, the importance of the fact that Hardy did not know Sussman when he called, but she agreed to meet with Sweeney along with Sussman. The following questions are based on the rules and laws of probability. If Hardy fights the questions, she loses more than if she accepts them.

Q: You had met with Mr. Sweeney before Mr. Sussman called you?

Q: At the time Mr. Sussman called you, you had no pending appointments with Mr. Sweeney?

Q: The Ironworkers remained on the list of desirable customers for Blue Cross/Blue Shield?

Q: When Sussman called you, he was a stranger to you?

Q: Sussman suggested that you and he meet with Mr. Sweeney?

Q: You knew that Sweeney was a co-chair of the trustees of the welfare fund?

Q: You knew that you had already provided Sweeney information about Blue Cross/Blue Shield?

Q: You agreed with Mr. Sussman to go with him to meet Sweeney?

Q: You agreed to go with Mr. Sussman because Mr. Sussman persuaded you that he was very close to Mr. Sweeney?

Q: You were persuaded that Mr. Sussman was very close to Mr. Sweeney by what Mr. Sussman told you?

Q: You knew the first time that you spoke with Mr. Sussman that he was a broker?

Q: You say that it was unusual for a welfare fund to use a broker in seeking health insurance?

Q: Because it was unusual for a welfare fund to use a broker to seek health insurance in your experience, it was important to you that Mr. Sussman really was close to Mr. Sweeney?

Q: Mr. Sussman told you that not only was he close, but that he had brokered the Preferred Care contract and receives a commission on it?

Q: In fact, it was his claim regarding Preferred Care that led you to believe that Mr. Sussman might be able to deliver the Ironworkers contract for Blue Cross/Blue Shield?

The point we make is that the cross-examiner needs to consider facts that cannot be denied: Hardy and Sussman were strangers. Hardy wanted the Ironworkers contract and would not have risked going to Sweeney, with whom she had met, with just anyone. Hardy herself claimed it was unusual for a welfare fund to use a broker. Hardy nonetheless agreed to go with Sussman and let Sussman do the talking. Why would she do this? Why would she risk going with a stranger to seek an important account? The logical answer is because of what Sussman told her about Sussman's relationship with Sweeney and his success in getting the Ironworkers to accept a health insurance package that he had brokered.

Another line of cross-examination could have focused on Blue Cross/Blue Shield's profit on the contract. Hardy claims not to know whether Blue Cross/Blue Shield made a profit. On this point, her testimony could be made to look silly, but the cross-examiner does not make the point. It should have been easy to address Blue Cross/Blue Shield's profit and to undermine to a considerable extent the point made about Hardy's commissions on direct examination. Consider the following questions:

Q: You testified that you hope to earn a commission on renewals of the Ironworkers contract for many years?

Q: You hope to earn a commission for many years?

Q: You hope that this contract will continue?

Q: You hope that this contract will continue because it is profitable for Blue Cross/Blue Shield?

Q: Blue Cross/Blue Shield cannot stay in business if it loses money on contracts?

Q: Blue Cross/Blue Shield cannot pay commissions for long on contracts that lose money?

Q: If Blue Cross/Blue Shield loses money on a contract, Blue Cross/Blue Shield may not renew a contract?

Q: No one has told you that Blue Cross/Blue Shield is losing any money on the Ironworkers contract?

Q: No one at Blue Cross/Blue Shield has told you that your commission is in jeopardy?

Q: So, as far as you know, Blue Cross/Blue Shield is satisfied with the contract?

Q: You are satisfied with the contract?

Q: Now, Blue Cross/Blue Shield pays you and others salaries as well as commissions?

Q: You have received salary increases from time to time?

Q: Blue Cross/Blue Shield's ability to pay salary increases depends on whether it has money for increases?

Q: Blue Cross/Blue Shield's ability to pay salary increases depends on whether it earns money?

Q: If Blue Cross/Blue Shield earned no money, it could not pay salaries?

Q: If Blue Cross/Blue Shield earned no money, it could not pay your salary?

Q: If Blue Cross/Blue Shield earned no money, it could not pay you a salary increase?

Q: If Blue Cross/Blue Shield earns a lot of money, it has more money available for salaries?

Q: If Blue Cross/Blue Shield earns a lot of money, it has more money available for salary increases?

Q: If Blue Cross/Blue Shield earns a lot of money, it has more money available to pay commissions?

We could go on, but the point is already made. A cross-examination is a chance to make the points that the cross-examiner wants to make. With the right questions asked, the witness is the excuse for asking the questions.

The cross-examiner correctly felt that Ms. Hardy was evasive in explaining why she testified that she had talked about Sussman with Maresca. However, Hardy is never adequately confronted with the contradiction in her testimony, and is permitted to make a speech about why it really doesn't matter whether she spoke with Maresca, Sweeney, or both.

Finally, there is the matter of the 1 to 3 percent commission that Hardy's notes show she spoke to Sussman about. It seems pretty clear that she did not tell Sussman that it would be odd for him to receive such a commission. In fact, she led him to believe that such was a standard commission. The most important point that could have been made is that she never told

Sussman that she thought there was anything unusual or improper in his receiving the standard commission, and that he obviously was led to believe that he was eligible for that commission if the deal was done.

TEXT OF THE REDIRECT EXAMINATION

THE COURT: Redirect?

MR. SONNENFELD: Very briefly.

[Comment] This is an interesting decision. If one is ahead after direct and cross, then one should stop — because if there is redirect, there will be recross and the fire must be endured again. In our judgment, although Blue Cross was not ahead, it might have been wiser to get Hardy off the stand.

BY MR. SONNENFELD:

Q: You were asked about U.S. Healthcare and whether you would be surprised if there was no broker of record letter if they had a group agreement. If they had individual contracts with the retirees, would you expect a broker of record letter?

A: I honestly don't know, because I'm not familiar with individual contracts, but perhaps they pay commissions, I just don't know.

Q: And you were asked about this arrangement that Mr. Sussman says he has with Preferred Care, where he gets a percentage of the saving as his commission. Does Blue Cross ever enter into a commission arrangement like that?

A: Not to my knowledge.

[Comment] Notice, on redirect most courts allow far more leading than on direct itself.

Q: And with respect to this 1 to 3 percent that you discussed with Mr. Sussman in September of 1994, you never told him that that was going to be his commission, did you?

A: No, I did not.

Q: And you never reached any <u>agreement</u> with him, on the terms of the commission, did you?

A: No.

[Comment] This much is good. And then he opens the record to her.

Q: And why was that?

A: He just asked me what our—you know, how they were paid, and I shared with him what I found out, <u>after making a call. I made the call to Brian Sullivan's boss, a gentleman by the name of Poore. And he told me that it's around 1 to 3 percent, and it depends on the size of the case</u>, and it depends on the type of financial arrangements that they have and suggested that they would have to look at their primary broker.

[Comment] Here is a problem. He has undermined her own $1800 by establishing that outsiders get far more, and that it is regularly paid. More troublesome, the focus has shifted from a commission for Sussman being a union decision to a Blue Cross decision—and that is not where the defendant should want to be. Worst of all, she has elevated the discussion beyond her level at Blue Cross. And now counsel exacerbates the situation by pursuing it.

Q: And is there also a cap or a large group?

A: There is, but I do not believe that I shared that with—I don't think that I said that to Mr. Sussman. Perhaps I didn't get that piece at the time.

[Comment] She now is not sure what she told him.

Q: If you brought in General Motors for thousands of people, you would cap it somewhere?

A: Absolutely.

Q: All this would be the subject of some <u>negotiation</u>, would it not?

A: I believe that's the way that it's done, that it happens with the primary broker.

Q: And you never had those <u>negotiations</u> with respect to Mr. Sussman?

A: No.

Q: And you never <u>got</u> to that?

[Comment] Not such a good question, you "never got to that," for obvious reasons.

A: No.

[Comment] In our view, counsel might have been better advised to return to his central point: any commission was a union decision, and the union made it without conferring with Blue Cross—and remind us of the Sweeney testimony. Now he finishes his redirect on what seems to us to be relatively unimportant points.

Q: And as far as meetings, you testified very clearly that you had one meeting with Mr. Sussman and Mr. Sweeney, correct?

A: That's correct.

Q: That's the one in May of 1994. And then you also, then in June of '94, had one meeting with Mr. Sussman alone; is that right?

A: Very brief.

Q: And that's when you gave him—

A: I didn't even get out of the car.

Q: And that was at a diner in New Jersey and you gave him the directories that he asked for?

A: That's correct.

Q: Finally, on the subject of leasing a network, can you just tell us what you mean by leasing a network?

[Comment] At this stage, does anyone care? Can this possibly interest the jurors?

A: To my understanding, most of the companies that have—that are P.P.O. companies, and there are several of them, Multi-Plan is one, Preferred Care, I think it is, I'm not real familiar, but that's one. There's another one called Americare. I believe that primarily what they do is rent or lease their networks, to my knowledge, and they may, but to my knowledge, they don't necessarily pay the claims. They generally will have an arrangement where they can lease the networks. Now, they may pay claims, I'm not—I just don't know that much about them. But we don't. We base—we sell a product. We sell the total package, where we provide the discounts, but we also administer the claims.

Q: So, the subject of leasing the network that you were discussing with Mr. Sussman back in May or June of '94, would have involved the Ironworkers Fund continuing to administer the claims themselves, but just taking advantage of the discounts hospitals and providers negotiated by Blue Cross; is that right?

A: Yes.

Q: That's not something that Blue Cross does?

A: That's correct. We do not.

[Comment] We think that the jurors—the prisoners in the box—are likely hoping this is all on this subject. But the witness wants to go on and on.

Q: You would want to pay and process and administer the claims, as well?

A: Yes. Can I continue?

Q: Sure.

A: In fact, the contracts that we have with our providers, specifically the hospitals, well, it can be the doctors as well, requires that we pay the claim directly, that another third party cannot pay that claim and get that discount. There cannot be that repricing.

Q: That is something different from what Mr. Sussman was discussing with you back in May of 1994?

A: As I understand what he was trying to accomplish with this Fund, yes.

Q: What this Fund is now doing is Blue Cross administers the claims and gets the discounts and pays them and then charges that administrative [fee] to the Fund for that service?

A: That's correct. They actually bought what we would say a product, they bought the whole package.

Q: <u>That's not what you were discussing</u> with Mr. Sussman back in May of 1994?

A: That's correct.

[Comment] So why are we listening to all of this?

Q: And as far as the discounts with the hospitals, is it correct that Blue Cross negotiates separate contracts with each hospital?

A: Yes.

Q: And each one is a different discount, they vary by hospital?

A: Yes, they do.

Q: That's a competitive negotiation; is that right?

A: Yes.

Q: But there's a so-called plan-wide discount of 55 percent, correct?

A: Yes.

Q: And that's what is guaranteed in the five-county area?

A: Correct, that is per hospitals.

Q: Hospitals?

A: Correct.

Q: And it's something different for medical and surgical, doctors' bills and so forth?

A: Right. That's a range, 40 to 45 percent.

Q: That also varies by provider?

A: That is correct.

Q: Depending upon what you were able to negotiate with the provider?

A: That's correct.

Q: The reason you keep those discounts secret is you don't want your competitor coming in and knowing what discounts you have negotiated; isn't that right?

A: Partly, yes.

Q: That's one of the reasons?

A: Yes.

[Comment] But we guess that the secret is out of the bag now—if anyone cares.

Q: Finally, speaking of negotiations, you're now involved in negotiations with Mr. Maresca of the Segal Company over the renewal of this contract, aren't you?

A: Yes, we are.

Q: And one of the issues in the negotiation is the amount of the retention or administrative charge?

A: That's correct.

Q: And there's no guarantee as to how that will turn out, is there?

A: No. Last year it stayed the way it was, and we need to evaluate it again based on Mr. Maresca's request for us to do that, and we will and we are.

*[Comment] We suggest it is not wise to end on this point,
which gives the impression of a focus on damages.*

MR. SONNENFELD: Thank you.

ANALYSIS OF THE REDIRECT EXAMINATION

At this point, we have no doubt that the jury has made up
its mind about the witness and whether Sussman had a reasonable expectation of a commission, and whether one was
held out to him, at least within certain parameters. The examiner establishes powerfully that Hardy communicated to
Sussman that 1 to 3 percent was a standard commission and
probably did not bother to get into details about things like
caps. Thus, even though the witness testifies that there was no
actual agreement about the amount of the commission, the
jury will clearly understand what Sussman understood the
usual range to be—and all this is not so good for a direct examiner. Better he should have let the witness go after cross.

It seems to us that neither the witness nor the defense case
is helped at all by this examination. Emphasis on the standard
nature of the commission is more likely to strengthen the
plaintiff's case than the defense case. Also, the suggestion that
what Mr. Sussman was inquiring about in 1994—renting the
network—is oblique and likely to be lost on the jury.

The largest mistake, though, might well have been opening the door to why the percentage discount is kept secret. The
examiner suggests that the reason is to protect Blue Cross
against competitors. But this witness has already testified that
Blue Cross was the only game in town. Thus, the door was
open for the plaintiffs to demonstrate that the real reason for
secrecy was to prevent consumers like the welfare fund from
finding out what Blue Cross was earning. This was the point
that Craggs made early in the case. Raising the secrecy issue
at this stage is incredibly risky.

TEXT OF THE RECROSS-EXAMINATION

THE COURT: Recross?

MR. LONGER: Yes.

[Comment] Let us see whether the decision to again examine is a wise one, given where we are.

BY MR. LONGER:

Q: His request is that the retention charge be reduced, Mr. Maresca?

A: Yes.

Q: And that is his concern to you?

MR. LONGER: Just for the benefit of the record, I'm showing the witness Exhibit Number-26.

BY MR. LONGER:

Q: Have you renegotiated the retention charge or is that still to be negotiated?

A: For the first contract year it stayed as it was, and now the second contract year Mr. Maresca has asked us to take another look at it. He is of the opinion that it is higher than what it should be. So, we are evaluating that and most likely we won't make a change, but we'll certainly respond to him.

Q: So, his opinion last year was that this fee was excessive, you didn't do anything about that. And this year, he still believes that it's excessive and you're going to think about that; is that right?

A: Well, it's not that we did not do anything about it. We provided him with information that confirms the appropriateness of that retention and we'll do the same this year.

[Comment] So far, nothing worthwhile seems to have been done. But now counsel scores by returning to his strong points.

Q: And just so I'm clear about the conversation that you had with Mr. Sussman about commissions, you talked about a range of 1 to 3 percent being negotiable; is that right?

A: It was 1 to 3 percent. I don't recall that I used the word negotiable with him. It was a very brief conversation.

Q: Well, 1 through 3 percent implies that it is a negotiable number?

A: <u>I agree with that</u>.

[Comment] That is a superb use of the rules of probability. Vol. III, pp. 177–184. Watch him do it again.

Q: And 1 percent is the <u>bottom</u> line, right?

A: As I understood the <u>commission</u>, yeah.

[Comment] He has struck strong blows. We are left with the impression that Sussman would have received at least one percent — and he got there by moving from "negotiable" to "bottom line" to the notion of "at least." Very well done indeed.

MR. LONGER: Thank you.

ANALYSIS OF THE RECROSS-EXAMINATION

The examiner succeeds in making the point that 1 percent is "the bottom line." That is a success. Then the witness buys into "commission." Notice how counsel keeps to the main point of his case.

TEXT OF THE RE-REDIRECT EXAMINATION

THE COURT: Counsel.

[Comment] The defendant has been hurt by the last, and so he feels the need to bandage the wound. But does he, with this one question?

BY MR. SONNENFELD:

Q: Subject to a cap?

A: Subject to a cap, which I said I did not share with him, but I believe he has a primary broker or a primary brokerage firm that he works with and they would certainly have the details, and I did suggest that he needed to go to them to talk about it in more detail.

MR. SONNENFELD: Nothing further.

MR. LONGER: I have no further questions.

THE COURT: Thank you, ma'am. You may step down.

[Witness excused.]

ANALYSIS OF THE RE-REDIRECT EXAMINATION

This brief examination demonstrates how unlikely it is that further direct examination will be useful, and how easy it is to make a mistake in asking a few questions hurriedly. The witness says she did not explain the "cap." She also says that she suggested to Sussman that he seek more information about the usual terms of a commission from a primary broker. Why in the world would she have made this suggestion to Sussman if she did not think he was going to receive a commission? And why does counsel want to end his entire case on the point that Sussman's commission is subject to a "cap"?

THE DEFENSE RESTS AND EXHIBITS ARE ADMITTED

THE COURT: Defense.

MR. SONNENFELD: Your Honor, the Defense rests subject to moving into evidence the various exhibits that we have identified.

THE COURT: Very well. Why don't we take a short recess, because the next thing that will take place are the closing arguments. But let's take a short recess because that will take about an hour and then we'll take a short break and my points for charge will probably take about a half hour, 20 minutes, and then you'll be ready to deliberate and eat lunch. Let's take a short recess.

THE CRIER: Everyone remain seated while the Jury leaves the room.

[Jury exits.]

[Short recess.]

[Discussion on the record.]

MR. LONGER: Your Honor, at this point in time, the Plaintiffs would like to move into evidence several of the exhibits that we've used today, and I believe that they are coming in without objection and I'll read them off, if I may. Exhibit P-1, Exhibit P-2, Exhibit P-4, Exhibit P-7, Exhibit P-3, Exhibit P-9. Did I miss one? P-5?

MR. SONNENFELD: I don't care if you put it in or not.

MR. LONGER: P-5, Exhibit P-10, Exhibit P-11, Exhibit P-3, Exhibit P-14, Exhibit P-15, Exhibit P-17, Exhibit P-18, Exhibit P-19, Exhibit P-26, Exhibit P-28, Exhibit P-29, Exhibit P-30, Exhibit P-31, Exhibit P-32. That is the exhibits that the Plaintiffs have moved into evidence.

THE COURT: Okay.

MS. BENNETT: Your Honor, Defendants would like to have the following exhibits into evidence, assume without objection from Mr. Longer.

MR. LONGER: We have agreed to it.

MS. BENNETT: Defendant's Exhibit-4, Defendant's Exhibit-5, Defendant's Exhibit-7, Defendant's Exhibit–8, Defendant's Exhibit-9, Defendant's Exhibit-11, Defendant's Exhibit-12, Defendant's Exhibit-13, Defendant's Exhibit-14, Defendant's Exhibit-15, Defendant's Exhibit-17, Defendant's Exhibit-18, Defendant's Exhibit-20, Defendant's Exhibit-22, Defendant's Exhibit-23. That's all.

THE COURT: Thank you.

Chapter Fourteen

Final Motions, Closing Argument, and Verdict

MOTION FOR JUDGMENT

The Motion

> THE COURT: Thank you. And there's a motion for directed verdict, I believe.
>
> MR. SONNENFELD: Your Honor, I would like to hand up a motion for a directed verdict. I have given a copy to Mr. Longer.
>
> THE COURT: Do you want to incorporate your prior arguments?

[Comment] You can bet that the judge wants him to "incorporate" rather than the judge having to listen to the same argument again. Counsel agrees, but it is not wise for him to do so. Watch.

> MR. SONNENFELD: I'll incorporate the prior arguments and the briefs that we submitted yesterday and moved for a compulsory nonsuit. And this should be directed to Count 1 of the Complaint, and in particular, I would like to draw the Court's attention to the arguments with respect to damages.
>
> THE COURT: Denied.
>
> MR. LONGER: Thank you, Your Honor.
>
> [Jury enters.]

Analysis of the Motion

The defendants' motion is one that usually must be made to preserve a claim on appeal that a case should not have been sent to the jury. Defense counsel wisely recognizes that the judge is not going to want to delay submitting the case to the jury, and so puts his argument in writing. At the court's invitation, he incorporates the previous written and oral arguments that were successful in dismissing the negligence count. But, in our view, waiving argument in this instance is not such a good thing.

It is true that defense counsel has preserved his record in the event he loses and he has done so without straining relations with the court. Nonetheless, a good argument would not have turned the judge into a raging seeker of revenge. In this case, counsel, now that all the evidence is in, has a strong argument to make: where is *any* evidence that Hardy told Sweeney or any union employee not to give Sussman his broker's letter? If there is no such evidence, why go to the jury on the one count left in this complaint, which charges Blue Cross with tortious interference?

At this stage of the case, it cannot be a surprise that the judge denies the motion, particularly because the judge has not been made to deal with this argument.

INSTRUCTIONS ON CLOSING ARGUMENT

Text of the Instructions

THE COURT: Ladies and Gentlemen, now you have heard all of the evidence which is going to be presented in this case. The next step is for counsel to give you their closing arguments. Even though these arguments do not constitute evidence, you should consider them very carefully. In their arguments counsel call to your attention the evidence which they consider material and will ask you to draw certain inferences from that evidence. Please keep in mind, however, that you are not bound by their recollection of the evidence. It is your own recollection which must guide your deliberations. If there's a discrepancy between your recollection and that of counsel's, you are bound by your own recollection.

You are not limited in your consideration of the evidence to that which is mentioned by counsel. You must consider all of the evidence which you consider material to the issues involved in this case. To the extent that the inferences which counsel asked you to draw are supported by the evidence and they appeal to your reason and judgment, you may consider them in your deliberations. Counsel may also call to your attention certain principles of law in their arguments. Please remember, however, that you are not bound by any principle of law mentioned by counsel. You must apply the law in which you are instructed by me and only that law to the facts as you find them.

In the Commonwealth of Pennsylvania, the Plaintiff's attorney will speak first, followed by the Defendant's attorney and then a final rebuttal by the Plaintiff's attorney.

Following that, I will instruct you in the law which you will apply to the facts as you find them.

Counsel for the Plaintiff, you may address the Jury.

Analysis of the Instructions

Now that the judge has instructed the jury on the purpose of closing arguments and on the order, the lawyers can stand up and do their arguments. No introduction to closing arguments is necessary or desirable.

In federal courts and in some states, judges will instruct the jury on the law prior to the closing arguments. Federal Rule of Civil Procedure 51 permits the judge to instruct before or after argument, or twice. This is not the case here. The judge will instruct only after the argument. Also, in some states, the defense will argue first and the plaintiff last. Here, plaintiffs have the right to go first and last.

PLAINTIFF'S FIRST CLOSING ARGUMENT

[Comment] Remember, as you read this, it is our view that closings do not tend to persuade — at least not in lengthy trials. This was a fairly short one. Nonetheless, as you shall see, even here summation could not have mattered much. What, then, is the purpose of summation? Until we have asked and answered

*that question, we can have no real conception of how a summa-
tion should be "done." The function of the closing is to arm your
friends on the jury for the truly final argument, which will take
place in the jury room. Therefore, the purpose of summation is
to equip and teach your friends the arguments to make in the
jury room, and how to use the testimony and exhibits in making those arguments. See Vol. IV, pp. 27–36. Summation is thus
not a time for you to argue your case; that time is over. It is an
opportunity for you to use the exhibits and the* actual *testimony
to simultaneously show your friends on the jury how to argue,
and to make it difficult for their (and your) enemies to exercise
denial, in terms of what the evidence has been. And, if the burden of proof is on your adversary, now is the time to mention
that, to further arm your advocates in the jury room and give
them the ability to be unpersuaded by their adversary. See Vol.
IV, pp. 36–38. Let us see how well counsel executes this.*

Text of the Argument

MR. LONGER: Thank you, Your Honor. Thank you,
Ladies and Gentlemen.

Without you, this can't happen at all. We appreciate
your time, and I know I appreciate your time and I'm
sure Mr. Sussman and the Court and everyone in the
courtroom thanks you for your time.

Three weeks ago or thereabouts you all received your
summons and here you are today and we are giving our
arguments. You have heard the evidence and here we are
now about to close, and this is my closing argument.

I'm going to tell you as best I can, what you have
already heard, and to summarize for you Mr. Sussman's
case against Blue Cross/Blue Shield.

What you have heard is a tale of two cities, of a big
corporation, Blue Cross/Blue Shield, against a very small
operation in New Jersey, which is run virtually alone by
Mr. Sussman. He has five other employees. Blue Cross/
Blue Shield is big and it's getting bigger and it's getting
bigger off of the back of <u>my client</u>.

[Comment] Not bad, except for the "my client." Indeed, it is clear that he is making an effective emotional appeal, but now he deals with the burdens of proof. Let us see how he handles it.

Judge Kafrissen is going to tell you after we are done that because I am the Plaintiff—and because I represent the Plaintiff, it's my burden of proof. I have to show to you by a preponderance of the evidence that Mr. Sussman has proved his case.

And at the beginning of the trial, both the Judge and myself used the analogy of the balance scales. Preponderance of the evidence means <u>if you put a feather on one side of the scale and it tilts it this much [indicating], I have satisfied my burden</u>. I submit to you, after you put the evidence on the scale, <u>I haven't put a feather</u> on this side, <u>I have leaned this scale over</u>.

[Comment] We think this is very well done. He is not defensive about the topic, but raises it affirmatively. See Vol. I, pp. 147–151; Vol. IV, pp. 36–38.

Mr. Sussman brought Blue Cross/Blue Shield to see Mr. Sweeney because he knew, because of his relationship with Mr. Sweeney, that Bob Sweeney would give him a Blue Cross/Blue Shield contract. Bob Sweeney could deliver, just as he had with the Preferred Care contract. Blue Cross/Blue Shield's efforts were led by Ms. Hardy.

Ms. Hardy, and I showed you the documents, had a status report, and indicated a total lack of interest in Blue Cross/Blue Shield. She told you that she met with Bob Sweeney at the beginning of 1994. When Mr. Sonnenfeld asked her, she was prompted, and she said it was in April of 1994, and she says, "It was a very positive meeting." Do you remember that? "It was a very positive meeting."

Mr. Sweeney says, "I have an open door policy. I don't even remember her practically." I mean he says it was a 15-minute meeting. I don't know what she was doing.

[Comment] This is the right place to begin: the need of Blue Cross to sell the union and its inability to satisfy that need. He might have done better to have used the status report—that is, to have shown it—rather than merely summarized it. See Vol. IV, pp. 35–36.

Mr. Sussman, however, brought Ms. Hardy into that meeting and Mr. Sweeney denies that it was a very positive meeting, but you know that it wasn't. Mr. Sweeney is not a friend of Mr. Sussman. He was a friend but he is not anymore. He is embarrassed about this situation. And he denied anything to do with Mr. Sussman. It's a shame that that happened. But Mr. Sussman was coming in to service his friend and client. He had provided to Mr. Sweeney a contract which the Ironworkers appreciated, the Preferred Care contract.

Mr. Sussman brought in a partner, Mr. Halverson. The two of them shared their commission with Preferred Care, each of them getting 10 percent. They had a 20 percent commission, they were willing to split. Mr. Sussman was willing to share, Ladies and Gentlemen.

[Comment] Yes, he had a commission, but the point is not that Sussman was willing to share it with this partner, the point is that he was willing to give it up entirely for his client, to be replaced by another from Blue Cross. Unfortunately, instead of making points by grouping events, counsel seems to have fallen into a chronological telling of the events.

He then understands, through Mr. Sweeney, that he's not entirely satisfied with the networks for the outlying Locals. He wants a bigger network. Mr. Sussman knew to go to Blue Cross/Blue Shield. He spoke to the Head of the Health and Welfare Department, Ms. Hardy. He told her, I can get you a favorable audience with Bob Sweeney. And did she jump at that chance? You bet she did, because she had not been able to get beyond Nick Craggs. And you heard Mr. Craggs, Mr. Craggs has a total dislike for the Blues, he didn't like them way back when, he doesn't even like them right now.

[Comment] Excellent. No doubt this is correct, and now he will make a point of it, at least in the first two sentences that follow.

Mr. Sussman got this train moving. The Ironworkers were moving towards Blue Cross. Mr. Sweeney needed time to get Preferred Care's experience. So, after that meeting in June of 1994, Mr. Sussman returned in 1995, but between then, Mr. Sussman had provided Mr. Sweeney with Zip—I'm sorry—Blue Cross/Blue Shield with a Zip Code listings.

He had provided Mr. Sweeney with the directories so that Mr. Sweeney could understand the extent and the reach of Blue Cross/Blue Shield across the Tri-State Area, because that's what the Ironworkers needed. They are a big Health and Welfare Fund.

Ms. Hardy had conversations with Mr. Sussman all through 1994. In September of 1994, she's talking to Mr. Sussman about what he can expect as his commission on this contract. She's telling him it would be 1 to 3 percent of the premium paid. Mr. Sussman says, we'll come back in the future. In 1995, we'll do it again.

[Comment] All of this is correct. But again, is it an argument or a recitation of fact in chronological order?

In 1995, Mr. Sussman, Ms. Hardy and Mr. Sweeney meet again, in March of 1995, and this train is rolling. No one wants to admit that these people were meeting. It's going to be up to you to decide who is telling the truth here, but Mr. Sweeney is not admitting to it and Ms. Hardy is not admitting to it. Ms. Hardy is not admitting to a lot of things here.

When she heard Mr. Maresca yesterday say, "I never talked to her about commissions with Mr. Sussman, when we were conspiring to shut him out, I never heard about it." Today she comes in and says, "Oh, I have read my deposition transcript where I'm telling you, Mr. Longer, all about this conversation with Mr. Maresca, now, I'm confusing Mr. Maresca with Mr. Sweeney except in the same sentence I'm talking about Mr. Sweeney." So, somehow Mr. Sweeney is confused with Mr. Sweeney. It doesn't make any sense. She's backpedaling as fast as she can today, because somebody didn't get their stories straight.

Mr. Maresca was saying, I never talked to you about this. Yesterday she said, we did talk about it. Today she says, we didn't. Tomorrow she might have another explanation. I don't know. But you will have to decide who is telling the truth here.

[Comment] He does very well with this here. Better than when he was crossing Hardy—but if the jurors did not get it then, will they get it now? And this is the allegation at the heart of his case, as framed by the complaint, that Blue Cross interfered with the union paying a commission to Sussman.

And what were they talking about? They knew that in July they were going to have a meeting. Mr. Maresca is the Fund's consultant, was and is. Mr. Sweeney was going to have Mr. Maresca appointed to evaluate Blue Cross/Blue Shield. At the June 23rd, 1995 meeting, of the Board of Directors, a motion was presented to evaluate a P.P.O. Mr. Craggs told you whose motion that was. It was the Union's motion, the Union's Trustees. The Management Trustees, co-chaired by Mr. Reith, they are not involved in this. This was a presentation by the Union side, where Mr. Sweeney is the co-chairman. Mr. Sweeney says, I'm one vote of 11, I've got no influence over anybody else. That's not the way it works in unions. We know unions. Your Business Agent, when he is a co-chairman, you're happy that he is the co-chairman because he has power and influence, he can direct how the votes will be done, he controls the agenda of the meetings. You even hear that out of Mr. Sweeney's mouth.

Now, he couldn't bring up the motion, but he could be sure that the motion was brought up. And they knew that the motion was going to brought up for a P.P.O. and that

P.P.O. was only one insurance company, and that was Blue Cross/Blue Shield.

[Comment] We seem to have left the commission track and are on to something else. But now we are suddenly wrested back to the topic.

And at that point in time, they already knew that Mr. Sussman was on his way out, because at some restaurant in South Jersey, Mr. Maresca <u>was told</u>, we're going to have a meeting in the future <u>and he's out, no commissions to Mr. Sussman</u>. We're not going to pay him a dime because we want to get the cheaper premiums that we can from Blue Cross/Blue Shield.

[Comment] Who is telling Maresca this? If it is the union representatives talking among themselves, where is the interference by Blue Cross? Counsel must know he needs to put them in too, and so he does.

Blue Cross/Blue Shield doesn't want to cut its retention fee, the charges that it is going to make the profit on, that it could share with Mr. Sussman, but it's not willing to because it's a big corporation and it's getting bigger. It's got a new president. They have got new programs. We heard 40 or 50 minutes of testimony at the end of the day yesterday, Ladies and Gentlemen, about the wonders of Blue Cross/Blue Shield. It's a great company. It's great because it's on—it's getting bigger and bigger on the backs of little people. Union members, Mr. Sussman, all of those.

[Comment] Now, that's entertainment! He gave the defendant a real lick. But where is the evidence of all this? And is the interference with the relationship between Sussman and the union Blue Cross's refusal to cut its own fees and profits? Nevertheless, counsel, without the evidence, has substituted advocacy—and very well too. See Vol. I, pp. 87–93.

<u>A lot of us</u>, at least, <u>have Blue Cross/Blue Shield insurance and that is where this company is making its</u>

money. Well, it's <u>wrong</u> for them to do it on the backs of the union workers. It's <u>wrong</u> for them to do it on the back of my client. He got them in there, he was doing his job. He was working hard to help his friend and to make some money. He's not going to deny that. He's here because he was trying to make a commission on this contract. He expected to make a commission on this contract.

[Comment] Excellent! Simply beautiful. We will even forgive the "my client." Everybody can relate to what he first said although the reference to the jurors' personal contracts with the Blues is objectionable. Now he is arguing, not simply telling a story. And he is operating effectively on an emotional level. He can only hope that neither judge nor jury understands that he has shifted from an interference theory to a kind of claim for quantum meruit from Blue Cross.

He talked to Ms. Hardy about a commission on this contract. It was understood what was going on. <u>And that the big Health and Welfare Fund leaders, after they talked to their consultant, who spoke to Ms. Hardy about shutting Mr. Sussman out of this deal</u>, before that July meeting, <u>they</u> wanted him out and <u>they</u> agreed to get him out and then after that the rest is history.

[Comment] Well, now he is back to his tort theory. He has also taken Hardy's testimony that she merely asked Maresca if Sussman was still involved, and implies, without quite saying it, that she was part of a conversation with the union to shut out Sussman. But even at that, counsel has this coming from the union to Blue Cross, not the other way around. Still not good enough.

Mr. Sussman tried to work around Helen Hardy. He brought in Mr. Sullivan. Why would he go to Mr. Sullivan if he knew he needed a broker of record letter? Does that make any sense? He wouldn't have gone to him to try to end-run Ms. Hardy.

He went to him because he knew that brokers can get a commission and that commission doesn't have to be on the backs of the union members, it can be on the back of Blue Cross/Blue Shield's profits. Blue Cross/Blue Shield could share that money with him just like he shared with Mr. Halverson on the Preferred Care contract.

The Preferred Care contract is not being—Preferred Care is paying Mr. Sussman commissions, not out of the money or monies of the union members. It is not building up. They're saying, we'll share with you also. Preferred Care sounds like a decent company. Blue Cross/Blue Shield is doing anything it can to get this plum contact, one that it's been looking after since it lost the account in the 1970s. It lost this account. Mr. Craggs didn't like them and he wanted them to stay out, and they have been fighting to get into it and they couldn't.

[Comment] He still does not make the argument that Sussman, in helping Blue Cross/Blue Shield, is losing a commission on Preferred. Now for some of the very best of the summation, which is very good indeed.

And, Ladies and Gentlemen, it's just <u>not decent</u> what they did once they got in the door through Mr. Sussman and shut him out. That was <u>wrong</u>. And you are the voice of the community here today. Today you can tell Blue Cross/Blue Shield what they did was wrong. You can say to them, when someone is nice to you, when someone is trying to help you out, you share with them. Mr. Sussman shared with Mr. Halverson. Preferred Care shares with both of them. Blue Cross/Blue Shield doesn't want to share with anybody. They are making money and they are going to make more money.

[Comment] Wasn't that just spectacular? If he achieves the purpose of this last, the jurors will not likely care that he has sued on a theory for which there is little or no evidence in support. They will give him a verdict.

And Mr. Maresca is telling them, we think your charges are excessive, and they are not willing to renegotiate until the next year. That letter I showed you the big blowup, was January of '96, that was last year. And Ms. Hardy today says, we didn't do anything about that. We're now talking again. Maybe we'll change it or not.

Now, I submit to you, Ladies and Gentlemen, we have proved to you that these people came in with the intent of driving Mr. Sussman out. Mr. Sussman was going to get that contract as long as Blue Cross/Blue Shield was willing to share.

Mr. Sweeney concedes to that. He saw to it with the Preferred Care contract, and he was willing to do it until he heard that Blue Cross/Blue Shield was not willing to share, and then he changed his story. And it's because Blue Cross/Blue Shield talked to Mr. Maresca, and that conversation is critical and they're denying it takes place now because they know how critical it was, that it is essential for them to deny that it occurred.

Now, as I said afterwards, once the Board has authorized this contract, it went forward, and you see the contract that Mr. Sussman had been developing with Mr. Sweeney in 1994, and then again in March of 1995, came into existence. This is a claim, by the way, for a prospective contract, but there is no prospect here. This contract is in existence. It has been in existence for a year and a half now. It has been renewed for a second year. It's going to be renewed again.

Ms. Hardy hopes that it stays on until she retires, because she makes a commission on that contract. She's making money on it. She's not willing to share that.

Mr. Sussman is getting paid nothing. Nothing. But he brought them in. He opened the door for her and he was influential with the co-chairman of the Board and he did that work, Ladies and Gentlemen, and that's why there's a contract today.

[Comment] Notice how he wisely returns to his point of greatest power and persuasion, and *protection. No Sussman, no contract — and the probabilities are with him on that.*

Now, you're going to see that there is a battle of calendars here. Mr. Sussman has a calendar which indicates his meetings with these people. Everyone else denies those meetings took place. Why? The only reason is because they don't want to acknowledge Mr. Sussman was involved.

But Ms. Hardy, in her testimony at her deposition, admitted that there were meetings. She's denying today that there were meetings plural. She's saying that there's just one. You're going to have to decide, because clearly there's a big untruth being told.

[Comment] Wow. He never addressed the legal stuff that the judge will instruct them on. He keeps after the only item that he can raise to support a claim that Blue Cross interfered between Sussman and the union, that there are some inconsistencies in Hardy's testimony about the number of meetings she had with union people.

Now, the Judge is going to tell you about the legal aspects of this case, the law that applies to this claim. I have a burden. I told you that when I began. I have to prove to you beyond a preponderance of the evidence four simple elements to prove my claim. I have already done that. The evidence has proven my claim out.

The Judge, I'm sure, will instruct you that I have to prove that a prospective contractual relationship existed between Tower Financial Planning, Mr. Sussman, and the Ironworkers. I have proven that. Mr. Sussman already has a contract with Preferred Care. He could get a contract with the Ironworkers, and look at what happened, there's a contract with the Ironworkers. He could have done it, and we know it.

Mr. Sussman has to prove as a second element, that these people acted with intent to interfere with that contract. Blue Cross/Blue Shield wanted this contract. Ms. Hardy had been trying to get this contract for years. Every year she comes back. "Mr. Craggs, what can I do for you?" Mr. Craggs to Ms. Hardy, "You can get out of my face."

Ms. Hardy, "What can I do for you, Mr. Sweeney?" "I can forget about this meeting. I don't remember you. I had a 15-minute meeting with you."

She says it was the best thing that could have happened. Well, I forget what she said, but—"It was a very positive meeting." That's right. "It was a very positive meeting."

I asked Mr. Sweeney, "Was that a positive meeting? Did you give her reason to believe that that was a positive meeting?" What did he say? "No." Mr. Sussman got her in there and things changed, and when things changed, they went to their consultants and their consultants spoke to Ms. Hardy <u>and Ms. Hardy says "We've got to get Sussman out of here because I can give you a lower premium," and Mr. Maresca goes, "He's out of here</u>." That is intent, Ladies and Gentlemen. <u>He's going to deny it</u>. <u>She's going to deny it</u>. No one is going to tell you, "Yeah, I did that." It's up for you to decide whether or not they lied to you.

[Comment] Here it is! Counsel has supplied the conversation which no one has testified to and which there is no direct evidence in support of. Any verdict for him will be based on advocacy, utilizing that inference, not evidence. See Vol. I, p. 141. And yet, he can get into difficulty here—is he saying that the union should have paid the commission, instead of saving on the premium, or that Blue Cross should have cut its profits?

The third element that I have to show to you is the lack of privilege or justification. That's an easy one. I have already done it. I just told you why. Is it right for them to squeeze Mr. Sussman out, just blow him away? That's all privilege is. They used him. They used his services. They used his connections, and then they abused him. They told him, "Get out of here. We won't deal with you. We're not going to share with you. We're going to get greedy and we're going to keep this money to ourself. We are Blue Cross/Blue Shield. We don't have to talk to you. We can make money the old fashioned way. We can steal it from you."

[Comment] And now we are ready for the final thrust, the question of how much? Here counsel has a problem. This is a watery area.

The last element is one that I have to spend a little bit of time with you because it is damages. You have to understand how Mr. Sussman is damaged. I have proven that there are damages here.

A broker makes a living by selling insurance and getting a commission from the insurance company that is grateful to the broker for giving him the business. This company is not grateful about much at all. They say we can do it ourselves, but they couldn't. They tried for years and they couldn't do it. The money at stake here was a big contract. Millions and millions of dollars were at stake in this contract.

Mr. Craggs told you and Ms. Hardy confirmed it, that we were talking about a six million dollar contract. Six million dollars. They both said the same figure. There's not that much dispute. I had shown you the Federal reporting form, that Form 5500. Mr. Craggs—I showed it to Mr. Sussman, because Mr. Sussman understood that this was a 15 or 17—I'm sorry—17 million dollar Fund in terms of the benefits that they paid. What we found out from Mr. Craggs was that that number was really every benefit paid. It's not just health and—doctors and hospitalizations. It included dental and eye glasses and other things so that big figure was reduced.

And we heard that it was about six million dollars, and it was about six million dollars this past year. And what we did, was a little bit of multiplication. And we found out that with the retention charge, Blue Cross/Blue Shield has a 10.2, according to Mr. Craggs, but Mr. Maresca's letter here to Ms. Hardy, shows that it's actually 10.3 percent. Not a big difference, but I think you should be aware of

that. And that results in the retention charges that Blue
Cross/Blue Shield gets its profits from.

Now, while you were out, I did a little drawing, and
you can see my sloppy handwriting. We're talking about 6
million dollars. Mr. Sussman had a conversation with Ms.
Hardy, she admits it—no one is denying it. They were
talking about 1 to 3 percent range with respect to commissions. I have done the math.

One percent of 6 million is 60,000. Two percent of 6
million is 120,000. Three percent of 6 million is 180,000.
That's per year and it would be—it would be that every
year for as long as this contract continued.

[Comment] OK, but how much is he supposed to get?

Now, Mr. Sussman, when he got into this, he was trying to negotiate an agreement with them based on the
Preferred Care way, which was 20 percent of the saving.
The savings here is the 10.3 percent retention charge. It's
the equivalent. That—I'm just using round numbers—10
percent, 10 percent of 6 million is $600,000. Mr. Sussman
wanted 20 percent of that savings. Twenty percent would
have been $120,000.

Ladies and Gentlemen, it is pretty clear that as far as
negotiation goes, we are not talking about a big difference. $120,000 is right smack in the middle. $120,000 is
probably where they would have ended up.

*[Comment] Excellent . . . for a negotiation. But this is sup-
posed to be a verdict for a sum based on a* promise. *We suggest
that this argument might have drawn an objection, too.*

But, you, Ladies and Gentlemen, if you believe that
the evidence shows that there was an intentional interference with this contract that my client developed,
worked for and obtained, you can find that it could have
been anywhere. You could find that it would have only
been a one percent commission; you could find that it
would have been a three percent commission; you could
find it would have been right in the middle. You can find

that he might have been able to do better. And you can find that this commission would have continued for as long as Ms. Hardy was working until her retirement, and she's going to get a commission until she retires. She's not willing to share it with Mr. Sussman. He was willing to share it with her, but she's not willing to share it with him, at least until she retires.

[Comment] So . . . how much is he asking for? In the words of the King of Siam, "Is a puzzlement."

Mr. Craggs, yesterday, felt that this contract was going to continue and continue. Ms. Hardy backpedaled today. I laughed when she said that, that was just me, I knew that she was—she had spoken last night with Mr. Sonnenfeld and they wanted to put a little doubt into your mind as to how long this contract was going to continue.

[Comment] We suggest that the last was improper, without any evidentiary foundation, and could have been objected to.

But now, after redirect, or on cross-examination, she is now going to say, yeah, I hope it will continue. I expect that it will. We agree that this thing is going to continue and if it does, it's $120,000 on. She's now putting in a cap. It's news to us.

At any rate, if you find that you should—that there should be an award of damages, I'm asking you to recognize that at least there are two years right now under our belts. You have got 1996 passed, and we're into 1997, this contract was renewed, we're at two years. Mr. Cragg expects it to go to at least next year. You can keep going for as long as you want. And I'd be very happy and very grateful and I know that my client would also. But if you do that, you have to be honest and recognize that money in hand now, because of interest, is worth more now than it would be over time.

So, you have to reduce the present value, what that future stream of income is. And it is in your good conscience to do that if you were to award damages.

[Comment] Now, how is the jury going to reduce that to present value without an expert witness? None was presented. In any event, he seems to be asking for at least two years, at $120,000 a year, for a total of $240,000, for the past, plus whatever future there may be. And now the counsel does an excellent thing. He carefully explains to the jurors just how to fill out the interrogatories.

Now, the Judge is going to instruct you on the law. You're going to hear what it is that I have proven. You're going to hear the law, you're going to know that I have proven and met my burden. We put the evidence on the scales and we didn't just tip it, we slammed it down.

One last thing. You're going to get the documents called Special Jury Interrogatories and you're going to take it into the jury deliberating room when you consider this. And I want you to be clear as to what it is that you have to do if you're going to award my client his just compensation. There are going to be four questions. You have to answer each one yes. Yes, I have proven beyond a preponderance of the evidence that there was a prospective contract out there that he would have gotten. Yes, beyond a preponderance of the evidence that there was an intentional interference with that contract. Yes, Blue Cross/Blue Shield had no right to squeeze my client, wring him out, take everything that he could give them and give him nothing in return. Yes, beyond a preponderance of the evidence that he was damaged. And then at the end, it's up to you, Ladies and Gentlemen, you have to put in the number figure that represents the just compensation that is reasonable to compensate Mr. Sussman here, for doing the labor, for doing that leg work, and for that greedy corporation sitting over there, making the money off of his back.

It has been an honor to present this case to you, and I thank you very much.

THE COURT: Thank you, Counsel.

Analysis of Plaintiff's First Closing Argument

Counsel makes a powerful argument based on inference as to liability, but wavers as to the amount of damages.

DEFENDANT'S CLOSING ARGUMENT

[Comment] The argument in response comes next. But it must not respond, at least not to a picture already painted. You should begin with a blank canvas and draw a new picture, your way, picking up the other's points as they naturally arise in yours. See Vol. IV, pp. 143–146. See if he does that.

Text of the Argument

MR. SONNENFELD: May I proceed, Your Honor?

THE COURT: Please.

MR. SONNENFELD: Good afternoon. I hope this is the last time I have to greet you, and I'm sure you hope this is the last time I greet you, as well.

MR. LONGER: I like that.

MR. SONNENFELD: I know you like that.

MR. SONNENFELD: I want to thank you, as Mr. Longer did, for your time. I know this is an imposition on all of you. You have come here from various parts of the City, and you have been here with us now three days. You have listened to some testimony, some I hope interesting, some perhaps not so interesting. All of you, I'm sure, would have had other things you would have rather done and we appreciate your role in the judicial system.

I would submit to you that what this case is about is someone, Mr. Sussman, trying to get something for <u>nothing</u>. Trying to get something for which he had done no work, <u>conferred no benefit</u> on anyone and claiming what we would call a windfall, a lot of money for doing nothing. You saw the numbers up on the blackboard <u>that I turned around</u>.

[Comment] Apparently, plaintiff's counsel used a blackboard. That was good. And the defendant's counsel got rid of it. Also very good. But is it true that Sussman did nothing? *We have suggested several times that advocating a weak point will not strengthen, but will only weaken, stronger points. See Vol. I, p. 75.*

For Mr. Sussman to claim that he's entitled to compensation because of the agreement entered into between the Ironworkers and Blue Cross and Blue Shield is like trying to take credit for the sun rising and asking for a commission on it. If it is greed anywhere, it is greed that Mr. Sussman asking you to award him hundreds of thousands of dollars for what, even taken at best his own testimony, was five short meetings that went nowhere, playing on what he claims were his contact with a friend that he had, and that he feels should require you to award him of Independence Blue Cross, hundreds of thousands of dollars.

[Comment] He is better on the disproportion of the money claimed for the work done than his argument that nothing *was done. Now he makes an effective argument, going close to the prohibited golden rule by placing the jurors' personal interests at issue, and going outside of the record by referencing their personal expertise.*

Now, Mr. Longer talked to you at length about Independence Blue Cross and Pennsylvania Blue Shield, <u>my clients</u>, and made some nasty comments about them. But, who is Blue Cross/Blue Shield? They are no stranger to any of you. <u>Five of you</u> have your health insurance with Independence Blue Cross, <u>two of you</u> get that health insurance through your unions or your Health and Welfare Funds. <u>You know</u> Blue Cross. It's a non-profit corporation, meaning it has no shareholders that makes it profits, <u>its owners are in essence the members</u>, the people that get their insurance through Blue Cross. Its Board is not a bunch of greedy people. Its Board are representatives of its members, including, as Ms. Hardy told you, several of the unions, and several of the construction trades unions that serve on the Board.

They negotiate discounts with hospitals and other providers and <u>pass those benefits on to its members</u> in terms of lower hospital and medical costs, than they otherwise could get.

[Comment] Normally, none of this would be allowed. However, it was plaintiff's counsel that referred to the jurors' personal insurance contracts, and termed Blue Cross greedy, and so forth, so. . . . Remember: Both sides of every case have an emotional appeal. See Vol. I, pp. 87–94.

It has a social mission, as Ms. Hardy said. It's the only health care insurer in which anybody can walk in off the street and get health insurance without regard to their medical history, prior condition or otherwise. No one, Ms. Hardy told you, is turned away.

Pennsylvania Blue Shield, likewise, a non-profit corporation located in Harrisburg, providing a similar service with respect to hospitals and medical bills. Blue Cross and Blue Shield, Independence Blue Cross and Pennsylvania Blue Shield didn't get where they are today riding on the backs of little people, as Mr. Longer would lead you to believe. It is made up of little people, that provides insurance to little people, that's the purpose and reason for its existence and it reinvests back into the people of this region and that's why the people of this region support it.

[Comment] Appeal to emotion has been met by a similar response. Nevertheless, the jurors are likely to decide that issue based on their personal experience with their own insurance companies, and that does not usually bode well for the defendant.

Now, who is Mr. Sussman? Mr. Sussman is a broker across the river in New Jersey, whose experience has been primarily with life insurance not health insurance. And to the extent that he has been involved in health insurance, by his own words, it was primarily with small groups. The Ironworkers, as you know, from various testimony, has some 2500 members located in the Tri-State Area and is comprised of all different Locals, far beyond anything in Mr. Sussman's experience. His largest two groups were 500 and 900-member groups, and all the rest were below 100.

Moreover, prior to the Ironworkers, Mr. Sussman had no experience working with a union health and welfare fund, something foreign to him, and had only one experience working with the Tri-State Area, or a group expanded beyond the bounds of the Tri-State Area.

[Comment] These are not very persuasive points. But then, the facts are difficult for him, because the equities seem to favor something for Sussman. Counsel is best focusing on the odd nature of the claim, which sounds in tort rather than quantum meruit. And so he does.

Now, it's important to keep focused on what this case is about. And what this case is about is the claim by Mr. Sussman, and Tower, that my clients, Independence Blue Cross and Pennsylvania Blue Shield, intentionally interfered with his prospective contractual relationship.

Now, those are a lot of big words, and I'm going to cross it out into four parts and later on Judge Kafrissen will instruct you on the law, so his words will be final on this. But just so you understand my argument, I want you to understand what the four elements are, of the claim that my client intentionally interfered with a prospective contractual relationship.

First, Mr. Sussman has to prove that there was a prospective, that is a future, relationship between him or between Tower, his company, on the one hand and the Ironworkers. That's the future relationship that he claims was interfered with. So, first he has to prove that he had an expectation of a future relationship with the Iron-workers.

Second, he has to show that Blue Cross and Blue Shield intentionally interfered with that relationship. And third, he has to show that there was no privilege or justification for Blue Cross to do that. And fourth, he has to show that he was damaged as a result.

[Comment] All well and good. But that sure is a lot of information to be giving the jurors all at once. Better he should deal with each separately, and the only one that we think he should deal with is the second: for there was a relationship and he sure did lose out when he no longer had it to enjoy. But there really is no evidence, at least no direct evidence, of an "intentional interference" by Blue Cross. The third element he should not even deal with, for to do so implies that the second has been established.

Now, I would submit to you that the evidence in this case establishes none of those four elements. Moreover, I submit to you that at the end of the case, you're going to receive a verdict form to fill out. And what I would ask you to do on this form is to say no. And just by saying no, that none of these four elements were established.

Going back over them, a prospective contractual relationship, I think it's clear from Mr. Sweeney and from Mr. Maresca and from Mr. Reith and from Mr. Craggs, that the Ironworkers didn't want Mr. Sussman and Tower involved. Their testimony was all consistent on that.

[Comment] He separates the first here, and makes the point clearly. But the point really is not that there was no relationship, but that the union folk wanted to terminate it.

Secondly, I think it's clear from Ms. Hardy's testimony and corroborated from anyone else, that Ms. Hardy never interfered in the relationship and, if anything, inquired as to whether or not the Ironworkers wanted to work through Mr. Sussman and was told rather clearly that they did not.

[Comment] And that is simply the entire issue of the case as framed by the complaint. *Did they tell* her *or did* she *tell* them *that Sussman was out?*

Third, in terms of justification, what else was Blue Cross to do in this situation? Think of the situation they are in as the Ironworkers moved forward in entering into a relationship with Blue Cross and Blue Cross is told that no, the Ironworkers don't want Mr. Sussman as their broker. What is Blue Cross to do in that situation, other than honor what the Ironworkers have told them, which is that they don't want Mr. Sussman.

[Comment] This last is an excellent point, given the legal theory of the plaintiff. But it is not justification *for interfering (third element). It is rather that there was* no interference, *which is the second element.*

Finally, in terms of damages, to claim entitlement to a percentage of the medical bills paid by Blue Cross for the members of the Ironworkers, would be to award Mr. Sussman the money which he is just not entitled to. And bear in mind, you heard from Ms. Hardy that her own commission, the one that Mr. Longer complains today that Mr. Sussman—that Ms. Hardy won't share with Mr. Sussman, her own commission as an employee of Blue Cross or incentive pay was $1800.00, a one-time payment for signing of the contract and because of the retention of the contract, she gets a payment of roughly $30.00 a month. A far cry from what Mr. Sussman is seeking here, and I'm sure not what he genuinely is looking to have shared with him.

[Comment] Now he is making hay. The contrast between her commission or incentive pay and what Sussman is seeking is enormous. It sounds out of proportion. But, of course, she is a full-time paid employee of Blue Cross/Blue Shield and the

"incentive" is an extra goodie, whereas Sussman gets nothing at all without a commission. But nobody made this point during the testimony. Now he uses an illustrative aid to engage the jurors' eyes and to pull the testimony together. See fuller discussion Vol. I, pp. 237–240.

Now, I would like to show you a time line that I have prepared. Hopefully, this is large enough for you to see, and if it's not large enough for you to see—I always like to arrange the dates once you get done the evidence, to see how its relates.

And, Your Honor, I apologize if I'm blocking your view of the jurors, but you have seen each other for three days. Late May of 1994 was the first meeting between Ms. Hardy and—the first entry on the chart is the meeting between Ms. Hardy and Mr. Sussman with Mr. Sweeney. What we already know, and is not in dispute, is that even before this May, 1994 meeting, Ms. Hardy has already met with Mr. Sweeney. She has already had access to him. She had a meeting that Mr. Walton arranged. She met with him. She also met with another representative of the Ironworkers, another local, Mr. Dougherty, a business agent for another local in this Fund. And as Mr. Sweeney said, he has an open door. And the fact that Mr. Sussman arranged this meeting, this meeting following the meeting that Ms. Hardy had arranged, was no big deal. Anybody could get a meeting from Mr. Sweeney and go in and see him.

[Comment] Well, maybe anyone could. But she was happy enough to go back with Sweeney's pal, Sussman, and willing to talk commissions with him. We suggest it would have been wiser to stay on the main point: that the union *did not want to give Sussman a commission, ergo, no* interference *by Blue Cross, rather than arguing weaker and really irrelevant points, given the complaint.*

The important point is that nothing became of the meeting, June 16th or 17th, Mr. Sussman informed Ms.

Hardy that the Ironworkers Fund was not interested in Blue Cross and instead they went into the arrangement with something that was called Preferred Care.

So, the meeting was a non-event, it went nowhere. And in any event, as Ms. Hardy said, the meeting was no more or less positive, the meeting with Mr. Sussman, than the previous meeting that she had alone just with Mr. Sweeney.

[Comment] We can almost see counsel going down his time line chart. But now he approaches the principal factual dispute between the parties: the issue of whether the plaintiff made any contribution. As we have repeatedly noted, this is a much weaker point for the defendant than the issues of who benefited, who should pay (if anyone), and who made the decision not to pay Sussman. Is it really necessary to set up the conflict as to the actual number of meetings, especially given Hardy's two different accounts?

Moreover, both Mr. Sweeney and Ms. Hardy are consistent in telling you that that is the only meeting that they had, even though Ms. Hardy and Mr. Sweeney was consistent in telling you that is the only meeting that they had that was arranged by Mr. Sussman. You have to weigh whose recollection you want to put your weight on and whose you don't. I would submit to you that you should accept the testimony of Ms. Hardy and Mr. Sweeney.

And you also heard the testimony both from Ms. Hardy, from Mr. Sweeney and from Mr. Craggs, that following this meeting, all the way through 1995, contrary to what Mr. Sussman has told you, Mr. Craggs never provided information to Ms. Hardy. Mr. Craggs never met with Ms. Hardy. And the little information that Ms. Hardy had received from Mr. Sussman, the Zip Code listing was not useful. Indeed, Mr. Sussman never asked for or received from Ms. Hardy a proposal, never presented a proposal to the Ironworkers from Blue Cross, never presented a contract, never provided to Ms. Hardy the information that would have enabled, that would have enabled Blue Cross even to submit a proposal.

We then come into an interesting area of controversy, which is March 31st, 1995. There Ms. Hardy testified, and you saw her calendar, Mr. Longer passed that around, that on March 31st, 1995, a tentative meeting with Mr. Sussman and Mr. Sweeney never took place. And you saw in her calendar it showed tentative and she testified that it was never confirmed, and, therefore, she didn't attend.

Mr. Sweeney, on the other hand, contends that he had two meetings with—Mr. Sussman contends that he had two meetings with Mr. Sweeney and Ms. Hardy in March of 1995. Both Mr. Sweeney and Ms. Hardy denied those meetings, have no recollection of them and indeed, there is no documentation that those meetings took place, no letters afterwards confirming the meetings, no letters of thanks for the meetings, no follow up.

[Comment] We can see that even counsel became confused about the number of meetings claimed by one or the other. This will not help his point. Again, we wonder whether it is helpful to the defendant to set up a credibility contest on this point, forcing the jurors to find that one or the other side is lying, particularly as it does not—or should not—matter to the defense of intentional interference with a prospective contract.

What then is interesting is that on April the 7th, Mr. Sullivan and Mr. Sussman meet with Mr. Sweeney. That is Mr. Sussman called up Brian Sullivan of Blue Cross, and you remember yesterday morning, you heard Brian Sullivan's testimony. He called up Brian Sullivan and arranged for a meeting with Mr. Sweeney on April 7th. And Mr. Sussman admitted that in doing that, he was going behind Ms. Hardy's back.

Now, Mr. Longer said in his speech to you about a half hour ago, that why would Mr. Sussman ever arrange for this meeting on April 7th with Mr. Sullivan and Mr. Sweeney, if he knew he needed a broker of record letter?

He said that. He said why would he arrange this meeting, suggesting to you that as of April 7th, 1995, Mr. Sussman didn't know he had a need for a broker of record letter.

Well, let me show you Mr. Sussman's testimony. On cross-examination, I asked Mr. Sussman: "As of April 7th, when you had your next meeting, you knew then, did you not, that in order for you to receive a commission, you would have to have a broker of record letter?"

Answer: "By the time I met Brian, yes, I knew I needed a broker of record letter." And indeed later on, Mr. Sussman acknowledged that. He's also got a dispute with the New Jersey Blue Cross plan, and I asked Mr. Sussman, "And, in fact, wasn't it back in November of 1994 that you knew that to get a commission from New Jersey Blue Cross, you would need a broker of record letter from the New Jersey Ironworkers?" And his answer was: "Yes."

So certainly regardless of what Ms. Hardy told him, Mr. Sussman knew back in 1994, and certainly by his own admission, knew as of April of '95, that he would need a broker of record letter in order to get a commission from Independence Blue Cross.

[Comment] Excellent. It is imperative to use the actual testimony during summation. Why? Because your enemies will not remember it the way you merely summarize it, if you do not read the actual words, and your adversary may be emboldened to object to your summarization as inaccurate. The judge is not likely to rule but instead to tell the jurors to fall back on their own recollections, and then each side's jurors will be left to their druthers. For a full discussion of this most important technique, see Vol. IV, pp. 31–33.

Now counsel goes to the heart of what should be one of his two important points. Who should pay for what Sussman did?

Now, a lot has been said about broker of record letters and I would like to review with you what a broker of record letter is and the significance of it. It is not something that is unique to Blue Cross. It is not something that is intended to shut out a broker from getting a commission, if he has earned it. The purpose of the broker of record letter is to protect the group. In this instance it is to protect the Ironworkers, because in the final analysis they are the ones who would be paying the commission. Because as virtually every witness explained to you, the commission would be loaded in the rate. That is, it would be included in the rate. It would be included in the administrative fee which Blue Cross charges the Ironworkers. It would be added onto that 10.3 percent that Mr. Maresca thought was excessive, and then, therefore, paid by the members.

Therefore, in order to make sure that the group wants to work with the broker, Blue Cross requires that the broker produce a broker of record letter from the group saying that he is authorized to be the broker for the group. And this group simply didn't want Mr. Sussman to be their broker and Mr. Sussman knew that. He knew from Ms. Hardy back in the first meeting in May of '94, he needed a broker of record letter, by his own admission in his dealings with the New Jersey Blue Cross plan, he knew that in November of '94, and certainly as I mentioned, as I read his testimony, he knew as of April of '95, that he need a broker of record letter.

[Comment] Well done! Now, isn't that a better argument than that Sussman did nothing and that no one should pay him anything?

Now, Mr. Longer keeps stressing Mr. Sussman's ties with Mr. Sweeney. But Ms. Hardy knows the union people. She knows the various funds. Blue Cross provides health insurance to most of the unions in the Delaware Valley, including most of the construction unions. And on April 26th, Ms. Hardy met with Mr. Fratalli, another one of the Ironworkers Fund Trustees and met with him.

Finally, we see that in June of 1995, the Ironworkers Fund authorized the Investment Committee to meet with the Segal Company to review a new P.P.O. program and report their findings at the September 1995 meeting of the Board of Trustees. That is June 23rd. We then know that on July 26th, representatives of Segal, Blue Cross and the Fund met here at the offices of Independence Blue Cross, over at 19th and Market Streets, and then, five days later, on July 31st, Mr. Maresca of the Segal Company, requested in writing, a proposal from Blue Cross and Blue Shield. And Ms. Hardy got that letter some time after August—after July 31st, 1995. Now, what I think is interesting is what Ms. Hardy then did after getting that letter. What she did was to call Mr. Sussman. Assuming Mr. Sweeney—excuse me, call Mr. Sweeney and ask him, what about Mr. Sussman. She went out of her way to find out what it was that the Ironworkers wanted to do.

[Comment] These slips between "Sussman" and "Sweeney" are not helpful, but now he does something very helpful indeed. Watch as he uses vividness and the actual exhibits introduced during trial. See Vol. IV, p. 35.

And you will remember Mr. Longer earlier today said he wished he had a blowup of the notes that Ms. Hardy made of that phone call. Well, I have had one made. Here is the August 7th, 1995 phone call, 8:45 a.m., that Ms. Hardy had, that is her handwriting, with Bob Sweeney and says, "Ironworkers, talked to Len Sussman to advise him that he is not involved." That is the decision of the Ironworkers, the decision of Mr. Sweeney, not a decision dictated by Blue Cross and not a decision suggested by Blue Cross.

The Ironworkers simply didn't want him involved, and indeed what had Mr. Sweeney, you know—excuse me, what had Mr. Sussman even done up to this point?

[Comment] Counsel is nailing the point now. Blue Cross owed Sussman nothing, which is why there is no contract between them and no sum certain even claimed. And Sussman had no contract with the union for Blue Cross to interfere with. Unfortunately, now he goes back to the point that Sussman did

nothing, *which we doubt anyone would agree with, and so suffocates his own best argument.*

Up to this point, Mr. Sussman had done <u>nothing</u> more than to arrange a meeting back in May of 1994 between Ms. Hardy and Mr. Sweeney with whom Ms. Hardy had already met, and then later on, in April of 1995, April 7th, they go around Ms. Hardy's back, and he admits, to bring in Brian Sullivan of Blue Cross to meet with Mr. Sweeney. And again nothing came of either of these meetings. Everyone agrees that nothing came of the May 1994 meeting. Nothing came of it because a month later the Ironworkers decided to go with Preferred Care and not with Blue Cross. And we know nothing came of the April 7th meeting, because what Mr. Sussman told us of that meeting, was that he and Mr. Sullivan and Mr. Sweeney were discussing something called Blair Mill, a third party administrator owned by Blue Cross and that is not what the Ironworkers went with.

So moving on after this phone call, on August 17th, Blue Cross provided Segal with a proposal and you saw the thickness of that, it was the size of a phone book. And certainly Mr. Sussman has never requested or received a proposal from Blue Cross. And then the Segal Company analyzed the proposal and prepared a memorandum analyzing the proposal from Blue Cross and sent that to the Investments Committee.

Meanwhile, in between, Mr. Sussman again tried to inflict himself into a situation in which he was not involved, called up Mr. Sullivan and got him to meet with Mr. Sweeney again, not telling Mr. Sullivan fully what was going on with Ms. Hardy, and Mr. Sweeney told him it was out of his hands and in the hands of the Segal Company. It is clear the Ironworkers didn't want to be involved with Mr. Sussman. He had done nothing, he had really arranged one meeting that anyone could have arranged, sent a Zip Code directory that was of no use, and received back from Blue Cross, back in May, June of

1994, a listing of doctors that anybody could have provided by calling up Blue Cross on the telephone.

No benefit conferring on the Ironworkers or on Blue
Cross and the Ironworkers didn't want him involved and
they repeatedly made that clear. The next event is
September 5th, the Investments Committee recommends
the Blue Cross/Blue Shield Program, and that Committee
meeting, as you know, took place here in Philadelphia
over at the General Building Contractors Association
office, Mr. Reith's office, and he's the management co-
chair.

*[Comment] In our view, it is again a difficult argument that
Sussman conferred no benefit on anyone. Why, then, the talk of
1 to 3 percent between Hardy and Sussman? Isn't the point
here, for the defendant, that Sussman was the agent of the
union (his pals), got them better insurance than he had gotten
them before, but that they did not want to pay him because it
would be in the rates and so they would not give him the broker
letter?*

And as Mr. Reith explained to you, going with Blue
Cross is not really a union proposal, it's not something
that the Union and Management was devising, everyone
supported going with Blue Cross. That's one of the amazing things, I think about Mr. Sussman's whole argument.
He acts as though going with Blue Cross was some kind
of mystery, like finding some kind of secret organization,
as though were it not for him suggesting Blue Cross to
Mr. Sweeney that the Ironworkers wouldn't ever have
thought of it. So, it was like discovering the answer to a
mystery. Everyone has heard of Blue Cross/Blue Shield.
You can't drive down the street without seeing the posters
on the billboards with Coach Vermeill. And you can't
watch TV without seeing the ads. Everyone has heard of
it, everyone is familiar with it, but more importantly the
Ironworkers having had the Segal Company as their consultant for some 40 years, and Mr. Maresca for nearly all

that time, involved with other health and welfare funds in the area using Blue Cross are aware of that contract.

And to suggest that having what is called a fiduciary duty, a duty of trust, that the Trustees would go to Blue Cross merely because at one time Mr. Sweeney had a friendship with Mr. Sussman, is ridiculous. I think it asks you to leave your common sense at the courthouse door and to put blinders on as to common sense. In any event on September 22nd, we see that the Trustees resolved to implement the Blue Cross/Blue Shield proposal, relied on the Segal Company's analysis and the contract went into effect on January 1st, 1996.

[Comment] We are not so sure that, put this way, the jurors would find the use of influence irrelevant. Better to argue that Sussman, on behalf of his friends in the union, found the union better insurance. That, we believe, is what he really means to say. Does the remainder of his argument further this point?

Now, the contract that went into effect, as you heard from Ms. Hardy's testimony, has nothing to do with the renting of a network idea, a goofy idea that Mr. Sussman was discussing at his meeting back with Mr. Sweeney and Ms. Hardy in May of 1994. The idea of renting a network, as Mr. Sussman wanted to have, was to give the Ironworkers the benefits of the Blue Cross discounts of the hospitals, but to have the claim still processed up at the Fund's office up at Castor Avenue in the Northeast.

And Ms. Hardy explained no, that's not the way Blue Cross worked. They don't just give you a discount and then have the group still administer the claims. Blue Cross sells a whole package.

And what the Ironworkers finally went with, as shown in the January 1st contract, was a total package, Personal Choice, giving access to hospitals and doctors in the five-county area and beyond to other Blue Cross plans in Pennsylvania and South Jersey and Delaware, and administering these claims, thousands of claims per year, at the Blue Cross Headquarters here in Philadelphia, and not at the Ironworker's Fund's headquarters up on Castor Avenue. The fact of the matter is, that, none of this was information that Mr. Sussman was familiar with. He wasn't familiar with the products of Blue Cross. He wasn't able to explain to Mr. Sweeney. He had no interest in them in his conversation with Ms. Hardy, and his one and only interest is apparently in what he calls having a big payday.

[Comment] Is this argument helping the defendant? If Blue Cross did nothing to stop the union from authorizing a commission, why is it so darn important for counsel to continually argue that no commission was earned or deserved?

Those were the words that Mr. Longer used in his opening Monday morning, Tuesday morning, and the words that Mr. Sussman used of his own testimony and denied by Ms. Hardy. What incentive would Ms. Hardy have to cut out Mr. Sussman, if he generally [sic] were involved and genuinely entitled to a commission? Blue Cross is the only game in town, as you heard from her testimony and from Mr. Maresca. No one else is able to provide the package of benefits that the Ironworkers wanted. The only choice was to continue to be self-insured as they were, and administer their own claims, which they didn't want to do because they were losing money. They weren't competing on the basis of price. And as indeed you heard from Mr. Maresca and others, this was not a situation where Blue Cross was competing with another insurer and, therefore, had to cut the price down by negotiating as to Mr. Sussman's commission. There was no incentive. The commission would have been built into or loaded into the rates passed onto the Ironworkers Fund. Whether the Ironworkers wanted Mr. Sussman involved or didn't want him was their decision and of no concern to Blue Cross.

[Comment] Well, if he wasn't finding insurance for the union, because he knew nothing of Blue Cross, and Blue Cross was the

only game in town, why would anyone *be talking 1 to 3 percent with him?*

And indeed, why would Blue Cross want to mistreat a broker? If they were to mistreat a broker, wouldn't the word get around in the broker community and wouldn't that dissuade other brokers from wanting to deal with Blue Cross? Do you think that Blue Cross would get to the point where it is right now, as Ms. Hardy told you with some 2.8 million people insured in the Southeast Pennsylvania area, if it had a policy of mistreating brokers or not paying commission when they were properly earned and authorized? That's ridiculous, and again, asks you to leave your common sense at the courthouse door.

[Comment] Do you think this is a good argument, that Blue Cross would never cheat anyone? Do you think that all of the jurors have always felt that their health insurers have treated them fairly? How about you?

Unfortunately, we are now about to circle back to the number of meetings and to set up what we believe to be a needless credibility choice.

Now, what Mr. Longer is asking you to do, basically, is to conclude of the seven witnesses you heard testify, six in varying ways were lying and only one was telling the truth, and that one being, of course, Mr. Sussman. I submit to you, that the testimony of the six witnesses that you heard, Mr. Maresca, from the Segal Company, Mr. Sweeney, from the Ironworkers, Mr. Reith, the management co-chair from the Ironworkers, Ms. Hardy, Mr. Sullivan and Mr. Craggs, as entirely consistent and Mr. Longer, I think, makes a big deal out of points that are simply beside the point.

[Comment] Very good. But, we suggest, not on the point of how many meetings, which he will use it for; rather, on the point of who made the decision not to award Sussman a commission. Watch.

For example, Ms. Hardy and Mr. Sweeney both testified that there was only one meeting between Mr. Sussman, Ms. Hardy and Mr. Sweeney and that was the meeting of May of 1994. And Mr. Sussman says, "Oh, but in her deposition at point, Ms. Hardy referred to meetings plural." Well, sure there actually were two meetings. There was one meeting in May of 1994 with Mr. Sweeney and Mr. Sussman and Ms. Hardy, and then we know that after that, Ms. Hardy drove over to New Jersey and met only with Mr. Sussman and gave him the directories that Mr. Sussman asked for. Those are the directories anybody could have gotten from calling Blue Cross. But never has Ms. Hardy said that she had two meetings with Mr. Sweeney arranged by Mr. Sussman.

[Comment] And now for what we believe to be the major error of the argument. See if you can catch it.

But in any event, so what? Even if there had been two meetings of a half an hour in length, is that enough to justify giving Mr. Sussman a commission of hundreds of thousands of dollars a year for the rest of his life? And is that what you and the five of you, as people insured by Blue Cross want to see your money going to do is to pay him a commission of hundreds of thousands of dollars a year for the rest of his life?

[Comment] Bang! The "But even if" argument. Who is he arguing against now? Himself, of course. See Vol. I, pp. 71–75. It is lethal to do so here, on the credibility conflict that he himself set up. First, he tells us that Sussman is lying whereas all of the defendant's witnesses are telling the truth; then he tells us "even if" Sussman is telling the truth (presumably his own people are lying), Sussman should still lose. In our judgment, this is not an argument to make.

And then Mr. Longer makes a big deal about whether Ms. Hardy's conversation over whether Mr. Sweeney was to be involved—I mean whether Mr. Sussman was to be involved was with Mr. Sweeney on August 7th, 1995, as reflected by her handwritten notes, Defendant's Exhibit-9, or whether she had that conversation with Mr. Maresca a couple of weeks earlier as she had testified at her deposition. What is the difference? The conversation is the same conversation. She was confused at her deposition.

There's no question, it appears in her notes and there's no question that that is entirely consistent with the testimony that you have heard from Mr. Sweeney when he said yes, he had a conversation with Ms. Hardy, and he told her that it was the decision of the Ironworkers that Mr. Sussman was not to be involved. And you also heard Mr. Maresca testify that Ms. Hardy had not discussed it with him. This was a decision of the Ironworkers.

[Comment] We are back in the saddle now.

What Mr. Longer is asking you to do is to disregard the testimony you heard by six witnesses, assume that they are lying and assume that things that Mr. Sussman <u>imagined</u> occurred. And again, I would just like to refer you back to Mr. Sussman's own testimony, and the cross-examination. Towards the very end, I asked Mr. Sussman did Mr. Sweeney ever tell you that any representative of Blue Cross or Blue Shield told any representative of the Ironworkers to avoid dong business with you or Tower and the answer was no. And likewise I asked Mr. Sussman, did Ms. Hardy ever say anything to you that made you think she was trying to negotiate with the Union, the Welfare Fund, based on your commission— excuse me. <u>This was Mr. Longer's question, his own lawyer. "Did Ms. Hardy ever say anything to you that made you think that she was trying to negotiate with the Union, the Welfare Fund based on your commission?" And I objected and the Judge overruled my objection and Mr. Sussman said: "No." No, he had no reason to believe that Ms. Hardy was negotiating over his commission with the Fund. They simply didn't want Mr. Sussman.</u>

[Comment] This, for us, is the high point of his argument. It is very well done. His use of testimony is excellent, and it is good that he is attempting to return to his main argument. But this confusion, and his use of "but even if," have hurt him. Had he begun with this point, and stayed with it for his entire argument, relating it to the second element of the judge's instructions, we think it would be more effective. He has also gone on too long, and he seems to know that he has.

I know you have been patient. You heard me for three days. If you're as hungry as I am, the last thing you want to do is hear me talk any further, so I won't, other than to say when the Judge gives you the verdict form and you go back in the jury room after you have heard the Judge's instructions and deliberate, just say no, this is an outrage for Mr. Sussman to be asking you to award him money for having done nothing or to suggest that my client Independence Blue Cross and Pennsylvania Blue Shield in any way intentionally interfered with his prospective relationship with the Ironworkers and caused him damage.

So, I would just ask you to say no on the verdict form, and I thank you very much for your time.

THE COURT: Thank you, Counsel.

Analysis of Defendants' Closing Argument

Again, we have a windup. And this time counsel may be too cute. It is inconsistent to thank the jury and to say at the same time I hope this is the last time I have to speak to you. The problem with warm-ups is that they go nowhere and can be insulting or condescending.

Counsel returns to the central theme that Sussman did nothing to earn a commission. Is the jury going to buy the fact that he did nothing, that he was irrelevant in this process? If not, the central theme will run against the facts that the jury will believe. Counsel argues that, if there was greed anywhere, it is Sussman who is greedy. But will he look greedy in seeking some commission—letting the jury decide how much—on a contract that may last forever for Blue Cross/Blue Shield? If the main defense is that the issue of commissions was irrelevant to Blue Cross—not the union who would pay it—then why is Blue Cross so adamant that Sussman did not deserve one?

In making the case that Sussman is greedy, counsel argues that Sussman is asking for hundreds of thousands of dollars. Is that a fair characterization of the plaintiff's closing argument? The fact is that Sussman is asking for something by way of commission. That is why there is a suit. Sussman's theory is that he is entitled to something. It is the defendants' theory that the amount is zero. The plaintiff's theory does not require any given number for damages; only the defendants' theory does. This may not be lost on the jury in light of the plaintiff's approach to damages in the first closing argument.

Defense counsel points out that five of the jurors are insured by Blue Cross/Blue Shield. In making this point, he runs the risk that they may have found the insurer too big and unresponsive at some point. This is the same insurer that Maresca believes is charging the Ironworkers too much, and the same company that Hardy says is unlikely to lower its charges to the Ironworkers. The social conscience and the social program of the company may not play so well against this backdrop. Also, the evidence strongly suggests that Blue Cross/Blue Shield is the only game in town for certain kinds of health insurance. It is not going to be easy to convince these jurors that the company is not interested in profit.

It is not going to help the defendants that counsel keeps referring to them as his clients, reminding the jury that he is being paid to make this closing argument. See Vol. I, pp. 36–44. It is also unlikely to help him in attacking Sussman on the ground that Sussman had never dealt with any organization as large as the Ironworkers, when the evidence is absolutely clear that Sussman helped broker the deal, along with Halverson, for the Preferred Care contract for the same welfare fund.

The jury is asking itself whether it believes what the lawyer is arguing. When counsel says that "the fact that Mr.

Sussman arranged this meeting, this meeting following the meeting that Ms. Hardy had arranged, was no big deal," the jury will ask whether Ms. Hardy thought it was a big deal: a chance to land the Ironworkers and to have a hearing with Sweeney in which Sussman, the man who had arranged the Preferred Care contract, would make a pitch with Hardy present. This was a potential way around Craggs. Was it an important meeting? We think the answer is clearly yes, and that arguing facts that the jury will not believe will not help the defendants' case.

Counsel for the plaintiff has called Ms. Hardy a liar about several matters. One is whether she and Sussman met twice or only once with Sweeney. Sweeney's memory, according to his deposition, is not good on the point. Defense counsel argues as follows: "Moreover, both Mr. Sweeney and Ms. Hardy are consistent in telling you that that is the only meeting that they had, even though Ms. Hardy and Mr. Sweeney was consistent in telling you that is the only meeting that they had that was arranged by Mr. Sussman. You have to weigh whose recollection you want to put your weight on and whose you don't. I would submit to you that you should accept the testimony of Ms. Hardy and Mr. Sweeney." Sussman had a calendar which would have to be wrong along with his testimony for the jury to disbelieve him. Is Sussman telling the truth, or is Hardy? The closing argument for the defendants "submits" that the jury should accept the testimony of Hardy and Sweeney. He strongly implies that Sussman is lying—but then he says the issue is immaterial. The "but even if" is bad. He might go with the argument that the discrepancy does not matter, or he might choose to argue that the plaintiff is a liar and his people are truthful, which shows fundamental dishonesty—*not both*. This buffet theory of advocacy, designed to pick up all the votes, the jurors who believe Hardy-Sweeney as well as those who believe Sussman, may well lose them all.

The argument goes from "Sussman did nothing or nothing important" to his not having a broker of record letter back to his not having done anything. Interspersed is the argument that the Ironworkers did not want Mr. Sussman involved. Then, in passing, counsel argues that Sussman had a "goofy" idea about renting a network.

The theme that comes through most clearly is that Sussman was not entitled to money because he did not do enough to earn it. In many respects, the broker of record letter interferes with this theme, because even if Sussman were solely responsible for the Ironworkers contract, the fact remains that he had no such letter. In other words, the broker of record letter is an argument that does not depend on the amount of work done. It is the issue as to who the plaintiff was representing and for whom he is an agent that controls whether he needs the letter.

The defense closing is less consistent than the plaintiff's. We have already pointed out the inconsistency between the broker of record argument and the theme that Sussman did nothing important, as well as the poor "but even if" argument on witness perjury. Moreover, the defense makes the point a couple of times, close to the end of the argument, that Blue Cross is the only game in town. This point is made at the same time defense counsel is asking why Blue Cross would cheat a broker. The jury's answer may be arrogance and greed, which is the plaintiff's theme.

The argument is at its very best—and that is very good indeed—when focused on the fact that every witness has sworn that there was no interference and that even Sussman admitted that he has no evidence to the contrary. This should, in our view, have been the entire theme of the defendants' argument, and, before that, its entire case.

PLAINTIFF'S FINAL CLOSING ARGUMENT

[Comment] The plaintiff is now about to get an opportunity to rebut. He has a golden opportunity to hammer these openings, which the defendant has handed him. Let us see if he takes them.

Text of Plaintiff's Final Closing Argument

THE COURT: Well, Mr. Longer.

MR. LONGER: I'm hungry, too, Ladies and Gentlemen, and I'm going to be short and I appreciate your time and I'll be done before 2 o'clock, just nine minutes away.

I've seen the advertisements that Mr. Sonnenfeld is talking about. I've seen them, they say "Lean on the Blues." The Blues leaned on Mr. Sussman, and now they're leaning on him in a big way to get him out. And you know what? Right beside those advertisements for Blue Cross/Blue Shield, Lean on the Blues, is U.S. Healthcare, and a bunch of other insurance companies. And when Ms. Hardy tells you that there's no other game in town, that is not the case.

Mr. Maresca told you that when the Ironworkers up in North Jersey needed insurance in 1995, they got competitive bidding, so that the Trustees didn't violate their fiduciary duties. How many insurance companies did Mr. Maresca investigate in this situation with these Ironworkers? One. Only one. There's competition in town, Ladies and Gentlemen. But the reason that only one was looked into, was because there was only one contract going down and there was only one contract going down because of one person.

Mr. Sussman had this company, had this company in with the Ironworkers, and he was telling them, "Let's go, Bob, this is your opportunity and this is the right thing to do for your union members." And what happened? Blue Cross/Blue Shield came in and Ms. Hardy squirmed and Mr. Sonnenfeld just told you that her squirming was for a good reason because he just admitted that in her deposition, she was confused about Mr. Sweeney and Mr. Maresca. She knew that it was Mr. Maresca that I was talking about and Mr. Maresca is denying it and these two people were getting together to shut him out and the Blues were leaning on him, Ladies and Gentlemen, and I'm asking you to lean on the Blues. I thank you.

[Comment] *Unfortunately, counsel chooses a flip phrase, "lean on the Blues," rather than hammering his adversary for telling the jurors that Sussman lied and his own witnesses told the truth, but it really does not matter if it was the other way around.*

      THE COURT: Thank you.

Analysis of Plaintiff's Final Closing Argument

One of the common mistakes in litigation is to assume that what your adversary thinks is good for *its* case is not good for yours. The only game in town is something that seems to work better for Sussman than for the defendants. He understood how important Blue Cross could be to the Ironworkers. He started with Preferred Care but recognized that no one could provide the coverage afforded by the defendants. The insurer that views itself as the only game can be arrogant. It can be greedy. These are possibilities that favor the plaintiffs. What is the point of arguing that there was competition among insurers for a New Jersey local's business? Or that Mr. Maresca only investigated Blue Cross? The only game in town is not bad for the plaintiff. It is consistent with his theme.

THE COURT'S INSTRUCTIONS

[Comment] *And now for what could be important, but rarely is: the judge's instructions on the law. These could be vastly important, particularly in a case like this, in which the legal definitions of duty, contract, and so forth can be outcome-determinative. Unfortunately, the instructions, usually read in a monotone, will convey more information in half an hour than is taught in a month of law school. Whatever might be significant in the case will be drowned or suffocated in an outpouring of material that will likely only bewilder the lay jurors. In a more sensible system, key instructions should be delivered at the outset of the trial, and the jurors continuously instructed throughout.*

Text of the Instructions

THE COURT: Thank you. Now that you've heard all of the evidence and the arguments, it is my duty to give you the instruction on the law applicable to this case.

It is your duty as jurors to follow the law as I shall state it to you, and to apply that law to the facts as you find them in the evidence in the case.

It is your sworn duty as jurors to follow the law as I will state it to you and to apply that law. You are not to single out one of my instructions alone as stating the law, but must consider these instructions as a whole. Neither are you to be concerned with the wisdom of any rule or law stated by me.

Regardless of any opinion you may have as to what the law is or ought to be, it would be a violation of our sworn duty to base a verdict upon any view of the law other than that given to you in the instruction, just as it would also be a violation of your sworn duty as judges of the facts to base a verdict upon anything other than the evidence in the case.

In deciding the facts of this case you must remember that our system of law does not permit jurors to be governed by sympathy, prejudice or public opinion.

All parties to this case and the public experts that will carefully and impartially consider all of the evidence in the case, follow the law as instructed by the Court and reach a just verdict regardless of the consequences.

As I have said, it is your duty to determine the facts, and in so doing, you must consider only the evidence that I have admitted in the case. The term evidence includes the sworn testimony of the witnesses that you have heard, the deposition testimony that has been presented, the facts stipulated to by the parties and the exhibits admitted in the record. You have heard the testimony of the witnesses who have been present here.

In addition, during the trial of this case, certain testimony has been read to you from depositions. These are sworn recorded answers to questions asked of the witnesses in advance of the trial by one or more of the attorneys for the parties to the case.

The testimony of a witness who for some reason cannot be present to testify from the witness stand may be presented in the form of a deposition. Such testimony is entitled to the same consideration and is to be judged as to credibility, weight and otherwise considered by the Jury insofar as possible in the same way as if the witness had been present, and then testified from the witness stand.

The exhibits which have been admitted into evidence will come to the jury room with you. Thus, you will have those exhibits available to inspect as you desire. These exhibits may be discussed by you and your fellow jurors.

Remember, that any statements, objections or arguments made by the lawyers are not evidence in the case. The function of the lawyers is to point out those things that are most significant or most helpful to their side of the case, and in so doing, to call your attention to certain facts or inferences that might otherwise escape your notice.

In the final analysis, however, it is your own recollection and interpretations of the evidence that controls.

I also want to tell you that when counsel, as they have done in some instances, have objected to questions which have been asked or have objected to something else which has gone on during the trial, they were doing their duty. It was up to them to make objections under proper circumstances. It is up to the Court to rule on such objections when made. And you have heard me rule on them. Sometimes one way; sometimes another.

Occasionally, when during the trial I have thought it was appropriate, I have tried to tell you why I have ruled in a particular way. But if I had not so told you, please do not speculate on why I ruled in a particular way on an objection or motion to strike or anything else.

If you infer from anything I have previously said, anything I said on the day you were chosen for jury service, anything you have heard me say since the trial commenced, anything you have heard me say up to this point in the charge or that you may hear me say before concluding the charge that I have any views with regard to the facts of this case, please, understand that my views with regard to the facts are not binding on you.

[Comment] How much of all of this rote are the jurors likely to remember in the jury room? Or likely to need? Unfortunately, one of the authors mouthed these identical words at the end of every trial he presided over for thirteen years.

While you should consider only the evidence in the case, you are permitted to draw such reasonable inferences from the testimony, exhibits and other evidence as you feel are justified in the light of common experience. In other words, you may make inferences and reach conclusions which reason and common sense lead you to draw from the facts which have been established by the testimony and evidence presented in the case.

At the beginning of the trial, I gave you some preliminary instructions about evidence, what you could consider to be evidence and what you must disregard as not being evidence. Now, I would like to talk to you about evidence in more detail. At this point I'll review some of the points that I made earlier and I'll elaborate on other points. There are two kinds of evidence, direct and circumstantial.

Direct evidence is direct proof of a fact. It includes the testimony of an eyewitness, someone who personally saw or heard something. Thus, if someone looked outside and saw it was snowing, that person would later testify from his own personal observation that it snowed. Such testimony is direct evidence. Circumstantial evidence is inferred proof of a fact. It includes testimony which is not an eyewitness account, but instead, you may infer or conclude from that testimony, that other facts exist. Thus, if the same person went to sleep at night and there was snow on the ground but awoke in the morning to see fresh snow on the ground that person could testify to his observations of those facts. This testimony is circumstantial evidence, but from such, you can reasonably infer that it snowed while the person slept.

You may consider both kinds of evidence. The law makes no distinction between the weight given to either direct or circumstantial evidence. The sworn testimony of a witness is evidence. This is regardless of which party may have called the witness. However, you have a right to determine the credibility of each witness. That is for every person who took the stand to testify, you determine which witnesses are worthy of belief and the weight which you feel should be given to their testimony.

In a few moments, I'll be giving you some guidelines to help you determine credibility or witnesses. Any documents or exhibits which have been accepted by the Court are evidence. On the other hand, exhibits which have been marked for identification but which have not been received in evidence by the Court or material brought forth only to refresh a witness's recollection, may not be considered by you as evidence.

[Comment] Gosh! Think the jurors are with him?

Stipulations made by an attorney are evidence. Stipulations contain facts to which all the lawyers agree. You must accept the facts or the fact included in the stipulation as evidence. Stipulations can also be agreements between the attorneys limited to a statement that a witness would testify to certain things if that witness were called to testify in person. In that case, you may treat that stipulation as you would treat any other witnesses' testimony as we discussed above.

It is within your province to accept or discount the stipulated testimony, just as you would the testimony of any witness who took the stand to testify in person.

[Comment] They all have this clear, right?

When evidence came in and I instructed you to disregard it, you must put it out of your mind, as if you had never heard it, you are absolutely bound to do that.

I have invited your attention to various factors which you may consider in evaluating a particular witness's testimony or other of the evidence for each of the parties. In doing so, I have not attempted to indicate any opinion on my part concerning the weight which you should give to the evidence or any part of it, and I would not want you to think that I had. In any event, it is for you, and you alone, to determine the credibility of each witness.

Statements made by attorneys are not evidence. This is because the attorneys are not witnesses. What the attorneys have said to you in their opening statements and in their closing arguments, is intended to help you understand the evidence so that you may reach a verdict. If at anytime your recollection of what was said here during the trial differs from an attorney's statement, your recollection must control.

Admissions of facts made by the parties in the complaint, answers to the complaint and other pleadings, documents, statements or transcripts of testimony have been offered by the opposing party and received in evidence. The parties against whom the admission is offered is bound by these admissions. And if you will recall, I brought to your attention some admissions that were read into the record.

[Comment] One can only imagine what the victims in the box are thinking about all of this. But it is about to get worse.

I said you must consider all of the evidence. This does not mean, however, that you must accept all of the evidence as true or accurate. You are the sole judges of the credibility or believability of each witness and the weight to be given to his or her testimony.

In evaluating the witnesses' testimony which has been presented in this case, you may apply those standards for the testing and accuracy of the facts which you have found to be reliable in your everyday life, based upon your own good common sense. You may consider many factors. For example, ask yourself what interest or lack of interest any witness has at the outcome of the litigation.

Also, in determining the credibility or believability of witnesses, you should consider their manner of testifying, their apparent candor, frankness and fairness or lack of it; their bias or prejudice in the case, if any was shown; their means or opportunity for having obtained information concerning matter to which they have testified and corroboration of their testimony by other witnesses or by other evidence presented in the case.

Consider all of the surrounding circumstances in determining which witnesses to believe and what weight to give to their testimony. Inconsistencies or discrepancies in the testimony of a witness or between the testimony of different witnesses, may or may not cause you, the Jury, to discredit such testimony.

Two or more persons witnessing an incident or transaction may see or hear it differently. An innocent misrecollection like failure of recollection is not an uncommon experience.

In weighing the effect of a discrepancy always consider whether it pertains to an important detail or unimportant detail. Also, consider whether the discrepancy results from an innocent error or intentional falsehood.

[Comment] We are sure that all the jurors will keep all these factors in mind.

After making your own judgment, you may give the testimony of each witness such credibility, if any, as you may think it deserves. You are not required to accept any witness's testimony, even though the testimony may be uncontradicted and the witness has not been impeached.

You may decide that because of the witness's bearing and demeanor, or because of the inherent improbability of his or her testimony, or for other reasons sufficient to you that such testimony is not worthy of belief in whole or in part. Such a decision is solely within your province.

If a witness is shown to have testified falsely concerning any one particular material matter, you have the right to distrust such witness's testimony as to other matters. You may reject all of the testimony of that witness or give it such credibility as you think it deserves.

Also, the weight of the evidence is not necessarily determined by the number of witnesses testifying as to the existence or non-existence of any facts. The law does not require any party to call as witnesses all persons who may have been present at any time or place involved in the case, or who may appear to have some knowledge of the matters in issue in this trial. Nor does the law require any parties to produce exhibits, all papers and things mentioned in the evidence in the case. The test is not which side brings the greatest number of witnesses or presents the greater quantity of evidence, but which witnesses and which evidence appeal to your minds as being more accurate, trustworthy, reliable and credible. You may find that the testimony of a smaller number of witnesses as to any fact is more credible than the testimony of a larger number of witnesses to the contrary.

[Comment] Better and better. Now we are going to really help them.

This is a civil case, and therefore, the Plaintiff Tower Financial has the burden of proving the essential elements of its claim by preponderance of the evidence. And the reason that it is important that you understand this is a civil case is, forget all the stuff that you saw on television about Simpson or anybody else. This is not a criminal matter, it is not beyond a reasonable doubt. I'm going to describe now what it is, okay.

A contention is established by a preponderance of the evidence, if you are persuaded that what is sought to be proven is more likely true than not. Okay. So that a preponderance of the evidence, because you're going to see this in the question, has it been proved by a preponderance of the evidence, or more likely true than not, that is all the same thing.

A contention is established by a preponderance of the evidence, if you are persuaded that what is sought to be proved is more likely true than not.

To put it another way, if you will, of an ordinary balance scale, with a pan on each side. As to each claim, on one side of the scale, place all of the evidence favorable to Tower Financial; on the other side, place all of the evidence favorable to Independence Blue Cross and Blue Shield of Pennsylvania. If, after considering the comparable weight of the evidence, you feel that the scales tip to the slightest degree in favor of Blue Cross and Blue Shield, or are equally balanced, your verdict must be for Blue Cross and Blue Shield. If the scales, however, tip in favor of Tower Financial, then your verdict must be for Tower Financial.

[Comment] And now come the instructions that the jury really needs: the law applicable to the actual claims. But what kind of shape are the jurors in by now? They have heard three arguments and all the instructions up to this point. Our hearts go out to them.

Tower Financial has alleged that Blue Cross and Blue Shield intentionally interfered with its prospective contractual relations with the Ironworkers District Council Health and Welfare Fund. One who intentionally and improperly interferes with another's prospective contractual relations is subject to liability to the other for the pecuniary or financial harm resulting from the loss of the benefits of the relationship, whether the interference consists of, one, inducing or otherwise causing a third person not to enter into or continue the prospective relations, or

two, preventing the other one from acquiring or continuing the prospective relations.

[Comment] Wow! Well, we can hope that they got that one.

In order to establish a cause of action for intentional
interference with respect to prospective contractual relations, Tower Financial must prove several elements: One,
Tower Financial must prove the existence of a prospective
contractual relationship between Tower Financial and the
Ironworkers Fund. Tower must demonstrate that there
was a reasonable likelihood or probability that the
Ironworkers Fund would have entered into the contract
with Tower Financial had it not been for the actions of
Blue Cross and Blue Shield.

*[Comment] Interesting. Do you think the jurors understood
that to prevail the plaintiff must prove it more likely than not
that Blue Cross stopped him from having a* contract with *the
union? Particularly where, here, he is suing Blue Cross for a
commission that Blue Cross promised to pay him,* from *Blue
Cross.*

Two, Tower Financial must prove that Blue Cross and
Blue Shield acted with the purpose or intent to harm
Tower Financial by preventing the relations between
Tower Financial and the Ironworkers Fund from occur-
ring.

Three, Tower must prove the absence of privilege or
justification on the part of Blue Cross and Blue Shield.

And four, Tower must show that it has suffered actual
damages as a result of the conduct of Blue Cross and Blue
Shield.

In determining whether Blue Cross and Blue Shield
were privileged to act, you should consider a number of
factors. You should consider the nature of the conduct of
Blue Cross and Blue Shield. For example, you should consider whether their conduct was otherwise wrongful
under the law or tortious. You should also consider the
motive of Blue Cross and Blue Shield, whether they acted

for the purposes of causing the interference or whether it was merely incidental to another purpose. Further, you should consider the interest sought to be advanced by Blue Cross and Blue Shield. For example, an economic interest on the part of Blue Cross and Blue Shield normally will outweigh a similar interest by Tower Financial as long as Blue Cross and Blue Shield do not act through wrongful means.

[Comment] We suggest that the defendant should have considered waiving instruction on all the elements, except the second. That would focus the jurors on the real issue. In any event, we think that the third factor is not helpful to the defendant; indeed, we think the instruction hurt it.

Tower Financial's interests with which the Defendant's conducts interferes should also be considered. You should consider society's interest in protecting business competition, as well as its interest in protecting the individual against the interference with his pursuit of gain.

Next, you should consider the proximity or remoteness of the conduct of Blue Cross and Blue Shield to the interference. Finally, the relationship between the parties should be taken into account in determining whether the conduct of Blue Cross and Blue Shield was justified and proper.

[Comment] We suggest that these last series of instructions are beyond anyone, and everyone, particularly considering how much has gone before. But there is more. There is the damage instruction.

Tower must also prove the damages it claims to have suffered as a result of the conduct of Independence Blue Cross and Pennsylvania Blue Shield by a fair preponderance of the evidence. That is what I just explained to you, what a fair preponderance of the evidence was.

Damages are not recoverable if they are too speculative, vague or contingent and not recoverable for a loss beyond an amount that evidence permits to be established with reasonable certainty. While damages need not be proven to a mathematical certainty, sufficient evidence must be produced by Tower Financial, so that you can arrive at an intelligent estimate without conjecture.

If you determine that Tower Financial has sustained its burden of proof with regard to its claim, Tower Financial is entitled to be fairly and adequately compensated for all of the pecuniary loss of the benefits and prospective contractual relationship between Tower Financial and the Ironworkers Fund, and for all other pecuniary losses suffered by Tower Financial as a result of the Defendants' actions. The amount which you award today must compensate Tower Financial completely for damages sustained in the past as well as damages Tower Financial will sustain in the future.

[Comment] The judge has finished his specific instructions. And we suggest that there is not much here to help the jurors. He is now going back to the general instructions. One thing must be made clear: we are not criticizing this judge. He has done nothing out of the ordinary, nothing different from what hundreds and thousands of judges routinely do. It is not even the system that we criticize, although it needs criticism and reformation. It is rather to demonstrate the utter unimportance of jury instructions, as presently routinely given, notwithstanding appellate court tendencies to regard any error here as of great importance. Instructions that are given in this way—and they almost always are given as they were here—are simply not a factor, because they simply cannot be understood.

I have now outlined for you the rules of law applicable to this case and the need for you to weigh the evidence and determine the facts. Upon the conclusion of my instructions, you will retire to consider your verdict. You must determine the facts from all the testimony that you have heard and the other evidence which has been received during this trial. You are the sole and exclusive judges of the facts. And in that area, neither I nor anyone else may infringe upon your responsibility.

Any comments I may have made as to my recollection of the evidence during the trial or in these instructions may be disregarded entirely by you, if your recollection of the evidence is different than mine, since you are sole judges of the facts.

On the other hand and with equal emphasis, I will instruct you that you must accept the rules of law as I have given them to you and apply that law to the facts as you have found.

*[**Comment**] Undoubtedly the jurors hope that he is done. But no, there is more.*

The attitude and conduct of jurors at the outset of their deliberations are matters of considerable importance. Upon retiring to the jury room, your deliberations should begin and proceed in an ordinary fashion. Your first order of business in the jury room will be to select one of you as foreman to preside over your deliberations. Normally, No. 1 Juror acts as foreman, but you are free to select any of you to act as foreman. The foreman's vote is entitled to no greater weight than that of any other juror.

If, in the course of your deliberations, you should find yourself in serious doubt concerning some portion of my instructions to you on the law, it is your privilege to return to the courtroom for further instructions. In such event, you will transmit a note to me through the Bailiff signed by the foreman. No juror should attempt to communicate with the court by any other means than a signed writing, and the Court will not communicate with any juror on any subject touching the merits of the case, other than in writing or orally to him or her in open court. You should not at anytime reveal to the Court how the Jury stands numerically until you reach your verdict.

Your function to reach a fair conclusion from the evidence and the applicable law is an important one. Your verdict should be reached only after careful and thorough deliberations, in the course of which you should consult with each other and discuss the evidence and reasonable inferences to be drawn therefrom, freely and fairly, in a sincere effort to arrive at a just verdict.

It is your duty to consider the issues with a view towards reaching agreement on a verdict, if you can do so without violating your individual judgment and your conscience. You must each decide the case for yourself, examining the issues and the evidence with candor and frankness, and with proper deference to and regard for the opinions of each other. Mature consideration requires that you be willing to re-examine your own views and change your opinion if convinced that it lacks merit or validity. While maintaining this flexibility, you are not required to surrender your honest conviction as to the weight or effect of evidence solely because of another juror's opinion, or for the mere purpose of returning a unanimous verdict.

Your verdict must represent the Jury's final considered judgment. While it is important that the view of each of the jurors be considered, it is not necessary under the laws of this commonwealth that your verdict be unanimous.

By an act of the Pennsylvania Legislature, a verdict in a civil case rendered by at least five-sixths of the Jury shall constitute the verdict of the Jury and shall have the same effect as a unanimous verdict of the Jury.

Consequently, when after your deliberations at least seven of your members have agreed upon a verdict, that decision shall constitute the verdict of the Jury. You will then inform the bailiff that the Jury has reached a verdict so that you can be returned to the courtroom to render your verdict. So, seven out of eight is a verdict.

Keep in mind that the dispute between the parties is for them a most serious matter. They and the Court rely upon you to give full and conscientious deliberation and consideration to the issues and evidence before you.

You should not allow sympathy or prejudice to influence your deliberations. You should not be influenced by anything other than the law and the evidence of the case. All the parties stand equally before the Court and each is entitled to the same fair and impartial treatment at your hands.

Now, I need a copy of the verdict sheet. These are Special Interrogatories which will be provided to you. They really form something of a worksheet and they will help you move kind of through the case. If you just follow the directions, they are about as self-explanatory as they can be. I'm going to go over them with you, however.

The first question is: "Has Tower Financial Planning Associates, Inc., proven by a preponderance of the evidence, that a prospective contractual relationship existed between Tower Financial and the Ironworkers District Council Health and Welfare Fund?"

You have to answer that yes or no. If your answer is no, you don't answer any further questions. You inform the Court that you have finished and you come back.

If your answer is yes, you proceed to Question Number 2.

Question Number 2: "Has Tower Financial proven by a preponderance of the evidence that Independence Blue Cross and Pennsylvania Blue Shield acted with the purpose or intent to prevent a contractual relationship between Tower and the Ironworkers Fund?"

Yes or no. If it's no, you come back. If it's yes, you continue.

"Has Tower Financial proven by a preponderance of the evidence an absence of privilege or justification on the part of Independence Blue Cross and Blue Shield?"

Once again, you will answer that yes or no.

And then the final question, Number 4—not the final question, the final Interrogatory, as you will see in a moment: "Has Tower Financial proven by a preponderance of the evidence that it suffered damage as a result of Independence Blue Cross and Blue Shield?"

And if you have answered yes to that, then you have answered yes to all of them and you continue to Number

5: "How much do you award Tower Financial Planning Associates, Inc., in compensatory damages?" Which means how much money do you give them. And that is just one number, don't do it by years. You come to one number that represents what that number—that represents your conclusion. Okay.

Counsel, do you want to see me about anything?

[Comment] What the Court is asking, in a code that the lawyers know but that the jurors do not, is whether there are any objections or "exceptions" to his instructions.

MR. SONNENFELD: No, Your Honor.

MR. LONGER: Thank you, no, Your Honor.

THE COURT: And with that I'm going to ask that you be taken out to deliberate and we'll send out copies of the Jury Interrogatories with you. Just tear off the first page, the instruction.

[Jury exits at 2:30 p.m. to deliberate.]

Analysis of the Court's Instructions

Our guess is that these instructions, which are typical in jury cases, must be almost mind-numbing for a jury. Why, other than tradition, do we define for juries *direct and circumstantial evidence,* only to tell them that the definition is of no importance because they can give any evidence the weight they believe is appropriate? Tradition is the answer. We spend enormous amounts of time telling juries that they can do virtually anything they want in assessing the evidence before them. Of course, by the time they are instructed, they already have made their judgments.

Most jurors can understand the court's instructions on credibility and weighing evidence, because these instructions are little more than common sense, and the judge actually tells the jury to use common sense. The instructions on the law are another matter. We suggest that no lay person and not many lawyers could possibly understand the instructions that the judge gave in this case on privilege, the third element of the plaintiff's cause of action. The judge tells the jury that Tower and Sussman must prove the absence of privilege. Take the instructions that the judge gives on privilege and hand them to anyone—a lawyer in your firm, a family member, a friend, a stranger, anyone—and ask what they understand the law to be. We would tell you what we think the law is, but for the fact that we don't understand the instructions.

As we have said throughout our analysis of this trial, we doubt that the jurors will care much about the technical definitions we judges and lawyers use. The plaintiff claims he was cheated. The defendants say he wasn't. That is what this case is about, and it is how the jurors will decide it.

We do think that it is likely that the defendants suggested the use of the special interrogatories, and that this was sound legal strategy. In standard jury instructions, it takes so long for the judge to get to the law that the jury may not focus on the law as much as a party might want (and the jurors may not understand anyway). But with all these questions, all the defendant needs is just one no. The plaintiff needs all yeses. That is why lots of questions are usually good for defendants.

In this particular case, though, a focus on one element— whether Blue Cross interfered with any relationship that the Ironworkers wanted to have with Sussman—might have been to the defendants' advantage. We suggest in our analysis that the defendants might have waived an instruction on privilege, and we believe had they done so they might have clarified and sharpened the only issue that really should matter, given the nature of the plaintiff's claim.

THE JURY'S VERDICT

The Verdict

[Jury enters at 3:30 p.m. with verdict.]

[Comment] Note: After all these arguments and instructions, the jury was out less than one hour.

THE CRIER: Jurors, do you have a verdict?

THE JURY: Yes.

THE CRIER: Your Honor, may I take the verdict?

THE COURT: Yes.

THE CRIER: Question Number 1: "Has Tower Financial Planning Associates, Incorporated proven by a preponderance of the evidence that a prospective and contractual relationship existed between Tower Financial and the Ironworkers District Council Health and Welfare Fund?"

Answer: "Yes."

Question Number 2: "Has Tower Financial proven by a preponderance of the evidence that Independence Blue Cross and Pennsylvania Blue Shield acted with the purpose or intent to prevent the contractual relationship between Tower Financial and the Ironworkers Fund?"

Answer: "Yes."

Question Number 3: "Has Tower Financial proven by a preponderance of the evidence an absence of privilege or justification on the part of Independence Blue Cross and Pennsylvania Blue Shield?"

Answer: "Yes."

Question No. 4: "Has Tower Financial proven by a preponderance of the evidence that it suffered damage as a result of the actions of Independence Blue Cross and Pennsylvania Blue Shield?"

Answer: "Yes."

Question Number 5: "How much do you award Tower Financial Planning Associates, Inc. in compensatory damages?"

Answer: "$120,000."

THE COURT: Thank you very much. Do you want the Jury polled?

MR. SONNENFELD: Yes, Your Honor.

THE CRIER: Juror No. 1, do you agree with the verdict as read?

JUROR NO. 1: Yes, I do.

THE CRIER: Juror No. 2, do you agree with the verdict as read?

JUROR NO. 2: Yes.

THE CRIER: Juror No. 3, do you agree with the verdict as read?

JUROR NO. 3: Yes.

THE CRIER: Juror No. 4, do you agree with the verdict as read?

JUROR NO. 4: Yes.

THE CRIER: Juror No. 5, do you agree with the verdict as read?

JUROR NO. 5: Yes.

THE CRIER: Juror No. 6, do you agree with the verdict as read?

JUROR NO. 6: Yes.

THE CRIER: Juror No. 7, do you agree with the verdict as read?

JUROR NO. 7: Yes.

THE CRIER: Juror No. 8, do you agree with the verdict as read?

JUROR NO. 8: Yes, I do.

THE CRIER: Thank you.

THE COURT: Ladies and Gentlemen, thank you very much for your time and service and effort. We greatly appreciate it. Now you can speak about the case with anybody you'd like, and anybody you don't like for that matter. And really, in this case, both counsel were excellent lawyers. These three attorneys have really done a very good job.

Analysis of the Verdict

The jury was out only an hour before returning a unanimous verdict for the plaintiff. The jury agreed with the plaintiff that he was cheated and should be compensated. The award of $120,000 can be explained by some of the alternatives put forward by plaintiff's counsel, but it is certainly less than the $240,000 for the past two years he suggested on a 1.5 percent, "smack in the middle," of 1 to 3 percent per year. It amounts to that computation for just one year, with no consideration for future years. Plaintiff's counsel was clear in summation that he wanted *at least* two years—that is, $240,000—to be really happy. In any event, the jury picked the number he mentioned most often, $120,000, and then got on home.

The fact that the jury was out only an hour suggests that they likely had few disagreements and were all or almost all convinced of the justness of the plaintiff's case. For those who think that jurors wait to begin deciding the case until deliberations, we offer this verdict as evidence to the contrary. This jury had to leave the courtroom. It had to organize itself. It had to choose a foreperson. It had five interrogatories to answer. It had to agree on a precise number of dollars in a case in which the plaintiff had not demanded a specific sum. Yet the jury was back in the courtroom within 60 minutes of leaving. Each of these jurors surely had reached a personal judgment on the case before deliberations began, and before hearing the judge's instructions as well.

Chapter Fifteen
Epilogue

For us, this is an interesting case. It is interesting not because of the fame of the persons or the vast amounts of money involved. It is interesting because it is a case that might have been won by either side. It is a case in which the lawyers were good. They were prepared, and they knew what they wanted to accomplish. Most of all, it is interesting because it is a very ordinary dispute, a run-of-the-mill case that enables us to test out the maxims and lessons of the underlying work, *Trying Cases to Win,* against the routine work of our courts.

Looking back, it seems clear that plaintiffs had a central theme that they carried forward with some consistency. It is the theme that Sussman and Tower were cheated by a greedy large insurance company. That theme emerged in the opening argument and was developed as each witness testified. If you compare the plaintiff's opening with the plaintiff's closing argument, you will see that the opening might have presented the theme even more clearly and persuasively than it was presented.

The defendants' central theme was somewhat less clear. At times, the focus was on Sussman's failure to do enough work, at times it was on the absence of a broker of record letter, and at other times it was a direct assault on the tortious interference notion. As we point out several times, there is an inconsistency between these defenses. If Sussman did no work and that is a defense, it ought not to matter whether he had a broker of record letter. If the letter is key, it ought not to matter how much work he did. Moreover, whether he did any work or had any broker of record letter, the defendants' claim is that they never interfered with Sussman's relationship with the union. This last point is virtually uncontradicted, but its force is lost because it is buried under other arguments.

All in all, if it was Blue Cross's position that any commission, *earned or not earned,* was the responsibility of the union, then its continual proclamation that no commission was due (because no work was done) undercut that basic position. It also infected the entire defense with a factual claim unlikely of success. With the enormous advantage of hindsight, it seems to us that the defendants' difficulty was in not pointing the finger at this union. The broker letter, if given by the union, would have entitled the agent to a fee. But the union, even after Sussman's efforts to get it better insurance, did not want his commission built into its rates. As we see it, any jury is very likely to conclude that Sussman played an important role in breaking down a barrier that had prevented Blue Cross from regaining the Ironworkers contract that it lost some 20 years earlier. To deny this is to deny something that the jury will very likely find, and to rest a central theme upon it is precarious. A central theme must account for those facts the jury will find to be true.

A central theme—that Sussman had done the work, that the company was prepared to pay a 1 to 3 percent commission, but that the union would not agree to it and so refused the letter—would have explained why he and Sweeney were no longer friends and could have been supported by every witness in the case. No part of trial work is more difficult than predicting what the jury will believe and what it will reject. This prediction requires lawyers to evaluate the evidence without favoring their version of the case, and that is something many lawyers have difficulty doing.

The first question then is: will the jury believe that Sussman is entitled to *something* from *somebody*? If we are correct that most juries will believe Sussman was relevant to bringing the Ironworkers and the insurance company together, then the defense must work to develop a theory of the case that does not require it to claim that Sussman was irrelevant. They, in our view, should have focused on one single issue: the decision by the union—which, after all, would pay the plaintiff's bill through higher rates—not to pay Sussman, and that the union made this decision *alone,* without consulting Blue Cross.

Thus, we think that one reason the plaintiff received a verdict is that the defense rested much of its case on a factual contention that ran against the rules and laws of probability, based on common experiences of humankind. That contention was not only unnecessary to, but appears to cut against, the real issue: that there is no evidence that *the company told the union not to agree to a commission and thus no evidence that it interfered with Sussman's arrangements (prospective contract) with the union, which is the only claim that the plaintiff has made.*

Our review of this trial leads to a conclusion that is not surprising, which is that the lawyers sometimes thought they were making points clearly when they were not. This is a common problem at trial. Lawyers prepare their cases for months. They interview witnesses, compile exhibits, and have a keen eye for how everything fits together. But jurors have not been part of the process. They hear things for the first time. What is obvious to the lawyers is not always obvious to the jurors.

This means that it is vital for lawyers to argue their cases to the jury through the witnesses. This is the job of the direct examiner and it is the job of the cross-examiner. Lawyers should not expect jurors to find their way on their own to conclusions. Lawyers should lead them down the path so that the conclusions not only become obvious, but are clearly stated by the advocate at the outset and throughout the trial.

At various points in the book, we have suggested how direct examiners and cross-examiners might have developed lines of argument and bolstered the themes of their case. This is important because it enables readers to decide for themselves whether these arguments would persuade them. It also shows how questions can be molded to form an argument. If the reader practices with the lawyers and with the critiques, the exercises will tone the muscles of the advocate, irrespective of agreement with all of the critiques.

We move to the end with a final thought. Who won the case? The plaintiffs won, in the sense that the verdict is for the plaintiff, but the jury could have awarded more than $1 million if it thought that the contract between the Ironworkers and Blue Cross/Blue Shield would last for many years, and it seems clear to us that plaintiff's counsel was asking for at least $240,000, although obliquely. In all fairness, to some extent the argument that Sussman did not do enough to earn a commission, which we raise questions about, might have worked to establish that he did not do enough to earn a life-time commission, or even one in the amount of $240,000. But then, it is also true that as the case for liability weakens, the amount of damages for even the same injury decreases as well. See Vol. I, pp. 83–84. In any event, it seems clear, at least to us, that the jury simply wanted to give Sussman *something*—and a significant something at that—and plucked the $120,000 figure out of a low suggestion by counsel as to what one year of the contract was worth, simply because they wanted to and never really understood either the actual theory of the plaintiff or the precise defense to it.

Deciding whether a case has been won or lost requires a judgment about what the parties expected would happen or wanted to happen. If Sussman expected a jury verdict of several times what he received, he may view the case as a loss, especially if his counsel takes a contingent percentage as well as the costs of the case. If Sussman is concerned with establishing that he was cheated regardless of the amount that is paid, he has won. If Blue Cross/Blue Shield wanted to minimize the amount it paid and always thought it would pay something, it might view the case as a win or at least as a wash. If, however, Blue Cross/Blue Shield expected to prevail, it must view the case as a loss. For example, a case that yields a verdict of $100,000 is a loss if the settlement offer was $150,000, or even $102,000. See Vol. I, p. 9. We, of course, have no knowledge concerning any settlement difficulties or pretrial party expectations.

In our judgment, though, there is one clear winner here. Who is it? It is each one of us who went through this record with a critical eye, testing each question and answer against what we might have done, imagining ourselves asking questions or making objections to these questions. All of us—the authors as well as the readers—who have done this exercise have, in our view, developed some muscle as advocates. And if that is not a win, we do not know what is.

Index

CPSIA information can be obtained at www.ICGtesting.com
Printed in the USA
BVOW03*1058210515

401053BV00004B/6/P